*Puerto Rican Citizen*

HISTORICAL STUDIES OF URBAN AMERICA

*Edited by Timothy J. Gilfoyle, James R. Grossman, and Becky M. Nicolaides*

# Puerto Rican Citizen

History and Political Identity in Twentieth-Century New York City

## Lorrin Thomas

The University of Chicago Press *Chicago and London*

The University of Chicago Press, Chicago 60637
The University of Chicago Press, Ltd., London
© 2010 by The University of Chicago Press
All rights reserved. Published 2010.
Paperback edition 2014
Printed in the United States of America

20 19 18 17 16 15 14     2 3 4 5 6

ISBN-13: 978-0-226-79608-6 (cloth)
ISBN-13: 978-0-226-15176-2 (paper)
10.7208/chicago/ 9780226796109.001.0001

Library of Congress Cataloging-in-Publication Data

Thomas, Lorrin.
   Puerto Rican citizen: history and political identity in twentieth-century
New York City / Lorrin Thomas
   p. cm.—(Historical studies of urban America)
   Includes bibliographical references and index.
   ISBN-13: 978-0-226-79608-6 (cloth: alk. paper)
   ISBN-10: 0-226-79608-6 (cloth: alk. paper)
1. Puerto Ricans—New York (State)—New York—Social conditions.
2. Puerto Ricans—New York (State)—New York—Economic conditions.
3. Puerto Ricans—New York (State)—New York—Political activity.
I. Title. II. Series: Historical studies of urban America.
   F128.9.P85T463 2010
   305.868'729507471–dc22

                                                        2009035824

♾ This paper meets the requirements of ANSI/NISO z39.48-1992
(Permanence of Paper).

# Contents

# Acknowledgments

To describe the debts of gratitude accrued in the process of making a book, to narrate these years of creation via the names of the people who helped me on my way, is to recollect the best parts of the experience. The story of this journey begins and ends with my family, a large and loving mix of in-laws, steps, and blood relatives whose generosity in both practical and emotional matters has been constant. From Maine to Alabama and several spots in between, family members have welcomed, fed, and entertained my husband and children and me during extended summer visits, finding quiet places for me to write and never failing to express sincere interest in what I was doing. I especially thank my parents, Janet Thomas and Bill Thomas, for a lifetime of support and sometimes unreasonable faith in me, which each has conveyed mostly patiently during these many years of book writing—even though my father, an efficient publisher of his own research, simply could not understand what was taking me so long, nor could my mother, who always believed I could do anything with one hand tied behind my back and thought I could finish the book before the last baby started walking. (She was a few years off.)

Of the many gifted and generous teachers who influenced my thinking as I worked on this project, I first thank Elizabeth Blackmar, my undergraduate adviser at Columbia University, for the ways she opened my eyes to some of the issues that would become central to this project—and then gave her ear to my early efforts to sort them out. In particular, I trace my interest in the "broken narratives" of citizenship and inclusion back to Betsy's undergraduate seminar on republicanism in the nineteenth-century United States, whose themes resonated so well with my other coursework in Latin American literature and history. When I got to graduate school at the University of Pennsylvania, my dissertation committee enthusiastically embraced my ideas as I pursued a more formal study of the Americas as a region. That committee turned out to be a magical trio. Michael Katz, a prolific scholar who is widely admired in his field, should be famous by now also for his gifts as an attentive and loyal adviser. Ann Farnsworth-Alvear nurtured my curiosity at every turn, and her creative intellectual aesthetic inspired me tremendously during my training at Penn. Tom Sugrue shared generously of his historical imagination and helped me think my way out of many a narrative or conceptual rut. One of the major benefits of landing a job in the Philadelphia area is that I am now able to count each of these mentors as colleagues and friends. Also at Penn, I benefited from exchanges with and advice from Russel Kazal, Barbara Savage, Walter Licht, Ewa Morawska, Lynn Lees, Julie Franks, Rogers Smith, and Doug Massey, all crucial to the early development of this project. In addition to many great teachers, my friends at Penn made graduate school a joy. Yanna Yannakakis and Aiden Downey, Abby McGowan, Ian Petrie, Paulina Alberto and Jesse Hoffnung-Garskof, Idana Goldberg, Fran Ryan, Margaret Pugh O'Mara, Gabriela Ramos, Hilary Dick, and Christina Wirtz offered a combination of fun collaborations and serious hilarity. Completing my degree was made possible by the support of a Benjamin Franklin Fellowship and, in my last year of writing, from a Chimicles teaching fellowship, both funded by the University of Pennsylvania.

At Rutgers-Camden, my colleagues in the history department and in Latin American studies have been a great source of support and have helped make the balance of teaching, writing, and other faculty responsibilities consistently enjoyable. I especially thank Laurie Bernstein, Janet Golden, Carla Giaudrone, Howard Gilette, and Phil Scranton for their mentoring and encouragement. My colleagues in the department of Latino and Hispanic Caribbean studies in New Brunswick have likewise sustained me with both friendship and academic wisdom for which I thank each of them. I was fortunate to have begun my career at Rutgers as a Woodrow Wilson Postdoctoral Fellow in the Humanities, and I am extremely grateful for the financial support and extra writing time the fellowship gave me. I also would like to thank Margaret Marsh, a fellow historian and dean of the Rutgers-Camden Faculty of Arts and Sciences, who has provided tremendous support for the faculty during her tenure both as dean and as interim chancellor of the Rutgers-Camden campus.

There were many scholars in a variety of disciplines whose comments and feedback during workshops and conferences, and many other casual exchanges, shaped my thinking in invaluable ways. I thank Silvia Pedraza, Christina Duffy Burnett, Marc Rodríguez, Mae Ngai, Gary Gerstle, David Gutiérrez, Linda Bosniak, John Beckerman, Judge José Cabranes, Imani Perry, Larry La Fountain-Stokes, Persephone Braham, Ray Rocco, Ana Ramos Zayas, Suzanne Oboler, and other participants at the Princeton conference on Repositioning North American Migration History, the

University of Delaware Latin American Cities conference, and the *Latino Studies* conference on citizenship at the University of Illinois–Chicago. I would also like to thank participants and audience members at a number of other venues where I presented my work, including the Program in American Culture at the University of Michigan, the Department of Latino and Hispanic Caribbean Studies faculty research roundtable at Rutgers, the Lees History Seminars at Rutgers-Camden, and the program in Latino and Latin American studies at the University of Pennsylvania. I especially thank the colleagues who invited me to present my work at these events.

I managed to make immeasurable improvements in the book manuscript because of the keen insights and incisive critiques of the many wise and generous scholars who read it. Carmen Whalen and Ruth Glasser each read an early draft of the full manuscript and pushed me to think about questions I hadn't adequately answered. Aldo Lauria Santiago read more than one version of the entire manuscript and, often starting with a deceptively simple query, helped me work through some of the trickiest aspects of the book's conceptualization—even though he didn't always agree with the directions in which I was headed. Many other friends and colleagues read parts of the book along the way and offered invaluable suggestions. I thank Eric Schneider, Iris Morales, Thea Abu-El Haj, Brooke Coleman, Jesse Hoffnung-Garskof, Jerry Vildostegui, José Cruz, Victor Vázquez, Kathy Peiss, Barbara Savage, and Félix Matos Rodríguez. I also deeply appreciate the close reading and suggestions provided by George Sánchez and two anonymous readers for the University of Chicago Press. My editor at the press, Robert Devens, has been extraordinarily helpful at every stage of this process and always a joy to work with. I also thank Jim Grossman, the series editor, for his early encouragement and interest in this project. I'm grateful to Anne Goldberg and Mark Reschke for their expert assistance in getting the book to press, and to Susan Cohan, Suzanne Sherman Aboulfadl, and Stefania Heim for superb help with, respectively, copyediting, indexing, and proofreading.

The Philly and New York friends who have provided me with so much spiritual sustenance during these years—moral support and sympathy, child care and playdates, coffees out and dinners in, and diversion of all kinds—may have had no idea that they were contributing concretely to this book, but indeed they were; and though they are too numerous too mention here by name, if they read this, they will recognize themselves and will hear my resounding shout of gratitude. Even beyond this everyday support and friendship, a number of friends in New York have generously (and tolerantly) hosted me for a decade now—at times long-term and sometimes at a moment's notice—during my regular research trips to the metropolis. I couldn't have managed without their hospitality. Tom Hilbink, Anne Kahn and Scott Alexander, Heather Serepy, Lisi de Haas and Sandra Contreras, and Simone White and Anthony Leslie gave me places to sleep, food to eat, and loving companionship when I poked my head out of the archives. I especially thank Sandra not only for her sofa, and for her many gifts of friendship and inspiration over the last two decades, but because she taught me my first words of Spanish in 1989, Dominican contractions and all; and Simone, too, my oldest intellectual compatriot, because I am sure that her writing advice to me when we were fifteen continues to resonate in my prose.

My research in New York was quite literally made possible by the fabulous staff at the Library and Archives of the Centro de Estudios Puertorriqueños at Hunter College. Nélida Pérez, a visionary librarian who helped create the Centro library, and Pedro Juan Hernández, archivist extraordinario, along with an incredibly knowledgeable staff, including José Camacho, Jorge Matos, Félix Rivera, Yosenex Orengo, and Mario Ramírez, supported my research at every turn and made me feel welcome during every one of the many days I spent with them. For years, the members of this great team answered every question I had and found every source I wanted if it was possible to find, all while sustaining the invaluable research agenda of the Centro. Xavier Totti, editor of the *Centro Journal*, and Pedro Pedraza, Centro researcher, also provided helpful advice during exchanges about this project. Unless otherwise noted, all translations of the Spanish-language sources I used, many from the Centro archive, are my own. I benefited as well from the assistance of the staffs at the Balch Institute of the Pennsylvania Historical Society, the New York City Municipal Archives, the Tamiment Library and Robert F. Wagner Archives at New York University, the Brooklyn Collection at the Brooklyn Public Library, and the Manuscripts and Archives Division of the New York Public Library. I am also very grateful to the various people who permitted me to interview them about their experiences in Puerto Rican New York in the 1940s, 1950s, and 1960s. Anita Vélez-Mitchell, Carmen Osiakowski, Anthony Bermudez, the late Joseph Montserrat, Susana Cabañas, José Morales, Pedro Rodríguez, and Iris Morales all shared with me their time and their memories.

Last of all, I thank the three amazing people I live with, for their forbearance and their boundless love. I joyfully dedicate this book to Daniel, Tasso, and Reed, for all they give to me and to the world.

# Puerto Ricans, Citizenship, and Recognition

‖‖‖‖‖‖‖‖‖‖‖‖‖‖‖‖‖‖‖‖‖‖‖‖‖‖‖‖‖‖‖‖‖‖‖‖‖‖‖‖‖‖‖‖‖‖‖‖‖‖

In 1994, Juan Mari Bras, a lawyer and Nationalist leader in Puerto Rico, renounced his United States citizenship at the U.S. Embassy in Venezuela. The U.S. State Department confirmed his denaturalization within a year, but a more complicated issue remained: was Mari Bras, then, a Puerto Rican citizen instead? Attaining legal recognition of Puerto Rican citizenship—with full political rights, including the ability to vote in Puerto Rican elections—was Mari Bras's goal, and it took him several years to win his case in the Puerto Rican Supreme Court. Throughout the twentieth century and until Mari Bras became the first true citizen of his island nation in 1997, there was legally no such thing as a "Puerto Rican citizen."[1] Eight decades earlier, Bernardo Vega, another well-known critic of U.S. empire, also struggled to sort out the details of his citizenship status. Vega, a *tabaquero* from Cayey, Puerto Rico, traveled by ship from San Juan to New York City in August 1916, an immigrant full of immigrant dreams. At that point, the year before the U.S. Congress extended U.S. citizenship to all Puerto Ricans, Vega was technically a U.S. national, coming from the "unincorporated territory" that was a prize of war taken by the United States following its defeat of Spain on behalf of Cuba in 1898.[2] In the memoir he wrote forty years later, Vega recounted his experience, soon after he arrived in New York, in an evening English class at a public school on Manhattan's Upper East Side. Vega recalled how his Irish teacher instructed the class on preparing to become U.S. citizens:

*US grants puerto ricans citizenship in 1917*

> "How can I become an American citizen?" I asked. She replied that you just have to follow the steps she had outlined. I responded by pointing out that, unlike our Hungarian and German classmates, Puerto Ricans do not really have any citizenship. Outside of Puerto Rico our natural citizenship is not recognized. Without any citizenship to give up, it would seem pretty hard for us to become Americans.

A bit flustered, the teacher could only restate what she had said before: that you just have to give up your own citizenship, follow the steps, and there you have it. And it was the same for everyone who was a resident of the United States!

"Yes, for everyone," I said, "except Puerto Ricans."

Vega and the teacher continued their circular discussion until the teacher called in the school's principal to settle the matter. "After hemming and hawing, he concluded that the problem was that so little is known about Puerto Rico here in the United States."[3]

Less than a year later, President Woodrow Wilson signed the Jones Act into law, granting broader governing powers to a new Puerto Rican legislature and conferring U.S. citizenship on all Puerto Ricans.[4] After the First World War, inspired by the postwar boom in U.S. industry and the steady constriction of the island's subsistence economy by North American sugar interests, Puerto Rican migrants would begin arriving in New York

Figure 1. Bernardo Vega, photographed for an identification card issued by the New York Branch of the Bureau of Commerce and Industry of Porto Rico in 1936, at age fifty-one. Records of the Offices of the Government of Puerto Rico in the United States, Archives of the Puerto Rican Diaspora, Centro de Estudios Puertorriqueños, Hunter College, CUNY.

by the boatload, now at the regular ports of Brooklyn and lower Manhattan instead of at Ellis Island, and with citizenship in hand. By the end of the 1920s, the Puerto Rican population of New York City reached around forty-five thousand, forming a complex and unique community of migrants who were "foreign in a domestic sense," as a Supreme Court justice had described the island itself in 1901.[5] But what to call them? They were foreigners with U.S. citizenship, immigrant-citizens but not Americans. Unlike other immigrant groups that would become known as "hyphenated Americans" over time—Italian-American, Japanese-American—Puerto Ricans in the United States were never referred to as Puerto Rican–Americans. Their relationship to the United States was spelled out awkwardly, instead, in phrases like "American citizens of Puerto Rican origin," and observers occasionally, using an imprecise shorthand, referred to them as "Puerto Rican citizens." For most of the twentieth century, though, this was an impossible category, suggesting quietly the unresolvable tension between its two terms: *Puerto Rican* and *citizen* fit together only when mediated by the United States. Although Bernardo Vega's 1916 citizenship conundrum would soon be solved, the problem of Puerto Rico's invisibility in the United States—rooted in the island's colonial ties to a democratic liberal nation that would acknowledge that relationship only via euphemism—remained. And the corollary of that invisibility, the persistent political marginalization of Puerto Ricans in the United States, would never cease to confound Vega and his compatriots.[6]

This book's narrative begins shortly after the passage of the Jones Act, tracing Puerto Rican migrants' interpretations of their United States citizenship and what it promised in terms of civic, political, and social rights. This seemed to me to be the place to begin my inquiry about the political identities of the United States' first and only citizen-immigrants. Citizenship became a central preoccupation of political and policy history during the 1990s, following the fall of the Berlin wall, and inspired reassessments of foreign policy and immigration issues around the world. It also has become a real analytical problem for social history, sociology, and anthropology. Scholars have become as interested in the subjective interpretations of citizenship, what citizenship actually means to people, as in its formal dimensions, especially to members of groups marked by some form of exceptional position in the nation. Historical sociologist Margaret Somers argues, for instance, that citizenship is important not as a status per se but as a set of "institutionally embedded social practices"—in other words, that citizenship in practice involves people making claims on the state via institutions like courts, schools, the legislature, and the less formal institutions of the public sphere.[7] This praxis is, for all who engage in it, geared toward achieving the equal status that is explicitly promised by liberal citizenship. Central to Somers's definition is the idea that groups develop and pursue their own expectations of citizenship rights, expectations that emerge not only from their sense of rights promised to citizens by the nation-state but also from their relationships to local institutions and the local economy. While Somers's analysis gave me much clearer insight into the changing social and political practices of Puerto Rican migrants vis-á-vis their citizenship, I began to notice that their skepticism about citizenship as a guarantee of equal status in the United States increased over time. Initially I had simply asked how Puerto Ricans sought to make claims on the basis of these rights. But I began to notice that, by the late 1930s, many of my sources complicated this analytical focus by articulating their political identities and aspirations in ways that ranged far beyond the category of "citizen."

Following the admonition of anthropologist George Marcus that social scientists "follow the thing" and formulate their research around the dilemmas of people in "actual fields of social conflict" and in historical time, I had to adjust my questions about citizenship and think about what goals really guided Puerto Ricans in defining their political identity in New York. Bernardo Vega was only one of thousands of Puerto Ricans who had begun, by the early forties, to worry less over the frailties of his American citizenship—to which he had only an ambivalent attachment from the start—than over the actualization of the larger commitments of a liberal democracy, particularly promises of justice and of sovereignty, the latter in both its metaphoric and politically concrete senses. Vega's contemporary and friend, Jesús Colón, a community activist, writer, postal worker, communist, and erstwhile politician who had migrated to New York from Puerto Rico in 1917, placed great emphasis on the value of citizenship in the 1930s. But by the mid-1950s, he was more prone to expressing Puerto Ricans' goals as political actors in terms like this optimistic lament: "The community is struggling to express itself more forcefully, to unite itself, to gain recognition and the rights it is entitled to, in the city at large."[8] In invoking the idea of "recognition," Colón was talking not only about claiming a voice, being "recognized as speakers," or attaining what historian Rebecca Scott calls the "dignitary components of citizenship," though these were important dimensions of his claim. Colón was also, implicitly, asserting the legitimacy of Puerto Ricans' critiques of liberal democracy: after three decades of activism and political organizing, members of his community were no longer sanguine about the actual power of their citizenship.⁹ It seemed increasingly clear to me that recognition was a more coherent "thing" to examine, a thing encompassing a broader set of aspirations and demands than citizenship.

As with many of his interpretations of the political life of Puerto Ricans in New York, Colón was before his time: *recognition* was a term that Puerto Ricans and observers of the Puerto Rican community (and African Americans and other marginalized groups as well) would begin using regularly, if not consistently, by the mid-sixties to talk about the political and social goals of their struggling neighbors in New York's *barrios*. Their demands for recognition were demands to address what the liberal theorist Jürgen Habermas has referred to as the "collective experience of violated integrity."¹⁰ They were also assertions of a political identity that pushed beyond citizenship, since their status as citizens in the liberal democracy had proved unable to deliver on its promises of equality, and was certainly not potent enough to reverse the violations of justice that marked their colonial past. Puerto Ricans' claims for recognition also, then, represented a distinct challenge to what theorist Wendy Brown identifies as the most enduring conceits of American liberalism, "expos[ing] the legitimating function" of liberalism's "foundational presuppositions, including progress, rights, and sovereignty."¹¹ By the mid-sixties, the term *recognition* was firmly linked to new iterations of human rights discourse and "the politics of universal dignity" that had begun to coalesce in the wake of the Second World War.¹² Discourses of human rights and recognition shared a sometimes paradoxical balance of demands: both called for universal equality as well as the acknowledgment of particular group difference. More important, though—and this was the draw for Puerto Ricans and other groups involved in struggles for justice in the sixties—both sought to elevate the idea of a legitimate and egalitarian political status above the limitations of the category of "citizen" in a flawed liberal democracy.

## The Problem of Citizenship

United States citizenship was a problem for Puerto Ricans even before they possessed it. During the nearly two decades of debate over whether or not to turn Puerto Ricans into United States citizens, which began shortly after the 1898 Treaty of Paris and lasted until the passage of the Jones Act in 1917, most jurists and lawmakers saw no need to hide their racist judgments about Puerto Ricans behind the coded language of foreignness.

Their notions about the "mongrel" Puerto Rican people, and the presumed incapacity for self-government that resulted from their racial deficits, were repeated ad nauseam throughout debates over Puerto Rico's status in relation to the United States. A series of essays in the *Harvard Law Review* in 1899 drew attention to the fact that it was precisely these legal scholars' perceptions of Puerto Ricans as "an alien and inferior race" that lay at the heart of their reluctance to extend U.S. citizenship. One contributor, Judge Simeon Baldwin, described islanders as "the ignorant and lawless brigands that infest Puerto Rico."[13] Not much had changed by 1917, when, in the final debates over the Jones Act, a representative from Connecticut continued to object that "the people of Porto Rico have not the slightest conception of self-government. . . . Porto Rico is populated by a mixed race. About 30% are pure African . . . and fully 75 to 80% of the population *was* pure African or had an African strain in their blood."[14]

Objections to extending U.S. citizenship to Puerto Ricans came not only from the American political elite but also from many Puerto Rican *independentistas* (supporters of Puerto Rican independence) who saw the imposition of citizenship on the island as a device to tie it permanently to the United States. Bernardo Vega, for instance, refused to support "that campaign [for citizenship] because I felt that what we should demand was a resolution to the problem of our sovereignty."[15] More moderate supporters of independence, like Luis Muñoz Rivera, were willing to tolerate the idea of incorporation into the U.S. nation-state because of the perceived benefits of membership in a democratic society but warned of the dangers of an unequal status within the nation. In 1917, the pragmatists in Congress—many of whom were as openly racist as those who explicitly opposed the extension of United States citizenship to black and brown people—finally won out, conferring U.S. citizenship on an island whose residents had gone to sleep one night in 1899 as subjects of the Spanish crown and awoke the next day as the United States' first colonials.

The Jones Act did not, of course, reverse assumptions about Puerto Ricans as "unfit" for citizenship in a liberal republic. On the island, one measure of that judgment was a property and literacy requirement (the former restriction abandoned in the United States in the early nineteenth century) that disfranchised almost 70 percent of the population.[16] Nor would they have the right to vote in federal elections, meaning that the terms of the Jones Act did not amount to "taxation without representation" but worse, as *independentistas* argued, governance without representation. In 1900, Senator Joseph B. Foraker had said, about his first proposal to extend citizenship to the island, "In adopting the term 'citizens' we did not understand . . . that we were giving to those people any rights that the American people do not want them to have."[17] And Puerto Ricans in the United States—who could vote in any election on the mainland as soon as they took up residence there—would ascertain within little more than a decade that Muñoz Rivera's fears were legitimate: their informal exclusion from the full privileges of citizenship amounted to, indeed, "a citizenship of an inferior order, a citizenship of a second class."[18]

By the late twentieth century, it would become a commonplace to call exclusion a hallmark of citizenship in the United States and in all liberal democracies. A century and a half earlier, Karl Marx, in distinguishing between political emancipation and what he saw as the ultimate goal of human emancipation, derided "the fake, ersatz universal" of liberal citizenship.[19] But exactly how is this exclusion to be understood in the context of the United States, where the idea of inclusion in the nation evolved into a feint of "liberal values"? Rogers Smith and others since the 1990s have convincingly argued that the democratic liberal foundation of U.S. citizenship is fundamentally uneven, and its philosophy unevenly applied, because it has always been mediated by less tolerant dimensions of an American "creed": a republicanism rooted in homogeneity and "ethnocultural Americanism" given to racist nativism.[20] African Americans very clearly suffered the worst of this American creed in practice, but Puerto Ricans in the United States collided with it, too, and not just because of their mixed-race origins but because their status as former colonials marked them as "dependent," citizens who were failures by republican standards before they even arrived on the mainland.[21]  ↳ ala locke's 2 treatises

Puerto Rican migrants themselves did not see their political identity as overdetermined in the first decade of substantial settlement in New York. In that era, Puerto Ricans were hopeful that they would become important to local politicians and gain a foothold in formal mainland politics the way the Irish, Italians, and Jews had before them. Their optimism was sustained for a time by the relationship that the early migrant community in East Harlem developed with their state representative, Sol Bloom, who in 1925 was interested enough in his Puerto Rican constituency to make a trip to their island and promise his support—soon reversed—for Puerto Rican independence.[22] When Puerto Ricans experienced the first of countless waves of ethnic violence in New York a decade after they became U.S. citizens, during a series of street fights and other clashes (*choques*) with Jews in East Harlem, one migrant told a *New York Times* reporter that "the source of the problem is that people don't realize that we Puerto Ricans are American citizens."[23] This was a naïve view, of course; misapprehension of their status hardly explained the roots or the extent of the conflict. The *choques* marked the beginning of the conscious struggle by Puerto Rican activists to articulate a meaningful political identity as citizens in the United States. What they sought was a status that would protect them from the harms of discrimination and empower them with the freedom of self-determination, both for themselves as individuals (just like other citizens of the liberal democracy) and for their homeland (just like other nations recognized as sovereign by the United States).

### Rights, Liberalism, and the Problem of Colonialism

The 1930s marked a turning point for Puerto Ricans living in the United States. The economic depression that blindsided migrants in New York sharpened their awareness of the disadvantages of their position in the city's labor markets and, by the mid-thirties, in its new institutions of public relief as well. Puerto Ricans complained to city officials, the mayor, and one another about the relentlessness of the discrimination they faced, a real departure from the optimism so many had expressed even in the face of adversity in the twenties. The hardening of a new racial identity, categorizing Puerto Ricans more or less as Negro, added to their pessimism. Whereas observers of the 1926 *choques* attributed the conflict to "ethnic rivalry," Puerto Ricans by the early thirties could see the outlines of a racial ideology that was adapting with lightning speed to the radically changed social terrain of New York in that decade. Recently purged of new European immigrants and now drawing black migrants from the American South as well as from the Hispanic and Anglophone Caribbean islands, New York worried observers like the chairman of the House Committee on Immigration and Naturalization, who warned in 1931 against the sudden expansion of the "black colony in Harlem, N.Y."[24] It was a quotidian and local reality of racial identity in New York that Puerto Ricans struggled to understand in the thirties and whose power they struggled to hold at bay. Their anxiety about the debased racial identity ascribed to them in the media and in the streets—ranking them "lower than the colored worker" and making much of the presumptive signs of their blackness—intensified migrants' anxiety about their failure to secure rights as full citizens in the United States. Infuriated by a New York tabloid's article that cast Puerto Ricans as the city's most dangerous newcomers, Nationalist activist María Más Pozo, known for her strident letters to the Spanish-language daily *La Prensa*, prodded her compatriots to join her in asserting that *"we do not want a North American citizenship that humiliates us, depriving us of our dignity, after having been stripped, in the name of humanity, of our blessed land"* (emphasis in the original).[25]

It was not uncommon for *independentistas* to invoke their U.S. citizenship as a straw man to knock down in debates about Puerto Rico's political status.[26] That citizenship was, to them, a false guarantee proffered by the colonial power disguised as a liberal democracy promising rights to all its members, and in their view it actually weakened the island's chances for national sovereignty. But even migrants who were not *independentistas* articulated a sharpening awareness of the frailty of their rights as citizens in this era. While laments about the failed protections of their citizenship initially focused on the traditional dimensions of liberal citizenship (the "negative rights" it promised, in the form of freedom from discrimination, for instance), increasingly Puerto Ricans emphasized the evolving social rights ("positive rights") promised by the New Deal, including, most important, access to state-funded benefits.[27]

Alongside their African American neighbors, Puerto Ricans in the thirties were articulating an early form of what other scholars have identified as a New Deal–era "language of rights," demanding equal access to the benefits the state was in the process of creating for its citizens under the New Deal. Historian Daniel Rodgers writes that in this moment, Americans began "unbundling" abstract words like *freedom* into "the hard, specific language of rights"; they were increasingly focused on the institutionally grounded nature of their rights as Americans.[28] Rodgers agrees with Alan Brinkley that the postwar tumult of rights-based claims emanated "from below," gathering "not in the centers of power but on its margins"—as with the African American and Puerto Rican residents of Harlem and other New York ghettos. Although scholars like Rodgers and Brinkley have assumed that such demands for rights developed later in the New Deal, this book's narrative of this era makes it clear that both Puerto Rican and African American activists were making explicit arguments by the early thirties that citizenship meant something concrete, arguing that the status promised power in the material sense (access to New Deal social benefits) as well as in a symbolic sense (recognition as equals).[29] They could still see, of course, how the discursive framing of that status was warped by the realities of racism, which was part of what they were fighting against.[30]

Puerto Ricans were already important actors in a burgeoning movement of antifascist and anti-imperialist activism after 1935 when the politics of

Puerto Rican nationalism exploded on the island in a number of violent confrontations that began in 1936 and then, within months, spread across New York's *barrios*. In this context, Puerto Ricans enacted a form of political engagement that anthropologist Michel Laguerre calls, in reference to Haitians in the United States, "diasporic citizenship." Diasporic citizens are marked by their dispersion from the homeland, though their distance does not prevent members of the displaced group from participating in homeland politics, remaining effective (if not actual, in all cases) citizens of the homeland.[31] Seeing the late thirties' rhetoric of antifascism and wartime concerns about imperialism as an opening, Puerto Rican activists pushed with new energy for resolution of Puerto Rico's status problem. Paying less attention now to the issues of local, individual rights and equality that had animated them earlier in the thirties, they focused on anti-imperialist politics, almost exclusively, for several years. In pressing for the resolution of their island's sovereignty dilemma, alongside claims to individual rights in the liberal democracy, they crafted a language of rights that stretched outside the purview of liberalism's individual-rights protections and borrowed from the nascent discourse of human rights that would be more fully developed in the wake of World War II. Puerto Rican critiques of liberalism suggested that the practice of the liberal ideals of both the state and its people was warped by the racist and colonial presumptions of their liberal democracy. By the end of the decade, Puerto Rican activists—almost alone—would identify colonialism as another shadowed part of the American creed, a critical if less prevalent dimension of their avant-garde language of rights that has remained almost entirely invisible in narratives of New Deal liberalism.

While leftist Puerto Ricans by the late thirties were asserting that the problem of colonialism gave the lie to the United States' liberal discourse of rights and respect for other nations' sovereignty, liberals stayed as far away as possible from the word *colonialism*. The only lawmaker who openly and consistently referred to Puerto Rico as a colony in this era was Vito Marcantonio, the radical leftist who represented his East Harlem district for nearly two decades in the thirties and forties. This context of silence on the question of a U.S. empire made it all the more surprising when the New Dealer statesman Rexford Tugwell, appointed governor of Puerto Rico by Franklin D. Roosevelt in 1941 (he served until 1946, when Roosevelt appointed Jesús Piñero as the island's first native governor), admitted the centrality of colonialism in the relationship between the United States and Puerto Rico thus in *The Stricken Land*, his 1947 memoir of his time in Puerto

Rico: "This is what colonialism was and did: it distorted all ordinary processes of the mind, made beggars of honest men, sycophants of cynics, American-haters of those who ought to have been working beside us for world betterment—and would if we had encouraged them. . . . Puerto Rico was a colony just as New York and Massachusetts had been colonies. . . . And this last was the real crime of America in the Caribbean, making of Puerto Ricans something less than the men they were born to be."[32]

Liberals' denial of the United States' colonial relationship with Puerto Rico made the political invisibility of Puerto Ricans in the United States by the end of World War II something approaching a foregone conclusion. In denying the real nature of the United States' relationship with the island, they also denied the burdens of political identity borne by its people in the metropole. By the early forties, politicized Puerto Ricans could see clearly their own invisibility, and in fighting against it, they developed a newly complicated relationship to liberalism, continuing to rely on its discourse of inclusion, belonging, and rights, and seeming to take some of its promises at face value, but at the same time critiquing the realities of the actually existing liberal democracy in the United States.[33]

## Puerto Ricans and the Challenge of Recognition

Jesús Colón's framing of the political and social goal of recognition in the 1950s emerged out of a number of failures of Puerto Ricans' aspirations for empowerment as citizens by the end of World War II. Talk about citizenship and citizenship rights had drifted off the table by the fifties, in part because the emancipatory promises of the World War II era were, at best, a wash for both Puerto Rico and Puerto Ricans. Puerto Ricans in the United States had settled quite clearly into the new social category of "minority" by the end of the war. It was a category that sociologist Louis Wirth had defined in 1945—"Minority status entails exclusion from full participation in the life of the society"—and fixed, adds historian Phillip Gleason, "the element of *victimization*" to its subjects.[34] Having become visible as a social "problem" by the late forties, and an increasingly popular subject of academic study by the early fifties, some Puerto Ricans began to take note of the ways in which their "excess visibility" produced a new form of invisibility for them in American society—indeed, as victims.

Others remained hopeful about Puerto Ricans' incorporation into American society. Many mainstream Puerto Rican activists in the fifties got caught up in the promises of postwar liberalism, the newly powerful institutionalization of liberal political goals to "save" both Puerto Rico (through the developmentalist plan called Operation Bootstrap) and "our Puerto Rican neighbors" in the United States. This was also the moment when Puerto Rican leaders at the Migration Division, the largest and most powerful social service agency for Puerto Ricans in New York City, coined the phrase "Juan Q. Citizen" and used it in materials to promote voting and civic engagement among other tools of assimilation. On the other hand, to dissenting political actors within the community, the exclusions of the American creed were obvious and concrete enough by this point that activists like Colón were beginning to articulate a notion that had hovered on the fringes of debate since the late thirties: citizenship in itself was not a status worth arguing over. A broader recognition as equals, as valid social actors, was the thing to aspire to, even if it did not promise a materially or even politically equal status. What this framing of their political identity did do was to push beyond liberalism's limited promises of negative individual rights.

Like the words *inclusion, belonging,* and *membership*—used carelessly, often, throughout much of the twentieth century to describe the goals of incorporating diverse groups of newcomers into the liberal democratic nation—*recognition* can sound vague and imprecise, reaching for a description of social and political relationship that it may not attain. A more specific sense of the term, common in the language of statecraft since the nineteenth century, refers to acknowledgment of a group or a state as a legitimate political entity. Apart from its more popular uses, *recognition* also has a particular set of meanings within political theory and critical social theory, rooted in a wide-ranging and complex debate that originated with philosopher Georg Hegel's phenomenology of consciousness in the nineteenth century.[35] Hegel argued that "intersubjective recognition" was constitutive of a person's sense of self, a necessary prior condition for subjectivity and therefore for the production of what philosopher Charles Taylor calls "full human agents."[36] Only a few nonphilosopher scholars were interested in the social and political implications of Hegelian recognition before the 1950s, in the United States most notably Chicago school sociologists Robert Park and Ernest Burgess, who discussed, in a 1921 textbook, the immigrant's "struggle for recognition" in the sense of the quest for inclusion. By the early 1950s, Martinique-born psychiatrist Frantz Fanon was arguing that white supremacy in colonial societies denied African-descended peoples the attainment of recognition in the Hegelian sense. Together with Jean-Paul Sartre, Fanon sought to turn the idea of recognition into a "topos in the critique of colonial oppression" in the fifties and sixties.[37]

The Hegelian origins of the trope may have been opaque to all but its theorists, but during the revolutionary anticolonial explosions of the sixties, Puerto Rican activists, along with African Americans and Chicanos, began to appropriate the sensibility, if not the precise meanings, of recognition as a "grammar of social conflict."[38] In this context, *recognition* took on precisely the idea of demanding a voice, of insisting on acknowledgment as valid and legitimate social actors. In 1961, the secretary of the Puerto Rican Bar Association wrote to New York's mayor Robert Wagner, informing him that "Puerto Rican students, their parents, and the entire Hispanic community would like to see its role changed from that of a voiceless subject of sociological thesis and studies, to that of equal citizens with a share in the policy making of a system so vital to themselves."[39] His emphasis on the "role . . . of equal citizens" sounded like the typical liberal rights discourse of the previous generation, but his rejection of "voicelessness" and demand for "a share" brought his claim in line with the more comprehensive challenge embodied in the idea of recognition. In many instances, Puerto Rican activists of this era adopted language to talk about their dilemmas that would only later be used by scholars in debates over what they called the "politics of recognition." In 1967, for example, when journalist Peter Kihss interviewed Ted Vélez, the twenty-eight-year-old director of the East Harlem Tenants Council, about the recent riots in his community, Vélez explained, "Violence comes out of frustration, nobody listening, not having organizations effective enough, not having recognition, respect, dignity."[40] Outside observers used the language of recognition as well: a *U.S. News* article about Latinos in 1970, titled "A Silent Minority Starts to Speak Out," announced that "millions of Spanish-speaking Americans—traditionally quiescent—are suddenly shaking off old restraints, making a bold bid for recognition and opportunity."[41]

These scattered invocations of "recognition" signaled an agreement, not just on the Left but among more centrist observers as well, that demands for social change were pushing past the boundaries of a traditional liberal discourse of "civil rights" to encompass a larger set of claims. These claims were larger in both a discursive and a geographic sense, and were more accurately described as "human rights." Indeed, the rearticulation of human rights as a problem in the era of worldwide anticolonialism became an important if unevenly invoked component of the language of justice, fixing attention on the human, experiential costs of colonialism and racism.[42] In the early postwar period, African American activists—whose cause soon became more narrowly defined as "civil rights"—had expressed many of their claims about racial justice, and the failed promises of liberal societies, in the language of human rights, although it was only after a long decade's battle against legal segregation in the United States that activists began returning to a human rights discourse. In 1962, for instance, New York City officials renamed the city's Commission on Intergroup Relations, an antidiscrimination review board, the "Commission on Human Rights."[43] Around the same time, Malcolm X began to call for an expanded political agenda that would focus on human rights more than on civil rights. He also, at times, linked his human rights claims to the language of recognition, as in a speech at the Militant Labor Forum in New York in the spring of 1964: "[America] has colonized twenty two million Afro-Americans by depriving us of first-class citizenship, by depriving us of civil rights, actually by depriving us of human rights. She has not only deprived us of the right to be a citizen, she has deprived us of the right to be human beings, the right to be recognized and respected as men and women."[44]

Particularly amid what looked like the implosion of the civil rights movement by 1970, the language of equal citizenship had come to seem somewhat anachronistic and naïve to claimants in many social groups. The languages of recognition and human rights were more elastic and capacious, and more precisely descriptive of the growing connections among worldwide justice movements. Those discourses reflected the breaking apart of boundaries—challenging the pieties of liberal discourse and the emphasis on state-centered reform—to make room for the explosion of grassroots energy like that of the Puerto Rican movement, which its activists hoped would continue to gain ground into the seventies.

### Puerto Ricans and the Struggle for Recognition: An Argument against "False Novelty"

In spite of its potent start, the discourse of recognition remained somewhat diffuse in Puerto Ricans' political claims by the late seventies. For one thing, "recognition" was not as easily encapsulated into sound bytes as were, for instance, the traditional complaints about "second-class citizenship." Another reason for its underdevelopment as an explicit discourse was the splintering of social, political, and cultural claims that had been successfully unified by the Puerto Rican movement activists in the late sixties. In Puerto Rican New York in the mid-seventies, there were Nuyorican poets creating radical street theater, education activists working on issues like bilingual programs and the community control of schools, and socialist nationalists pursuing an independence agenda increasingly removed from the New York *barrios*. Certainly many of these people were connected to one another in their communities, and many activists worked on multiple agendas, but not with the same level of commitment to linking their diverse goals as during the heyday of the Puerto Rican movement. And there was a related decline in public awareness of their struggles. The mainstream press and the white literati paid little attention to the Nuyorican artists whose cultural projects paralleled those of the Black Arts movement, and there was only sporadic public discussion of the continuing battles over adequate schools and housing in Puerto Rican neighborhoods. Even the cause of Puerto Rican independence fell into the shadows of political life in the city, except during one instance in 1977 when a group of nationalist activists managed to reach the top of the Statue of Liberty and fly a Puerto Rican flag from her crown.[45]

In the face of the political fragmentation of that decade, a small but growing number of Puerto Rican activists in universities (many in the Puerto Rican studies departments they had fought to establish) tried to maintain an integrated analysis of social, political, and cultural issues facing Puerto Ricans in the United States. They were, indeed, demanding to give voice to "voiceless subjects," in their academic communities as well as in their neighborhoods. Through the creation of Puerto Rican studies programs, these activists made a claim for the intellectual significance of Puerto Ricans' experience in the United States and insisted on the centrality of colonialism to that history. Like the work of practitioners within other new ethnic studies movements, however, Puerto Rican studies remained "ghettoized" within the academy well into the 1980s.[46] Efforts to make sense of the explosion of rights-based claims in the wake of the sixties' liberation movements had begun to generate debate about what was increasingly (and usually derisively) called identity politics, and critics of identity-based political and intellectual work dismissed it as rooted in "personal" complaints that did not count as legitimate public discourse. On the other side, proponents of identity-based political agendas argued that society's failures to respect difference produced political harm—an irrefutably public matter. As philosopher Linda Martín Alcoff explained, invoking Nancy Fraser, "We [minorities and white women] are 'denied the status of full partner in social interaction' precisely *because* of our identities."[47]

The rancorous debate over identity politics inspired a new and lively discussion about the idea of recognition among political theorists. The ideological differences among them, defined at times as liberal versus communitarian, or more generally as center versus left, generated conflict over the meaning of "recognition" and "identity" in the context of postsixties rearrangements. All agreed on the basic social need for intersubjective recognition, as Hegel had defined it, but theorists argued about motivations for recognition claims. Did they entail "just" the recognition of group members' identity position—their "difference"—or did they invoke the expectation of redistribution of resources? In other words, what was at stake? Was it simply "acknowledgment" in the cultural and social field, or was it actual redistribution of economic resources and social and political power? Scholars argued over whether recognition of difference for disadvantaged groups could be achieved without upsetting the balance between traditional liberalism's values of individual rights and freedoms on the one hand and communitarian, multiculturalist values of group respect and cultural survival on the other.[48] Responding to the seminal essay "The Politics of Recognition" by his communitarian colleague Charles Taylor, Jürgen Habermas conceded that it was not just "identity politics" but "historically unredeemed claims" that formed the basis of modern struggles for recognition, and that such struggles were linked to "collective experiences of violated integrity," not just to the denial of rights on the individual level.[49] This was, of course, exactly what activists in the sixties' justice movements had argued.

Philosopher Nancy Fraser pushed forward the debate over the politics of recognition by calling the liberal-communitarian divide a "false antithesis." She argues that recognition should be understood fundamentally as a matter of group justice, rectifying historic wrongs through the honoring of individual rights and made concrete through redistribution of resources. "What requires recognition," she says, "is not group-specific identity but the status of individual group members as full partners in social interaction." Or, as philosopher Iris Marion Young put it, "most group-conscious political claims . . . are not claims to the recognition of identity as such, but rather claims for fairness, equal opportunity, and political inclusion. A politics of recognition, that is, usually is part of or a means to claims for political and social inclusion or an end to structural inequalities that disadvantage [its practitioners]." It was the status as "full partners in social interaction" that would allow the leverage to achieve some level of equitable distribution of resources; and, indeed, this leverage was what the young activist Ted Vélez was talking about in 1967 when he spoke of his community's need for recognition in order to achieve more effective advocacy on issues like housing, employment, and education.[50]

A rather predictable irony of the discussion about recognition among theorists in the 1980s was that among the handful of North American examples of identity-based politics they tended to draw on—those of women, homosexuals, Quebecois, and African Americans—they entirely overlooked the example of Latinos' struggles for recognition. Axel Honneth, one of the central theorists of recognition, asserted that "if social theory is to provide an adequate account of actual fields of social conflict, it will have . . . to situate the motivation for these emancipatory struggles within the social world." Especially for those scholars who advocated the examination of their theories in the context of the actual fields of conflict in the United States, Latinos' absence from that field was quite a loss.[51]

And, of course, it was noted acutely by scholars working in the field of Latino studies. In 1992, anthropologist Renato Rosaldo remarked with mordant humor on the "recent praise songs of insightful, moderate, and sensible Canadian philosopher Charles Taylor's writings on multiculturalism." "What happened," asked Rosaldo, "to bell hooks . . . Gloria Anzaldúa, Cornell West, Mari Matsuda, Gerald López . . .?"[52] At the same moment, when political theorists were examining the idea of recognition more systematically, an interdisciplinary collective of scholars in Latino studies was developing a parallel conversation about identity and rights in the United States. Pointing to the practical and theoretical constraints of citizenship as a formal status, just as Puerto Rican and Chicano activists had argued over a generation before, this group of scholars sought to push the discussion of rights and social belonging for Latinos beyond the realm of the state, strictly speaking. Some of these scholars would argue, instead, that "those who labor and contribute to the economic and cultural wealth of the country . . . [should] be recognized as legitimate political subjects claiming rights for themselves and their children, and in that sense as citizens." Renato Rosaldo, a member of the collective, had proposed a theory of "cultural citizenship" that he defined as "the right to be different and to belong in a participatory democratic sense"; and it was this idea that the Latino Cultural Studies Working Group used as their framework for a collection of essays published under the title *Latino Cultural Citizenship*. Although few members of the group used the term *recognition* in an explicitly theoretical form, their definition of "cultural citizens"—equal members of American society by virtue of their real contributions to that society—fit readily within the framework of the recognition theorists. They also argued that a more equitable distribution of resources should follow that recognition, for undocumented migrants and legal citizens alike.[53]

The Latino Cultural Studies collective had started out with an avant-garde project, but by the time their book was published, they had some company. In history departments, for instance, "majority scholars" and graduate students had begun to take note of new scholarship that cast Latino historical actors as part of larger narratives of American culture, labor, and urban life.[54] In a broader frame, the collective's novel approach was being echoed in other "new citizenship" scholarship around the Americas in the early nineties. Much of this work emphasized the importance of not just broadening native peoples' access to traditional citizenship rights but also delivering on the promise of human rights. In the decade or so since, Latin American scholars across the region, along with Africanists and other scholars of postcolonial politics, have continued to expand questions of non-state-centered citizenship practices. They, too, have sought to connect these practices to a broader conceptualization of human rights and recognition, "the right to be seen and treated as human beings."[55]

This scholarship represents more than just a revival of Fanon's "topos" in critiques of colonialism. The theory and discourse of recognition also connect struggles for justice in the "global south," the areas of the world most burdened by the legacies of colonialism, with new iterations of minority group politics in Europe. And, as with the Puerto Rican case that I explore here, these questions have been posed not just by academics but by activists on the ground: the emergence of the Zapatista movement in the nineties in Mexico, a direct response to NAFTA (the North American Free Trade Agreement), drew on a discourse of recognition, and so have recent campaigns for ethnic justice and equality in various African nations.[56] Linda Martín Alcoff is one of the first to begin connecting the dots that link the rough continuum of Chicano and Puerto Rican grassroots politics since the sixties to other examples of recognition struggles in the United States and "to global identity-based movements." Her arguments present more than just a powerful "plea for empirical investigation" of the theorists' claims. They also offer a starting point for thinking more expansively about past and present rights discourses as claims for recognition.[57]

I argue in this book that Puerto Ricans articulated goals as political and social actors in the United States throughout the twentieth century that represented something more than a simple demand for equal citizenship. Politicized Puerto Ricans increasingly pointed to the necessity of their compatriots' recognition as equal partners in social interaction, with rights that extended beyond the limitations of actually existing liberal citizenship. Earlier in the century, in the 1920s and 1930s, Puerto Ricans in New York often focused on citizenship rights as the primary goal of their local politics, although arguably the debates about challenging discrimination, for instance, or about the costs of being identified as "Negro," or even complaints about Puerto Rico's lack of sovereignty in this era, were also efforts to be recognized as valid political actors with a legitimate critique of U.S. racism and imperial aspirations. After World War II, once Puerto Ricans' experience in the thirties had shown that the promised rights of liberal citizenship were no match for the weight of their identity as dark-skinned colonials, it was increasingly clear to politicized Puerto Ricans that a more forceful "grammar of social conflict" was required for them to achieve any measure of equality in the United States.[58] Such a framing of the political identities and political goals of Puerto Ricans throughout the twentieth century highlights how the struggle for recognition defined their path well before the late sixties, the era in which most scholars locate the beginning of the politics of recognition in the United States.

In fact, by testing the theory of recognition primarily in the context of identity-based politics during and after the sixties, scholars have limited its heuristic power, misinterpreting "the politics of recognition" as a contemporary phenomenon central to only the most recent chapters of a longer and broader history of freedom struggles. In a similar vein, philosopher Axel Honneth argues that "the conceptual framework of recognition is of central importance today not because it expresses the objectives of a new type of social movement, but because it has proven to be the appropriate tool for categorically unlocking social experiences of injustice as a whole." Likewise, Craig Calhoun, who has written about political identity and recognition during the labor struggles of the early-nineteenth-century United States, admonishes fellow scholars not to fall for what he calls "the false novelty of the new social movement." Calhoun's point is that a sense of history is key to seeing the continuities in what people actively look for as they construct and revise their political selves and group identities in specific contexts.[59]

The blindness about the past that Calhoun warns against is not merely presentist, as historians like to say. It also comes from privileging abstract theoretical perspectives over the reasoned interpretations of historical actors about their own time. (In her introduction to Charles Taylor's volume on recognition, *Multiculturalism*, Amy Gutmann asks, for instance, "Is Aristotle's understanding of slavery more enlightening than Frederick Douglass's?")[60] Recognition, I am arguing here, is actually an old way of structuring claims about political and social goals and the identities from which they emerge. Particularly when recognition is theorized as a set of claims about both identity equality and resource equality, it is an accurate frame for understanding the popularly defined goals of historical actors, and it is one that Puerto Ricans in the United States developed increasingly throughout the twentieth century.[61]

Just as important as the historical sensibility, interpreting Puerto Ricans' political goals in terms of recognition allows us to see how, often, those goals were framed beyond the boundaries of liberal citizenship discourse. Puerto Ricans' demands for recognition in the United States, as well as those of many other minority groups, were not just demands for special group rights. More important, Puerto Ricans insisted on the legitimacy of their particular and historically specific claims to inclusion and equality. In making these claims, activists did not always wish to define themselves primarily as equal participants in the liberal polity—since, in many eras, what they were demanding was recognition of the legitimacy of a view that was actually critical of liberalism. This was true to an extent of the Puerto Rican "old left" of the thirties (socialists, internationalists, island nationalists), whose claims as political actors were expressed primarily in terms of equal citizenship rights. It was more true of the young radicals of the sixties, who drew from heterodoxical ideologies of socialism and nationalism and the increasingly popular discourse of human rights to craft these capacious claims for both individual equality and group recognition.

I am also asserting, then, that the goal of recognition is not limited to a strictly liberal vision of society. American liberalism had certainly become "protean" by mid-century, as historian Gary Gerstle argues, flexible and able to incorporate many new ideas, especially racial justice in certain forms. But it still was bound by assumptions about the acceptable range of political critique, particularly for those whose collective complaints of violated justice rested on the imperialist crimes of liberal democracies.[62] The conventional recognition framework presumes a shared liberal worldview and language, when actually those demanding recognition often selectively used liberal discourse (inclusion, justice, equality, rights) but were motivated by goals that lay beyond—sometimes far beyond—the scope of American liberalism.

Recognition, conceptualized in this way, was a real goal of political action that Puerto Rican activists in New York pursued. Implicitly and explicitly, their claims for recognition questioned the coherence and consistency of what theorist Wendy Brown calls the legitimating narratives of liberal democracy, including those that focus on "rights" and "sovereignty."

"What happens," Brown asks, "when these narratives and assumptions are challenged, or indeed simply exposed in the legitimating function?"[63] The history of Puerto Ricans and their struggle to define a cohesive political identity in twentieth-century New York provides one set of answers to that question. Beginning sporadically in the 1930s, and gaining full momentum by the late sixties, Puerto Ricans combined demands for traditional liberal individual rights, like equal access to housing, employment, and education, with the assertion of particular group rights, like ballots and civil service tests in Spanish and bilingual education; and through both categories of claims, they challenged the United States' liberal democracy to acknowledge the reasons that their group experienced such persistent failures of justice.

In attempting here the intricate work of reconstructing this history of Puerto Rican activism in twentieth-century New York, I have relied on the insights of countless other scholars and contemporary observers. But more important, my central arguments borrow heavily from what the most incisive Puerto Rican voices were saying all along about their struggles: that their island's unequal relationship to the United States had wrought the disadvantages Puerto Ricans suffered throughout the century, both in their home society and on the mainland, and that the "injustices of recognition" they experienced were rooted in the failures of a democratic liberal society to acknowledge this history. The chapters that follow narrate the effort of Puerto Rican New Yorkers to secure what many framed as the human right to be recognized as equals in the nation that had made them, begrudgingly, into Americans.

Chapter One

# New Citizens
# of New York

Community Organization and Political Culture in the Twenties

⊩⊩⊩⊩⊩⊩⊩⊩⊩⊩⊩⊩⊩⊩⊩⊩⊩⊩⊩⊩⊩⊩⊩⊩⊩⊩⊩⊩⊩⊩⊩⊩⊩⊩⊩⊩⊩⊩⊩⊩⊩⊩⊩⊩⊩⊩⊩⊩⊩⊩⊩⊩⊩⊩⊩⊩⊩⊩⊩⊩⊩⊩⊩⊩⊩⊩

### Puerto Ricans in *la Colonia Hispana*, 1916–29

On the day he arrived in New York in the summer of 1916, after riding the
ferry from Staten Island to Manhattan and then boarding a West Side elevated train bound for Twenty-third Street, Bernardo Vega entered the
vibrant New York world of Spanish-speaking immigrants. It was a world
about which outsiders knew little. Indeed, Jesús Colón, a compatriot and
later friend and ally of Vega's who landed across the river in Brooklyn's
"Puerto Rican ghetto" in 1918, would observe that "only those who lived
there knew it existed."[1] Manhattan's first *barrios latinos* had sprung up in
Chelsea and along lower Second Avenue before the turn of the century but
soon shifted uptown and, by 1920, became a Spanish-speaking island in
what was then the largely Jewish and Italian neighborhood of East Harlem.
This enclave, too, occupied the margins of the city both geographically
and socially. Residents of the *colonia hispana* (as Spanish speakers referred
to their Brooklyn and Manhattan neighborhoods together) formed a lively
and diverse community of working-class and middle-class aspirants in New
York. Skilled and unskilled laborers lived alongside merchants and shopkeepers, together with a handful of professionals that included lawyers,
doctors, and dentists who served the surrounding community of *hispanos*.
In terms of political interests, El Barrio would become increasingly heterogeneous over the course of the twenties, but the earliest residents of Puerto
Rican East Harlem never forgot that its roots lay in the lively exile community founded in New York by Cuban and Puerto Rican independence
fighters in the 1860s.[2]

When Vega and Colón first landed in New York, the Puerto Rican population in the city was tiny, with Spaniards and Cubans dominating the *colonia*. "I remember when we had just one Puerto Rican grocery store, one
Puerto Rican restaurant and one such barbershop in all of New York City,"
Jesús Colón wrote, recalling his first years in the city. "No matter where you

lived you had to take the old nickel IRT to 125th St. and Madison Avenue if you wanted a haircut in a Puerto Rican barbershop so you would not be discriminated against because of race, color, nationality or accent."[3] Within a few years, however, Puerto Ricans would overtake other Spanish speakers in number.[4] Contemporary estimates of the population of Puerto Ricans from within the *colonia* placed the migrant population at around 30,000 to 40,000 in 1925, although Bernardo Vega thought there were almost 35,000 Puerto Ricans in New York already in 1919.[5] In 1927, Puerto Rican Resident Commissioner Córdova Dávila pronounced that the "40,000 votes" of Puerto Ricans in New York "constitute a respectable force." More grandiose was the Porto Rican Brotherhood of America, which claimed in its 1927 annual bulletin that "our conservative estimate shows the number of Porto Rican residents in NY to be 100,000." The U.S. Bureau of the Census estimate put the Puerto Rican population at about 45,000 by 1930.[6]

The several *hispano* communities into which Puerto Rican migrants settled around 1920 comprised a heterogeneous world. Colón described the *colonia* of the twenties and thirties as a crazy quilt of racial, economic, and political identities: "In this pilgrimage in search of a better economic well-being, have arrived Puerto Ricans who are poor, middle class, white like some inhabitant of a Nordic forest, *trigueños*like good descendants of Chief Aguaybana, black like a shining citizen of old Ethiopia." "And," he added, "all of them carry with them a mind that surely doesn't think alike in terms of politics, prejudice, etc., which adorns the present social organization."[7] This diversity of mind flourished within a context of sharply drawn class distinctions in the *colonia*. By the time the post–World War I Puerto Rican migration began, some of the earlier migrants, who in the nineteenth and early twentieth centuries settled first in Chelsea and in the Upper West Side, had opened shops and restaurants, doctors' offices and other businesses in the area of Harlem bounded approximately by Eighth Avenue to Lexington, and 110th Street to 120th.[8]

Carlos Tapia, a leader of the Puerto Rican community in Brooklyn in the twenties and thirties, noted that while most Puerto Rican migrants in that period settled in the Borough Hall and Red Hook sections of Brooklyn, the "cream" of the Puerto Rican migrants "elected to live in Harlem." He recalled bitterly what he saw as the differences between the Manhattan and Brooklyn enclaves: "The Brooklyn Puerto Ricans were the ones who fought and struggled to establish the foundation of the Puerto Rican political, social and economic force. . . . [Puerto Ricans in Manhattan] did not participate in these battles . . . in their sanctuary [but] they reaped the po-

Figure 2. Portrait of Joaquín Colón, brother of Jesús Colón, taken in New York in 1919, at about age twenty-three. Jesús Colón papers, Archives of the Puerto Rican Diaspora, Centro de Estudios Puertorriqueños, Hunter College, CUNY.

litical and economic benefits conquered by blood, and fire, death and tears by fellow 'countrymen.'"[9] Bernardo Vega, who remained in Manhattan, also reflected on the boroughs' distinct class identities. He observed that middle-class Puerto Ricans living in Yorkville (south of East Harlem's *barrio latino*) and other middle-class parts of Manhattan tended to call themselves "Spaniards," or avoided speaking Spanish in public or reading Spanish papers, and forbade their children to speak Spanish. On the other hand, Vega insisted that in working-class neighborhoods, residents were "proud" to be Puerto Rican—"no one cared if they were called 'spik.'"[10]

Ramon Colón, a cousin of Jesús Colón, recalled that "in those days Brooklyn was more or less poor in comparison with [El Barrio]."[11] Only about a third of residents in the Manhattan *barrio* worked as unskilled laborers, while in Spanish-speaking Brooklyn, over two-thirds of residents worked in low-skill jobs; 15 percent of Manhattan residents worked in offices or owned businesses, while less than 3 percent of their Brooklyn compatriots did so. Many of the men who counted as skilled laborers worked as *tabaqueros*, or cigarmakers. Most women who worked for wages were also skilled workers, though they were more likely to do sewing piecework at home.[12] There were also differences in the racial profiles of the Brooklyn and Manhattan communities. Of those Spanish speakers categorized as "black" by state census takers, a higher percentage lived in Brooklyn than in Manhattan, a fact not unrelated to the class structure of the two communities since, in Latin America as in the United States, racial and class hierarchies ran parallel to each other. Some Manhattan Puerto Ricans referred with disdain to the *"negros"* settling across the river, suggesting their sense of privilege as residents of a neighborhood into whose white population they hoped they would soon blend. Their judgment was challenged by two of the Brooklyn *barrio*'s best-known leaders, Jesús Colón and Carlos Tapia, who considered themselves black and embraced the many-hued complexions of their Brooklyn compatriots.[13] Arturo Schomburg, who would become the most famous of these early Puerto Rican New Yorkers as a bibliophile and collector of a world-class library of Africana, took a different approach to navigating the city's racial landscape. After migrating to New York in 1891, Schomburg "crossed over" to the African American community that he married into in the early twentieth century, and lived the rest of his life largely separate from his compatriots.[14]

The heterogeneity of migrants' worlds could be measured not only in the class and racial differences but also in the multitude of nationalities represented in the Spanish-speaking *colonia.* Before the turn of the century, Spanish immigrants vied with Puerto Rican and Cuban exiles for dominance in both the Chelsea and East Harlem centers of *hispano* life in New York, but the Antillean nationalists had dispersed by the beginning of the Spanish-Cuban-American War in 1898, many of them returning home to fight in the final imperialist struggle against Spain. The very small numbers of Dominicans, Mexicans, Venezuelans, and other South Americans living in New York before World War I also began to increase in the years after the war.[15] In 1913, a Colombian immigrant founded what would become the *colonia*'s newspaper of record, *La Prensa*, as a four-page weekly; by 1918, a Spaniard, José Comprubí, started running the paper as a daily to meet the needs of the expanding *colonia*. Ten years later, *La Prensa* reported an average daily readership of fifteen thousand. The paper covered headline news from across Latin America as well as local news deemed relevant to its immigrant readership. The editorial sensibility of *La Prensa* was a subject of some dissension in the *colonia* among members of the working class, who regularly accused Comprubí of representing the interests only of the bourgeois sector of the community. The editors would occasionally make a show of running a front-page interview with a working-class leader or providing page-one coverage of a dockworkers' strike (many Spaniards and Puerto Ricans were maritime workers).[16] Puerto Ricans in particular also complained, from time to time, about the paper's bias in favor of its Spanish readers.[17]

In its early years, Spaniards dominated the *colonia* not only numerically but also culturally. While Puerto Ricans often referred to the United States, and New York City in particular, as *"la metrópoli"*—the center of political power over the island—Spain remained, to many, the *"patria."*[18] Spanish origins conferred greater social status, both in and outside the *colonia*, and it was a common practice for Puerto Ricans to "pass" as Spanish when they could. Pedro Juan Labarthe, a Puerto Rican teacher at Xavier College in Chelsea, and later author of the first published memoir of a Puerto Rican migrant in New York, lamented that even other Spanish speakers in the *colonia* looked upon his compatriots with disdain and suggested that Puerto Ricans suffered from an "inferiority complex." Labarthe illustrated his point with a story about visiting an American barbershop with a Puerto Rican friend. When the barber asked Labarthe's friend—"a cultured, refined man, well-respected in our country"—if he was Puerto Rican, the friend replied that no, he was Spanish. Labarthe, "wounded," interjected, "I am Porto Rican." Upon leaving the barbershop, the friend explained, "It's that we have such a bad reputation here."[19] Many migrants asserted that for people of other ethnicities in New York to refer to Puerto Ricans as "Spanish" was a term of "respect."[20]

The Spanish-speaking *colonias* in East Harlem and Brooklyn were not only heterogeneous internally. In each borough, they also formed part of a larger mixed community of immigrants and second- and third-generation "ethnics." In the East Harlem *barrio*, Jews comprised the "old" residents, having settled in the blocks above 110th Street, east of Fifth Avenue, beginning in the late nineteenth century. Italians had begun to migrate north from southern Manhattan around 1910 and were well established in the neighborhood by the time Spaniards and Puerto Ricans began settling there in larger numbers after World War I.[21] Some Puerto Ricans recalled conflict between ethnic groups. Lorenzo Homar, who arrived in East Harlem as a child in 1928, said that "there were fights with Italian-Americans and with the blacks, because [Puerto Ricans] were the new ones, they were the new immigrants." His father, he recalled, took a look around El Barrio and said, "'No, I'm not staying *here*.' He believed that it was pretty much a ghetto." So the family moved north and west, to the less crowded Jewish and Irish district of Washington Heights.[22] Others remembered El Barrio in the early twenties as a peaceful place where neighbors of different nationalities got along well. "We didn't find so much discrimination at that time because we [Puerto Ricans] were only two families [in the building]," recalled Louise Delgado, who lived on the fringes of East Harlem when she migrated to New York with her family in 1923—although she did recall hostility from her Italian neighbors, both on the streets and at the dress factory where she worked, later in the thirties.[23]

Some residents of Brooklyn also remembered less ethnic conflict in the early years of the twenties. Mercedes Díaz, who arrived in Brooklyn in 1923, remembered ethnic relations there in the twenties as Louise remembered them in Manhattan: "There was no racism because there were very few of us."[24] But most of those who recounted halcyon days of early settlement also related memories that contradicted their rosier ones. Although Mercedes asserted an absence of racism in that era, she admitted that "there were fights, the Italians against the Puerto Ricans." Another early Brooklynite, Félix Loperena, said that his Irish neighbors were the most hostile to Puerto Ricans; Ramón Rodríguez concurred, postulating that "the Irish hated the Puerto Ricans because they envied their ability to come and go freely as citizens."[25] A number of the people who recalled an atmosphere of ethnic conflict pointed to skin color as a factor. Loperena remembered problems with his Irish neighbors most acutely, but he also observed that "Italians treated *trigueños* worse than light-skinned Puerto Ricans." Juan Ramos, who first said that Puerto Ricans were treated fine because there were few of them, later added that Italians were very prejudiced toward "blacks" (meaning African Americans) and toward Puerto Ricans whom they perceived as black.[26] Clemente Torres talked about a general attitude of racial discrimination among Jews and Italians: "In that time, it wasn't easy for Puerto Ricans to live together with these people. . . . When I arrived in this country [in 1925] people of my skin color . . . [weren't] allowed in many places in that time."[27]

A migrant's class identity shaped how he or she remembered social relations in the *colonia* in the early years. Within El Barrio, unskilled workers and their families lived in close proximity to shopkeepers and professionals, they shopped together at *la marqueta*, an open-air market that stretched beneath the Park Avenue railroad trestle, and they gathered at the Teatro Latino for Spanish-language movies. Although residents of both classes worked to organize mutual benefit societies and other associations to improve their "lot" in a crumbling district of the city, Bernardo Vega felt that the elite "always seemed to turn their backs on the working people."[28] A larger proportion of the "working people" lived across the river, near downtown Brooklyn, close to factory jobs and to the Navy Yard, where many worked on the docks, but far from the shops and services of El Barrio, where they could find Spanish-speaking clerks and familiar products like *plátanos* and *habichuelas* (plantains and beans).

Some migrants later recalled fondly the smallness of this Brooklyn world, the intimacy of the few Puerto Rican families who resided there in the early 1920s, and the plentiful work; others, though, said they felt isolated and were acutely aware of the aspersions that many Manhattan Puerto Ricans cast on their less "cosmopolitan" counterparts in Brooklyn. Ernesto Sepúlveda was a member of Brooklyn's small Puerto Rican petty bourgeoisie who settled there in 1926 and lived next door to his friend Ramon Colón, Jesús Colón's cousin, on Lafayette Avenue, where he operated a small grocery store.[29] Sepúlveda claimed in a 1974 interview that "at no time in the fifty years since I came here have I felt rejected or discriminated against because I was Puerto Rican." His working-class compatriots, on the other hand, described clashes with Jewish and Italian coworkers in the wire factory, the Campbell Soup factory, and National Biscuit Company—places where they might have struggled to find work in the first place. They steered clear of the Irish police, "who were like a gestapo for the Puerto Ricans"; they "couldn't cross Columbia Street" into the Italian district because "they would throw stones"; and relied regularly on the informal aid of the Brooklyn *colonia*'s "Robin Hood," Carlos Tapia.[30]

### La Vida Cotidiana

"Jobs for Puerto Ricans were painting boats and cleaning boilers at the docks," said one Brooklyn man, recalling the twenties. "We work our fingers to the bone, but why complain? We all have to work to improve our situation," wrote a migrant woman to *La Prensa* about her work as a seamstress in a small Manhattan garment factory.[31] The majority of the Puerto Rican migrants living in New York City in the 1920s spent their days working at factory jobs or doing piecework in their small apartments, largely unaware of rivalries among the elite leaders of the *colonia* and rarely participating in their *fiestas*.[32] In 1922, *La Prensa* had begun printing a daily column called *"Vida obrera,"* or "Worker's Life," an olive branch extended to the laboring Puerto Ricans who complained of their exclusion from public life in the *colonia*. It was probably not a surprise to *La Prensa*'s working-class readers that the letter selected for the first run of the workers' column advocated a politics of compromise among the working class—an approach that should, said the writer, be modeled after the teachings of Jesus Christ.[33] Many migrants who actually lived a *"vida obrera"* took a less conciliatory view of their struggles in New York. One member of the Ateneo Obrero Hispano wrote, in the weekly paper *El Pueblo*, that while many immigrants had hoped to find "the promised land" in the United States, the land of gold and fortune, they found in America "the land of hard and punishing work where almost all doors were closed and the gold and the fortune were in the hands of giant monopolies."[34]

The young and middle-aged Puerto Rican workers who migrated to New York around 1920 had come of age in Puerto Rico in a period of intense labor struggles. Dockworkers, agricultural workers, and urban artisans like carpenters, shoemakers, and *tabaqueros* conducted work stoppages as well as dramatic strikes countered by violent repression from both employers and the U.S.-dominated island government. Throughout the 1910s and 1920s, conflicts between workers and bosses played out in a context of widespread tension over the transformation of the island's economy. U.S.-based corporations were buying up huge tracts of mixed-use agricultural land to turn them into profitable sugar plantations, causing dramatic dislocations in the agricultural sector and creating a new kind of unemployment on the island. Socialists and workers began organizing the Federación Libre de Trabajadores, a craft-based labor union, which by the early 1920s had forged close ties with the American Federation of Labor. As the popularity of the Socialist Party increased dramatically among workers, government persecution of Socialists escalated.[35]

The Socialist Party played a major role in workers' efforts to consolidate power in labor struggles, both on the island and in New York City. In Puerto Rico in the twentieth century, socialism developed along a particular trajectory that followed the idiosyncratic career of its primarily leader, Santiago Iglesias, who was resolutely pro-American and would become a proponent of statehood by the early thirties.[36] In New York, however, Puerto Rican workers who allied with Socialist groups engaged in an internationalist sphere of working-class politics. Vega recalled his role in founding the first Puerto Rican committee of the New York Socialist Party in 1918, along with Jesús Colón and Eduvigis Cabán, among others. Vega's activism as a Socialist in New York, and that of several of his *compañeros*, extended far beyond the boundaries of his relationships to other Puerto Ricans. He regularly attended meetings of the Eastern European socialist groups in New York, where he made contacts with Czechoslovakian and Jewish comrades with whom he would make a failed attempt to set up a small cigar shop.[37] Few migrants of the working class occupied such a cosmopolitan political world, but groups like the Alianza Obrera Puertorriqueña and the Porto Rican Brotherhood of America nevertheless asserted their commitment to working-class concerns beyond just *"la política puertorriqueña"* and proclaimed that they would make "no distinctions of color, class, religion, or political creed" within their memberships.[38] They also welcomed the support of non–Puerto Rican workers; according to one member of the Alianza Obrera, "over 200 Jewish Socialists" attended a 1925 meeting to address the implications for workers of the political situation in Puerto Rico.[39]

Among Puerto Rican workers in New York, it was the *colonia*'s cigar-

Figure 3. Banquet sponsored by the Porto Rican Brotherhood of America, Las Flores restaurant, Brooklyn, 1928. Erasmo Vando papers, Archives of the Puerto Rican Diaspora, Centro de Estudios Puertorriqueños, Hunter College, CUNY.

makers who engaged most intensively in cross-national labor organizing in this period, motivated in part by the challenges they faced from the mechanization of their industry in the mid-twenties. By 1925, following the lead of their *compañeros* in Puerto Rico and Tampa, Puerto Rican and other immigrant cigarmakers in New York had begun to organize to improve working conditions. A small group of Spanish-speaking *tabaqueros* established "el Comité de Reconstrucción Social y Económico" in 1925, initiating a campaign of "agitation and workers' propaganda" to improve the working conditions of *tabaqueros* in New York. One of the leaders of the *comité*, Pedro San Miguel, reflected on the nascent campaign in a piece for the "Vida obrera" column, in which he asserted that the working conditions for cigarmakers in the city's large tobacco firms were "abominable." San Miguel said that his hopes for successful struggle in the tobacco industry lay with the *latinos*, although they comprised only 12 percent of the cigarmaker workforce, because they were the ones who, he said, possessed a group history of struggle, striking numerous times in both Puerto Rico and Tampa before 1920. Under San Miguel's leadership, *tabaqueros* in New York allied with their counterparts in Philadelphia and New Jersey in 1926 to form a union local of cigarmakers, affiliated with the International Cigarmakers of America.[40] A primary goal of the New York–based local involved organizing opposition to mechanization in the bigger tobacco firms, which found cheaper labor in Passaic, New Brunswick, Perth Amboy, and other New Jersey towns.[41]

Women make a few appearances in the scant stories of Puerto Rican *tabaqueros*' organizing in the twenties.[42] *Comité* activist San Miguel, in a letter to *La Prensa* on the struggle for unionization in New York, discussed at length the difficulties women presented in the struggle to unionize. San Miguel estimated that the majority of women working in the tobacco shops were over the age of sixty and asserted that since "their lives are a race nearing its end," these *tabaqueras* were docile and willingly adapted to "whatever working conditions were imposed on them," thus hindering the efforts of other workers to protest working conditions and build a union movement.[43] Other male *tabaqueros* may or may not have agreed with this attempt to scapegoat women as the weak link in their effort to unionize. And those who would pin the blame on women workers may or may not have taken note when, about eighteen months later, a considerable number of these women turned out for a rally in support of striking cigarmakers in Puerto Rico. Not only did women in the *colonia* participate—and presumably many of them were *tabaqueras*—they were also represented on the platform by "*señorita*"

Rose Schneiderman, head of the Ladies Trade Union League.[44] Luisa Capetillo, "a tireless militant" and one of Puerto Rico's most famous Socialist radicals whose itinerant activism kept her traveling between cigar factories in Puerto Rico, Cuba, and the United States, also took part periodically in labor struggles in New York City.[45] (Both Schneiderman and Capetillo became women's suffrage activists in the early twentieth century.)

Women's participation in public life was more willingly recognized by *colonia* leaders when it stayed within the traditional boundaries of women's roles. Already by the early twenties, elite men had begun expressing anxiety about the instability of women's place in the New York *colonia*. A writer for *El Caribe*, a weekly paper, included the following admonition to *colonia* women in his meandering and impressionistic column on life in New York: "And you, Puerto Rican woman, whatever your station in life in your village, when you arrive in this land of OPPORTUNITY, do not forget that you were born there; and on this spacious stage upon which you spin, do only what elevates and dignifies you as a superior woman, without ceasing to be from there [Puerto Rico]; without ceasing to be who you are, the honorable wife, the tender mother, the sensitive sister, the heroic and simple Puerto Rican woman."[46] Periodically over the next several years, men in the *colonia* wrote to *La Prensa*, fretting over the moral perils that Puerto Rican women faced in the metropolis. One writer asserted that the real problem was that after Hispanic women had tried and failed to become "*americanas*," they would languish in a middle ground of a "confused identity." Maximiano Ríos Ríos, a Puerto Rican literature scholar, wondered whether "*nuestras virgencitas de Hispano América*" ("our little virgins of Hispanic America") could handle the "liberty" of life in the city that more worldly American women enjoyed.[47]

The focus on family culture and gender norms described by Ríos Ríos was not peculiar to his class. Working-class men in the *colonia* had an interest as well in guarding the boundaries of women's roles in the family and their participation in public life. By the mid-twenties, several working-class organizations, including the Ateneo Obrero Hispano and the Porto Rican Brotherhood of America, established a "*reinado de obreritas*," or working girls' beauty contest, turning a familiar celebration of women's traditional roles into a display of the new Puerto Rican migrant womanhood.[48] The New York *reinados* placed a new emphasis on the moral superiority of migrant "girls" who worked to contribute to the economic and social well-being of their families. The largest such contest of the decade, with seventeen candidates winning ten thousand votes combined, according to *La Prensa*, took place with great fanfare and publicity in the spring of 1926.⁴⁹ The desirable characteristics of *obreritas* were sketched out in *La Prensa*'s announcement: "girls" would win votes "not only for their beauty, charm, and attractiveness" but also for their virtues, especially devotion to their families. "They, in their way of life and with their virtues as Hispanic women, create constantly, humbly but effectively, a subtle and honorable propaganda of the spirit that inspires our homes and nurtures our children before sending them out into the world, even among the modest classes."⁵⁰

The successful *obrerita* candidate would represent her class, displaying her humility, hard work, and respectability. She would also represent her *compañeras* (female coworkers); her family; and, not least, her "race." Modesty was a critical element of her virtue; many of the *reina* candidates' short biographies emphasized, for instance, their lack of interest in dating. *Reinado* officials (most were men) wanted to make it clear that although these girls worked and socialized away from the watchful eyes of their families, especially protective brothers and fathers, they were not in danger of picking up the unsavory habits of American working girls in popular culture. This formulation of a working girl's respectability suggested that it was possibly bolstered by her public identity as a worker outside the home. In the formulation of the *reinadas*, the "struggle for existence" of working girls never endangered their "virtues as Hispanic women," nor were their virtues threatened by their proficiency with English or their success in the social world of work in "rough and strange" New York City. All this meant that, while the working girl's identity was more flexible than that of elite women, working-class women were still recognized, within the Spanish-speaking community, primarily as symbols of cultural honor and purity.

While *colonia* men expressed openly their anxiety about gender and family roles in the twenties, they had little to say, publicly at least, about the place of religion in their new communities. Like other former Spanish colonials, Puerto Ricans were Catholic, if not always in terms of regular religious practice then at least in terms of cultural identity. But the Catholic Church was not visibly a central institution in the *colonia* in the twenties.⁵¹ Several observers from outside the *colonia*, writing in the 1930s, suggested that migrants' alleged irreligiosity had to do with their "lower-class" and "rural" origins. Lawrence Chenault, a Columbia-trained sociologist who conducted the first book-length academic study of Puerto Rican migrants in New York, cited the similarly dismissive perspective of the Puerto Rican social worker who "finds the cause for the lack of religious influence in the many attractions of the large city which divert the Puerto Rican from religious service and an interest in Church affairs." Another social worker whom Chenault talked with offered a more concrete reason for migrants' distance from the Catholic Church: it was "due to the work of Protestant and non-sectarian organizations among them." There was some truth to this observation.[52] But other sources suggest that even as Protestant groups vied for converts among Puerto Rican migrants—American Protestant denominations had established a precedent for evangelizing Puerto Ricans on the island not long after 1898—migrants' attraction to Protestant and Pentecostal churches in New York also stemmed from a lack of access to the city's Catholic churches.[53] The New York archdiocese built one Puerto Rican church in Harlem, La Milagrosa, in 1926 in a converted synagogue; the Brooklyn *colonia* had no church of its own until the 1940s. One migrant recalled that her family had begun attending a Pentecostal church in Brooklyn in the 1920s because, she said, "it was about the only place" where Spanish speakers felt comfortable.[54]

Religious scholar Joseph Fitzpatrick also attributes Puerto Ricans' uneasy integration into the American Catholic Church to structural factors related both to Puerto Rico's colonial history and to the timing of the Puerto Rican migration to the United States. The first problem for Puerto Rican Catholics was that there were so few native priests on the island in the early years of the migration (prior to 1898, the majority of priests and all but one bishop in Puerto Rico were Spanish) that none were encouraged to join the migration and establish a specifically Puerto Rican parish in New York—as the German, Irish, and Italian clergy had done during their nations' peak periods of immigration to the United States. The second issue, according to Fitzpatrick, was that most Puerto Ricans who attended church, lacking churches led by their own clergy and providing services in their own language, had to join "integrated" parishes that served Catholics from diverse national backgrounds.[55] Although some of the clergy spoke Spanish or tried to learn it, many migrants did not feel welcome or comfortable in such parishes and let go of (or never established) their institutional connection to the church. In 1934, a Puerto Rican Trinitarian nun, Sister Carmelita Bonilla, would help to establish Casita María, a Catholic settlement house in East Harlem that served thousands of Puerto Ricans each year, but migrants gravitated to Casita María as much for its provision of social welfare services as for its pastoral services.[56] For new migrants in the twenties, a formal relationship with the Catholic Church played a relatively insignificant role in public life in the *colonia*. Unlike their Italian predecessors in El Barrio, whose community activities had centered from the start on the church and its religious festivals, Puerto Rican migrants' public life emerged around a complex and politicized associational sphere and an emerging political culture wherein migrants struggled to balance the pull of island politics with an increasing focus on what one migrant leader would call "the politics of here."[57]

### La Vida Política and La Vida Pública

Ernesto Sepúlveda, the successful Brooklyn grocer, viewed the social economy of the Brooklyn *colonia* in the twenties and thirties through the eyes of a small business owner and hoped to see his community and his business prosper together; later, in the 1940s, he would help establish and serve as president of the Puerto Rican Merchants Association. Puerto Ricans who came to New York in the twenties encountered a few of the surviving civic and political groups of their nineteenth-century compatriots, but leaders of the 1920s' *colonia* elite put great energy into organizing their own clubs, which combined their political and cultural interests. The Alianza Puertorriqueña, the Club Latinoamericano, and the Club Betances (joined under the banner "La Liga Puertorriqueña" in 1922) regularly sponsored public galas that celebrated *"la Raza"* and members' "Hispanic roots."[58] Members of working-class organizations were rarely invited to participate in such events, and their exclusion was a source of tension in the *colonia*. The working-class Porto Rican Brotherhood of America (PRBA) in one of its pamphlets in this era, described the divisions inscribed into the community by "social categories," meaning that the "better off" Puerto Ricans sequestered themselves in East Harlem and shunned their working-class compatriots in Brooklyn.[59] The PRBA exaggerated the degree of intentional residential segregation by class, though segregation did substantially shape the dynamics of the migrant community in that decade.

More important than class alone in dividing migrants in this era, however, was the conflict generated by island political ideologies, which these activist migrants brought with them as they settled in New York.[60] The question of Puerto Rico's political status had shaped the outlines of the island's political party system from the time of the Foraker Act of 1900.[61] This legislation established the framework for a civilian, U.S.-dominated government in Puerto Rico without actually defining the island's status vis-à-vis the United States; the Jones Act, in 1917, would name Puerto Rico "a territory incorporated into the United States."[62] Political parties in Puerto Rico formed around various positions on the status question. The Union

Party, a 1904 reincarnation of the Federal Party led first by Luis Muñoz Rivera, supported independence, although its leaders as well as its constituency held a variety of opinions about the means by which to achieve that goal. *Unionistas* held the dominant position in island politics through much of the early twentieth century. The Republican Party (with no ties to the U.S. Republican Party), from its inception in 1900, advocated the full integration of the island into the United States via statehood. The Socialist Party began as the Socialist Workers Party in 1901, linked closely with the island's largest labor union, the Federación Libre de Trabajadores, and later with the U.S.-based American Federation of Labor. Socialists played a consistent role as the underdog third party in electoral politics, although their leader, Santiago Iglesias Pantín, achieved considerable power in insular politics and would be elected to represent Puerto Rico in Washington as resident commissioner in 1932.[63]

At different moments in the island's political history in its first half century as a U.S. territory, Puerto Rican political leaders forged alliances with other parties' members, fragmenting and realigning their parties' membership along a central axis of political status positions. The most enduring of these alliances was the one between the Socialist and Republican parties. These apparently unlikely political allies would join forces numerous times in the decades before the creation of the Commonwealth of Puerto Rico in 1952. Although their constituencies occupied opposite poles of Puerto Rico's class system (working class and business elite, respectively), the leadership of the two parties agreed on the fundamental question of U.S. involvement in the island's affairs. Republicans strongly supported the expansion of U.S. corporate interests in Puerto Rico's sugar industry, since they saw U.S. control of that industry as the surest route to its profitability—and saw a profitable sugar industry as the only route to island prosperity. Many Republicans worked closely with, or directly for, U.S. businesses and tended as well to be the firmest supporters of Americanization programs in island infrastructure, education, and social programs. Although the majority of the Socialist constituency worked as skilled and unskilled laborers, typically the antagonists of big capital, the Socialist leadership was willing to overlook ideological differences to work with Republicans because it believed that a pro–United States policy in the Puerto Rican legislature would secure the most lasting material gains for labor from a U.S.-influenced political system. Iglesias, whose vision for Puerto Rico looked more like a "labor democracy" than a Socialist workers' state, argued that the status question should be a secondary concern for workers but backed statehood by default.[64] On the opposite side of the Socialist-Republican alliance of 1920 were the Unionists, who controlled the legislature by a firm majority. The Union Party represented primarily the landed elite who stood to lose most in the transfer of power from Spain to the United States, with the influx of U.S. corporate control of the sugar industry and agricultural lands. Their leadership and constituency opposed statehood but struggled to formulate policy positions that would balance sometimes-conflicting goals: political independence, a liberal democratic government like that of the United States, and the economic benefits of friendly relations with its powerful neighbor.

The flux of party alliances had intensified in the several years following the passage of the Jones Act, as the creation of the island's bicameral elective legislature in 1917 spurred greater competition among the parties for electoral dominance and the opportunity to influence the policies of the presidentially appointed governor.[65] The party structure confronted a new crisis in 1922, when Representative Philip Campbell of Kansas proposed a bill to create an "associated free state" of Puerto Rico, with continuing ties to the United States but an independent political structure.[66] Unionists initially opposed it and in doing so ran afoul of the anti-*independentista* governor E. Mont Reily. Socialists and Republicans, on the other hand, came out strongly in support of the bill, and of Reily, in spite of a widespread and relatively nonpartisan dislike for this bumbling appointee of President Warren G. Harding.[67] Under pressure to maintain a place in the legislative game, Unionist leader Antonio Barceló eventually reversed his position on the Campbell bill, revising the historically *independentista* position of his party and infuriating those who supported independence. As soon as Barceló vowed that "the creation of the Free Associated State of Puerto Rico is from this day on the Program of the party" and hailed "an Association of a permanent and indestructible character, between the Island and the United States of America," a faction of *Unionistas* bolted the party, establishing Puerto Rico's Partido Nacionalista by September of 1922.[68]

These developments in island party politics reverberated deeply in New York's *barrio latino*. Bernardo Vega recalled that a number of his working-class compatriots—men who were nominally Socialists and supported Iglesias out of loyalty to their class but who also wanted independence for the island—furiously protested Barceló's move. The Manhattan-based Asociación Nacionalista Puertorriqueña, with its membership of elite *independentistas*, called an emergency general assembly that fall.[69] Bernardo Vega identified this moment as the point at which the Puerto Rican Nationalist movement in New York began. "They came together to organize a protest demonstration," he said, "and they have remained together ever since."[70] Vega's recollection illustrates the complexity of island ideological influences among politicized migrants in New York. Vega himself supported independence for Puerto Rico and objected strongly to Barceló's sudden shift of position, but as a working-class activist and a Socialist (who frequently criticized the statehood politics of Iglesias), Vega did not count himself among the group of migrants in New York "who had begun to call themselves nationalists."[71]

The first Nationalist organizations in Puerto Rico had been formed by members of the predominantly Hispanic (that is, "white") landed elite, who, like the Unionists from whom they split in 1922, stood to lose most from the growing dominion of U.S. capital on the island. The class identity of Nationalists in New York mirrored for the most part that of their island counterparts; if migrant Nationalists differed from nonmigrants, it was primarily in terms of a heightened emphasis on their Hispanic identity as a marker of social status, perhaps to compensate for the loss of the concrete markers of status that they had left behind: land, servants, and the obligatory respect shown to the social elite. The *colonia*'s Nationalist elite may have shared views on independence with many of their working-class compatriots, but differences in status dictated that the two groups create distinct camps for themselves within the new *puertorriqueño* political culture in New York. The negotiation of migrants' political allegiances involved an intricate balance of class and ideology, complicated by what Theodore Roosevelt Jr., the island's governor from 1929 to 1932, would call the "kaleidoscopic" structure of Puerto Rican politics: "They chop and change, combine and split, with great regularity."[72]

The central dilemma among politicized New York Puerto Ricans in the twenties was the question of how best to further their various political agendas in the homeland while building political relationships in the metropole. The majority of prominent working-class leaders viewed an alliance with the Democratic Party as the most effective means to represent the "real" interests of most Puerto Rican migrants, which they defined as both everyday concerns of working people as well as autonomy for Puerto Rico. The Porto Rican Brotherhood of America, for instance, announced that its purpose was to promote the mutual protection of Puerto Ricans "on the Continent" and to contribute to the welfare of "our brothers residing on the Island." The organization would rely on its members' citizenship to reach those goals: "using our power and our influence among the American people and government to demand justice for the people of Puerto Rico."[73] The membership of the more elite Liga Puertorriqueña (the "leading Puerto Rican intellectuals in New York," as Bernardo Vega described the mostly Unionist *independentista* journalists, professors, and businessmen who comprised its membership) had more or less ignored the Democratic Party until the 1922 controversy over the Campbell bill inspired them to seek local political alliances via their newly formed organization.[74] Inspired by the island fracas, Liga members now sought direct engagement in U.S. party politics. Certainly the agenda of the *independentista* Liga members would be furthered if Democrats in the U.S. Congress could help oust Reily, a Republican. The Liga produced a "Manifesto" that year, which emphasized migrants' participation in New York politics, using their right to vote to influence the outcome of island conflicts. "Here we are American citizens with indisputable rights, and as such . . . we will actualize for the benefit of Puerto Rico, as well as that of the City of New York, and the state of New York and the Republic of the United States," proclaimed the manifesto.[75]

José Comprubí, *La Prensa*'s editor and a supporter of the nationalist ideology of the Puerto Rican elite, hailed the newly reformed Liga as "a compact nucleus for the exercise of [Puerto Ricans'] political rights within the Constitution of this country." He urged all Puerto Ricans to pursue the rights that belonged to them due to their "inescapable American citizenship."[76] Working-class migrant leaders, on the other hand, complained that the "proletarian Puerto Rican element" had been excluded from the Liga's activities and accused its leadership of ignoring the political labors of their working-class counterparts across the river, who had been involved in Democratic politics for several years already.[77] Shortly thereafter, *La Prensa* printed a "manifesto" summarizing its attitude toward *colonia* politics, "Los portorriqueños y *La Prensa*," a reminder that the paper would defend itself as the representative of both the working-class and elite communities. The manifesto asserted that *La Prensa* "does not ally with any particular Puerto Rican society, comprised of proletarians or capitalists, no matter what their title." On the same day, the paper also ran a front-page story profiling Brooklyn's working-class Porto Rican Democratic Club, whose president, José Alonso, asserted that its "proletarian elements" adhered to a nonpartisan ideology focused on "being useful . . . to the faraway *patria*." Alonso claimed that although the club's three hundred members had participated in different political parties in Puerto Rico, now that they lived in New York, they abstained from island politics. Instead, "thanks to the . . . utilization of their citizenship rights," they could achieve "'the intervention of the club in the politics of here for the benefit of Puerto.'"[78] This was an obvious jab at the Liga, a challenge to the elite's pretension that it represented the interests of all Puerto Ricans in New York.[79] The controversy over local organizational politics inspired Jesús Colón to comment, mildly, that "trying to unite the Puerto Ricans of New York from a political point of view . . . , wanting all to participate in a certain party, is a utopia."[80]

Regardless of their leaders' class divisions and ideological disagreements, the majority of Puerto Ricans had some relationship with the Democratic machine in New York. Like other immigrant groups in the city, Puerto Ricans were introduced quickly to the world of machine politics in the city by its vote-seeking leadership, and working-class members of the group were the most readily drawn to the machine's promises. Democrats managed to win the allegiance of the majority of *colonia* voters during Al Smith's gubernatorial campaign in 1918; Bernardo Vega claimed that seven thousand Puerto Ricans—almost half the migrant population at that time— registered to vote in that campaign, most of them to vote for Smith. Within a few years, a number of working-class groups in the *colonia* began to forge ties with the Democrats, who controlled most of the patronage in the city. This allegiance on the part of Puerto Ricans may have been partly ideological, but it was also practical. Immigrant groups before them had accepted the advances of machine leaders, especially Tammany Democrats, as a way to secure basic goods and services (a Christmas turkey, garbage collection) as well as economic advancement and neighborhood power through patronage jobs; Puerto Ricans were learning to do the same.[81]

But many migrants also expected their support of local politicians to be repaid in the form of some action on the various issues vexing Puerto Rican–United States relations, ranging from U.S.-sponsored hurricane relief and other economic aid to U.S. congressional pressure to resolve the status question. In the Porto Rican Democratic Club's 1923 *La Prensa* profile, PRDC head José Alonso had asserted that "the Brooklyn Club doesn't hide its objective. They give votes to American Democratic candidates, in exchange for the help that the latter can offer to the Porto Ricans."[82] Alonso denied that members of his organization were interested in using their votes to influence "Puerto Rican politics," but testimony about *colonia* activists in this era belies that claim. Perhaps the most famous of the Brooklyn *colonia*'s Tammanyites, Carlos Tapia, described by a compatriot as "the hero of the Puerto Rican beachhead in New York," asserted in 1924 that one of the primary goals of the Puerto Rican Democratic organizations was to elect officials "who in exchange for our help to elect them will have to help our

beloved Puerto Rico." "The only way for our island to get political recognition," he asserted—leaving the meaning of *recognition* open, not, in any case,
a direct statement of support for independence—"is through the 'Puerto
Ricans' here in New York and in other states of the Union."[83]

Carlos Tapia had arrived in Brooklyn around 1920, an imposing but
personable *"hombre de color"* from Puerto Rico.[84] By 1922, he had opened a
grocery store on Second Street near the Brooklyn Navy Yard and quickly
became known as someone who would open his home to any newly arrived
migrant who needed a place to stay. Tapia housed and fed many recent
migrants and then helped them find jobs and advocated for them in conflicts with police, landlords, and sometimes-hostile Italian neighbors.[85] He
achieved a singular degree of fame in the Brooklyn *colonia* in the twenties
and thirties, seen by some as a slightly shady Robin Hood figure (he headed
Brooklyn's *bolita*, the Puerto Rican numbers racket), by others as a benevo-
lent *"papá* of everyone around him," as one woman called him. "Whoever
asked him for a favor," Doña Gregoria Lausell said, "he would go [to them]
right away.... He would go and fix everything."[86] When Puerto Ricans in
Brooklyn reflected, decades later in oral history interviews, on Tapia's presence in their community, women and men tended to remember him differently. Many women emphasized his paternalism in ways similar to Doña
Gregoria; one, Doña Gloria Rodríguez, recalled emotionally: *"Ay dios mío....
M'hija* [Girl]... this man was so good that he was like my father.... It was he
who protected the first Puerto Ricans who came here. He gave them food,
shelter, and everything when they came here."[87] On the other hand, it was
Tapia's masculine power that figured most prominently in migrant men's
recollections of him. One recalled that Tapia was very "loyal" to his fellow
Puerto Ricans and that "he liked to fight." "When they [members of other
ethnic groups] would beat up a Puerto Rican or some other injustice [Tapia]
would get together two or three friends and go and fight for him."[88] Another
man asserted that Tapia "always protected the Puerto Ricans and I heard a
lot about the fights he would have with various people, defending others."[89]

In the process of fashioning himself the protector of Brooklyn Puerto Ricans, Tapia became an informal district leader of the Tammany machine by
the early twenties. Although he would not participate in the leadership of
the Brooklyn *colonia*'s growing network of Democratic clubs until the early
1930s, when his friend Luis Weber started the Baldorioty Democratic Club
in their district, Tapia supported these clubs informally and mediated between Democratic politicians and his compatriots. During the 1924 presi-

dential election, Tapia reportedly told fellow migrant Ramón Colón that he invested so much in the Puerto Rican Democratic organizations

> so that when some unfortunate "Puerto Rican" is arrested by the police, I can ask some politician to talk to the judge on his behalf. So that I can ask the same politician to help some poor "Puerto Rican" who needs medical attention in some municipal hospital. . . . As long as these political clubs remain politically strong . . . so long as I can go to any one of the numbers game operators, according to the circumstances, to ask him to provide money for the funeral of any "Puerto Rican" who dies and has no life insurance . . . money to help widows and their children . . . to provide food and shelter for the unemployed and sick. . . . These numbers game operators have strong-arm men whom I can use . . . in defense of any "Puerto Rican" when abused or attacked by hostile groups.[90]

In describing his motivations to act the part of neighborhood hero, Tapia linked the familiar relationship of the immigrant and the political machine to the neighborhood politics of *la bolita*, which played an important role in the informal economy of many working-class urban communities in this period. This relationship meant that he was not solely dependent on bosses and party leaders: his position as a *bolitero* gave him the flexibility to deliver financial aid and protection from other sources and the ability to put pressure on his Tammany contacts not just with the promise of votes but also with the backing of his "strong-arm men." Tapia expressed, obliquely, that the most important benefit of Puerto Ricans' investment in the Democratic machine was the dividends in terms of protecting their rights, so often ignored by judges, doctors, and other officials. As Jesús Colón's brother Joaquín put it, "These poor, hardworking people had nowhere to go with their complaints"—so they went to the Puerto Rican representatives of the *maquinaria*.[91]

Voting was the currency in which all favors were traded between neighborhood leaders and city officials. Because they arrived in the United States with citizenship in hand, Puerto Rican migrants had a head start in the patronage game compared to other recent immigrants; yet they also arrived with little or no knowledge about the workings of the U.S. political system, and few Puerto Ricans actually voted on the island.[92] To encourage voting in the United States, the editors of *La Prensa* printed a series of articles in the fall of each election year in the twenties, urging Puerto Ricans (as well as all naturalized *hispanos*) to use their power as citizens to make the voice of *la comunidad hispana* heard.[93] Many migrants who settled in Brooklyn in the 1920s and were interviewed fifty years later recalled how, right away, they understood the importance of voting—and voting Democratic. One woman remembered that a handful of well-known *colonia* Democrats "would help to orient people . . . register them to vote . . . and teach them that they must use their votes."[94] José Alonso had organized the first Puerto Rican Democratic club in his district in 1923, and other migrant Democrats followed suit in the later twenties, setting up two more such clubs in the First Assembly District and several others in parts of Brooklyn into which the Puerto Rican population had begun to expand, particularly Greenpoint and Williamsburg.[95]

By most accounts, Puerto Rican Manhattanites lagged behind their Brooklyn counterparts in forging ties with the city's political machines. In Manhattan, the small favors of patronage did not intersect with the clout and cash of *boliteros* as they did in Brooklyn. The Puerto Rican *bolita* was less established in El Barrio than in Brooklyn because the Italian and African American numbers men in Harlem left few openings for new Puerto Rican *boliteros*. Also, a higher proportion of Puerto Rican residents were shopkeepers or professionals who were less in need of the city jobs (most in the street-cleaning department) that patronage provided.[96] Juana Weber Rodríguez, a Brooklyn resident and sister of the well-known *bolitero* and Democratic leader Luis Weber, remembered that a prominent Manhattan doctor used to travel to Brooklyn for meetings of the Betances Democratic Club, of which she was a member. She said that Dr. Antonio Sesteros "lived in New York [Manhattan] but came to all the meetings and was very active in the [Brooklyn] community. . . . In New York they hadn't formed [clubs]. . . . There was nothing. So he used to come from New York to Brooklyn."[97] But Tammany Democrats had made significant inroads in El Barrio by the mid-twenties. Domingo Collazo, an early *independentista* in New York, became a prominent figure in the Democratic politics of East Harlem by the early 1920s and directed the "Spanish department" of the Davis-Bryan presidential campaign in 1924. Bernardo Vega remembered Collazo as Tammany Hall's "representative of the Puerto Rican community" in the twenties.[98]

Juana's recollection about Sesteros begs the question of women's roles in public life and political culture in the early *colonia*. Though it was a relatively small role they played, women enthusiastically joined *colonia* organizations, both leftist and elite, most often via "women's auxiliaries," which took charge of the social- and charity-oriented functions of the organization while the men conducted the civic or political business. A handful of women, members of both the working class and the bourgeoisie, attained significant leadership positions in several of the important migrant organizations. Leftist groups in particular seemed willing to include women in their leadership ranks; for instance, the Alianza Obrera Portorriqueña listed a woman treasurer, Señorita Emilia Hernández, in 1923, its first year of operation. Many of these women were wives, sisters, or daughters of important community figures: the names Concha Colón (married to Jesús) and Emilia Vando (married to Erasmo, a leftist writer and performer) appear in various records of a number of leftist associations, and Isabel O'Neill (married to Gonzalo, a prominent Nationalist) appears as a top leader in several elite organizations.[99] Yet even when they occupied important administrative positions in *colonia* organizations, women only rarely gained mention of their participation in records of important associational events and conflicts.

A few of these women quickly developed public identities of their own, a step apart from the male-dominated associational sphere in the *colonia*. In Brooklyn, Doña Antonia Denis attained a notoriety in the community to the extent that one migrant who remembered her recited her name alongside the two best-known leaders of the working-class Puerto Rican neighborhoods there: "Carlos Tapia, Jesús Colón, Antonia Denis." One woman recalled how Denis served early on as president of Hijos de Borinquén, "Sons of Puerto Rico" (ironic, in her case), the largest mutual benefit society in the Brooklyn *colonia* in the late twenties. Many others remembered her prominent place in the Brooklyn Democratic organizations in the twenties and thirties, especially the Betances Democratic Club. "[She] knew every big leader politically and every Puerto Rican . . . was well backed by that group," said one.[100] In Manhattan, several elite *colonia* women used their participation in *La Prensa* debates and letters to the editor to achieve a powerful voice and public recognition throughout the twenties, belying the image of womanhood represented in *La Prensa*'s column "Para las damas," which was limited to issues like entertaining, sewing, and childrearing.[101]

The best known of these female voices emerged in debates about independence, which continued to occupy the greatest amount of space in *La Prensa*'s op-ed pages and inspired hundreds of public events through the middle of the 1920s. A new round of controversy over the status question emerged early in 1924, when two major realignments in the island party system took place. First, Unionist leader Barceló and head of the Republican Party José Tous-Soto, seeing past their differences to agree on the vague goal of "self-government," forged what would turn out to

be an enduring *"alianza"* that they hoped would help them secure control of the island legislature. Then the leaders of the Socialists and the
Constitutionalist-Republicans (who had split from the Alianza Republicans) joined forces, an unlikely alliance of left- and right-wing leaders who
had found common ground in their denunciation of Barceló, Tous-Soto, and
any form of independence—the Socialists because they believed justice for
workers needed to come first, and the Constitutionalist-Republicans because statehood was the only status option they would support.[102]

In the months leading up to the party realignments, Puerto Rican Socialist leader Santiago Iglesias had ignited a firestorm when he announced,
during a visit to Washington, D.C., that "the popular masses of Puerto Rico
do not desire independence."[103] Although statehood had been a consistent
plank of the Socialist Party platform (partly a function of its close ties with
the American Federation of Labor), the party had tried to avoid alienating
constituents who straddled the divided camps of labor and independence
by couching its position in terms of the benefits to workers of allying with
U.S. labor and progressive forces.[104] Never before had the Socialist Party
definitively denounced independence. Iglesias stood before the House
Committee on Insular Affairs as he claimed to speak for the "masses" of
Puerto Ricans, sounding the familiar theme of economic justice for workers. He argued that Puerto Rico deserved "a status that would permit
better development" on the island, implying that independence from the
United States would work against such "progress." He also elaborated on
claims about the value of Puerto Ricans' American citizenship, asserting
that "citizenship must signify something like what [it means] for those who
live on the mainland of the United States." He continued, "The masses of
the people of Puerto Rico do not want to establish an independent government; this is merely a conversation among a few politicians. . . . [The
masses] want to have the opportunity to share in the benefits of the North
American form of government, of its institutions and its citizenship."[105] The
"real" status issue for the majority of the Puerto Rican people (both islanders and migrants), Iglesias asserted, involved the conditions of daily life and
access to the promised benefits of their U.S. citizenship.

In New York, *independentista* migrants excoriated Iglesias for his pronouncement. A group of *colonia* leaders who were members of the Nationalist Association and the Liga Portorriqueña, among other elite-dominated
organizations, wrote a letter to John Weeks, secretary of war, asking that
Iglesias be removed from the delegation of Puerto Rican leaders scheduled to appear in Washington in January 1924. Invoking the specter of

working-class radicalism, the letter writers accused Iglesias of misleading the "excitable working masses" with "incendiary Communist and Bolshevik propaganda."[106] They employed a recurring trope in the political discourse, claiming to represent *"el anhelo del pueblo,"* the yearning of the people, just as Iglesias had in asserting that he spoke for "the masses": "we reflect the sentiment of the representative element of the Porto Rican *colonia* in this city." In the *colonia*, the controversy quickly transformed into an argument not so much about which status was best for Puerto Rico but about who got to decide what "the Puerto Rican people" wanted.[107] Answering their Nationalist rivals in New York, the Federación Portorriqueña (as the group of New York–based Puerto Rican Democratic clubs now called itself)—most of whom shared the *independentista* ideology of their Nationalist neighbors—addressed the question of representation in the *colonia*: "we do not know with what intention these Porto Ricans abrogate the representation of the 45,000-plus compatriots residing in New York . . . because they were not called to express the opinion of our *colonia* in this country."[108]

Iglesias did not alter his position and would within weeks formally join the Republicans in the new pro-statehood Alianza Puertorriqueña. Nationalist and Democratic migrants in New York squabbled over who got to articulate, on behalf of the rest of the community, the goal of sovereignty for Puerto Rico. Their ideologies were similar, both focused on independence, but there was a distinct difference in terms of what they expected and hoped for from their relationship with the United States. The Socialist leadership wanted, in Iglesias's words, "to have the opportunity to share in the benefits of the North American form of government, of its institutions and its citizenship." Nationalists occasionally would invoke the promised benefits of U.S. citizenship as well, but often as a straw man, to underscore what the United States failed to live up to in its colonial rule over the island.

Even for many Nationalists, however, "sharing in the benefits" of their U.S. citizenship was most East Harlem Puerto Ricans' primary goal in supporting their U.S. congressional representative, Sol Bloom. When Bloom first ran for election as a Democrat in the Nineteenth District in 1922, he convinced Puerto Ricans voters there—of whom there were almost two thousand, according to *La Prensa*—that he took an interest in Puerto Rican politics and would stand behind their goal of increased sovereignty for the island. Bloom won the election by a narrow margin, and his Puerto Rican constituents took partial credit for his victory. Migrants elected him again in 1924, seeing him as a key player in, as Brooklyn Democratic leader José

Alonso had put it, "the politics of here for the benefit of Puerto Rico."[109] Bloom's constituents applauded him when he visited Puerto Rico in the spring of 1925 and noted with pride his comment to a Puerto Rican journalist that the island was "extraordinarily advanced and progressive." But in another interview, Bloom allegedly reversed his previous support for independence, advising Puerto Ricans to give up their struggle for autonomy and comparing *independentistas* to "children who refuse to take their medicine, and in the end will have to take what the doctor . . . gives them." A coalition of New York Puerto Ricans, including both Nationalists and Democrats, wrote a furious letter to Bloom about the incident, defending their political goals and renouncing his hypocrisy and abuse of his constituents' support. They also threatened Bloom that, since Puerto Ricans in the Nineteenth District "hold the balance of power," they could, "at a moment's notice . . . decide the victory of a candidate" in the next election. Bloom's reply denied the statements attributed to him. After a meeting was arranged between the migrant coalition and Bloom by the Sephardic Democratic Association, a Jewish Democratic club in East Harlem, coalition members informed *La Prensa* that Bloom "assumed an aggressive attitude," and that "it was evident that [he] did not come in peace but ready to verbally abuse the Puerto Ricans gathered there."[110]

Several months later, when *colonia* journalist Domingo Collazo established the first Puerto Rican Democratic club in Manhattan, he cited the Bloom incident as a cautionary tale: migrants should pick their candidates carefully and exercise their rights as citizens with gravitas. Bernardo Vega noted that "the incident caused much dissatisfaction among Puerto Rican voters and led many to wonder if they could ever expect anything from a Yankee politician if this was the behavior of one who claimed to be liberal."[111] Even as Bloom's narrow victory, and his visit to his constituents' homeland, showed Puerto Ricans that they had become important players in New York politics, his unreliable support for their concerns warned migrants that American politicians could be counted on only to make strategic use of the issue of Puerto Rico. Indeed, as Bloom approached his campaign for reelection during the summer of 1926, he introduced a bill to allow Puerto Ricans to elect their own governor starting in 1928. Saying that he upheld "the liberal recognition of autonomous rights of small nations and groups of people," Bloom asserted that the passage of his bill "would, I feel, do very much to stimulate the aspirations of native Porto Ricans by way of improving their government and in a commercial sense also."[112] It was a transparent move to regain the support of his East Harlem constituency; on this point, the divided *colonia* could agree.

Their real disagreement, which only intensified during the course of the twenties, was over how much weight to give to the problem of island sovereignty versus the struggle for the resolution of local problems, like housing and employment. Although many migrants disavowed Iglesias's claim that "the masses" of Puerto Ricans did not want independence for the island, his broader political message was one that the *colonia* could rally around and that many of its activists would amplify during the thirties. Even as he alienated most *independentista* migrants, Iglesias articulated a potent idea of what Puerto Ricans' political struggle was really about: being recognized as equal to Americans, possessed of a "citizenship that must signify something like what [it means] for those who live on the mainland of the United States." A new series of local problems in 1926 and 1927 brought political rivals in the *colonia* together and motivated them in new ways to make claims on their status as citizens.

### Choques among Citizens

By the mid-1920s, Puerto Ricans had established a complex commercial and residential network in the neighborhood that had come to be known as "*el barrio latino*," along the western half of East Harlem. The Porto Rican Brotherhood of America conducted a survey of the community in 1926 and in boosterish tones reported that *barrio* residents now claimed ownership of more than twenty-five grocery stores; fifteen restaurants; twenty-five barbershops; and various pharmacies, shoe stores, and other establishments that catered to a Spanish-speaking clientele.[113] Prior to the arrival of Puerto Rican migrants in the early twenties, this part of East Harlem had been dominated by Eastern European Jews, and the transition to a vibrant Spanish-speaking community produced tensions with other ethnic groups in El Barrio. As part of the same "souvenir" pamphlet, the PRBA also asserted the growing power of *la colonia portorriqueña* alongside its rapid commercial growth. Not only were Puerto Ricans "indisputably . . . the most numerous" of the Spanish speakers; the Brotherhood also claimed that "we speak English and we are citizens of the United States, attributes very valuable in the defense of our individual and collective interests."[114]

The Brotherhood's claims about "the defense of . . . collective interests" were prescient. In July 1926, the growing commercial rivalry between Jewish and Puerto Rican shopkeepers turned suddenly into a violent demonstration of resentment on both sides, marked by sporadic street fighting, attacks on both Jews and Puerto Ricans, and the smashing of shop windows over the course of several days. The "July disturbances," as *La Prensa* called them—or *choques* ("clashes")—lasted for almost two weeks. By the time the neighborhood settled down, fifteen people were estimated to be seriously injured, and business owners on both sides suffered untotaled losses in sales, merchandise, and property damage. Several reports by Spanish-language groups also warned that the aggression of the Jews against the Puerto Ricans was spreading and that "bands" of Italian youths in Brooklyn were also beginning to assault Puerto Ricans in that neighborhood.[115]

None of the observers who reported on the incidents suggested a particular spark that ignited the conflict; all agreed simply that "religious differences" and "racial antagonisms," sharpening over the years, had led to the confrontations. But different camps of observers had differing opinions about whom to blame for the *choques*. *La Prensa* reporters accused "armed bands of Hebrews" for transforming a commercial rivalry between old and new residents into a violent struggle for economic survival. In this new war zone, "bands of Israelites" took up arms against innocent Puerto Ricans and other Spanish speakers. *La Prensa* also took pains to emphasize that many other ethnic groups in New York had experienced similar incidents of intergroup conflict on the city's streets—in other words, this incident did not represent a problem that was unique to *hispanos*. Later, the Porto Rican Brotherhood of America would call the incidents "the Hebrew-Hispanic conflict" and referred to the Jewish residents involved as "disruptive elements."[116] *La Prensa*, and several Puerto Rican leaders who spoke publicly after the incidents, also emphasized the inaction of the police when called to protect Spanish-speaking *barrio* residents.

On the other hand, the *New York Times* described the "Porto Ricans" and their "large numbers" in ominous tones. The most menacing element of the stories reported in the *Times* was the "large force of Porto Ricans" from outside the neighborhood that planned to "invade the district" and retaliate against the "old settlers," though city police managed to intercept the "advance guard of the Porto Rican army" before it did too much damage.[117] *La Prensa* failed to cover this detail of the *choques*, but Carlos Tapia later recalled leading a group of his Brooklyn compatriots ("gangsters," as a later police report called them) to El Barrio in a show of force directed against the Jewish aggressors in the *choques*. It was also a demonstration of defiance against East Harlem's Puerto Rican elite. Tapia was known to rail against his "*blanquito*" countrymen, as he called the *colonia*'s bourgeois sector, accusing them of profiting from their compatriots' poverty and dividing the *colonia* politically through their obsessive attention to the Nationalist politics of the island. *Blanquito* meant "little whitey" and, as an epithet emerging out of Puerto Rico's complex racial system, referred not to the actual color of a person's skin but to his tendency to treat others as subordinates, as if he were white. "I am afraid that these ingrates will never do anything to help either our people's struggle for integration here or our brothers' cause for civic dignity in Puerto Rico," he said, "because this kind of Puerto Rican, as long as their bellies are full and their bank accounts keep growing, do not care for our civic dignity or progress."[118] According to Tapia, if the powerful elite cared only about partisan intracommunity political battles, then they spent little of their social capital on matters of concern to "the people": improving the day-to-day conditions of life for Puerto Ricans in New York.

Most observers of the *choques* did not emphasize the element of class tension, as Tapia did. Instead, *colonia* members framed the events as a problem of ethnic conflict arising from neighborhood succession, noting that the experience of Puerto Ricans with such tensions was no different from what other immigrant groups had experienced before. *La Prensa* reported that it had received numerous letters calling attention to anti–Puerto Rican discrimination or to discrimination against Latinos in general. However, José Comprubí, the paper's editor, called such complaints "absolutely false" and warned that "our people who believe themselves to be persecuted, hated, and despised here, will never succeed in developing themselves as they should and could." In other words, the perception of discrimination arose from a self-defeating attitude—a subtle message about the differences in terms of respectability between Puerto Ricans and other Spanish speakers in the *colonia*.[119] J. M. Vivaldi, a well-known Puerto Rican Democrat, defended Puerto Ricans, obliquely countering Comprubí's editorial with an elaboration on the idea that "Puerto Ricans are not foreigners" and reminding his readers of Puerto Ricans' respectability. His intention, he said, was "not only to clarify but to repeat once and again that we are *American citizens* with the same rights and duties as those born in this land."[120]

By mid-August, before the dust had settled and before all the store windows were replaced, most of the Puerto Rican–affiliated organizations in New York had banded together in a show of cross-class unity. *La Prensa* praised the "cohesion of the community," while the Porto Rican Brotherhood of America hailed the prospects of "*la gran familia hispana*, without any class distinctions." This moment of *colonia* unity was remarkable for its

Figure 4. Liga Puertorriqueña e Hispana, Brooklyn, late 1920s. The Liga was formed in the aftermath of the 1926 conflicts between Jews and Puerto Ricans in East Harlem. Jesús Colón is holding the banner on the left. Jesús Colón papers, Archives of the Puerto Rican Diaspora, Centro de Estudios Puertorriqueños, Hunter College, CUNY.

leaders' pointed and repeated articulations about Puerto Ricans' status as citizens. The Brotherhood made its claims about respectability by arguing that Puerto Ricans "are citizens respectful of the law and lovers of order." When a number of the *colonia*'s working-class organizations formed a new coalition of politicized community organizations called the Liga Puertorriqueña e Hispana, a spokesman announced that the purpose of the association "was not to promote further antagonism . . . but to prove that the Spanish-speaking people are willing to be, and are Americans." Victor Fiol Ramos, the organization's first secretary, told a *New York Times* reporter that the real problem was "that people do not realize that we Porto Ricans are American citizens in the fullest sense of the word. . . . We believe that we have readily adapted ourselves to American standards and ideals and there is no reason why we should be looked upon with suspicion." The Liga's constitution, printed later that year, emphasized the "exercising of due influence among all members of the *colonia hispana* who hold American citizenship."[121]

Class and ideological divisions continued to destabilize the apparent unanimity behind these articulations of Americanness and "belonging."

Jesús Colón, Bernardo Vega, and some of their fellow working-class activists organized a new association, the Ateneo Obrero Hispano, which announced its purpose as "a useful instrument in the preparation of the '*latino*' worker for his identification with national and international labor."[122] It was a message framed in distinctly working-class terms, one that explicitly embraced *latinidad*, or "Latin-ness," as a challenge to *hispanidad*, or "Hispanic-ness." *Hispanidad* encompassed the cultural symbols of the Spanish-speaking elite, hearkening back to Spain and the romanticized European past of Latin America; the notion of *latinidad*—an idea that sought to deemphasize the role of Europe in Latin America's identity—aimed to include those who, by virtue of their race or class, were not part of the elite.[123] The *choques* had opened up a space for debate over the language of identity and place, and the question of belonging, particularly as it applied to the Puerto Rican members of the *colonia*. The Puerto Rican leaders of the Ateneo Obrero defined an identity for *latinos* that was internationalist, or at least panregional, and suggested a class-based belonging that was situated in both the United States and Latin America.

On the other hand, a spokesman for the Porto Rican Brotherhood of America, in a postmortem on the year 1926 in the *colonia* that emphasized the East Harlem *choques*, reminded his readers of the more specifically local tensions of identity, place, and class. The "primary problem" of the Puerto Rican *colonia*, this writer said, was internal prejudice among residents. He beseeched all Puerto Ricans in New York "to confront—it pains me to say this but it is necessary to do so—the dishonor that some Puerto Ricans, who live in other parts of the city, stupidly and maliciously hurl at our community. . . . It is not unheard of that in their conversations with foreigners, they discredit their compatriots and even their own homeland."[124] But framing this lament about internal community tensions was a more encompassing claim about Puerto Ricans' identity as American citizens: "we uphold and defend the laws of this Nation, of whose citizenship we boast," wrote the brotherhood.[125]

A year after the 1926 *choques*, Puerto Ricans and other Hispanics experienced a new round of violent confrontations in East Harlem, which a *La Prensa* editorial described as another series of attacks committed by Jews, "without motivation and without scruples."[126] Then, in the spring of 1928, tensions spiked again in East Harlem, this time between Puerto Ricans and African Americans. An unnamed African American newspaper was reported to have printed an ominous announcement that a number of Jewish landlords in East Harlem were intending to try to evict Puerto Rican

tenants in order to raise rents. Concerned Puerto Ricans, including leaders of the Caribe Democratic Club, interpreted this announcement as an
aggressive move on the part of African Americans in East Harlem. The
club's leader, Isaac Irizarry Sasport, suggested that African Americans had
become resentful of the commercial competition of Puerto Rican shopkeepers and that they were trying to undermine Puerto Ricans' position
in Harlem by pitting them against Jews. This was a circuitous interpretation, perhaps, but it revealed the growing defensiveness with which many
Puerto Ricans had begun to approach their relations with neighbors in Harlem.[127] Puerto Ricans also worried increasingly about harassment by police.
Shortly after the *choques*, the Liga Puertorriqueña e Hispana requested a
meeting with East Harlem's police district captain to discuss the widespread complaints by Spanish-speaking residents, especially Puerto Ricans, about the aggressive treatment they felt they received from police in
their neighborhood. Puerto Rican organizations bemoaned Puerto Ricans'
reputation as a group with a disproportionate "criminal element," pointing
out that other non-naturalized Spanish speakers would claim to be Puerto
Rican if picked up for a crime, so as to avoid deportation to their native
country. As one migrant, Félix Loperena, put it, "The police were the first
who discriminated against us."[128]

Earlier in the decade, migrants tended to refer to their American citizenship as a useful political tool that could help them to shape the outcome of
the island's status dilemma. Their interest in getting Sol Bloom to recognize
them as a constituency in East Harlem had less to do with attending to local
issues in the *colonia* than with securing an advocate at the local level for the
cause of independence. For many *independentista* migrants, the mobilization
of Puerto Rican voters in New York seemed, as Tapia put it in 1925, "the
only way for our island to get political recognition." Migrants also invoked
their American citizenship in more abstract and symbolic ways in the early
twenties, such as when, during a dispute over World War I veterans' pensions, Resident Commissioner Félix Córdova-Dávila argued that the U.S.
government, having given Puerto Ricans "the title 'American citizens,'"
should treat Puerto Ricans "as equals and guarantee all their rights."[129]

But the tenor of migrants' invocations of citizenship changed substantially after 1926. *Colonia* leaders talked about the *choques* as a turning point,
a sign of rising interethnic conflict that exposed Puerto Ricans' social and
economic vulnerability and threatened their fragile place in New York. It
was an awakening that recent immigrants from Mexico were also experiencing in many communities in the southwestern United States in the same

period, in part because of the larger context of anti-immigrant sentiment in the nation.[130] In Puerto Rican New York, reaching a consensus about the meaning of local conflicts was easier in the late twenties, in part because divisions over island political conflicts had mellowed somewhat in these years.[131] Since their new sense of vulnerability united them as well, migrants continued to invoke their rights as U.S. citizens to defend themselves against the range of challenges to their respectability and their belonging in the polity. But both working-class and elite community leaders were more likely, now, to focus also on the limitations of their American citizenship and push for political empowerment to achieve recognition as equal citizens. In the fall of 1926, a columnist for *Gráfico*, a working-class weekly of which Jesús Colón was a founding editor, worried that Puerto Ricans were "the most vulnerable group" among the Hispanic immigrants in New York. "Truly it seems a paradox," he said, "that, being American citizens, we should be the most defenseless. While the citizens of other countries have their consulates and diplomats to represent them, the children of *Borinquén* have no one."[132] Within just a few years, as they found themselves struggling to survive in a foreign city in the midst of the Great Depression, Puerto Ricans would repeat countless variations on this lament.

### Chapter Two

# Confronting Race in the Metropole

Racial Ascription and Racial Discourse during the Depression

In August of 1930, José Celso González wrote a letter to the editor of *La Prensa* bemoaning the terrible impact of epidemic unemployment on his fellow Puerto Rican migrants, who suffered, he said, far more than other residents of the city. Indeed, Puerto Ricans were the fastest-growing group of foreign workers in New York's collapsing economy, and they felt the deprivations of the Depression earlier and more keenly than most. González claimed that over a third of Puerto Ricans could not find work, and their plight, he said, was due to prejudice pure and simple: managers of apartment buildings and hotels "only take Germans, Poles, and Greeks" as porters; factory owners "need Italians, Americans, and Jews"; and "for dishwashers they want Armenians and Italians." "When we say in an employment office that we are from Puerto Rico, they frankly reject us," he declared, in spite of the fact that "we are as American as they are." They were certainly accustomed to ethnic divisions in the workplace, but the social strains of the early thirties seemed to intensify interethnic hostilities, particularly in the job market.[2]

The Depression alone was not to blame. Demographic change had contributed substantially to the growing anti–Puerto Rican prejudice noted by González and many of his compatriots in the early thirties. Following the passage of the restrictive immigration laws of the 1920s, which did not limit immigration from the Western Hemisphere, Puerto Ricans and West Indians were beginning to stand out as the only groups of foreigners whose numbers continued to expand rapidly in New York City. Together with African Americans fleeing the violence and economic stagnation of the South, these largely impoverished migrants took up residence in the city that was experiencing, more than any other place, the social and political impact of restrictionist immigration policies that had radically reduced the number of European immigrants entering the United States by 1925.[3] The demographic shift was alarming to many observers, including the head of the

House Committee on Immigration and Naturalization, who lobbied (unsuccessfully) in 1931 for a bill to temporarily halt immigration from Latin America and the Caribbean. Though the bill was framed in response to the unemployment crisis, Rep. Thomas Jenkins focused on the racial impact of the migrations. "Several race problems are brewing," he warned his fellow lawmakers. "How many realize that a great part of the black colony in Harlem, N.Y., is from Jamaica, Haiti, and other islands of the West Indies? How many know that they can all be naturalized? How many know that the people of Porto Rico, including those in the New York colony, are already citizens?"[4]

This was, of course, only the latest version of an immigrant "race problem." Mexican, Chinese, and Irish immigrants, among others, had been called "niggers" and faced violence, segregation, and discrimination that varied somewhat by place and time but that consistently delineated the distance between themselves and "native" white Americans. For groups that were unlikely to find the privileges of white citizenship within their reach, as the Irish eventually did, a slippery spectrum from "black" to "other" would define their social identity and limit their prospects of achieving social equality.[5] By the late twenties, native whites were readily adapting their old racisms to target the darker-skinned newcomers from the South. Recent scholarship on the legal construction of race treats this period as a defining point in the establishment of modern categories of race and ethnicity in the United States. Historian Mae Ngai argues that while this new nativist moment promised European immigrants access to a "common whiteness," Japanese, Chinese, Mexican, and Filipino immigrants saw their racial inferiority reinforced, affirming their status, sketched out in the nineteenth century, as "unalterably foreign and unassimilable to the nation."[6] Puerto Ricans had been legally rendered part of the nation in 1917, but, as Representative Jenkins's comments confirmed, they were nevertheless viewed vaguely—by the relatively few whites who noticed their presence in the early thirties—as part of the foreign and unassimilable "black colony" of New York. Yet many Puerto Ricans would have described themselves as somewhere between the two normative categories of American race, categories whose hardening was signified in 1930 by the decision of the Bureau of the Census to dispense with the label "mulatto."[7]

In fact, most Puerto Ricans in the twenties had expected to be identified much like earlier immigrants, as outsiders only temporarily, people whose "difference" would fade over time. By the late 1920s, discrimination against Puerto Ricans had become a central concern for migrants in the heterogeneous neighborhoods where most of them lived, but explanations for social conflict tended to focus on differences of language and custom, not on racial difference per se.[8] Migrants worried about police harassment, and about the nascent stereotype of the Puerto Rican "criminal" in New York City, but they did not describe these problems as specifically racial. During the Depression, though, as their foreignness and their inscrutable racial origins seemed to hinder them in their competition with other New Yorkers for jobs and an increasing array of welfare funds, racial identity became a common subject of debate within the Puerto Rican community. Migrants' preoccupation with their ascribed racial identity was not limited to the light-skinned elite who felt they had the most to lose from being categorized as "black" in the North American binary scheme. Socialist internationalists and communist racial egalitarians participated in newspaper debates and public forums as well, worrying alongside their elite compatriots over the fact that the group was perceived not just as immigrants but as *Negro* foreigners vying for a place in the metropole.

The subject of race became an increasingly central public issue for many groups in the thirties, discussed more widely than ever before in the nation's cities, especially New York. By decade's end, the problem of racial prejudice and racial violence would force its way into the national consciousness: African American activists stepped up their campaigns against lynching and economic discrimination against black people; progressive and New Deal liberals began to recognize racial justice as a political issue in their platforms and policies; interracial coalitions of reformers and activists pointed to racism at home as a key dimension of the "fascist menace" on American soil, forcing American policymakers and intellectuals to try to define themselves against the racist precepts of Nazism. Anticolonial activists in Africa, the Caribbean, and the United States also began talking about racism as a problem for the way national membership was defined in nations with colonial interests.[9]

Aware to varying degrees of the racist power dynamics within their native society, migrants across the political spectrum talked about the pitfalls of "second-class citizenship," of being relegated to the inferior status of the Negro in the United States. During the thirties, Puerto Ricans began to see how, as American citizens upon arrival in the United States, the ascription of a nonwhite identity would exact a measurable cost. They began to express fears that if they became, like Negroes, "citizens without rights," they would be excluded from many of the benefits and protections that white citizens expected, demanded, and got. In his 1943 classic *Brothers under the Skin*, progressive journalist Carey McWilliams wrote that Puerto Rican migrants, upon arrival in the United States, "discover, rather to their amazement, that they are all classified as 'Negroes'; and must, perforce, buck the color line." McWilliams's observation would have sounded a bit melodramatic to most Puerto Ricans who settled in New York in the Depression era. The realization of their racial ascription in the United States inspired dismay for many, and perhaps a measure of surprise for those who were sure they were not, in Puerto Rican terms, *negro*. But coming from a society marked by the same basic race and class nexus, *amazement* was the wrong word. McWilliams was right, though, about their motivation to "buck the color line," and his assessment sums up what so many migrants sought to do, "perforce," in the thirties. Using a variety of strategies that reflected both their diverse ideological positions and the details of the local social terrain, Puerto Ricans struggled to disaggregate their political identity as U.S. citizens from the racial identity that was becoming more firmly ascribed to them during this decade.[10]

## "The Puerto Rican Must Not Be Seen as Worse Than the Native Blacks of this Country"

When Pedro Juan Labarthe, a Puerto Rican teacher at Xavier College, wrote to *La Prensa* early in 1931 to lament that Puerto Ricans suffered from an "inferiority complex"—illustrated by his friend who "passed" as Spanish—he concluded with a point about racial identity: that Puerto Ricans should be proud not just of their nationality in general but also of the fact that "we have people of color" on the island. "Americans have them too," he said, "in great numbers [in New York] and in the South." And, he added, "Our mulattos are more attractive because they have fine features and complexions the color of *café con leche*."[12] Labarthe's letter signaled a new subject of public debate in *La Prensa* by the early thirties, as migrants shifted from discussing a generalized anti–Puerto Rican prejudice to a distinctly racial prejudice against their compatriots. Readers were now writing letters not just about the general problem of a "bad reputation" in New York, the conversation begun in 1926; they were expressing worry about white Americans' conflation of Puerto Ricans with African Americans, which observers interpreted as a distinct threat to their still-evolving social status.[11] It was one thing for a Puerto Rican to identify another migrant as "*negro*," since the label *negro* implied an observation about color as a social fact not synonymous with the North American label "Negro." Categories of color, in Puerto Rican society, carried with them coded information on a person's probable class position and social status, but they did not ascribe an immutable social location. It was a different thing entirely for a white American to identify a Puerto Rican as Negro, a fixed category at the bottom of the social hierarchy of the United States that trumped all other markers of identity.

Although Labarthe did not mention a particular motivation for his letter, he probably was inspired to write by an article printed in the tabloid daily *New York American* several days earlier. "Newcomers in the Slums of East Harlem" called attention to the increased migration of Puerto Ricans to New York since the beginning of the Depression and referred to migrants as "wretched" and "the lowest grade of labor," "lower than the colored worker."[13] In concluding that it was better to be black in Puerto Rico than in the United States, Labarthe was responding obliquely to the reporter's charge that Puerto Ricans' lowly status in the United States resulted from their blackness. María Más Pozo, a Nationalist activist and one of the few visible women in *colonia* politics in this era, attacked the *Journal American* article more directly, with venom. "It is time to think long and hard about the situation of my compatriots in this country," she said. She continued, "The Puerto Rican must not be seen as worse than the native blacks of this country. *We do not want a North American citizenship that humiliates us, depriving us of our dignity, after having been stripped, in the name of humanity, of our blessed land.* We want to be pure Puerto Ricans, only proud of a single race; that which mixed her white blood with the passionate blood of the indian [emphasis in original]."[14] Although she elsewhere criticized the "imposition" of an unequal and debased form of U.S. citizenship on Puerto Ricans—a common Nationalist complaint—Más Pozo insisted here that that U.S. citizenship should function to protect Puerto Ricans against the ascription of a low social status, one that made them "worse than the native blacks" on the mainland. More to the point, for all Más Pozo criticized North Americans for their racial hypocrisy, her concern was not with racial injustice; she complained only about the specific injustice of Puerto Ricans' being paid "worse than Chinese and blacks" in the United States. A number of similar letters followed in *La Prensa*'s "De nuestros lectores" section, including one from East Harlem resident Fernando Arjona López, a self-identified *independentista* who railed against the "humiliation" of "comparing us with black Americans . . . putting us in a debased sphere"—one of the many insults of U.S. colonialism.[15]

Only a single reader criticized both the *New York American* article and the commentators who failed to challenge the hierarchy in which Puerto Ricans fell beneath Negroes and Chinese immigrants. Introduced by *La Prensa*'s editors as "a Puerto Rican of the black race," Gabriel Rivera also protested *"los insultos de los yanquís"* but questioned other readers' outrage over being categorized with black Americans: "I don't see the motivation to feel so profoundly injured because they see us as black Americans; since . . . I wouldn't want to be seen as a white Texan or Georgian, either; because . . . I am filled with contempt and disgust by the white man for his savage and heretical instinct, which the lynchings in the Southern states have shown us so recently."[16] Rivera's reference to "the lynchings in the Southern states" would not have surprised *La Prensa*'s readers in 1931, since the rise in racial violence in the South during the twenties was covered regularly in *La Prensa*.[17] More surprising, given the dominance of the slippery discourse of *mestizaje* in Puerto Rico—a discourse with a blind spot regarding the African component of the mixture—was the way Rivera took Más Pozo to task for her definition of Puerto Rican peoplehood: "What would my countrywoman do with black-blooded *Boricuas* . . . , whose blood is mixed as much as white blood is mixed with indian?" Más Pozo defended herself aggressively. "Many times in *La Prensa* and other New York periodicals, I have taken up the defense of the colored man with every ounce of my being."[18] Indeed, in previous letters to *La Prensa*, she had fashioned herself as a champion of the underdog and a proponent of racial enlightenment, though always in ways that carefully signified the distance between black Americans and Puerto Ricans *de color*.[19]

But there was more than just a grain of political expedience in these positions. It was one thing for Nationalists to criticize the United States for claiming to export lessons of liberty and democracy to Puerto Rico (and other "backward" countries) at the same time that the nation trampled on African Americans' civil rights at home. But for migrants like Más Pozo, whose house in suburban New Jersey and ties to the Manhattan migrant elite suggested origins in Puerto Rico's mostly white upper class, it was another thing entirely to connect racial injustice in the United States to the unequal racial order of their native society. Historian Miriam Jiménez Román refers to this problem as the "historical amnesia" of the "twice colonized" island elite, who found it useful to argue against U.S. colonialism with a romanticized vision of a gentler social order under Spanish rule.[20] "One could say that in Puerto Rico there is no racial prejudice," Más Pozo proclaimed in another letter. In fact, of course, there were many, many Puerto Rican migrants of color who not only complained of unequal treatment in the *colonia* but talked about experiencing it in their homeland as well.[21] Más Pozo, inhabiting a different social and ideological world, elaborated on her reply to Rivera's criticism with another romantic portrayal of Puerto Rican racial equality. It was a familiar Nationalist trope about racism and the moral corruption of the United States:

> A colored Puerto Rican man in New York, as long as he is in the *colonia*, is considered by other Puerto Ricans who are not colored to be "one of us." . . . Only the North American, to debase the Puerto Rican, insists on making comparisons between the blacks from [the United States], and our countrymen, which angered me so much that I wrote that article, not because they compare us, but because of how the colored man in this country is viewed. . . . I came to know these prejudices in this country, in the country of liberty and democracy, the only one in the world where black people are lynched.[22]

The several letter writers who followed Más Pozo's lead in decrying Puerto Ricans' social debasement argued for maximizing distance between the Puerto Rican and the American Negro.

In addition to sugarcoating the racial dynamics in her New York community, Más Pozo capitalized on a burgeoning discourse of the political dimensions of race in the United States. She contrasted blackness in Puerto Rico and in the New York community of Puerto Rican migrants, where supposedly it bore no stigma, to the North American context, where blackness carried with it not just the threat of discrimination but also the danger of real physical violence. Indeed, a new attention to the problem of lynching in the United States allowed nationalists like Más Pozo (and Rivera, too) to use the issue to support a claim about the moral corruption of the U.S. social structure and political system: lynching, though it did not affect Puerto Ricans directly, stood as a symbol both of North American hypocrisy (a "country of liberty and democracy" that tolerated the murder of innocent citizens) and of the potential oppression that Puerto Ricans suffered as second-class citizens in their own right.[23]

Shortly after the exchange between Más Pozo and Rivera, debate on the connections between Puerto Ricans' U.S. citizenship and their racial identity arose again in *La Prensa*'s letters columns in response to reports on President Herbert Hoover's vacation trip to Puerto Rico and the Virgin Islands in the spring of 1931. Newspapers in the United States covered every aspect of his voyage, from the menus of the elaborate meals he enjoyed on the cruise ship to a small mix-up with the president's luggage in St. Croix.

The reception he received from Puerto Ricans on the island was mixed. Nationalists refused to welcome him, but the Federación de Trabajadores Libres, Puerto Rico's largest labor union, greeted Hoover's entourage with cheers, expressing gratitude for recent legislation that would create an insular Department of Labor and provide aid for rebuilding schools and roads damaged in the severe 1930 hurricane.[24]

In New York, Nationalists raised a cry of protest against this "good will" visit. *La Prensa* printed a series of letters from Nationalist readers that reiterated arguments about the injustice of Puerto Ricans' debased citizenship and their categorization as "lower than black." "We don't have any rights because we are not 'straight Americans' and our countrymen in general are shamelessly attacked," wrote one. He continued with a familiar argument about how Puerto Ricans' American citizenship served the purposes of the U.S. government: "We will become 'straight Americans' when in the near future there is another war and then the *New York American* will proclaim: 'Portoricans we are in a big war, we need your services as americans; fight for your flag and fight for your own liberty.' Forgetting that portoricans in times of peace are 'whelps and dirty portoricans.' And I am lower than any black American, who are lynched in broad daylight by whites in the South."[25] Another reader, after a long invective against the imperialist politics of the United States, reiterated the previous writer's points: "With our citizenship here, we are called dirty and wretched, black and lowly, by a periodical like the *New York American*. How ridiculous, then, is the phrase in Mr. Hoover's speech to Puerto Ricans, 'Fellow Citizens.'"[26] Another reader, Josefa Muñoz Cruz, pronounced herself to be an "*independentista* by birth and by conviction" but expressed a more optimistic view of Hoover's visit to their homeland. "In his recent visit to the island," she declared, "the Hon. Pres. Hoover has placed us in a position we deserve, and has shown to the United States that we are not a nation of black savages as until now we have been judged by narrow-minded Americans."[27]

With this hopeful—and racist—view of Americans' softening judgments of their Puerto Rican neighbors, Puerto Rican *La Prensa* readers closed the first in a series of discussions about racial identity in the United States in the early thirties. With the relentless progress of the Depression by the summer of 1931, *La Prensa*'s editors dramatically scaled back the printing of readers' letters.[28] For a time, the few letters that did appear focused on other problems: migrants' difficulties in securing Home Relief benefits, the political tensions in Spain, and President Gerardo Machado's controversial rule in Cuba. If any readers commented on a series of bloody conflicts between Filipinos and "Spanish Americans" in Harlem in July of 1931, *La Prensa* decided not to make room for their letters. Nor did it print observations about more everyday ethnic conflicts like those reported by migrant Louise Delgado, who later described to an interviewer the "very bad state of affairs" as Puerto Ricans struggled to live and work in East Harlem in the early thirties: "You have to remember that at that time there was a big problem in East Harlem with the Italians and the Puerto Ricans, they were always arguing and fighting."[29] And the native racisms of various groups in the Spanish-speaking *colonia* persisted, of course. It was not uncommon for announcements for some social events, like a charity dance sponsored by the Mexican Club Azteca in support of victims of a hurricane in Puerto Rico in 1932, to specify "for whites only."[30]

The public discussion about racial identity in the United States resumed in the pages of *La Prensa* three years later, when another sensationalist piece on Puerto Rico appeared in the mainstream press. This time it was a photographic essay featuring dark-skinned Puerto Rico peasants in the nationally circulating *Literary Digest*—just the kind of snapshot of her country that migrants like María Más Pozo were afraid of. In fact, the *Digest* article may have brought to mind, among the older members of the migrant elite, an 1899 report about the island assembled by a U.S. observer that was amply illustrated with photographs of Puerto Rico's exotic racial types. (The report's title, moreover—*Our Islands and Their People*—offered a remarkably precise description of how the average congressional reader might have described the new political relationship.)[31] Dr. Augusto Arce Álvarez wrote to *La Prensa* from the then middle-class enclave of Washington Heights early in 1934 to lament that "the publication of such photographs in this country . . . has led the majority of Americans to believe that our island is populated entirely by Negroes." Álvarez called on Puerto Ricans to lean on their status as citizens—though exactly how, he did not say—to counter the putative racial insult: "We must defend our rights before the people, without fear; we must seek the protection of the citizenship given us by the Congress of the United States in 1917."[32]

This time the debate about the dilemmas of Puerto Ricans' racial identity in the United States played out differently. In 1931, all but one of the participants in the debate over the *New York American* article rejected comparisons of the Puerto Rican to black Americans and refused to acknowledge African roots in Puerto Rican history. Now, however, Dr. Álvarez's passionate expression of this latest "injury" against Puerto Rico "provoked immediate attention within the *colonia*," according to *La Prensa*'s editors, attention that pointedly criticized Álvarez for his racist views. "I was not born black," wrote one critic, identifying himself as M. Callejo, "but if I were I would be proud to be part of a race . . . whose struggle . . . is that of the oppressed masses." Using a logic familiar to Nationalists like Más Pozo, Callejo went on to deconstruct Álvarez's invocation of citizenship as a source of "protection" for Puerto Ricans. "I ask you: 'Is this the way to defend the rights of the people, insulting the majority of your people and bragging about the citizenship which the Congress of the Morgans and the Rockefellers used to send to their death their unlucky soldiers?'"[33] Callejo was referring here to an interpretation of the 1917 Jones Act, popular among Nationalists and anti-imperialists, which asserted that the U.S. Congress granted citizenship to Puerto Ricans when it did—after seventeen years of debate—in order to enable the armed forces to draft Puerto Ricans to fight for the United States in World War I.[34] More of a challenge to the status quo was Callejo's claim that "the majority" of Puerto Ricans were black or at least would identify with Negroes in the United States. Other readers also objected to the racism in Álvarez's letter but couched their criticism in more genteel terms. Said one, "That they see us as black does not affect our dignity as a people, does not tarnish our collective aspirations, nor impede . . . our ability to prove, living in this land, that we are conscientious about our responsibilities as citizens and will remain vigilant about our rights."[35] "We are what we are," said another reader. "They can spoil our language, impose their education on us, but they cannot take away our color."[36] In all of these 1934 letters, "our color"—to whatever extent North Americans viewed it as "black"—figured as a distinct source of pride for Puerto Ricans.

Many readers would have noticed that La Prensa's letters pages charted a significant shift in discourse about the political dimensions of race in the United States.[37] Elite readers like Más Pozo seemed to fall silent in the flurry of reaction to the Literary Digest photos. Were outspoken Puerto Ricans, migrants with less attachment to elite nationalist orthodoxy, beginning to embrace a strategy of demanding rights as "underdogs," shrinking the political distance between themselves and African Americans? The growing number of working-class Puerto Ricans would have been hearing—and perhaps beginning to agree with—the rising chorus of black activists in Harlem who were demanding expanded civil rights, many of them influenced by Communist Party discourse on race in the thirties and events like the Angelo Herndon case and later the trial of the Scottsboro boys.[38] The more progressive letter writers in 1934 suggested that they were willing to make peace with the idea that Americans might "see us as black." They also

Figure 5. Liga Puertorriqueña e Hispana, Brooklyn section, outing to Heckscher State Park on Long Island, August 26, 1934. Jesús Colón is fifth from the left. Jesús Colón papers, Archives of the Puerto Rican Diaspora, Centro de Estudios Puertorriqueños, Hunter College, CUNY.

tended to give less credence to the rigid divisions required by racial ideology in the United States: "We are what we are. . . . They cannot take away our color." This assertion could have been interpreted in terms of the idea of the distinctly *non*-African *"gran familia puertorriqueña,"* what María Más Pozo referred to as "pure Puerto Ricans." In the context of the series of letters criticizing Álvarez's antiblack racism, however, this statement actually suggested a challenge to that racist discourse, and a challenge to North Americans' binary racial ideology.

### "Complexion," Racial Categories, and Racial Identity in the *Colonia*

When José Celso González protested against the discrimination that his compatriots encountered in the job market in 1930, he did not suggest that Puerto Ricans faced a specifically race-based form of prejudice. Rather, he implied that Puerto Ricans suffered because, as newcomers in New

York City, they simply occupied the lowest place in the hierarchy of foreign workers in the city. It seemed to González that if employers could be
convinced of the fact that Puerto Ricans were "as American as they are,"
some of that prejudice would soften and migrants would encounter less
hostile rejection. In fact, responding to the general problem of prejudice
against Puerto Rican migrants in the labor market, Puerto Rican legislators, led by Socialist Party leader and Resident Commissioner Santiago
Iglesias, had already proposed the creation of an "Office of Employment
and Identification" (OEI) in Manhattan to serve the mass of Puerto Rican
migrants who arrived in the United States jobless, usually, with American
citizenship in hand but no passport to prove it.[39] The organization would be
staffed by Puerto Ricans, and the employment office would be able to help
its Spanish-speaking clients much more readily than the state-sponsored
or privately run employment offices. The identification office would issue
identification cards to migrants so that they could prove their American
citizenship to suspicious employers and thus (or so OEI officials hoped)
garner a slight advantage as they competed with other foreigners in New
York's depressed labor market.[40]

According to José González, though, lacking proof of citizenship hardly mattered if a Spanish speaker could not even get in the door to speak to a hiring manager. Other pessimistic observers pointed to the importance of this "urgently needed" service, not for the purpose of securing jobs but for protection against deportation in case of arrest.[41] Comments from *La Prensa* readers about the identification office were not glowing. One writer complained that "it is not providing the service for which it was created. What has been the good of the identification of Puerto Ricans who go to this office?"[42] The relatively small number of migrants who applied for ID cards during the thirties suggests that many migrants doubted their utility in the labor market. In the first ten years of the office's operation, which coincided with the long years of the Great Depression and the slow recovery that followed, barely more than four thousand migrants sought identification cards.[43] Depending on the population estimate of Puerto Ricans in New York, this represented anywhere from about 5 percent to 10 percent of the migrant population. Before 1935, the overwhelming majority of applicants were men, since the primary purpose of the ID card was to vouch for the holder's employment eligibility, and migrant women at the time participated less frequently in the formal economy. After 1935, however, with the passage of the Social Security Act and its various provisions for public assistance, the number of women applicants increased to between 5 percent and 10 percent of the total number of applicants; the majority of these women were over the age of sixty, and they probably were seeking proof of citizenship in order to apply for benefits of Old Age Assistance and Survivors' Insurance.[44] (Applications increased dramatically during the period of the Second World War, when the OEI processed about fifteen thousand requests for ID cards, although as much as 10 percent of this number represented reapplications after a card expired or a cardholder moved from one address to another. Much of the real increase was probably spurred by the need for enlisted men and draftees to prove their citizenship.)

Official purposes aside, the ID cards, which prominently featured a "complexion" label, highlighted the contrast between flexible Puerto Rican racial categories on the one hand and a rigid, binary North American discourse of race on the other. The complexion labels represented a sideways challenge to that binary system even while they signified an evolving adherence to the rules governing the social meaning of skin color and class position in the United States. The 1931 debate in *La Prensa* suggests that Puerto Ricans were thinking about the need to "buck the color line" as the OEI was getting established, and the ID cards' complexion labels might have presented one possibility for doing so. They also symbolized more complicated processes relating to race in the *colonia* in the thirties—power relations between the office's Puerto Rican employees and their poor clients, and both groups' efforts to negotiate how they hoped to be situated socially, as people whose racial identity was not yet firmly established.

The complexion classifications that appeared on migrants' ID cards were a combination of self-descriptions supplied by the applicants and determinations of the applicants' complexions made by OEI employees. They included labels like "dark," "light," "ruddy," "olive," *"regular,"* "brown," "light brown," and "dark brown"—some of them terms translated directly from the Puerto Rican vernacular, which interpreted racial identity fluidly, while others (like *"regular,"* meaning "average," or "ruddy," written in English) represented innovations on the part of the OEI staff.[45] Such elision between description and category in Spanish was characteristic of the way Puerto Ricans and other Latin Americans had talked about race since the seventeenth century; Puerto Rican writer Tomás Blanco described these terms, in his 1942 classic *El prejuicio racial en Puerto Rico*, as "deferential euphemisms" that had filtered down from the official language of Spanish colonialism. Blanco and North American sociologist Maxine Gordon made similar observations about the range of racial terminology in Puerto Rico in the thirties and forties, where the vernacular was still peppered with a half dozen descriptions of different kinds of brown skin.[46] The popular belief in the fluidity of racial identity in Puerto Rico was reinforced by many aspects of life in a mixed-race society, including the fact that a single family commonly contained members of a variety of racial "types." One migrant who settled in New York in 1929, for instance, described the colors of his fourteen children as "white, dark-skinned, and everything in between."[47] This kind of observation was often used as evidence for the assertion that there was no racial prejudice within the Puerto Rican migrant community, only prejudice from outsiders. To a degree, the ID cards' adherence to Puerto Rican categories seemed to reinforce this notion: ID cardholders were not divided into opposing racial groups marked by "black" and "white."

Comparisons between the racial systems of the United States and Puerto Rico abounded in that era, not only among Nationalists who sought to emphasize the weaknesses and hypocrisies of the United States' political culture. North American observers, too—especially the growing cadre of social scientists who were absorbed by questions of race and prejudice—were fond of retelling the story of racial democracy in Puerto Rico. In 1930, for instance, a Brookings researcher reported that "colored men and women are found in all walks of life, numerous in the teaching profession, and colored pupils attend on terms of equality public schools and higher educational institutions."[48] This was a partial and distorted snapshot, one framed by a misapprehension of the limits of racial fluidity in social life. Although there was no legal segregation of whites and people of African descent in Puerto Rico (or in other Latin American countries), dark skin or other physical markers of Africanness strictly limited access to institutions and occupations. Jiménez Román has argued that the island's "flexible" racial ideology allowed the existence of multiple contradictions: Puerto Ricans could uphold "the institutionally sanctioned and popularly reinforced belief in distinct races with identifiable, essential traits" alongside "a corresponding notion of a 'multiracial' society whose citizens enjoy harmonious relations." At the same time, they could cling to the notion—expressed, for example, by María Más Pozo in 1931—of "'la gran familia puertorriqueña,' a 'race' of mestizos that shares a common culture, language and history."[49] A different version of social reality was reflected in a story recounted by Lucila Padrón, who arrived in New York from Ponce in 1934. Padrón told an interviewer that a cousin of hers had worked toward a teaching degree in Ponce in the thirties but was refused teaching positions in the city and was sent to the countryside instead, "because she's dark-complexioned [prieta] . . . she was a bit dark."[50] This story, and countless others like it, belied Blanco's main conclusion about racial prejudice in Puerto Rico, that "our prejudice is more social than racial"—that is, related to class more than race.

It was true that a binary racial ideology did not hold sway in Puerto Rico as it did in the United States. But black and white still marked starkly opposing poles of the island's social hierarchy, and most Puerto Ricans tended to deemphasize their society's blackness, as in the 1931 La Prensa debates. The final word from Blanco, and the consensus among many Puerto Ricans even beyond the elite, was that "although the mixture of blacks and whites is considerable, the African element has had only a slight influence on cultural characteristics."[51] More slippery was the power of whiteness, especially for North Americans who had difficulty seeing it in a place where mixed-race people were not systematically discriminated against. A Federal Writers' Project field-worker quipped in the 1940 edition of the American Guide to Puerto Rico that "on the mainland a drop of Negro blood makes a white man a Negro; while in Puerto Rico a drop of white blood makes a Negro a white man."[52] The "one-drop rule" was an exaggerated but more or less accurate description of racial categorization in the United States, but it was wrong to assert the inverse about Puerto Rico. White skin and European ancestry were highly valued, and, while not considered impossible or even unlikely for persons of mixed-race ancestry to possess, they were carefully guarded symbols of privilege.[53]

It was hard to predict how the traditional patterns of white privilege would play out among Puerto Ricans in the United States. The 1930 Brookings report described an advertisement in an island newspaper placed by a Puerto Rican auto mechanic, living in upstate New York, who sought a wife "who among other qualifications must be either white or mulatto." The researcher interpreted this instance as a sign of "the changing race attitudes of the emigrants," not understanding that a person's search for a "white" spouse—the desire to "marry up"—was an old and unremarkable practice on the island.[54] On the other hand, there was indeed a distinct pressure to claim whiteness in the United States. From the perspective of migrants like González who saw other immigrants—those considered to be uniformly "white" by the twenties: the Germans, Poles, Greeks, Italians, Armenians, and Jews—getting and keeping jobs more easily than Puerto Ricans, the value of a white identity increased on entering the United States. Pi Santos, for instance, came to New York in 1933, having learned of a job opportunity there that would be an improvement over her work at a children's clothing manufacturer, and her boss in Puerto Rico had encouraged her: "Look, be persistent, you're white, you know how to work, so you see you're not going to suffer."[55]

It is remarkable, then, that none of the Puerto Ricans who applied for ID cards in the thirties wound up with the complexion label "white" on their ID cards, including those whose photographs showed very pale skin. OEI employees, perhaps reasserting their sense of island-based racial hierarchies in a more openly racist society (who was a peasant to say he was "*de raza blanca*" if his social superior might not even be able to claim such status in the metropole?), denied nearly all applicants' claims to be white. In some cases, the application was accompanied by a birth certificate designating the race of the applicant's parents as "*de raza blanca*," but none of these applicants wound up with a "white" complexion label on the ID card.[56] In well over half of these cases, an applicant who was said to be born of parents "of the white race" (or, at least, a mother "*de raza blanca*," in the absence of an identified father) was labeled "dark" or "medium" or even "colored" on the ID application. In the remaining cases, all of the applicants were "light" or "fair," but never "white." For applicants who were at first labeled "white" on the ID application (either by their own determination or by that of an identification office employee), "white" was crossed out by hand or covered with a typed "X" and then changed to a different label: "fair"; "light"; or, more frequently, and in greater contrast, "dark." When José Víctor Pagán applied for an ID card on October 22, 1931, he wrote "white" on the line next to the complexion category. At some later point, as his application was being reviewed in the identification office, an employee typed dashes through "white" and below typed "dark." Joseph Feliciano, applying for an ID card a year later, may have marked his complexion as "white" without thinking about it, since the birth certificate he brought with him to the Migration Office classified his mother as "*blanca*" as well. He was probably puzzled when, on receiving his new ID card, he noticed that his complexion, like José Pagán's, was "dark." In spite of the fact that hundreds of migrants, from the early thirties to the end of World War II, described their own complexions as white on their ID card applications, not a single applicant in my sample wound up with an ID card that read "complexion: white." ID office employees changed the complexion description in every case.

While complexion descriptions on migrants' ID cards did not map onto U.S. racial categories per se, those who assigned the sometimes quixotic labels, as well as those to whom they were assigned, understood their connection to the larger racial hierarchy in New York. The fact that applicants' complexion labels on the ID cards were decided by Puerto Rican employees raises important questions not just about differences between Puerto Rican and North American racial ideologies but also about the relationships between the office workers who applied the labels and the applicants who bore them. José M. Vivaldi, a powerful Democratic district leader in El Barrio the 1930s, became the first director of the OEI and had overseen its staffing with Puerto Rican migrants. This allowed him to distribute patronage among his compatriots, and since literacy and certain middle-class norms were required for the job, OEI employees were mostly members of the "better class" of migrants. Tensions of class and color carried over from island society and inflected social relations in the *colonia*, marking the relationship between the usually light-skinned, educated employees of the office and the darker, poorer migrants whom they served.[57] Yet OEI employees, depending on their skin color, would have experienced many of the same difficulties—discrimination predicated on "foreignness" as well as perceived racial difference—that their clients encountered in a new city, especially in an era of economic depression. Given the insecurity of all recent migrants in a faltering urban economy, staff members may have had

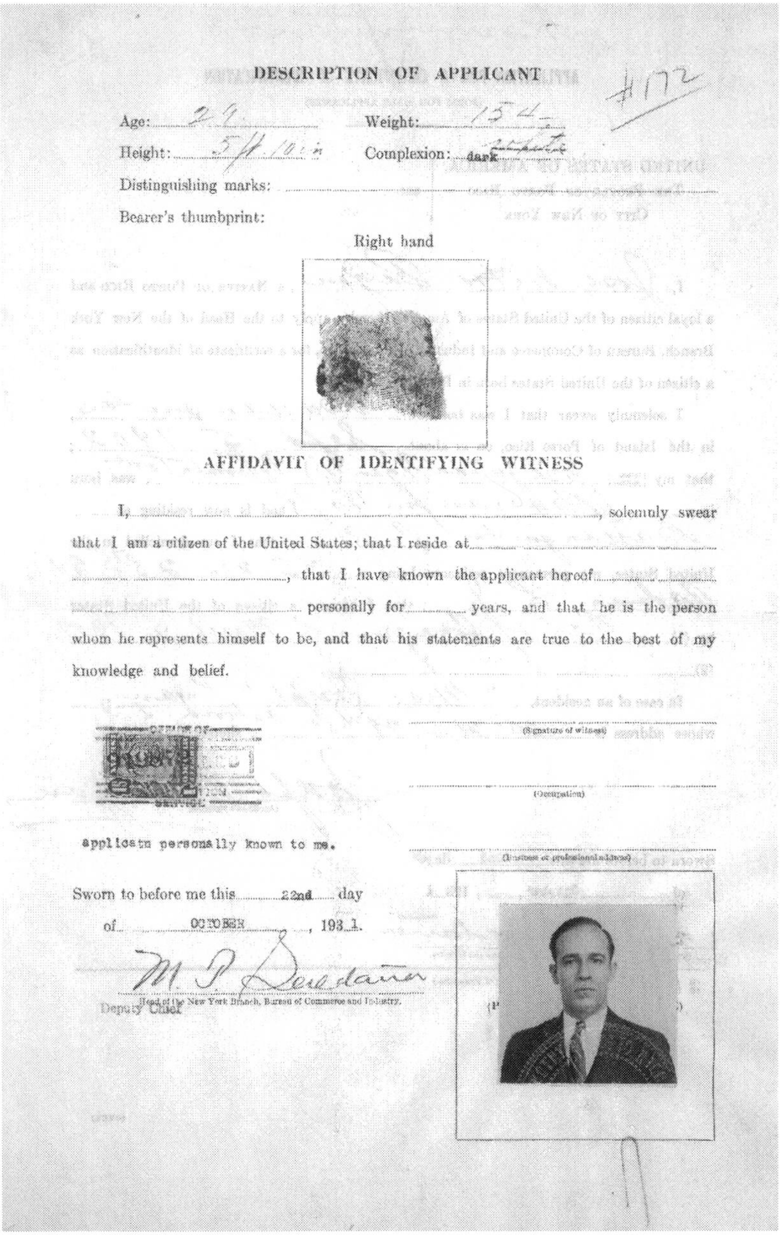

**DESCRIPTION OF APPLICANT**

Age: 29 Weight: 154

Height: 5 ft. 10 in Complexion: ~~white~~ dark

Distinguishing marks:

Bearer's thumbprint:

Right hand

**AFFIDAVIT OF IDENTIFYING WITNESS**

I, ............, solemnly swear that I am a citizen of the United States; that I reside at ............, that I have known the applicant hereof ............ personally for ...... years, and that he is the person whom he represents himself to be, and that his statements are true to the best of my knowledge and belief.

(Signature of witness)

(Occupation)

applicatn personally known to me.

(Business or professional address)

Sworn to before me this 22nd day of OCTOBER, 1931.

M. P. Deválaños

Head of the New York Branch, Bureau of Commerce and Industry.

Deputy Chief

#172

Figure 6. ID card application of José Victor Pagán, October 22, 1931. The complexion description, originally filled in as "white" by the applicant or his witness, was later changed by a clerk to "dark." Records of the Offices of the Government of Puerto Rico in the United States, Archives of the Puerto Rican Diaspora, Centro de Estudios Puertorriqueños, Hunter College, CUNY.

an increased interest in delineating the distance in social status between their clients and themselves.

Designating the mostly working-class applicants for the ID card as "dark" was one way to protect these social distinctions. Indeed, throughout the decade, a growing majority of migrants applying for ID cards— about 60 percent in the mid-thirties and 85 percent by the late thirties— were labeled "dark" or something similar, including "dark brown," "black," or "colored." Gender also shaped the patterns in complexion labels: in most years up through the end of World War II, the small number of women applicants (between about 5 percent and 10 percent of the total for each year of my sample) were three to four times as likely as men to be given a complexion label in the "light" range, a fact consistent with the discourses of racial danger in both the United States and Puerto Rico, which suggested that dark men were most threatening. The patterns in complexion category labels assigned over the course of the thirties indicates that ID office workers were responding to the hardening racial identity ascribed to Puerto Ricans during the Depression. Representing them as increasingly "dark" mirrored media images that increasingly asserted Puerto Ricans' similarity to African Americans. Sociologist Lawrence Chenault observed in 1938 that "the white Puerto Rican, after he has lived in New York for several years, takes up what is described as the 'American attitude' on the question of color"; and while this assumption can hardly be taken at face value, the evidence of the ID card complexion labels, along with anecdotal observations, shows its validity.[58]

With the ID cards' complexion labels, Puerto Rican employees of the OEI inserted their own "descriptive vocabulary" of quotidian social relations into a North American terrain marked by rigid and binary ideas about race. The complexion labels represent, then, both a certain refusal to adhere to the binary ideology and an interest in maintaining their native hierarchy. Historian Gary Nash has written about the historical denial of racial mixture in the United States, arguing that there is little discussion of racial mixing in North America, not because it didn't happen but because it was "ideologically repugnant." North American ideology had to support the absolute separation of the races and the belief that there were two races only. This dichotomy was even more strictly codified in 1930, the same year the first ID cards were issued, when the U.S. census dropped its long-used "mulatto" category.[59] While probably unaware of changes in the census, Puerto Rican New Yorkers of all social classes nevertheless experienced this rigidity—emphasizing the infamous North American "one-drop rule"—as confounding, neither entirely imaginary nor fully real. The assigning of complexion labels on the ID cards signified the diffidence (and confusion) of OEI staff and working-class clientele alike but also indicated the increasing conformity of the migrant elite to racial rules in the United States.

## Puerto Ricans and the Harlem Riot of 1935

In their letters to *La Prensa* about the racial representation of Puerto Rican migrants, several writers agreed that being categorized as "black" in the United States was tantamount to losing the most important benefits that U.S. citizenship was supposed to confer. Puerto Rican migrants were striving against mounting odds to secure for themselves the version of U.S. citizenship enjoyed by whites, not the citizenship possessed by the nation's largely disfranchised minority. In 1935, just at this moment of heightened worry about race in the *colonia*, a riot in Harlem confirmed the extent of Puerto Ricans' reluctance to align themselves with African Americans. One afternoon in March, Lino Rivera, a sixteen-year-old Puerto Rican boy, got caught stealing a penknife at a Kress five-and-dime store on 125th Street and Seventh Avenue, a few blocks from Rivera's home on Manhattan Avenue and 122nd Street. When the store's manager confronted Rivera and detained him, the boy resisted and allegedly bit the man on the hand. Someone called the police, and a crowd gathered outside and in the front of the store. After the manager decided to let the boy go instead of having him arrested, a police officer escorted Rivera through the basement to the back exit on 124th Street. When Rivera disappeared with the officer into the basement of the store, a rumor spread through the crowd that he was being beaten; and when an ambulance drove up to the back entrance of the store and drove away empty—having been called, some accounts noted, because of the hand wound Rivera inflicted on his captor—some in the crowd said that the boy had been beaten to death.[60]

The crowd consisted of shoppers in the neighborhood's busy commercial district as well as residents of Central Harlem, who were almost entirely African American, and it dispersed for a time after police arrested a woman accused of inciting the disturbance. Several hours later, a group of protesters began an impromptu public meeting about the alleged violence against a black child, and as the police were trying to remove a speaker from his soapbox stand and clear the sidewalk, someone threw a rock into the front window of the Kress store.[61] Thus began a full-scale riot in which several thousand Harlemites participated, an event that before long would symbolize the acute suffering and resentment of the country's most storied African American community. Writer Claude McKay remembered it as "a spontaneous community protest against social and legal injustice." "Harlem broke loose," he wrote. "The Black Belt ran amok along Fifth, Lenox, Seventh, and Eight Avenues, from 116th to 145th Street."[62]

In the end, seventy-five people were arrested, hundreds of windows were broken, and sixty-three people, including several policemen, were injured. One African American boy, shot in the back by a police officer, died several days later.[63] City investigators, reporting a year later, described the immediate sentiments that sparked the riot as linked to much deeper grievances: "The rumor of the death of the boy, which became now to the aroused Negro shoppers an established fact, awakened the deep-seated sense of wrongs and denials and even memories of injustices in the South. One woman was heard to cry out that the treatment was 'just like down South where they lynch us.'"[64] While it was immediately clear that the Kress store incident had struck a nerve with black Harlemites who saw an opportunity to publicize the suffering of their community, city officials and reporters took seriously rumors that the riot had been encouraged by external agitators with a political agenda. A group of mostly white communists called the Young Liberators looked most suspicious to investigators, since members had been spied distributing incendiary leaflets as the rioting began: "Child Brutally Beaten Woman Attacked by BOSS and COPS = Child near *DEATH*" and "WORKERS! NEGRO AND WHITE Protest against This Lynch Attack of Innocent Negro People," they trumpeted. With this evidence, many of the New York dailies pointed to the communists as the primary instigators of the riot.[65] A year later, though, writers of the Mayor's Commission final report disagreed, maintaining that it was simply residents' resentment over local conditions that had fanned the flames of protest in Harlem.[66] Whatever role the Young Liberators played in the riots, their flyers certainly sensationalized racial tensions in Harlem, simultaneously trading on fears of black-white conflict and promoting black-white unity. And in doing so, they used Rivera as the symbolic "Negro" who was the innocent victim of "This Lynch Attack."[67]

The *New York Amsterdam News*, New York's largest African American daily, failed to identify Rivera as Puerto Rican, referring to him instead as a "young Negro boy." The Jamaican-born writer and Harlem resident Claude McKay was one of the very few contemporary chroniclers to specify that Rivera was Puerto Rican. McKay's sensitivity to nationality as well as race is not surprising, since West Indian–born residents of Harlem often took pains to distinguish themselves from American-born blacks.[68] McKay wrote that "a rumor started that they were beating a colored boy in the basement," a description that suggests a way in which the ambiguity or error about Rivera's identity developed: to call Rivera "colored" could mean either that he was "Negro," born in the United States, or that he was "*de color*," a more elastic description in Latin American Spanish.[69] Perhaps African Americans elided the difference between an American Negro (or "colored boy") and a "*negro*" Puerto Rican to provide coherence in the narrative of the causes of the riot: to focus on Rivera's Puerto Rican identity would have diluted black Harlemites' message about racism and its effect on conditions in their neighborhood.

On the other hand, African Americans, and white observers, too, seem to have viewed the riot's participants through their own binary racial lens. Many may well have known that Rivera was Puerto Rican, but the only social fact that really mattered was that he was *colored*, and if he was colored, he may as well be called "Negro." To whatever extent Puerto Ricans took part in the riot, they remained a more or less invisible presence in all of its coverage by the citywide dailies. The *New York Herald Tribune* did note in its front-page article that "a Puerto Rican youth [was] the cause," and the *Brooklyn Daily Eagle*—whose headline warned of a "race war"—even preceded its introduction of the "Porto Rican" Lino Rivera with the assertion that he was "almost forgotten in the hullabaloo." The *New York Sun*, on the other hand, which printed a photograph of him standing with an African American police lieutenant, ran an article subtitled "Negro Boy Admits He Was Not Beaten in Store." The first *New York Times* report referred only to a "16 year old Negro boy" whose shoplifting precipitated the riot; a subsequent article pictured Rivera and gave his name but commented no further on his role.[70]

New York's Spanish-language daily *La Prensa* more carefully noted the distinction between the North American social category "Negro" and the descriptive Spanish term "*negro*," which referred to phenotype but did not necessarily represent a rigid social category. *La Prensa* reporters implied that the "disturbances" were attributable only to "*gente de color, americana*," and reported that most of the protesting and looting activity actually took place in Central Harlem, several blocks west of the East Harlem *barrio* where most Spanish speakers lived and shopped. If the African American press and city officials in New York agreed that the causes of the Harlem riot were rooted in the problems of Negroes, not Puerto Ricans, many

Figure 7. Lino Rivera, photographed with Lt. S. J. Battle at a Harlem police precinct following the riot that started with his detention for shoplifting at a Kress store on 125th Street on
March 19, 1935. The *New York Times* caption for this image, printed the day after the riot, noted
that "the report that the youth had been beaten to death started the trouble." AP / Wide
World Photos.

middle-class Puerto Rican and Hispanic residents were happy to support
that perspective. *La Prensa* reported on the rioting in Central Harlem in
distancing tones, calling the incident "race riots" among the "colored elements of that neighborhood."[71] Here the editors were using the term *colored* in a North American sense, meaning "Negro." The editorial printed
two days after the riot offered an explicit warning about the dangers of
Puerto Ricans' being implicated in the riots. "The fact that it was a Puerto
Rican boy who was the excuse for the noisy disturbances and clashes with
the police, could serve as the basis for a new, negative interpretation of . . .
the Hispanic community here," wrote the editors. They described the
"colored" sections of Harlem as characterized by "intense political activity" and "bizarre cults."[72] On the other hand, "entirely separate from this is
the Spanish-speaking group of the neighborhood, with distinct problems,
absolutely different interests, and ethnic characteristics that disassociate
Hispanics from their colored American neighbors." The editorial ended
with a warning that "events and situations created by the other half of the

district, not Hispanics"—not only the riot but also, for instance, the illegal numbers game—threatened to exacerbate the preexisting antipathy of "the authorities" toward Hispanics. The editors admonished their readers: "You must not ignore the fact that, once again, the discredit and unwanted notoriety generated by non-Hispanic Harlem, falls upon our part of the neighborhood."[73]

*La Prensa* also reported extensively on the damage done by rioters to Hispanic-owned businesses in Harlem, with detailed descriptions of window breaking and looting in stores owned by Hispanics.[74] Yet while the editors were anxious to defend the distinction between Spanish speakers and African Americans in Harlem, they assailed what they referred to as the "racial dividing line" erected by some black businesses, which "have in their shop windows signs that say 'colored,' indicating that people of the white race are not welcome."[75] This was a rhetorical sleight of hand, using an expression of concern about racial divisions as a way to increase the social distance between black Americans and Spanish speakers, declared to be *not* "colored." Indeed, *La Prensa* editors pointedly suggested that many Spanish speakers could be counted in "the white race," despite the fact that much of their actual readership—mixed-race Puerto Ricans—would be excluded from that category.

*La Prensa* profiled Rivera as a well-mannered, well-behaved boy from a home "characterized by an admirable cleanliness despite its modesty," who demonstrated loyalty both to his mother (he left high school to help support his family) and to his native country (he remained fluent in Spanish). One report declared that Rivera "involuntarily" caused the "racial clash" and "deplore[d] what happened." Apparently, Rivera had noticed some disturbances on the sidewalk as he was leaving the Kress store but was not aware that a woman had begun to scream about "a boy of the colored race . . . being beaten to death." The reporter described this as the "incident with the woman of his [Rivera's] race," suggesting that the skin color Rivera shared with both that woman and the other rioters was *only* skin deep and implied neither social kinship nor common cause. The main point of the interview emerged when the reporter asked Rivera whether he would have tried to pacify the crowd if it had been possible. "Of course!" Rivera replied, reinforcing the idea that Puerto Ricans had no investment in the "racial hatred" that "exploded" in Central Harlem.[76] In angling for that response, the reporter got Lino Rivera to affirm an unlikely interpretation of a riot whose impact would reverberate powerfully through the news, policymaking, and popular lore of the city for years afterward: that it was an unnecessary and meaningless upheaval that could have been averted by "pacifying" the crowd at the Kress store.

On the other hand, leftists in the *colonia* saw the riot as a predictable outcome. One *La Prensa* reader wrote to the editor after the 1935 riots with a passionate critique of the conditions created in Harlem by the *"explotadores capitalistas."* Libertad Narváez lived near the area of the rioting, outside of the boundary of El Barrio, and expressed deep sympathy with the plight and the grievances of the rioters: "Thousands of black workers, most of them unemployed . . . took to the streets of Harlem with the sounds of protest against the miserly aid distributed by the 'Relief' Administration, and the discriminatory . . . treatment by officials of this agency of which they are victims; against the high rents and unhealthy conditions of Harlem apartments; against the unconscionable . . . conduct of the rich business owners who refuse to give employment to those of [the colored] race, despite the fact that they represent almost the entirety of the shoppers." Narváez, who sympathized with and may well have belonged to one of the scores of communist organizations active in Harlem in the thirties, asserted that communists "are the only ones who defend the interests of the black worker in this country, and the only ones who sincerely represent and openly support . . . the highest social, racial, national and political aspirations of this oppressed race."[77]

Like virtually all of the other commentary on the riot, however, Narváez's letter was silent on both the place and plight of Puerto Rican migrants in Harlem. Not only did it fail to mention the large numbers of Puerto Ricans who would be identified—and might even identify themselves—as "Negro workers," it also ignored the fact that Puerto Ricans had been expressing for years the same grievances as African Americans concerning housing, relief, and discrimination. This writer's silence on these parallels recalls the pains taken not just by the elite but also by working-class, leftist Puerto Ricans to distinguish their countrymen from the black Americans whose plight they so often decried. Even the well-known radical activist Bernardo Vega stopped short of connecting Puerto Ricans' experience in Harlem to "all the pain and suffering of the black people [that] rose to the surface" during and after the rioting.[78] Vega was active in a variety of organizations in the thirties that sought to push back against "all the pain and suffering" of Puerto Ricans in New York, and he was certainly an outspoken proponent, along with Jesús Colón and many other dark-skinned working-class migrants, of racial justice in New York. But Vega's recollection of the riot in terms of the literal and figurative distance separating "Negroes" and

"Puerto Ricans" in Harlem speaks to the persistent problem of blackness in New York's Puerto Rican *colonia*. The price of accepting the ascription imposed by the United States' binary racial scheme—blackness as Negro, not just *negro*—was potentially too steep even for Puerto Rican radicals to pay willingly.

Mayor Fiorello La Guardia, who had a solid reputation as a racial progressive, formed a commission to investigate not only the immediate causes of the riot but the conditions in Harlem that constituted the underlying motivations for protest. Over the course of a year, the Mayor's Commission on Conditions in Harlem (MCCH)—whose members included ten men and one woman, six of them black, five white—investigated Harlemites' experiences with relief, housing, education and recreation, health and hospitals, and crime and the police. After twenty-one public and four closed hearings, including testimony of 160 witnesses, and months of research, the commission submitted its report to the mayor's office in March 1936. It concluded that the Harlem riot was a protest against the "intolerable conditions" wrought by five years of economic depression in an already poor community, "which made [Harlem residents] feel more keenly than ever the injustices of discrimination in employment, the aggressions of the police, and the racial segregation."[79]

In his first public statement about the riot, Mayor La Guardia had promised to appoint a commission of "representative citizens" to study its causes.[80] But the committee turned out to consist only of African Americans and white Americans, despite the fact that Puerto Ricans comprised the plurality of residents on about one-quarter of Harlem's residential blocks and were the second-largest group in the neighborhood.[81] In a memo suggesting areas of investigation for the Mayor's Commission, Walter White, secretary of the National Association for the Advancement of Colored People (NAACP), did refer to the presence of Puerto Ricans and advised that the "origin of population" in Harlem be examined along with housing, schools, health, and recreation. White proposed that the commission address the "interrelation of various groups making up [the] Negro community of Harlem," including Puerto Ricans, West Indians, and Virgin Islanders, as well as "the effect of friction or cooperation between various groups."[82] But no Puerto Ricans were appointed, and the specific problems of the group never made it into the commission's reports.

In spite of their apparent consensus that the riot was not a Puerto Rican affair—because of their geographic and social distance from the Negro community—leaders of a number of El Barrio's working-class and

Nationalist organizations expected to participate in the discussions about conditions in Harlem. Jesús Flores, head of Unidad Obrera (Workers' Unity), wrote to the MCCH two days after its appointment requesting that his organization be allowed to testify about the concerns of its members. He explained, "We have in our possession several cases of discrimination, denials of relief, deaths due to the carelessness of the officials representing the different aid societies, police terror against Spanish-speaking workers, corruption of police by using gangsters to provoke workers and especially the workers' organizations."[83] In a second letter, this time representing the Comité Pro–Puerto Rico, Flores reiterated, "So that you may hear the different slights and humiliations to which the Puerto Ricans are subjected, we expect . . . that you allow this Committee, which is composed of more than 60 organizations, Spanish-speaking and in their majority Puerto Rican, to testify."[84] Since the majority of the hearings held by the Mayor's Commission were public, Puerto Ricans were free to testify about their grievances along with all other residents of Harlem, although they were never included by invitation, as many African American leaders were.

Several other Puerto Rican leaders protested Puerto Ricans' exclusion from the MCCH. "We believe that excluding the Puerto Ricans from that committee was unfair if you will take in consideration the great number of Puerto Ricans not only unemployed but antagonized with so much prejudice against them," wrote Antonio Rivera, secretary of the Liga Puertorriqueña e Hispana.[85] Isabel O'Neill, a Nationalist activist, wrote to the mayor as a representative of the Junta Liberal Puertorriqueña de Nueva York with a harsh indictment of his treatment of Puerto Ricans:

> What is most displeasing—and . . . unwarranted—is not only the discrimination shown in the selection and/or appointment of members to the investigating committee, but also the complete ignoration [sic] of Puerto Ricans; of them, whose interest in Harlem and the betterment thereof is a vital factor . . . in their lives and general social welfare and being.
>
> It seems that we have been omitted from every civic activity that has presented itself . . . and the omission is even more flagrant in this instance, an act of political and civic indifference and unmindfulness at which we feel aggrieved.[86]

There is no record of how La Guardia's office responded, if it at all, to such charges. What is clear, though, is that Puerto Ricans' specific grievances—

despite their similarity to those of black American Harlemites—failed to make it into the commission's reports.

In the months following the Harlem riots, Puerto Ricans became the primary victims of a new "anti-Hispanic campaign" in Washington Heights, where middle-class Puerto Ricans had begun to settle earlier in the thirties. The Jewish and Irish landlords in the neighborhood had begun raising rents sharply in an alleged effort to "drive out" their Puerto Rican tenants. Spanish-speaking observers saw the landlords' coordinated action as a reaction to two perceived threats: first, that more and more of their Hispanic tenants were recent arrivals of the "lower classes" and, second, that these "brown-skinned or darker" new tenants would bring with them the kinds of problems that might turn Washington Heights into "a second Harlem." These observers saw a specifically racial prejudice against dark-skinned Puerto Ricans. "The situation in Washington Heights is not simply a situation of nationality, it is purely and unjustly a question of race," asserted one reader to *La Prensa*. Even the lighter-skinned among them should not feel immune to this kind of discrimination, he warned, since no clear line existed, here, between light and dark complexions; the only line was between *white* and dark. "If it could happen to them, it could happen to you," he warned.[87] That is, any Puerto Rican, no matter his or her complexion, could be discriminated against as a person occupying the nonwhite side of the binary—the black side. In spite of the growing public concern about race-based discrimination against Puerto Ricans, there remained a firm impulse, among all but the leftists in the *colonia*, to avoid complaining about the same injustices that African Americans objected to and, still, to avoid talking about the Harlem riot as a Puerto Rican issue. When the New York State legislature voted to assemble a "Temporary Commission on Urban Colored Populations" two years after the riot, *La Prensa* editors applauded the move. "[It is] certain that there are many thousands of persons of the colored race living in Harlem under the saddest of social conditions," announced the editorial, skirting any mention of Spanish-speaking residents, especially Puerto Ricans, in the area.[88]

### The "Subnormal" Puerto Rican Child

Sometime between the Harlem riot in the spring and the Washington Heights disturbances in late summer, the New York State Chamber of Commerce's Special Committee on Immigration and Naturalization commissioned two New York City psychologists to administer intelligence tests to Puerto Rican children in the city's schools. In December 1935, Dr. Clairette Armstrong and Dr. Edith Achilles released a report of their study of 129 Puerto Rican students at P.S. 57 in East Harlem. Based on their results, they argued that the children's poor performance on the Army Individual Performance Test and the Otis Group Test signified the basic intellectual inferiority of the Puerto Rican migrants settling in New York.[89] The investigators also concluded, ominously, that "Puerto Ricans are adding greatly to the already tremendous problem of intellectual subnormal school retardates of alien parentage, whence are recruited most delinquents and criminals," meaning, in their judgment, that "the majority of Puerto Rican children examined betray a family mentality which should not be permitted admission here." Furthermore, these Puerto Rican children would "deteriorate standards already so seriously impaired by mass immigration of the lowest levels of populations of many nations."[90]

Apparently, this was a pet topic of Dr. Armstrong's, a staff psychologist for the city's Children's Court. A year before beginning the study, she had described with frank xenophobia the dangers of immigrant children in a letter to the editor of the New York Times: "Juvenile delinquency on the whole results from the clash of civilizations. Low-grade, intellectually dull immigrants thrust into our complicated, highly organized civilization are unable to adjust their likewise intellectually dull offspring to the exigencies of such environment."[91] Although Americans' obsession with eugenics and scientific racism had peaked in the 1920s, Armstrong was not exactly an outlier in the thirties. Discourses about the racial basis of intelligence, with immigrants and African Americans situated at the bottom of the hierarchy, lingered well into the postwar era.[92] Mexicans in the west also were subjected to IQ testing throughout the twenties and thirties, with nearly identical pronouncements about their intellectual deficits and their undesirability, therefore, as permanent residents of their new communities.[93] Whereas the Harlem riot and earlier media representations of Puerto Ricans' blackness forced them to confront the pitfalls of being categorized with African Americans in New York, the controversy over the IQ tests represented a different kind of assault, one framed around their biological inferiority not as Negro but as foreign and "other," and articulated via the anti-immigrant language of the earlier twentieth century. One of the most notable aspects of this attack on Puerto Rican "immigrants" was its goal of scaring other New Yorkers and white Americans into lobbying for Puerto Ricans' exclusion. Since Puerto Ricans were colonial citizens who could enter the United

States without restrictions, this objective—pushed by Armstrong and other policymakers who should have understood the legal context—was irrational and futile. On the other hand, though, their arguments make more sense if they are interpreted as simply a goad to the folk logic of racist xenophobia, the goals of which were symbolic as much as actual exclusion.

The first media reports on the study addressed this most basic—if logically flawed—inspiration: to make a case for limiting the Puerto Rican migration, using the biological language of racial inferiority that had bolstered anti-immigration arguments in the 1920s. The *New York Sun*'s headline announced, "Puerto Rican Pupils a Problem," and noted that the study was commissioned "principally in connection with its consideration of immigration problems, and only incidentally to ascertain the conditions in the public schools."[94] *La Prensa*'s only coverage of the study was provided by its sports commentator, Julio Garzón, who addressed it as part of a discussion about the prejudice that Puerto Ricans confronted in the world of sports in the United States. While Garzón's objections to the study's methodology (particularly the testing of the children in English) were in line with those of other critics, his major complaint about its report was unique, placing the migration question in the political context of colonialism. Garzón argued that it was the colonial relationship between the United States and Puerto Rico—not the intellectual capacity of the island's children—that created a migration problem. He said that if, during the years of "American domination," Puerto Ricans had been able to profit in proportion to the "profits taken from [Puerto Rico] by American industrialists and businessmen," Puerto Ricans would not have had to use their "INARGUABLE RIGHT to emigrate to the country that exploits" them.[95] If the Chamber of Commerce viewed the "immigration'" of Puerto Ricans as a problem, it was a problem of their own—and other American exploiters'—creation.

A number of Harlem activists lodged more banal protests against the Chamber of Commerce report, including the Spanish Welfare League and Leonard Covello, a prominent East Harlem activist and educator who was the principal of East Harlem's progressive and multiracial Benjamin Franklin High School. Covello organized a "Racial Committee" following the release of the report, whose members prepared a thorough analysis of the methodological flaws of the IQ study.[96] These educators and defenders of Puerto Rican children did not explicitly take issue with the idea of assessing immigrants' suitability as "Americans" on the basis of their intelligence; they simply defended the right of immigrant children to be given tests that fairly measured their abilities. Covello pointed out that Italian immigrant children had been "attacked" in the press after a similar investigation of immigrant intelligence in 1921. "When the Binet tests were given to American children they had the same difficulty because of the foreign expressions and idioms. Only after the tests were revised was it possible to use them for American children," he said.

The group emphasized the difficulty of the intelligence tests used in the study and argued that the Puerto Rican children's poor performance was attributable entirely to their lack of familiarity with English.[97] The committee also argued that Armstrong and Achilles misrepresented their data when they called the small group of Puerto Rican children tested a "representative sample," since the children all lived in a small, poor section of East Harlem, attended a single poorly staffed school, and came from families "of the lower occupational levels," compared to the control group, described by the psychologists as "typically American children" who lived in a middle-class area in Westchester County, and which included "no children of unskilled laborers."[98] The Racial Committee evidently shared its report with Covello's close friend Vito Marcantonio, who was admired equally by East Harlem's Puerto Ricans and Italians and served as their U.S. congressional representative through much of the 1930s and 1940s.[99] Marcantonio stood before the House of Representatives in June 1936 and made an impassioned speech condemning the discriminatory and irresponsibly drawn conclusions put forth by the Chamber of Commerce investigators.[100] Particularly given his later record in Congress as a staunch anti-imperialist, it is notable that Marcantonio failed to comment on Armstrong and Achilles's misapprehension of the political status of the island and Puerto Ricans' U.S. citizenship.

One official who responded to the controversy interpreted it not just as an attack on Puerto Rican migration—this time from a statehooder perspective as opposed to the nationalist stance of La Prensa reporter Garzón—but also as an attack on the racial identity of Puerto Ricans. Puerto Rico's assistant commissioner of education, Pedro Cebollero, first made the obvious point that because Puerto Ricans were citizens, the study was "useless as a measure of the desirability of immigration control," which was the authors' most explicit argument concerning the implications of their findings.[101] More to the point, Cebollero said, to measure the merits of the inclusion of Puerto Rico in the United States according to the intelligence of migrants was "as absurd as if a psychological test of the immigrant Italian were to be taken as a measure of the ability of the Roman citizen generally." Most galling to Cebollero was the fact that, while 76 percent of the Puerto

Rican students tested in New York were "colored," Puerto Rican society in general, according to the 1930 U.S. census, was 74 percent white and 26 percent "colored." This discrepancy, he argued, was "evidence of the absolute disregard of the principle of 'representativeness'" on the part of the researchers; the overrepresentation of "colored" students in the study led to a real drop in the average score of the Puerto Rican children, since— according to one "expert" on intelligence he cited—"'all results show the negro decidedly inferior to the white on standard intelligence tests.'"[102] Cebollero used white supremacist logic, meaningful in only slightly different ways to a Puerto Rican as opposed to a North American audience, in order to refute Puerto Ricans' particular location on the race-bound terrain of both places. He was determined to prove—along with many of his compatriots, both on the island and in New York—that they were not a "majority black" population.

Perhaps the most notable detail of this controversy is that Armstrong and Achilles's report was the first widely circulated publication to employ a distinctly racial claim about Puerto Ricans—that they were biologically and culturally inferior to whites—without predicating their inferiority on their categorization as "Negro."[103] Armstrong and Achilles's argument drew on traditional anti-immigrant language, xenophobic and racist but in a way that was more dependent on the "subnormal immigrant" discourse than on the domestic discourse of black inferiority. The 1936 report sketched out the new ways Puerto Ricans would be vilified in the media when they began migrating to New York in much larger numbers after World War II. By the end of the thirties, Puerto Ricans had argued consistently, and with some success, that they were "not Negro" in the United States; Armstrong and Achilles, it seemed, did not disagree with them. But for migrants to claim a racial identity that would ensure Puerto Ricans' attainment of the privileges of full citizenship was another story entirely.

## Wartime Change and Continuity

During the fall of 1941, just before the Japanese attack on Pearl Harbor and the entry of the United States into the Second World War, New York dailies spent several weeks covering a new crime wave that rippled through Harlem. Observers unanimously identified the neighborhood's youth as the culprits but disagreed about their racial profile. Some presumed they were mostly Puerto Rican, while others said they were African American. As the incidences of looting, muggings, and vandalism died down, resurfaced the next summer, and then subsided again, city residents complaining to Mayor La Guardia and editorialists preaching to New York's citizens failed to reach consensus on the matter of the "hoodlums'" identity. But consensus wasn't the point.[104] At the height of the U.S. war on fascism and its racist terror in Europe, in the midst of the American liberal establishment's determined attack on racism and prejudice at home, racial politics in New York continued to unfold with bitterness and rancor. While the tabloids headlined the crimes in Harlem without distinguishing among the perpetrators, simply implying that all of the dark inhabitants of the area might be suspect, Puerto Ricans and African Americans squared off defensively, each group accusing the other of causing trouble. Whereas Puerto Ricans had remained largely invisible actors in the Harlem riot a few years earlier, they were now being cast as scapegoats along with African Americans in yet another racial drama of city life.

Anxious about the impact of their identification as Negro throughout the early thirties, *colonia* activists had equivocated on their connections to their African American neighbors and offered ambivalent interpretations of the place of Africanness in their Puerto Rican heritage. In their efforts to "buck the color line," they adopted strategies from multiple places and deployed them with a varying tolerance for the cultural and phenotypic Africanness that marked their native society. Many Puerto Ricans, especially members of the migrant elite, recognized the immobility of racial categories in the United States and focused their efforts in the 1930s on affirming their place on the powerful side of the binary. Even working-class radicals and self-proclaimed racial egalitarians, including Bernardo Vega, sometimes denied any common cause with their black American neighbors, fending off disadvantage by perhaps unwittingly following the rules of a powerful racist ideology. And then there were the majority who fit into neither of these groups, whose families on the island may have included members considered to be *blanco*, *negro*, and in between but who would have nervously observed the constraints on people living as Negroes in New York. Lino Rivera, for instance, who unwittingly incited the Harlem riot, rejected a black identity in asserting that he didn't want to be a protagonist in that drama. He—or the *La Prensa* reporter who told his story—minimized the importance of the events he set in motion, denying the validity of the anger expressed by "the [people] of his race."

By the end of the decade, popular understandings of race and racism had begun to change, reimagined mainly by the cosmopolitan intelligentsia. As Americans watched Nazism march across Europe in the late thirties and reached a peak of anxiety about racial divisions in their own society, few wanted to acknowledge the presence of another dark-skinned minority group in the United States. Implicitly, many Americans, and New Yorkers in particular, realized the truth of sociologist Louis Wirth's pronouncement that "minority status entails exclusion from full participation in the life of the society," and saw how problematic this fact was for the liberal democracy fighting for freedom abroad.[105] Along with these ideological changes came a small opening in the national discourse about inclusion in the nation and who benefited from its protections: liberals, cosmopolitans, and antidiscrimination activists sought to convince other Americans to endorse a more open and inclusive citizenship. In this context, claims to rights as citizens, particularly among African Americans and Puerto Ricans, as well as among Mexican Americans in the West, began to emerge in their New Deal form.[106]

Most important for Puerto Ricans in this period, U.S. lawmakers were forced to contemplate a solution to Puerto Rico's colonial status during the war, since the Allies were fighting a global conflict for "freedom" and allegedly supported decolonization movements all over the world.[107] The growing support for Puerto Rican statehood in this context made the racial composition of the island a more salient issue for Americans. If the United States was supposed to be a white country, it was better if Puerto Rico were seen as more or less white, too. Statehood supporters did a fine job of publicizing the phenomenon of "the vanishing Negro," a thesis about racial change that was allegedly substantiated by studies of the U.S. Bureau of the Census. Apparently, the proportion of the "white" population on the island had grown from about 62 percent in 1900 to almost 80 percent in 1940, inspiring a contemporary edition of the *Encyclopedia Americana* to suggest hopefully that "if this decrease should continue for a number of years, the black race would eventually disappear from Porto Rico."[108]

In the United States, these developments resulted in a reversal of the ID card trend by the beginning of World War II, wherein the number of migrants identified as "light" or "fair" tripled or quadrupled in the early forties, and between 1941 and 1949, the proportion of "dark" complexion labels declined to around half the applicants. Moreover, more than a third of the 1940s applicants whose complexion categorization was corrected, or whose complexion label changed upon reapplication, moved from a darker to a lighter complexion category, most often "dark" to "light." The majority of these cases were reapplications; the "darkness" assigned to migrants on their ID cards during the thirties now appeared to need revision.[109] On the other hand, except for the relatively few Puerto Ricans who attempted and managed to pass as Spanish (or those who, as historian Oscar Handlin put it, took their first chance to "lose themselves in the general category of whites"), Puerto Ricans' exclusion as a group from the category of "white" in the United States was nearly absolute.[110] Of the roughly forty thousand ID card applications that migrants filled out before the ID office dropped its complexion blank in 1956, only a handful identified the cardholder as "white."[111] These patterns made a convincing case that perceptions of Puerto Ricans' racial identity were based not primarily on the physical fact of their skin color but also on how they fit into the larger social and political terrain of the nation.

The backdrop of world war and early decolonization movements, together with the United States' rigidly binary racial ideology, may have defined Puerto Ricans' political identity in the national frame. But it was local racial dynamics, inflected by racial ideas that migrants brought with them from the island, that had shaped how Puerto Ricans navigated their place in New York in the thirties. Although their role in the city's various moments of racial tension during the thirties did not change the outcome of those incidents in obvious ways, Puerto Ricans' distinctive ideologies contributed to the changing ideas about race in that era, combining, on the one hand, an acceptance of their own racial heterogeneity and, on the other, a reliance on Latin America's old racial hierarchies. The concrete impact of Puerto Ricans' perspectives on the changing racial landscape of New York in the thirties is impossible to gauge. More visible is the discursive distance traveled, in the terrain of ideas about race, during that time within the Puerto Rican community. The Puerto Rican bibliophile, collector, and historian Arturo Schomburg's actual "migration" into New York's African American community, where he lived until his death in 1938, was an unusual if not unique embrace of African American identity; most Puerto Ricans struggled to define a place in the city somewhere between white and black. The antiracist counterideology of the working-class migrant Left also exerted a notable and growing influence on the racial discourse in the *colonia*. This new antiracist politics, and the more general push to acknowledge the validity and cultural importance of blackness among Puerto Ricans, developed amid the sometimes incompatible efforts by Puerto Ricans to present themselves as a racially distinct group that was neither black nor white.

This shift, uneven though it was, could be seen in a pair of letters to *La Prensa* early in 1940. Manuel Ríos Ocaña, who lived in East Harlem, wrote on Lincoln's Birthday to celebrate the "pride and dignity" of black Puerto

Ricans. A week later, Luisa Dessus Cruz, resident of Washington Heights, responded to Ríos Ocaña's letter with gratitude for his acknowledgment of the "valor" of Puerto Ricans of color. She asserted that the majority of the "intellectuals or educated Puerto Ricans" in New York were "of the colored race" (despite the fact that some, she said, try to pass for white), and she admonished young Puerto Ricans of color that they not forget that "we have to win the major battle of the century—[against] racial prejudice." Dessus Cruz concluded her letter with the first stanza of the poem "Indiana" by Luis Felipe Dessus, although she did not attribute the lines: "I am indian, African, *borincano* / Where passionate races come together."[112] Thus did both letter writers express Puerto Ricans' major interpretive innovation in the politics of race of this era: that Puerto Ricans could pursue equal rights in the United States without, necessarily, access to the privileges of white citizenship. Along with many other Puerto Rican New Yorkers, these two asserted, in spite of all evidence to the contrary, that citizens' racial identity should not determine their access to civic, social, and political power in a liberal democracy.

### Chapter Three

# Pursuing the Promise of the New Deal

## Relief and the Politics of Nationalism in the Thirties

In 1935, the middle of the Great Depression, almost four thousand hopeful Puerto Ricans arrived in New York City, seeking to escape the desperate poverty they had suffered on the island. One migrant who arrived that year was interviewed later by a field-worker for the WPA Federal Writers' Project as part of an ethnographic project on Spanish Harlem. This interviewee said, "Looking forward to better my living conditions, I came to New York. It has been an awful disappointment. Puerto Ricans who come to this city and return to the homeland usually exaggerate about the prosperous conditions existing here."[1] Another migrant told his interviewer that although he "never had any intention to leave Puerto Rico . . . the stress of economic conditions made me do it, very much against my will."[2] This man was lucky: he found a steady job as a dishwasher at a Harlem restaurant soon after his arrival, joined a union, and quickly worked his way up to head cook. But his was a rare success story. Although many migrants wrote to friends and relatives at home to tell them that "things were not as hard here as in Puerto Rico," and to entice their compatriots to risk the move north, Puerto Ricans were hit harder by the Depression than most in New York.[3]

During the worst years of the Great Depression, Puerto Rican migration to the United States slowed down dramatically, with half as many migrants entering the country between 1930 and 1935 as in the five years before 1930.[4] Grossly exaggerating the numbers, the *New York Evening Telegram* reported early in 1931 that "we now have around 150,000 nearly starving and sick Puerto Ricans in New York City. They live in hovels (like savages) in the tenements of Harlem, and only a few of them work." Puerto Ricans, the report alleged, presented a "problem of welfare and health to such a degree that forty agencies have united in a special committee to study their situation." María Más Pozo was one of several *colonia* activists who wrote to *La Prensa* denouncing the insulting tones of this publicity about her compatriots, though she did not deny the terrible conditions in which most Puerto Ricans lived.[5]

Other Puerto Ricans in New York lamented their situation with pathos and eloquence in countless letters to city officials and state representatives and to the editors of *La Prensa*. They asserted that they had as much right to aid and services as other Americans but attested that they were often denied access to both private and public assistance. The migrant community's many hometown organizations and mutual aid societies could hardly meet the increasingly desperate needs of their impoverished memberships. A Trinitarian nun, Sister Carmelita Bonilla, established the first Puerto Rican settlement house, Casita María, in El Barrio in 1934, but it could do little more than provide the occasional meal, along with spiritual and moral support, to the thousands of hungry migrants in its midst.[6] Although conditions on the island were indisputably worse than in New York, many who left longed to return to Puerto Rico and envied their immigrant neighbors whose consulates sometimes helped facilitate repatriation. Puerto Ricans lacked any aid for return to their homeland, and for those who stayed, the meager services of their island government's Employment and Identification Office hardly closed the gap.[7]

Furthermore, although unions grew in size and power during the 1930s and helped improve the lives of a growing number of working-class Americans (especially after the passage in 1933 of the National Industrial Recovery Act and its wages and working hours protections), Puerto Ricans were consistently excluded from mainstream labor organizations. While the American Federation of Labor had connected with Puerto Rican workers on the island by 1920, through the Pan-American Federation of Labor, that union—and even more notably, its progressive and inclusive incarnation of the later thirties, the AFL-CIO—assiduously shut out Puerto Rican workers in the United States up through the 1940s. The International Ladies Garment Workers Union (ILGWU), which successfully organized Chicana women in the Los Angeles garment industry starting in 1933, made some uneven efforts to organize the many Puerto Rican garment workers in New York, but the union leadership rebuffed migrant women's several efforts to create a Spanish-speaking local in the 1930s, leaving them at the mercy of union local heads who often discriminated against them.[8]

Many Puerto Rican migrants, barely scraping by, focused only on feeding their families, on their next paycheck or next job—or a threatened eviction—and paid little attention to labor politics, much less to electoral politics.[9] Not that migrants as a group lacked an interest in politics: many of them closely followed, and sometimes participated in, the turbulent elections, bitter political rivalries, and rancorous ideological battles of their homeland to the degree that one island observer would later remark, "The Puerto Rican *colonia* in New York is the eighth district of the island. (We all know that the island is divided into seven electoral districts.)"[10] Whereas the left-leaning working class had engaged in New York politics since the twenties, Nationalists tended to remain aloof from local politics. The island's Nationalist Party, headed since 1930 by Pedro Albizu Campos, had renounced electoral politics as a sham; and its mostly elite constituency in New York expressed few complaints about their life in New York in the twenties, focusing most of their attention still on the island's independence. In fact, Bernardo Vega noted that Nationalists in the *colonia* "even went so far as to insist that Puerto Ricans who became involved in the immediate social struggles in New York were betraying their primordial patriotic duty."[11] This disengagement with local issues caused regular conflict with left-leaning activists in the community, especially the growing ranks of Communists in Harlem.[12]

By the early thirties, though, *colonia* leftists had an easy time convincing their compatriots of the importance of everyday political struggles. The Depression itself was motivating thousands of migrants to focus on local issues, and the promise of New Deal politics changed many migrants' minds about the payoffs of political participation at the local level. In addition to the scores of hometown clubs, employees' unions, and various community defense groups they organized in this era to serve the unmet needs of Puerto Ricans in New York, *colonia* leaders and voters also began to intensify their focus on gaining the recognition of the major political parties.[13] If residents of the Puerto Rican districts could convince political bosses of their importance as an ethnic voting bloc, they would be in a position to demand their rights to the benefits of patronage and city services, as well as to the various protections (from victimization by landlords, business owners, and other ethnic groups in the neighborhood) that district leaders typically provided to their constituents. Puerto Ricans' immigrant predecessors in New York—the Irish, the Italians, and the Jews—had used their relationships with Tammany Hall to secure city jobs, Christmas turkeys, and favors from the police and judges, as well as protection from discriminatory landlords and business owners. The power of the vote loomed large for migrants who saw the other ethnics in their midst suffering less in the throes of the Depression.[14] Worry over signs of a hardening racial identity in the United

States was another issue that propelled activists in the 1930s to focus on the local political arena. One migrant, writing to *La Prensa*, reminded his compatriots in Harlem that after the "racial disturbances" of 1926 in East Harlem, "it was our ability to vote that saved us from being driven out of this district, that induced political leaders to defend us for the interest of gaining our votes."[15]

Yet, in spite of the determined engagement by *colonia* men and women in New York electoral politics in the thirties, it was not clear how much Puerto Rican voters mattered to major party leaders. Would increasing voter participation in the *colonia* be enough to gain access to the local political machines? "The Puerto Rican *colonia* finds itself devoid of representation," lamented one East Harlem man in 1934. He remained optimistic about his community's political energy if not about its political muscle: "We have struggled for more than fifteen years and we still have the spirit to keep struggling."[16] Sharpening their focus on their rights as citizens was one tendentious answer to migrants' dilemma of political empowerment in the thirties. As they lobbied and protested to secure equal access to relief funds and acknowledgment from city officials of their poor living conditions, migrants began to articulate demands for a broad range of citizenship-based rights. In pointing to their American citizenship as the basis for such claims, Puerto Rican migrants joined a long tradition of "rely[ing] on the rhetoric of rights to articulate their outrage," as Rodgers Smith has described rights claims by various groups in the nineteenth century.[17] But Puerto Ricans were also adding their voice to a new, twentieth-century variant of that tradition. Along with a growing number of African American activists and unionized workers who, during the thirties, breathed new life into the traditional American language of rights, Puerto Rican migrants articulated their claims on the state in a way that emphasized the new, "positive" rights of New Deal liberalism. It was a discourse that emerged, as historian Daniel Rodgers put it, "not in the centers of power but on its margins." Puerto Rican migrants joined a heterogeneous and dissonant chorus of people in framing a language of rights as citizens that would become the hallmark of political discourses in the post–New Deal era.[18]

Even if local party leaders were beginning to notice their growing Puerto Rican constituencies, New York's political terrain was undergoing dramatic ruptures and realignments in the thirties that cast a shadow over Puerto Ricans' hopeful vision of political advancement. One key change, stemming from corruption reform and the sustained success of La Guardia's Republican-Fusion Party, was the decline of Tammany Hall as the primary force shaping the city's ethnic politics. Tammany's loyal ethnic voting blocs, including Puerto Ricans, would have to learn other means of political survival after the early 1930s. New Deal politics also transformed New York's political landscape. New Deal liberalism seeped into city politics over the course of the decade and began to supplant the neighborhood "boss" and his patronage network with its reformist spirit, a growing bureaucracy, and a new concept of rights based on national citizenship—as opposed to the very local "ethnic-territorial" identities, as Ira Katznelson has so aptly dubbed them, upon which New Yorkers traditionally based their claims to political access.[19] Finally, another key development in the local political scene by the end of the 1930s was the ascent of a progressive coalition composed of prominent liberals, including many Jews and a number of African American leaders, that began trying to combat racism at home in the face of what looked like a growing Nazi threat abroad.[20]

According to its rhetoric, this rising tide of liberal action should have buoyed Puerto Rican migrants, too, in the quest for political recognition and protection from discrimination. But it did not, and inclusion in the city's new liberal order proved problematic for Puerto Ricans for reasons beyond their relatively small numbers (in 1940, the U.S. Bureau of the Census counted just over 61,000 Puerto Ricans living in New York City, while African Americans numbered over 450,000) or the faltering support of the political machines.[21] In the mid-thirties, intensifying agitation for independence in Puerto Rico, and several incidents of high-profile political violence, brought the question of the island's still-indeterminate status back to the center of *colonia* political culture. And, amid rising political radicalism among Spanish speakers in New York in response to the Spanish Civil War, migrant activists across the political spectrum began issuing calls for the end of U.S. colonialism in Puerto Rico. Migrants' sharpening anti-imperialist discourse further spurred the radicalization of the *colonia*, and some migrants accused even New Deal liberals of supporting imperialist policies regarding Puerto Rico.

This discourse highlighted a new tension in *colonia* political debates: while many migrants sought recognition by the major political parties, especially the Democrats, they also, now, supported a Nationalist agenda for Puerto Rico that was beyond the tolerance of mainstream liberals in the United States. The Puerto Rican status issue had become a political hot potato that very few U.S. lawmakers were willing to touch. Puerto Ricans had gained some ground as they deployed their New Deal–inspired language of rights, but the spread of nationalist politics in the migrant community by the late thirties suggested that Puerto Ricans could not easily be incorporated, alongside African Americans, in the nascent progressive-liberal coalition of that era. Island politics proved to be a distinct liability in the project of political empowerment.

While no New Deal Democrat was openly calling Puerto Rican migrants incapable of fulfilling the obligations of U.S. citizenship—as earlier lawmakers had in the debates leading up to the Jones Act—the silence with which New Dealers responded to migrant politics in the late thirties, and their anti-imperialist challenge to the liberal vision of the nation, expressed as much. So did their exodus from Puerto Rico in the wake of the tumult over Nationalist protests in 1936 and 1937. Migrant political activists soldiered on nevertheless in their battle for recognition as political actors. Many leaned further left by decade's end and invested even more faith in their stalwart advocate Vito Marcantonio, first elected to represent East Harlem in Congress in 1934. Earlier in the Depression, many of these activists had begun to embrace "the politics of here," initiating their first focused efforts at making demands of the state on the basis of their citizenship. Now, they framed their expectations of the state, as citizens, via a new set of diasporic political claims, combining demands for local rights and island sovereignty. It was a powerful vision, articulated in their own version of a New Deal language of rights, but it complicated their effort to create a niche for Puerto Ricans in mainstream city politics. They made few concrete political gains during this decade-long push for recognition by the major parties in the United States, leaving migrants more marginalized—if somewhat more visible—than they had been in 1930.[22]

### El Momento Político y los Hispanos, 1933–34

As the election season of 1933 approached, New Yorkers debated endlessly about the outcome of the contentious and divisive mayoral race. Mayor Jimmy Walker, the slick and popular Tammany candidate elected in 1925, had resigned in 1932 after Judge Samuel Seabury, a special investigator appointed by then governor Franklin D. Roosevelt, managed to convict scores of Tammanyites—including the mayor himself—on criminal charges ranging from pimping and gambling to office selling and bid fixing.[23] Democratic voters in the 1933 election split between John O'Brien, a traditional Tammany candidate, and Joseph McKee, the interim mayor who represented the putatively reform-minded Tammany offshoot called the "Recovery Party," so that the progressive Republican-Fusion candidate Fiorello La

Guardia easily won the contest with a plurality vote of 40 percent.[24] During La Guardia's three-term tenure, Tammany Democrats gradually lost their grip on the city, even in many of the immigrant neighborhoods that had been delivering Democratic votes faithfully for almost a century.

The La Guardia years coincided with a surprising reconfiguration of ethnic politics in New York, a shift only partly attributable to Tammany's problems with corruption and incompetent leadership on the eve of the Depression. The Jewish vote, a hard-won staple of Tammany power since the turn of the century, drifted toward the progressivism of La Guardia's Fusion Party and, after 1936, the American Labor Party (the latter was established in New York to create a coalition of Socialist and labor votes to back Roosevelt in the 1936 election). Italians, a strong force among immigrant voters by the 1920s, also threw their weight behind La Guardia, whose close ties with East Harlem's favorite son Vito Marcantonio, representative of the East Harlem district in the U.S. Congress for sixteen out of twenty years between 1934 and 1954, cemented his popularity in that Tammany stronghold by the mid-thirties. Even among the loyal Irish, Tammany's tight hold on a unified party slipped as more New Yorkers "moved up" into the outer boroughs, where traditional mechanisms of securing voter loyalty—handing out hundreds of Thanksgiving turkeys on a single block, for instance—were less appreciated by the aspiring middle class. Finally, with municipal funds dried up by depression, no longer could bosses and district leaders trade "ballots for bread" with their old magnanimity; federal work projects and federal welfare funds replaced patronage jobs and district politicians' handouts.[25]

Puerto Ricans fit uneasily into the ethno-political mosaic of the thirties. Hispanics were far less important to Tammany than its Irish and Jewish constituencies had been, although the gregarious Jimmy Walker occasionally courted the favor of his Puerto Rican voters during his time as mayor. In the first months of the Depression, for instance, Mayor Walker wrote an emotional letter of support to the organizers of a fund for starving children in Puerto Rico, promising that "the Mayor and his associates in the City Government will do all in their power to assist you." Now, under siege by the early thirties, Tammany leaders began making some preliminary advances toward their Spanish-speaking constituents.[26] In fact, though, Puerto Rican voters gave Tammany Democrats little cause for concern before the later years of the decade. While Italians in East Harlem rallied early for their native son La Guardia, their Spanish-speaking neighbors were much slower to come around. They had worked for the better part of ten years to make some headway with Tammany leaders, and they were not going to be easily convinced to abandon that effort.

The Puerto Rican districts in New York, both in Manhattan and in Brooklyn, voted loyally for one or another camp of the Democratic Party in the 1933 mayoral campaign, in spite of the fact that *colonia* leaders had had to struggle consistently to get Tammany bosses to make good on their promises to Puerto Ricans. Brooklyn in particular remained a "regular" Tammany (as opposed to Democratic Recovery Party) stronghold, with a network of clubs that toed the party line under the watchful eye of Luis Weber, the Puerto Rican neighborhood's de facto and well-loved boss. La Guardia, and the reformist projects of his Fusion Party, made little headway among Brooklyn's Puerto Rican voters, not so much because of their loyalty to Tammany politicians but because of their loyalty to Weber himself and to the leaders of the *colonia*'s political clubs. In the solidly working-class neighborhoods of Brooklyn, migrants gave their votes to the men who "would go and fix everything," as one migrant described Weber's associate Carlos Tapia. *La Prensa*'s political reporter, commenting in his column on "the Local Political Campaign and the Hispanic Electorate," noted that amid the diversity of political allegiances of Puerto Ricans across New York, "the Brooklyn *colonia* has always presented a united front in all its actions."[27] That front was, of course, Democratic.

Weber saw in this election an auspicious moment in which to push Tammany Democrats on their support for Puerto Ricans. He formed a committee of leaders of the Brooklyn Puerto Rican Democratic clubs to request a meeting with the major Brooklyn Democratic leaders and described to his audience the dire situation of his community in Brooklyn. He informed them that the loyalty and active participation of Puerto Ricans in the current campaign demanded proportionate recognition from the party. The assembled leaders reportedly agreed, "offering praise for the loyalty and discipline of the Puerto Rican voters of Brooklyn" and promising to "assist in the improvement and development of the *colonia*."[28] Manhattan Puerto Ricans were also more focused on relations with Tammany Hall than on La Guardia's message of political reform during the 1933 election. The prominent East Harlem doctor José N. Cesteros organized a "División Puertorriqueña" for O'Brien's "traditional" Tammany campaign and hosted a big rally for the candidate and his running mates at Harlem's Park Palace. Two thousand Puerto Ricans reportedly participated in the event, not daunted by O'Brien's arriving, "sweaty and exhausted," after midnight.[29] U.S. congressional representative James Lanzetta, who had ousted La Guardia from his seat in the Seventeenth District during the 1931 election, joined other speakers in hailing O'Brien as the crowd awaited the candidate's arrival. Lanzetta spoke in favor of the "adequate representation" of Puerto Ricans in the United States. He added a salvo against the opposition, asserting that La Guardia had not only not "succeeded in doing anything for [Puerto Ricans] during the eight years he was in Congress," but that he had tried to "undermine, put down, and scoff at the Puerto Ricans."[30] For many politically active migrants, support for O'Brien had little to do with the failings of the opposition candidate and much to do with their long-standing participation in the Democratic clubs that anchored many corners of El Barrio and of Spanish-speaking Brooklyn.

Puerto Rican Democrats were not a united voting block, however, and not all Manhattan Democrats in the *colonia* backed the "straight" Tammany candidate. Women voters in particular tended to support the Democratic Recovery Party candidate, Joseph McKee.[31] The elite *colonia* activist Isabel O'Neill provided spirited campaign support for McKee, and other women community leaders in the Seventeenth Assembly District organized campaign fund-raisers under the banner "Hispanic Women Voters for McKee." Laura Santiago de Cesteros, who headed the Harlem offshoot of the citywide Women Voters for McKee, bemoaned the "inertia" of Puerto Rican women in the *colonia*, who seemed to see politics as something "by and for men." Although some of her comments about the role of women in the campaign sounded like traditional ideas about women playing the helpmeet role in the "arduous but glorious" work of politics, she also insisted that Puerto Rican women "must realize the role that they play in the governing of this city, and that they awaken to the call of this duty."[32]

A much smaller number of Puerto Ricans did actually respond to the call to duty that Fusion Party reformers and progressives issued to New Yorkers—made even more notable by the fact that this was the only party in the 1933 elections, aside from the Communist Party, that actually nominated a Puerto Rican candidate to the ticket. José M. Vivaldi, an "old-time comrade" of Puerto Rican socialism, ran for alderman from the Seventeenth District on La Guardia's Fusion ticket.[33] In his formal announcement of his candidacy, Vivaldi reminded fellow Puerto Ricans (with some exaggeration of their numerical strength) that, "although eighty percent of the population in this district is Puerto Rican, the political leaders are not Puerto Ricans, the district representatives are not Puerto Ricans, in the hospitals there are no Puerto Rican doctors, in the courts of justice and in many other government agencies there are no Puerto Ricans, [and] there

Figure 8. Comité de Damas, Liga Puertorriqueña e Hispana, 1932. Jesús Colón papers, Archives of the Puerto Rican Diaspora, Centro de Estudios Puertorriqueños, Hunter College, CUNY.

are no Puerto Rican police or firemen."[34] In spite of this convincing call for support from his compatriots, and in spite of La Guardia's successful bid to oust the entrenched Democratic Party, Vivaldi lost to his Tammany rival.

Vivaldi's supporters were not the only Puerto Rican voters who were disappointed in November. Across the political spectrum, members of the *colonia* considered the 1933 elections to have been a failure in terms of possible gains for Puerto Ricans and other Spanish speakers who were struggling through the worst years of the Depression.[35] When those who had backed the "regular" Democrats or the Recovery Democrats saw their candidates trounced in the polls, they also saw their hopes for a return on their political investment—creating and joining the growing number of Puerto Rican Democratic clubs—dashed. The New Deal and its locally based programs, like Home Relief and work relief programs, had yet to be deployed by the Roosevelt administration; for Puerto Rican voters of all persuasions, this election season looked like a big step backward. As the *colonia* geared up for the 1934 state elections, *La Prensa* sponsored a formal exchange among political leaders, activists, and voters under the banner "*el momento político y los hispanos.*" A majority of commentators, most of them well-known *colonia* leaders, fretted about the problem of coordinating political action among Hispanic, and particularly Puerto Rican, voters. How could voters achieve

their common goal of Puerto Rican empowerment without unity of purpose? Leaders of elite and middle-class organizations had tried several
times in the twenties to bring disparate cultural and mutual benefit societies under a single organizational structure—and failed.[36]

Again in 1934, the trope of unity was trotted out by *colonia* leaders, but
it remained an elusive vision that failed to mask the various rivalries still
dividing the migrant community along lines of class and ideology. Whereas
leaders of the *colonia* cultural elite described their goals for group advancement in terms limited by a discourse of respectability, working-class leaders
defined "betterment" in terms of material as opposed to cultural advancement. Brooklynite Luis Weber, for instance, entreated Puerto Ricans to set
aside their normal political allegiances to vote for a candidate who would
help Puerto Ricans to secure employment, housing, and relief "regardless
of whether our representative is Republican, or Socialist or whether there
on our island he was the son of so-and-so or thus-and-such."[37] In other
words, it was time to let go of island rivalries and think about politics in
local terms: survival in New York. A number of other contributors agreed
with him. Pedro Rovira, a Puerto Rican leader of the Hispanic division of
the Recovery Party in Washington Heights, wrote that the "lamentable failure" of the last elections could be avoided if "disinterested persons," free of
"personal ambitions," could lead the *colonia* in the development of political
unity and organization. He seconded a nonpartisan push to elect Hispanic
leaders for the Spanish-speaking districts.[38] Puerto Rican Republicans, a
small minority among their compatriots, had the most to gain by supporting a cross-party campaign of support for Puerto Rican candidates. Oscar
García Rivera, who would become the first Puerto Rican elected official in
the United States when he won a New York State Assembly seat on the Republican ticket in 1937, proclaimed in 1934 that "the time has come to vote
for a Puerto Rican. This is not the time to fixate on whether the candidate
is a Democrat, Republican, or Fusionist. . . . We must . . . elect a Hispanic
who represents the collective sentiments of the 50,000 or more Spanish-
speakers who live in District 17."[39]

On the other hand, against the evidence of the recent election season,
many Democratic participants in the debate maintained that political empowerment for Puerto Ricans could only happen from within the Democratic Party. Traditional Tammany Democrats, including Brooklyn club
leaders Ramón Colón and Joaquín Colón, insisted that the solid popularity
of President Roosevelt—who allegedly had expressed support for the "re-
organization" of Tammany Hall—represented a rising tide that would lift

all Democratic Party boats; the usual patronage payoffs would follow, they said.[40] On the other hand, though, many more commentators on the *colonia*'s political prospects were beginning to blame the Democrats for its past and present political failures. Hispanic representatives of the Recovery Party blasted the entrenched and "false" leadership of the non-Hispanic Democrats in District Seventeen and insisted that "we Puerto Ricans must substitute the current democratic leadership with members of our own race."[41]

Predictably, members of the Republican minority in the district expressed even more trenchant critiques. One called Tammany Hall the "common enemy of all the Puerto Ricans in this district." Luis Ramos, a Republican who ran for the state legislature, noted bitterly that after "fifteen years of struggle and sacrifice" to gain political recognition from the major parties, it had come not from the Democrats, who had been collecting Puerto Ricans' loyal votes during those long years and given nothing in return, but from the Republicans. More interesting complaints about Tammany Hall came from *La Prensa* readers who were not major figures in the community. María Marín Reguero, from Washington Heights, reinforced the call of many *colonia* leaders to elect "one of us" to represent Puerto Rican neighborhoods, no matter what their party affiliation. She added a few critical words about the major parties: "If it is true that the Republican leader in this District has not treated us justly, it is no less true that the Democratic leaders have treated us still worse." Another writer complained, "For long years this community has blindly followed the principles and platforms of the Democratic Party, thereby making itself the unconscious victim of the disastrous manipulations ... of Tammany Hall."[42]

In the climate of reform that Fusionists and even Recovery Party members encouraged during the 1933–34 election season, *colonia* residents had begun to express more openly their criticisms of the powerful but ailing Tammany machine in East Harlem. A number of labor organizers and other progressives formed a "Puerto Rican Vigilance Committee" and set about documenting the numerous complaints collected from East Harlem residents who, for instance, had been denied work with the Tammany-controlled Sanitation Department on ad hoc jobs like snow removal. Diego Flores wrote to express his cynicism about the actions of machine politicians in poor communities and lamented the presence in the *colonia* of "opportunists" who allied themselves with political parties only for their personal gain. "It is sad to say, but politically speaking we are nobody," he said. "During the campaign they trick us with banquets, drinks, and false promises. Once in power they say in a nasty manner, when someone goes in search of assistance: 'I do not know you.' . . . Nevertheless these same politicians employ many of our compatriots to serve their purposes. There are numerous political clubs but none of them does anything."[43] As political empowerment continued to elude the *colonia*, the problem, according to Flores and many others, was not residents' apathy or political naïveté. It was that Democrats alienated Puerto Ricans by doing anything to get their votes but giving almost nothing in return.[44]

Much of *colonia* residents' resentment was directed not just at Tammany Hall and the Republican political machine; it was also targeted at the other ethnic groups that seemed to play the game of machine politics and patronage with more skill.[45] Puerto Ricans had nurtured a bitter rivalry with Jewish landlords and business owners in East Harlem since the mid-twenties, and these tensions had exploded into violent assaults from both sides during the summer of 1926. Although the Jewish population of Harlem was migrating steadily north into the Bronx by the thirties, Jewish business owners in El Barrio, with their material wealth and their firm grip on Democratic patronage, continued to rankle the growing Puerto Rican population of the neighborhood. In a letter reflecting on the strategies required of Puerto Ricans in the new political climate, one writer exclaimed, "Who are we going to serve? The Jews? American Negroes? NO. Puerto Ricans." Another railed against the manipulations of *"leaders—sajones* ["Saxons," as in Anglo-Saxon] and Hebrews who play with the Hispanic vote as they wish only to make a few little offerings during the electoral campaign." Jews—referred to by other Puerto Rican letter writers as *"caciques"* and "greasy businessmen"— were seen as saboteurs of political unity among their Puerto Rican neighbors, adversaries "who hate to see the successful resolution of our social and political problems."[46]

Many Puerto Ricans also expressed a deep reluctance about making common cause with African American voters to achieve their political goals. Part of this reluctance grew from the same kind of resentment that Puerto Ricans felt about Tammany's perceived favoritism toward the Jews in Harlem. American blacks, having struggled for three decades to win recognition from the Democratic machine in New York, had finally begun appointing their own district leaders and winning nominations to municipal and state offices; so in yet another equation of the machine's ethnic arithmetic, Puerto Ricans wound up at the bottom. More important, most Puerto Rican leaders feared being associated with "any other race especially those considered here to be inferior," as Luis Weber put it—"unless this is done out of expedience," he added. In spite of many Puerto Ricans' efforts to maintain social distance from their African American neighbors, however, some Puerto Rican Democrats—especially those who supported the Recovery Party—sought to join forces with African Americans during the 1933 campaign for mayor. A small group of leaders of the two groups, who so often competed for favors from Democratic leaders in their districts, co-organized what was reportedly one of the biggest Recovery campaign rallies in Harlem that year.[47]

But, as the letter writer quoted above indicated, many Puerto Ricans in New York felt that any political action that supported the agenda of Negroes in Harlem would hurt the *colonia*'s goal of electing "one of ours" to public office. This cynicism regarding cooperation with African Americans set the stage for a minor controversy during the 1934 elections. A leader of the Puerto Rican contingent of the Recovery Party, Dr. Pedro Ortiz, was criticized by other Puerto Rican Democrats for allegedly offering a public endorsement of the candidacy of African American Lester Taylor for State Assembly representative. In the interview in which he rather diffidently denied this accusation, Ortiz tried to smooth the feathers he had ruffled in the *colonia* by emphasizing how irresponsible such an action would be to the voters of the district. He did maintain, however, that "to reach an understanding with American Negroes to obtain mutual advantages in the approaching electoral campaign" might be the only way to "destroy the organized minority"—the Jews, he meant—"that rules this district without any electoral force."[48] In so many words, Ortiz was arguing for a political strategy in which Puerto Ricans in Harlem would join forces with their sometime rivals, African Americans, in order to edge out the neighborhood's more unanimously resented group, the Jews.

The 1933 elections had seemed "full of brilliant promise" for Puerto Ricans, but in spite of the *colonia*'s major political investment, the process "ended in complete failure, not just for the candidates of our race . . . but for the significance of the Hispanic vote in the city." Gearing up for the 1934 elections, Puerto Rican leaders continually reminded their compatriots of their power as voters, particularly in the Seventeenth District, where some claimed that Spanish speakers comprised up to 56 percent of the electorate, or sixteen thousand votes.[49] Ramón Colón, a Democratic leader in Brooklyn, wrote an open letter to *colonia* members as the 1934 elections approached, admonishing his neighbors to fight against the racial divisions that he observed within the community and to stop "imitating Yankees' racism."[50] Colón's point was clear: a successful bid for power as an ethnic bloc in New York politics required the resolution of the community's internal divisions. The 1934 elections, however, amounted to little progress on this front. The Republican Party, fighting hard to pull *colonia* voters away from Tammany, backed a Puerto Rican, Frank Torres, for State Assembly in the majority–Puerto Rican Seventeenth District. But Torres lost, and the 1934 elections were deemed, as one observer put it, "*otro fracaso*," another failure for Puerto Ricans. Such failures would make Puerto Rican voters far more receptive, in subsequent elections in the decade, to the Fusion platform and to the more leftist American Labor Party at its start in 1936. This particular "*momento político*" showed Puerto Ricans that the traditional immigrants' strategy of allying with Tammany was not working for them. They would have to develop a different approach to political empowerment.

## Politicizing Relief

While leaders at the top levels of *colonia* political culture were caught up in trying to win modest gains for Puerto Ricans in electoral politics in the early thirties, it was controversies over locally administered welfare programs that animated thousands of other migrants. In the absence of a federal safety net, which was not put in place until the Social Security Act of 1935, New York City had begun implementing small-scale "Home Relief" programs in the early thirties, providing food and cash assistance to needy city residents. Conflicts over relief centered on who was appointed to administer and distribute emergency funds, who was encouraged to apply for them, and who actually got them. Such tensions affected city life at every level throughout the Depression, from political maneuvering and accusations among high-level city officials to scandals in neighborhood Emergency Relief Bureau offices and stories of relief "chiselers"—such as the man collecting relief in Manhattan who was reported to have bought numerous hundred-dollar dresses for his mistress. In 1935, dogged by the complaints and rumors of corruption that had marked the Home Relief Bureau (HRB) since he took office in 1934, and spurred to act definitively by the recent Harlem riots, Mayor La Guardia finally called for an aldermanic committee to investigate the charges.[51]

African American Harlemites had become more successful in demanding attention from city officials since the 1935 riots, especially regarding access to relief, and the hearings provided a forum for their grievances and demands. Puerto Ricans would play a minor role in these hearings, and the claims they presented to local officials—regarding equal access to relief funds and fair treatment by relief workers—went unanswered. Newspapers did not report on Puerto Ricans' protests regarding relief distribution, and those who were lobbying on the *colonia*'s behalf reported little or no response from city officials. Their marginalization in these hearings, and in other conflicts over relief in the thirties, underscored their role as personae non gratae in the black-and-white political relations in Harlem and in the city at large. In the context of such controversies, Puerto Ricans in New York began to talk about citizenship beyond its utility for voting, articulating expectations of their status in terms of access to social welfare and to equal treatment by political and social institutions.

From the early days of the Depression, Puerto Ricans in New York reported that they were ignored by the city's relief administration and that local relief workers discriminated against them in the distribution of benefits. In 1932, *La Prensa* informed its readers that "we receive persistent and detailed complaints from destitute *hispanos* who, after speaking to relief station officials, either don't receive any aid at all or are given some indefinite date—which never actually arrives."[52] Not only did Puerto Ricans encounter delays, administrative mistakes, and refusals of their applications at Home Relief offices, many also complained that they were treated with outright disrespect and hostility. One applicant summarized his experience with the HRB with biting humor: "In this land to which we have come in search of new horizons, what we have discovered is insults and the opportunity to have our character assailed at the 'Home Relief' offices."[53] Other Puerto Ricans who applied for Home Relief or for assistance from private charitable organizations seconded the complaint that those who dispensed aid often dispensed judgments, as well, about the lifestyle of their clients.

In 1932, a group of migrants from the Seventeenth District organized a delegation of residents to meet with the Democratic city comptroller Frank Prial.[54] Members of the delegation laid out their grievances against the city for its failure to administer relief justly to Puerto Ricans and their grievances against private charitable institutions, which the delegation also charged with committing "injustices" and "prejudice." Prial reportedly expressed surprise at these revelations and was "taken aback" that "such a situation could exist in this city." The delegation would have viewed this reaction with some cynicism, given the fact that relief administration had been the object of various Harlem demonstrations for at least two years; *La Prensa*'s intrepid reporter of community news wrote archly about Prial's "sincerity" in an important election season.[55] If Prial was surprised at Puerto Ricans' problems in obtaining relief, he offered no formal response to the delegation's complaints, other than expressions of sympathy and the suggestion that he would look into the matter further. Migrants continued to encounter delays and obstacles at the Home Relief offices in Harlem, and it would not have surprised them to hear how the popular Puerto Rican singer Canario described their struggles with Home Relief in two of his *plenas*, recorded in New York in the mid-thirties. One of them, indeed, was titled "El Home Relief."[56]

Puerto Ricans and other *hispanos* in East Harlem, whose struggles to gain equal access to the city's relief funds and services went largely unnoticed by city officials, made it into news reports briefly during a scandal over relief administration that arose during the 1934 election season. James Lanzetta, a Democrat, was running for reelection as the U.S. congressional representative from East Harlem's Twentieth Congressional District (which encompassed the Seventeenth Assembly District, among several others). Although Lanzetta probably expected victory—given the majority of registered Democrats in the district whose votes had outnumbered Republican and Fusion votes by almost five to two—he knew that Vito Marcantonio, his Republican-Fusion opponent, presented a serious challenge to his prospects for winning.[57] Marcantonio was an old friend and staunch ally of La Guardia's (whom Lanzetta had beaten in the 1932 congressional race in the Twentieth Congressional District, riding FDR's Democratic landslide) and had been campaigning tirelessly in the district where he grew up. Lanzetta charged that city welfare commissioner William Hodson and his associate Edward Corsi, who directed Home Relief work for the Emergency Relief Bureau, were providing an unfair advantage to Marcantonio by allowing him to use their names at political gatherings. Moreover, Lanzetta charged, "Mr. Marcantonio, with the connivance, consent, and knowledge of Mr. Corsi, has struck terror into the hearts of the needy and destitute of the district by threatening to cut off their relief and take away their emergency jobs unless they supported him."[58] Lanzetta asserted that Puerto Ricans, the most "needy and destitute" of the district's residents, were pawns in the political games of Marcantonio, Hodson, Corsi, and even La Guardia. Hodson and Corsi scoffed at Lanzetta's charges. Marcantonio, calling Lanzetta's statements "scurrilous, wanton, and malicious," took the opportunity to attack the credibility of Tammany politicians in general. "My opponent's real complaint," he retorted, "is that he cannot use the relief administration to terrorize the district as he did when it was in the hands of Tammany Hall in 1931 and 1932."[59]

This was not the first time that Tammanyites had accused Marcantonio of manipulating the votes of his Puerto Rican constituents. (Nor was it the last. The most popular of his opponents' stories would claim, a decade later, that Marcantonio bought the votes of Puerto Ricans in his district by paying the airfares of residents' relatives to import additional votes from the island at election time.) Marcantonio's reputation as an advocate of the Puerto Rican people of his district did reach the point that, by the late thirties, even migrants' friends and relatives on the island began writing to him for assistance with their employment and relief problems. For instance, one widow from Mayagüez asked Marcantonio to help her obtain the benefits promised her by the Veterans' Bureau, "since I am a widow who is responsible for six legitimate small children, and as a widow of a veteran of the World War[,] I turn to you." Another man requested a "grant" from Marcantonio of one thousand dollars to go to the School of Aeronautics in Tulsa, Oklahoma: "I do not know you but I have heard about you and I know for sure that you are a good man." Other requests dealt with workmen's comp cases, teachers' pensions, requests for jobs from the Puerto Rican Reconstruction Administration (PRRA), and complaints of unmet promises by the PRRA to build housing.[60] Although they were never proved, the rumors about Marcantonio's padding his constituency with voters from Puerto Rico gained currency since they were grounded in a real pattern of contact between Marcantonio and his constituents' homeland. Because Hispanics, and Puerto Ricans in particular, struggled to gain access to any of the two hundred million dollars in estimated relief expenditures that New York City offered its residents in 1934, the political clout of a sympathetic representative could make the difference between hunger and subsistence.[61]

The city may have been ignoring them, but "needy and destitute" Puerto Ricans continued in their efforts to draw attention to their plight and to assert their social rights as citizens. In April 1935, a group of Hispanics staged a protest outside the Home Relief Bureau office at 116th Street and Madison Avenue. More than four hundred *colonia* members reportedly joined in the picketing, giving voice to the demands laid out in a flyer circulated by the protest organizers: that the value of relief "tickets" increase by 25 percent; that rents floated by the HRB be paid on time; that clothing be provided for whole families; that "closed" cases be reopened; and that moving costs be included among relief benefits. *La Prensa* reported that some thirty police officers patrolled the protest area, "perhaps worried about the occurrence of riots similar to the recent events on 125th Street." The reporter hastened to add, however, that "no altercations of any kind" had been observed at or near the protest.[62] Although the *World Telegram*, the *Daily News*, and the *Times* all covered news of the numerous protests staged at Home

Relief offices around the city in the mid-thirties, none of them considered the demonstration by "Spanish Harlem" residents important enough to report on.[63] With local officials' attention trained on the "explosive" nature of conditions in Harlem after the March riot, it was notable that any action, however orderly, by any Harlem residents would receive not even passing mention in the city's major media.

Hispanic Harlemites staged this demonstration just a week before the Mayor's Commission on Conditions in Harlem (MCCH) began a series of hearings to investigate charges of discrimination in municipal relief offices. In the "turbulent sessions" during which the MCCH heard testimony and complaints about discrimination from African Americans in Harlem, the identical grievances of Puerto Ricans and Hispanics in the same neighborhood went unheard. A. Philip Randolph, head of the Brotherhood of Sleeping Car Porters, presided over the largest of the hearings, attended by more than seven hundred people. It was no small task, according to reports, for Randolph to retain order as Edward Corsi, the director of the HRB, faced four hours of "a continuous barrage of questions from indignant Harlem residents who insisted, despite his denials, that Negroes had been victims of relief discrimination." Corsi defended himself by arguing that Negroes comprised nearly 20 percent of the HRB staff and that his bureau had made a concerted effort to staff Harlem offices with Harlem residents.[64] A central piece of testimony in the hearing came from James W. Ford, a leading organizer of the Communist Party in Harlem. Ford emphasized the discrepancies in the dollar amount of disbursements to Harlem residents versus disbursements to New Yorkers in other neighborhoods. He said that while the average amount of relief per family, across the city, was forty-two dollars per month, in Harlem the average was around twenty-eight dollars, or about 25–30 percent less. These were the very statistics cited by the Hispanic protesters at the 116th Street Home Relief office the week before, as they demanded an increase in relief payments to account for exactly this differential. Ford and the Hispanic protesters must have either shared this evidence or derived their figures from a common source—and either scenario makes it all the more puzzling that no residents of El Barrio gave testimony at the hearings.[65]

Ford, in his testimony, also complained about a Harlem Home Relief precinct administrator, Victor Suárez, who was Puerto Rican.[66] Ford mentioned other Relief Bureau officials in his testimony (aside from Corsi, who bore the brunt of the accusations) but singled out Suárez as the local relief official guiltiest of outright prejudice against his Negro clients. Ford alleged that Suárez had stated, "on the record," that 90 percent of Harlem's Negro relief recipients were "'fakers.'" Suárez had also reportedly explained that the low level of promotions among Negro HRB employees was due to the fact that "'Negroes were not educationally qualified to hold the better jobs in the Home Relief Bureau.'"[67] Neither James Ford nor any of his fellow complainants framed the accusations against Suárez in terms of his identity as a Puerto Rican; nor did any of the press coverage of the issue remark on the fact that Suárez was Puerto Rican. Nevertheless, the tensions between Puerto Rican and African American residents in Harlem during the Depression years defined the backdrop of Ford's narrative, and accusing Suárez of prejudice and discrimination against Negro relief recipients was one way to express that hostility without articulating it directly.

By the mid-thirties, African American Harlemites had engaged in countless battles for acknowledgment of the discrimination they faced in every aspect of life in the city, and that they were winning—finally—attention from city officials about the direness of conditions in Harlem represented a small but significant victory. The plight of Puerto Ricans, on the other hand, remained invisible to city officials and the mainstream media. A number of Puerto Rican activists had complained bitterly to La Guardia about their exclusion from the Mayor's Commission on Conditions in Harlem, including Isabel O'Neill, who had railed against that exclusion as "an act of political and civic indifference and unmindfulness at which we feel aggrieved."[68] In the English-language public record covering these years of conflict over Home Relief, Puerto Ricans appeared only as minor figures: as alleged political pawns in the contentious elections of the Seventeenth District; or, in the case of Ford's accusations against Suárez, as competitors or even oppressors of African American Harlemites. Indeed, "civic indifference and unmindfulness" was a rather restrained description of city officials' reaction to Puerto Rican concerns.

Behind the public silence that characterized their struggles in Harlem, however, Puerto Ricans were making explicit and increasingly concrete claims about their social and civic rights as Americans. Migrants' assertions about these rights emerged from their interpretation of the promises of democratic liberal citizenship in the United States, and they were claims that ran parallel to the incipient language of rights being formulated by African Americans on similar issues in the thirties. The right of access to city services, and to be heard by city officials, seemed particularly important to Puerto Ricans in the absence of effective political representation or the kind of recognition by the Democratic Party that African Americans were gaining by the late thirties. Certainly, African Americans were a more visible and numerically powerful constituency in city politics, and they were a constituency that was growing in importance as the politics of race intensified during the late 1930s. The official silence that met Puerto Ricans' claims, on the other hand, was not simply a result of oversight due to their relative weakness as a minority voting bloc; indeed, even when the *colonia* could boast barely thirty thousand residents in the mid-twenties, a number of politicians had noted its political significance. A more important explanation for their marginalization in city politics lies, rather, in the fact that these colonial citizens became increasingly troublesome to liberal politicians as Puerto Rico turned into a political minefield in the late 1930s.

## Nationalism and the New Deal

As *colonia* leaders reflected on the "failure" of the 1933 and 1934 elections—before the frustrations over relief and general conditions in Harlem took center stage in 1935—they focused on building greater political unity among residents and a stronger base of nonpartisan support for Puerto Rican and Hispanic candidates. In spite of their hand-wringing, leaders and voters seemed hopeful about building coalitions. After all, the community of Puerto Rican migrants in New York was still expanding during the early years of the Depression, and the number of political, social, and mutual benefit organizations was growing apace.[69] *Colonia* leaders referred more frequently to the power of migrants' American citizenship, and their votes in particular, and maintained that the push to nominate and elect Puerto Rican candidates was bound to succeed in the near future. But a series of political dramas in the mid-thirties sidetracked leaders' focus on local elections. The first involved the First Lady and a controversy about anti–Puerto Rican prejudice that she sparked inadvertently. Then, less than two years later, political violence in Puerto Rico pulled *colonia* activists more forcefully than before into the maelstrom of independence politics, pitting their political interests against those of many New Deal Democrats. One outcome of the conflict over island politics was that migrants embraced East Harlem's U.S. congressional representative Vito Marcantonio, whose political radicalism and support of Puerto Rican nationalism made him an outcast in Congress and outside of his home district in New York. There was, in this context, a general leftward shift among the many *colonia* activists who had sought political recognition for their community earlier in the decade. All these developments meant that Puerto Rican New Yorkers would confront real limits to their inclusion in the rising tide of political liberalism by the end of the thirties.

## The Roosevelts and the Puerto Ricans

Puerto Ricans in New York had supported President Roosevelt from the earliest days of his candidacy, and their devotion to the president only grew as the New Deal gained a foothold in the working-class neighborhoods of Depression-era New York. It was the expansion of the early New Deal programs, work relief and Home Relief, that cemented migrants' commitment to their president and bolstered their hopes about sharing in the benefits of recovery along with other Americans. When WPA Federal Writers' Project field-workers interviewed twenty-four Puerto Rican migrants to record their "life histories" and asked about their political beliefs, almost all interviewees spoke glowingly about Roosevelt and the New Deal. "President Roosevelt is my ideal of a great leader of peoples, politically and socially. His personality, courage and integrity, a product of his liberalism . . . ranges him amongst the greatest men of all time," said one. "In regards to President Roosevelt I believe that he is the greatest American ever born," pronounced another. One field-worker noted that his interviewee had hung pictures of Franklin Roosevelt, along with popular Mexican president Lázaro Cárdenas, in his living room, "clipped from newspaper and nailed to the walls."[70] (Mexican immigrants were also a devoted Roosevelt constituency. In his history of Mexican Americans in Los Angeles, historian George Sánchez quotes a Los Angeles social service provider who explained that "Franklin D. Roosevelt's name was the spark that started thousands of Spanish-speaking persons to the polls.")[71]

The First Lady was almost equally beloved. Puerto Ricans were delighted when Mrs. Roosevelt, known for her commitment to philanthropy, made a "goodwill visit" to the island in the spring of 1934. She planned to investigate the magnitude of poverty and depression there and also participated in a planning conference debating ideas for Puerto Rico's economic reconstruction. Accounts of the trip in newspapers like the *New York Times*, and in a biography of Mrs. Roosevelt written a few years later, emphasized the warm reception she received on the island and the appreciation that islanders expressed both for her attention to their suffering and for the hope she imparted to them. She "conveyed to Puerto Rico much of the buoyant optimism Washington has exhibited during the last year," announced the *Times*; the reporter gushed on that "her mere presence, bringing new hope of that fuller life of which the President is an exponent, was a greater tonic than anything she did or said." Puerto Rico's U.S.-appointed governor, Blanton Winship, proclaimed as well that "her gracious contacts with the people have universally charmed them and brought them to love her."[72]

These grandiose accounts were not inaccurate. Puerto Ricans, on both the island and the mainland, admired Eleanor Roosevelt and her husband and believed that their New Deal for America would extend not just to its newcomers but to its island possession as well. Some migrants did remark on a paternalistic inflection to her comments on the trip. One *La Prensa* headline noted somewhat sardonically that "Mrs. Roosevelt is surprised at the cleanliness of the houses and people of Puerto Rico."[73] Upon her return, Mrs. Roosevelt made the rounds of charitable events and public meetings to discuss her trip, including a one thousand–plate dinner held by the Women's Trade Union League. Mrs. Roosevelt had roused the sympathy of her audience with descriptions of the travails of Puerto Rican workers, especially the women who struggled to make a living by embroidering handkerchiefs at three cents per dozen. She then told her audience that "the colony of the islanders in New York" was "one of the worst in the city—not only for the unpleasant happenings but for diseases." She emphasized the "shockingly high" rate of tuberculosis on the island and claimed it was "just as high in their colony here." And, underlining the growing danger of the situation, she reminded her audience that there were no immigration restrictions on Puerto Ricans entering the United States.[74]

Hearing Mrs. Roosevelt's comments as an insult and a betrayal, migrants sent telegrams of "violent protest" and wrote letters to city newspapers objecting to her accusations. One writer to the *New York Times* said, "It seems to me that Mrs. Roosevelt is doing harm and embarrassing her illustrious husband, especially in making such an unwarranted statement against a group of law-abiding, hard-working American citizens." The Puerto Rico Spanish League informed her by telegram that her pronouncements had created a hysteria about tuberculosis that threatened both the jobs and future employment prospects of Puerto Ricans working in restaurants, hotels, and private homes. In her response to this protest, announced publicly at a social workers' dinner, she shot back sanctimoniously, "I think that the Puerto Rico Spanish League should face the fact that one never finds solutions until they confront a problem and accept the truth. If they continue to hide a condition, they will continue to have it. It is far better to bring it into the open and seek a cure."[75] Bernardo Vega, author of the telegram, followed up his communication to the First Lady with a long letter to *La Prensa* readers, explaining how and why her comments had hurt the *colonia*: "We continue to believe that a hostile atmosphere for the Puerto Rican element has been created unnecessarily, because those who do not go beyond the superficial in examining the statements of Mrs. Roosevelt, will feel inclined, when they see a Puerto Rican, to shun him the way one flees from pests or the plague." Vega went on to argue that Puerto Ricans' poor health and poor living conditions were largely attributable to the state of peonage to which they had been reduced by being displaced from the land, often at the hand of "compatriots of Mrs. Delano Roosevelt" who owned most of the sugar plantations in Puerto Rico by the 1930s. "The sons of Puerto Rico who live in this city are not here by choice nor desire. We live in New York by necessity." Finally, Vega wrote, "Our problems cannot be solved by doing what Mrs. Roosevelt has done and portraying Puerto Ricans as a racial group afflicted with contagious diseases so that a few charitable Americans can give us alms while the rest—the majority—do nothing but insult us."[76]

There is no way to determine how many migrants actually were fired or failed to land jobs in restaurants or private homes due to fears about their "contagion" in the spring and summer of 1934, although Vega asserted that the numbers were substantial. Toward the end of the summer, migrants realized that the insult to their community affected their children as well. Community leaders discovered that the agency that had for several years helped to send more than a thousand Puerto Rican children to church summer camps would not do so this year, "as we have been asked not to send any Puerto Rican children."[77] The Liga Puertorriqueña called a mass demonstration, and Vega wrote that "practically every social, political, and religious group in El Barrio showed up for the planning meeting." (It is notable, though, that the list of supporting organizations did not include any Nationalist groups, which still largely avoided local politics.) The protest, held at the Park Palace, took the form of a mock tribunal in which the offending organizations were tried before a jury panel of twenty-three delegates from "various labor and religious organizations" and two attorneys as judges. Jesús Colón acted as one of the district attorneys arguing on behalf of the Puerto Rican community. Colón and other Brooklyn community leaders also staged a mass demonstration to protest the discrimination against Puerto Rican children. The names of twenty-four organizations—including Democratic, Communist, and labor groups, not all of them Puerto Rican or even Hispanic—crowded the bottom of the circular that advertised the demonstration.[78]

Eleanor Roosevelt's name was not mentioned in the nine-paragraph "manifesto" included on the protest flyer, and she was not one of the "defendants" in the Park Palace mock trial, over which Bernardo Vega presided. But to *colonia* members, the respected wife of their president had rolled a large stone in what seemed like a new avalanche of recriminations against Puerto Ricans in New York. José Giboyeaux, a migrant who worked as a carpenter for the WPA, later told an interviewer that although he had supported Roosevelt "absolutely 100%," he sympathized with the numerous Puerto Ricans, many of them Nationalists, who had "split from Roosevelt and from Mrs. Roosevelt over this issue."[79] And although the controversy had nothing directly to do with the issue of Puerto Rican independence, protesters like Vega framed their local rights—to freedom from defamation and discrimination—such that they were linked to the problem of Puerto Rico's political relationship to the United States and the "necessity" of Puerto Ricans' migration to the United States. In doing so, Vega championed a complex framework for understanding Puerto Rican migrants' U.S. citizenship, one that presumed a necessary relationship between, on the one hand, their social rights as U.S. citizens in a local arena and, on the other hand, their political and civic rights as Puerto Ricans under the U.S. flag. Such a diasporic blending of local politics and the politics of U.S. imperialism would be reflected throughout the period of Nationalist fervor that erupted in the *colonia* less than two years later.

### Nationalism in Puerto Rico and "Political Upheaval" in New York

By late 1936, the most significant political issues animating the migrant community had little to do with New York City. Events in Puerto Rico that year sparked a new surge in nationalism on the island, as well as a popularization of *independentista* agendas in New York. Leading up to the political tumult that brought the question of independence to the center of Puerto Rican politics, the island's economic misery was spurring increasing anger about U.S. colonial policy. Legislators in Washington showed little interest in extending scarce recovery dollars to the island, and although President Roosevelt—influenced by the First Lady—ordered the creation of a Puerto Rican Emergency Relief Administration (PRERA) from National Recovery Act (NRA) funds in 1933, the average Puerto Rican gained little from the aid. By late 1933, workers in the sugar, tobacco, needlework, and trucking industries, along with dockworkers, had staged countless strikes for better working conditions and more government relief for the unemployed. In January 1934, sugar workers began a series of major strikes across the island, which disrupted the sugar harvest that year and caused significant losses in profits for the sugar companies. Strikes followed in other industries across the island. Nationalist Party president Pedro Albizu Campos took up the cause of the strikers, offering them practical and political support from his party. As island and federal officials sought to meet some of the strikers' demands to subdue their protests, they also began to redouble their efforts at repressing the Nationalists, whom they saw as rabble-rousers aiming to use the antigovernment sentiment surrounding the strikes to build support for independence.[80]

Yet, in spite of the increasing conflict, and against evidence that the New Deal in Puerto Rico had accomplished little in its first year—one man interviewed by reporters during Mrs. Roosevelt's 1934 visit complained that he and his large family were forced to live on fifty cents a day, saying that "the NRA treats us like dogs"—migrants' faith in the political goodwill of the Roosevelts remained largely unshaken.[81] The president's support for a new Puerto Rican Reconstruction Administration (PRRA), in late 1934, was a major step forward. Out of the Roosevelts' and Secretary of the Interior Harold Ickes's collaboration with a group of Puerto Rican Liberal Party leaders, including Luis Muñoz Marín and University of Puerto Rico chancellor Carlos Chardón, emerged what promised to be a powerful plan of development and economic recovery. The so-called Chardón plan involved the restructuring of the sugar industry, and a new and broader approach to development, that together would promote a more stable island economy.

But many saw the Chardón plan as inviable from the beginning, largely because the Socialist-Republican coalition that ruled the island legislature was backed by wealthy sugar interests and adopted a generally hostile stance toward New Deal programs.[82] A Federal Writers' Project field-worker later noted that the Chardón plan was defeated by "the large American corporations in control there." As important as the opposition of the *coalición* to the Chardón plan, though, was Roosevelt appointee Ernest Gruening's own political reversal over the course of his two years as director of the PRRA. According to Tugwell's memoir of his years working in Puerto Rico, Gruening's progressivism "melted quickly in the heat of tropical politics"; indeed, Gruening was instrumental in destroying the PRRA by 1937. As the WPA field-worker observed, "The Puerto Rican Reconstruction Administration which, with FERA [Federal Emergency Relief Administration] funds, was to revitalize the island's economic life, restore its undernourished people to health, modernize its cities and revive its wasted lands, has been systematically sabotaged by both the island's appointed administration and the American controlling interests."[83]

More precisely, it was the chain of events that followed the shooting of four young Nationalist demonstrators, in October 1935, that turned Gruening from a sympathetic collaborator with island Liberals to a hostile gatekeeper of continental dollars and influence. The Nationalists had been participating in a peaceful demonstration at the University of Puerto Rico at Río Piedras when police, allegedly responding to the sound of gunshots, fired on them. Albizu and his party promised to avenge these deaths, and, indeed, four months later, the police chief, Colonel Francis Riggs, was assassinated. The Nationalist Party did not publicly admit responsibility for the assassination, but the police arrested two Nationalist activists and charged them with the shooting. Shortly after their arrest, police shot the two suspects to death in the jailhouse, claiming that they had tried to escape. Puerto Ricans across the political spectrum expressed outrage over what they saw as naked political violence committed by the government to further its agenda of colonial control. Luis Muñoz Marín, the rising young leader in the Liberal Party and a staunch supporter of the Democratic administration in Washington, refused to condemn the Riggs assassination until the U.S. government condemned the police shootings of the young Nationalists.[84]

Suddenly, the Nationalist cause no longer looked like an extremist agenda nor one nurtured by a mostly elite minority. Across the island and in the New York *colonia*, sympathy for independence and its Nationalist proponents increased in inverse proportion to the declining tolerance of the U.S. presence in Puerto Rico.[85] These events radicalized migrants significantly and changed the way they expressed their views of *"nuestro presidente."* One East Harlem resident, who was not active in any of the Nationalist organizations but who described herself as a "Puerto Rican patriot," wrote to *La Prensa* that, given the power of the U.S. government across the world, "we must be friends of the United States, but we wish to apply the Monroe Doctrine to ourselves: Puerto Rico for the Puerto Ricans."[86] Many Puerto Ricans in New York would only reluctantly criticize Roosevelt for his approach to island politics. Two of the interviewees for the WPA Spanish Book followed their gushing praise for the president with diffident complaints. "I do not approve of his foreign policy, however I admit that perhaps I do not have the proper knowledge of his aims," said one. Another, the interviewee who had pronounced Roosevelt "the greatest American ever born," admitted that "I do not agree with . . . his foreign policies"—probably a coded reference to Roosevelt's handling of the recent island conflicts.[87]

While Roosevelt administration appointees battled Nationalists in

Puerto Rico, migrants in New York turned out in unprecedented numbers to join in Nationalist-sponsored demonstrations and rallies to protest the arrest and prosecution of eight Nationalist leaders on the island, including Albizu Campos, who were accused of sedition and conspiracy in the months following the Riggs assassination.[88] Infuriated by the Nationalist actions, Senator Millard Tydings of Maryland, a close friend of Riggs's, drafted a bill supporting the independence of Puerto Rico. There was no mistaking the bill's inspiration: it was not a concession to the *independentistas*, who had grown in number and in power since the early 1930s. Rather, Tydings and his supporters proposed the legislation as a quick solution to the political embarrassment that Puerto Rico was beginning to create for the United States, and its impossibly punitive terms confirmed the bill's intent. Tydings argued that the island's "disgraceful, corrupt, and fraudulent" elections caused American lawmakers to "question the worth of American institutions . . . being adapted to the people of Puerto Rico and to the conditions under which they live."[89] In other words, Puerto Ricans should be granted independence because they were not deserving of the American-sponsored political system that served them under the current colonial arrangement. If Puerto Ricans voted for independence in the plebiscite outlined by the bill, they would separate from the United States under the following terms: all federal assistance programs, including New Deal programs under the Puerto Rican Reconstruction Administration (PRRA), would immediately cease (Tydings told the Congress that "it seems as if the more we do the worse conditions become in the island"); the full U.S. tariff on imported goods would be imposed incrementally over four years at the rate of 25 percent per year; and the new government of the island would have to create its own military force and infrastructure within six months. In addition, Puerto Ricans would have six months to choose between Puerto Rican and U.S. citizenship, and thereafter Puerto Ricans entering the United States would be subject to U.S. immigration laws, which under the Tydings bill would allow only five hundred islanders a year to emigrate to the United States.[90]

Although Tydings told a *New York Times* reporter that the bill had the administration's backing, Roosevelt's connection to Tydings's proposal was not widely discussed. Six weeks before Tydings presented his bill to Congress, Secretary Ickes had issued a statement that "the people of Puerto Rico have a right within the limits of the Constitution to seek whatever form of government they deem best for themselves." Ernest Gruening, director of the PRRA, responded to Ickes with the suggestion that Puerto

Ricans be allowed to decide on the independence question in the elections that fall. He recommended that the legal division of the Interior Department be instructed to draft an independence bill for review by Ickes and by the president, one that could then be introduced to the Congress by Senator Tydings. Ickes approved of this plan, and evidently pushed it forward, but told Gruening not to talk to the press about its connections to the Roosevelt administration: it would be better if the public believed it originated with Senator Tydings himself. Tydings, however, did tell the press that the bill had the Roosevelt administration's backing.[91] In Puerto Rico, most political leaders reacted to the Tydings bill in more or less predictable ways according to their parties' stance on independence. Santiago Iglesias, the pro-statehood Socialist leader and resident commissioner, attacked the bill and presented a parallel bill to the Puerto Rican legislature supporting statehood. The leadership of the Republican Party, which remained in coalition with the Socialists, also opposed the bill as excessively punitive, while the pro-independence Liberal Party leader, Antonio Barceló, pronounced that "although we might die of hunger, we want independence!" Calling the terms of the bill "unjust" and comparing them to "highway robbery," the popular Liberal senator Luis Muñoz Marín offered a counterproposal amending the terms of the island's transition from colony to republic.[92]

Observing this highly charged sequence of events from New York City, the *colonia*'s most vocal and well-known Nationalists inundated *La Prensa* with their views, plying readers with invocations of island patriotism and calls to unified action. A smaller number of observers expressed skepticism about the economic implications of the bill and its possible effects on the daily life of Puerto Ricans. Most interesting about this sample of *colonia* public opinion was the number of women migrants who wrote letters to the newspaper in support of independence for Puerto Rico. Luisa Salgado, who had written several pro-Nationalist letters to the paper already, composed a celebration of the *independentista* writings of Luis Muñoz Rivera, Muñoz Marín's father. Luisa Quintero, Puerto Rican journalist and wife of Cuban journalist Babby Quintero, weighed in in favor of the Tydings bill despite its harsh terms because, she said, the "relief" that Puerto Rico got from the U.S. government—and stood to lose if independence won out— amounted to little in terms of improving the lives of islanders anyway. The stringent requirements for receiving relief from the PRRA, and the corruption in its administration, she said, simply underlined the fact that the island needed a sustainable economy rather than one controlled totally by U.S. corporations.[93]

Scores of other women and men wrote to *La Prensa* during the summer and fall of 1936 to express their desire for independence. Outrage at the U.S. regime in Puerto Rico spurred a new cohesion within the *colonia* and an outpouring of anticolonial discourse. A Federal Writers' Project field-worker observed that "the Tydings Bill, which raised all Puerto Ricans' hopes so high and then dashed them, seems to have lighted the spark that revived Lower Harlem's political life."[94] The renewed debate about Puerto Rican independence inspired some activists to revisit the promises of U.S. citizenship. Erasmo Vando, for instance, created Puerto Rican Citizens of the United States of America, whose first program announced, "You all know quite well that here, in the heart of this federal republic, we support and protect Liberty, the inalienable right of each citizen, to disseminate and defend their ideas. . . . And you also know well that here it is the COLLEC-TIVE FORCE, the same as in Puerto Rico, that determines the triumph of these Ideas."[95] Other *independentistas* were deeply cynical about their American citizenship, which many activists called a grossly inadequate re-placement for sovereignty. Nationalist Pilar Pacheco described mordantly how Puerto Ricans' experience of U.S. citizenship intensified their fight for independence. "Each Puerto Rican is a free and sovereign citizen of the United States," she began,

> free and sovereign to struggle against indigence and circumstance . . .
> free and sovereign to chase after his bread, . . . which he is denied. . . .
> The Puerto Rican in the United States has the privilege of clearing and
> scrubbing plates in restaurants; of rising at five in the morning on harsh
> winter days to line up at the factory, at the cafeteria, at the docks with
> the hope of being chosen among the hundreds of foreigners who com-
> prise the working masses of this people. . . . We are absolutely free to hear
> how they call us "niggers," to see how they ignore our rights as American
> citizens. . . .
>
> If this is the liberty and sovereignty that a people gives to loyal men . . .
> it is not strange that nationalist Puerto Ricans feel aggrieved and cry out
> for justice and equality and try to tear down with a valiant hand the veil
> of the hypocrites.[96]

In asserting that racism was one of the reasons that white Americans "ig-nore our rights as American citizens," Pacheco was not only echoing María Más Pozo's 1931 lament.[97] She was also connecting the weakness of their citizenship with the political conflict raging in Puerto Rico and in El Bar-rio, arguing that Puerto Ricans' debasement in racial terms was the central reason that Puerto Ricans were *not* "free and sovereign citizen[s] of the United States," citizens with rights.

In the days after Tydings presented his bill to Congress, both Muñoz Marín and the PRRA's Planning Division sent memos to Gruening outlining a series of proposed amendments to the legislation that would make its economic provisions less disastrous for the island. Gruening apparently ignored both. Then, within two weeks of Tydings's proposal, Vito Marcantonio presented to Congress his own bill for Puerto Rican sovereignty.[98] "The dignity of the American people as a freedom-loving Nation," Marcantonio declared, "demands that Puerto Rico be judged under the principle of self-determination of nations." The counterbill that he proposed called for a suspension of the tariff on Puerto Rican products shipped to the United States and open immigration of Puerto Ricans to the United States. Most boldly, the bill included a "substantial indemnity" to be paid to the "long-suffering people of Puerto Rico" as partial compensation for the estimated four hundred million dollars extracted from the island's economy by U.S. citizens and business interests. Typical of its hands-off approach on issues addressing the colonial status of Puerto Rico, Congress responded to neither, dissimulating with silence. Former governor Rexford Tugwell linked Congress's approach to Puerto Rico, vaguely, to "[the] general lack of equipment for the task of colonial government," which was, in turn, "obviously the result of our confused policy." "We had interests of which we could not let go," he admitted in his 1947 memoir of his years in Puerto Rico, "but at the same time we felt compelled to pretend that they did not exist."[99] Seeing the turmoil that his bill inspired beyond the walls of Congress, and perhaps nudged by the Roosevelt administration, Tydings actually withdrew the bill just a month after he introduced it.

While the fight over independence "lighted the spark" of political revival in El Barrio, in Puerto Rico it caused the New Deal coalition to crumble. Gruening, after an investigation into corruption and "anti-American" activity in the PRRA, systematically purged the organization of Liberal Party members, most notably Chardón, although they had been New Dealers' staunchest supporters on the island. Ultimately, the organization was stripped of its power to such an extent that its role in the island's economic reconstruction and recovery faltered.[100] The failure of the PRRA, which struggled to retain its funding through the late 1930s, signified not just the ideological reversal of its director. More, it represented the Roosevelt administration's divestment, both actual and symbolic, from Puerto Rican affairs throughout the remainder of the thirties.

In spite of the fact that neither of the 1936 independence bills was ever debated in Congress, the Marcantonio bill in particular lived on symbolically in the *colonia*. And Marcantonio continued to keep the independence issue alive in national politics by offering legal counsel to Albizu Campos and the other imprisoned Nationalists during a trip to Puerto Rico in the summer of 1936 (the first time he had traveled beyond the continental United States). The day Marcantonio returned from Puerto Rico, *colonia* leaders staged the largest public demonstration El Barrio had ever seen. The *New York Times* reported that ten thousand Puerto Ricans, "representing a score of political and social clubs in the city, paraded for three hours through the streets of lower Harlem . . . to protest the attitude and actions of 'Imperialistic America' in making 'slaves' of the natives of the island." "Free Puerto Rico!" "Down with Yankee Imperialism!" chanted demonstrators.[101] Many of the less politically active residents of the *colonia* participated in the wave of *anti-imperialismo* that spread across Spanish-speaking Harlem, and even Puerto Rican Communists grew more sympathetic to the Nationalist cause.[102] One member of the WPA Federal Writers' Project wrote about this moment that "Puerto Rican political groupings [have] crystallized to a degree never before attained."[103]

In these years of political turmoil, and amid migrants' growing crisis of faith in the national Democratic Party, Vito Marcantonio's devotion to solving the problems of his migrant constituency, and his staunch support for Puerto Rican independence, helped to rally the political energy not just of Spanish-speaking Harlemites in his district but of Puerto Ricans across the city. Marcantonio's Puerto Rican supporters would, however, pay a price for their allegiance to someone who was widely viewed in Congress as a dangerous radical; the more Marcantonio identified himself with the cause of Puerto Rican nationalism, the more he and his constituency were viewed as hostile to the U.S. government and American democracy.[104] However, while Marcantonio persevered as El Barrio's "maverick" representative in Congress in the late thirties, the Puerto Rican migrant Left thrived and expanded, galvanized by the anti-imperialist energy in the *colonia*. When civil war intensified in Spain in late 1936, broad-based support among U.S. Hispanics for the Spanish republican cause added to the intensifying debates about democracy and colonialism that were enlivening East Harlem and other Spanish-speaking neighborhoods. Puerto Ricans stood at the forefront of this movement, along with the Spaniards, whom they outnumbered by tens of thousands in New York, and alongside both white and black leftists who were native to the city. Pro-republican Spanish organizations across the city courted members of the Puerto Rican Left to help publicize their cause. One of the largest of the organizations mobilizing for the republican forces in Spain, supported by a number of Puerto Rican organizations, was headed by the Puerto Rican activist Erasmo Vando. At the peak of leftist organizing in support of democracy in Spain, *La Prensa* reported that seventy thousand people, the majority of them Hispanic, took part in the 1937 May Day celebrations, which that year were devoted to Spanish democracy.[105]

As the Puerto Rican community approached the challenge of another election season in the fall of 1937, its two major issues—democracy for Spain and independence for Puerto Rico—drew divided voters together, and the intra-*colonia* rapprochement would help migrants elect one of their own at last. But, as engagement in the politics of the Spanish Civil War and island nationalism pulled Puerto Rican voters further to the left, they moved further outside the realm of issues that leaders of the major parties were willing to address. Moreover, although Puerto Rican leftists in particular found in Marcantonio an important congressional advocate, their alliance pushed Puerto Ricans further from the goal of an empowered relationship to formal politics at both the local and national levels. As migrants demonstrated in reaction to island turmoil and increasingly demanded resolution of Puerto Rico's intractable "status question," the diasporic identity that had earlier made Puerto Ricans seem irrelevant in U.S. politics now made them look like a political liability to the Democratic Party. However, as Rexford Tugwell would later observe, Democrats' growing hostility on matters regarding Puerto Rico had to do as much with the administration's failings as a colonial administrator as with the constituency itself. "It was part of the general public hypocrisy which was naturally shared by the Congress," he wrote. "Americans generally had not come to think of Puerto Ricans as real citizens—rather, when they thought of them at all, as citizens of a sort of second class."[106]

### The Limited Victory of Oscar García Rivera

Puerto Rican East Harlem had indeed "come alive" in the mid-thirties, in the words of a WPA field-worker. "In the past few months," the field-worker went on to say, "Lower Harlem, the Puerto Rican neighborhood, has been undergoing a political upheaval. Until then our Puerto Rican's [*sic*] politics were quiescent with the exception of small groups whose politics were exilic and apparently non-contagious." He asserted that the "increase of independent political actions by Puerto Ricans in New York" was directly linked to the political tumult in Puerto Rico.[107] That tumult reached new levels in the spring of 1937, after island police fired on a demonstration of unarmed Nationalists at Ponce, killing twenty and wounding over one hundred people, an event thereafter referred to by Puerto Ricans as the "Ponce massacre."[108] Many migrants expressed dismay at how U.S. Democrats, and the Roosevelt administration in particular, handled the incident. Ramón Giboyeaux told an interviewer simply that "Roosevelt . . . committed a tremendous error. . . over the issue of [Ponce]."[109]

Far less contentious than island nationalism, or even than support for the republican cause in Spain, was the 1937 election campaign of their compatriot Oscar García Rivera for State Assembly representative in the Seventeenth District, a rallying point for Puerto Ricans across the political spectrum.[110] García Rivera's campaign was important not just because he was the first Puerto Rican elected to a state office in the United States, or because he sought to fulfill a more or less populist promise to represent the needs of the Puerto Rican community. His election, following on the heels of the tumultuous events on the island and in Spain and the leftward shift that both inspired, also represented a momentary refocusing of the *colonia*'s political energies on the traditional parties and their centrist politics in New York City. García Rivera's victory on the Republican ticket depended on an unprecedented crossover vote from Puerto Ricans in the Seventeenth District. Whereas registered Democrats in this district typically outnumbered Republicans by six to one in the 1930s, and Democratic candidates almost always defeated their Republican opponents, García Rivera beat out his three-term Democratic rival, Meyer Alterman, with almost 60 percent of the vote.[111]

Although García Rivera's victory signified Puerto Rican unity on voting day, migrant leaders were still fighting in the background about whether to stick it out with the Democratic Party. In the spring of 1938, *La Prensa* editors solicited input from readers on the question "How can the *colonia* organize itself politically?" recalling the paper's similar debate from several years earlier. A notable proportion of the responses came from Democratic leaders and voters who directly or indirectly admonished Puerto Ricans for betraying the Democratic Party, or at least said that it was a mistake for Puerto Ricans to turn their backs on the long-standing source of patronage to the migrant community. Several echoed the claim of the Puerto Rican Democratic leader, Dr. José Cesteros, whose radio address during the November campaign invoked "our savior" Roosevelt and proclaimed that the

Figure 9. Oscar García Rivera, representative in the New York State Assembly, 1937. García Rivera was the first Puerto Rican elected to political office in the United States. Oscar García Rivera papers, Archives of the Puerto Rican Diaspora, Centro de Estudios Puertorriqueños, Hunter College, CUNY.

candidates of the state Democratic ticket "represented the poor and the suffering." José Vivaldi, president of East Harlem's New Deal Democratic Club, faulted the "professional classes" among Democrats of East Harlem for "losing control" of their district.[112] Across the river, Puerto Rican leaders in Brooklyn remained staunchly Democratic and worried little about losing their district to a Republican ticket; they announced their plans to host a Democratic assembly "for the unification of *hispanos* in Brooklyn." There was talk of organizing a nonpartisan *"gran conferencia"* of political and community groups in both boroughs in the fall, and the Democratic Brooklynites hurried to spearhead the effort.[113]

Of course, such an event was actually rife with partisan jockeying, although García Rivera in particular claimed the mantle of nonpartisanship. "The Puerto Rican *colonia* living here must abandon the denigrating and outdated strong-man leadership of men associated with the political 'Bosses,' and unite themselves efficiently to select their own [Puerto Rican] candidates, those who best bring together their multiple interests," he declared. Other Republican readers seconded García Rivera's claim, one faulting his many compatriots who "for inexplicable reasons line up in droves for the Democrats." Another admonished her audience to "teach a lesson once again to those [Democrats] who deny us, after 25 years of exploitation, the right to have a representative that is genuinely ours."[114] Despite these partisan salvos, Puerto Rican Republicans participated in the "Congreso Borinqueño" along with community leaders across the political spectrum, the participants including not just Democrats and Republicans but also members of workers' organizations and nonpartisan community groups.[115] *Congreso* delegates said they would listen to "voices of the *colonia*" before setting their agenda and solicited *La Prensa* readers' input. A number of readers warned that political and social unity could not be realized without greater attention to the economic problems that still plagued the community. Some also blamed a lack of responsible leadership for the persistence of economic suffering among Puerto Ricans, citing leaders' tendency to bolster their personal power rather than spending political capital on making sure Puerto Ricans earned the benefits of patronage that was their due.[116]

Others disagreed that political weakness was the fault of party leaders, pointing the finger instead at the apathy and social disorganization of migrants. Elite class prejudice colored this point of view, although one such writer sympathetically if paternalistically pointed out that that the "masses in the workshops and factories" working "from morning to night" lacked both the physical strength and the "spiritual desire to pay attention to this or that candidate."[117] Many contributors agreed that poverty hindered community organization but argued that it was discrimination that kept Puerto Ricans poor, and that political and social power offered the only real weapons to protect "our orphaned and abandoned *colonia*." "We must make [leaders] understand the necessity of political brotherhood in a country in which, despite having the right to vote, they consider us foreigners, and the worst of all, [because] we were the last to arrive," said one contributor. This linking of socioeconomic status, identity as "foreigners," and political disempowerment constituted a popular discourse of politics in the *colonia*. It was also joined, now, by a more pronounced cynicism on the subject of recognition by major political parties in the United States. "Beware, brothers," Isabel O'Neill implored her readers, "because we are ALONE."[118]

Some *colonia* residents, and a few islanders who responded to *La Prensa*'s public opinion poll, took this opportunity to point out the necessary connections between island and migrant politics. And with the question of independence more intensely debated than ever before, migrants' U.S.

citizenship, especially their voting power, mattered even to their island compatriots, some of whom contributed to the *La Prensa* debate. Editors of *El Mundo* in San Juan wrote that this "movement for Puerto Rican solidarity" represented the only route to the "effective defense of [migrants'] rights" and "the enjoyment of a better citizenship."[119] Journalist Max Ríos Ocaña, an *independentista*, agreed that Puerto Rican organizations in New York had an obligation to orient their work toward the needs of the island, arguing that migrants constituted a legitimate sector of island political life.[120] Islanders on both sides of the independence question, Nationalist and pro-statehood, now argued that political organizing on the part of migrants in New York would further their respective causes. Santiago Iglesias, the pro-statehood Socialist leader and resident commissioner in Washington, gave the *congreso* a nod of approval. Two pro-independence Liberal leaders—the party president Barceló and a San Juan city official, José Ramírez Santibáñez—also wrote in support of the *congreso*, expounding on the the need for political support from New York if Puerto Ricans were to succeed in their campaign for independence.[121]

The more progressive, left-leaning sector of the *colonia* also backed the *congreso* but was skeptical of the group's "elite tendencies," as one activist put it. Members of the *colonia*'s Left focused on their own organizing campaign, one that would represent the needs of the politicized Puerto Rican working class. Working-class activism in the *colonia* had increased dramatically since 1936, spurred by involvement in the Spanish Civil War as well as in the cause of Puerto Rican nationalism. Although the major U.S. labor unions—most notably the progressive and now-powerful CIO—still largely excluded Puerto Ricans, migrants had persisted in labor activism, largely through the Communist Party. In fact, although the CIO continued to exclude Puerto Ricans in New York City, a group of migrants traveled to Los Angeles in April 1939 to attend the Congreso de Pueblos que Hablan Español, a collaboration spearheaded by a number of Los Angeles–area CIO union locals together with various leftist groups and Mexican and Mexican American organizations—and, behind the scenes, by Communists. The agenda was to build support for Mexican and Chicano workers in the region and confront the problems of naturalization and voting rights that continued to plague that community. Although the focus was on issues specific to Spanish speakers in California, more than a handful of the 136 participating union locals and other organizations came from the East Coast, incorporating as well the concerns of Puerto Rican and Cuban migrants in the United States, including their antifascist politics.[122]

Spanish-speaking leftists in New York redoubled their antifascist activism in the late thirties, still rooted in their support for the Spanish republicans. Jesús Colón and some of his Communist compatriots had built, over the course of the thirties, a strong Puerto Rican presence in the International Workers Order through a "Spanish Section" that claimed over twenty thousand members by 1939. Colón also helped establish a weekly newspaper for the IWO's Hispanic workers, *Verdad* ("Truth"), in 1939, which reported on local concerns (employment, housing, public assistance, and discrimination) as well as on the Puerto Rican status issue and worldwide antifascism. As "the voice of the Hispanic masses" in New York, *Verdad* backed Representative Vito Marcantonio and State Assembly representative Oscar García Rivera, supported labor unions, and applauded the infant Good Neighbor Policy as a way of creating "continental solidarity" against the possibility of fascist incursion. *Verdad* drew on the heterodox positions of not only the Hispanic left in New York (and its counterpart in Los Angeles) but also the larger progressive labor coalitions of the late thirties in the United States, particularly the CIO.

Echoing what historian Gary Gerstle calls "the language of Americanism" of this period's progressive working class, Colón and other *Verdad* writers praised the founding ideology of democratic liberalism in the United States even as they criticized liberals' practice, explaining their embrace of Socialism, Puerto Rican nationalism, and Popular Front goals. More specifically, they dwelled on how the New Deal had failed Puerto Ricans, both on the island and in New York: "To help the Puerto Rican people who see the benefits of the New Deal destroyed by the reactionaries in Congress, a clear agenda is necessary for the *colonia* whose political pressure can make possible, democratically, these improvements for the island. At the same time, the *colonia* here, without work, surviving on miserly relief money, without decent housing, deeply worried about the destiny of its children, needs a mouthpiece that heralds a program of improvement, of unity, and of action to obtain a decent standard of living and decent conditions."[123] It was a diasporic vision formulated by politicized Puerto Rican New Yorkers, one that identified democratic pressure as the antidote to the island's problem with colonialism, and activism as the antidote to the *colonia*'s problem with poverty.

In some ways, Puerto Rican migrants' rhetoric of unity in the *colonia*, and their approaches to local political empowerment, had changed little in the years of political tumult and intensive activism both on the island and in the New York *barrios*. The same class-inflected disagreements about party

Figure 10. Jesús Colón (*front row, fourth from the left*) with other members of the Hispanic Section of the International Workers Order, marking the publication of the antifascist weekly newspaper *Verdad*, 1939. Jesús Colón papers, Archives of the Puerto Rican Diaspora, Centro de Estudios Puertorriqueños, Hunter College, CUNY.

affiliations and electoral strategies shaped the newspaper debates in 1933 and again in 1938. Yet, during this decade, Puerto Rican migrants had in fact developed powerful new strains of political discourse, employing variants of a flexible and inclusive language by which they asserted their place as equal members of a political community of Americans. Invoking along the way the promises of democratic liberalism to its citizens, migrants demanded social equality in the metropole—through concrete claims like access to relief and decent housing—as well as attention to their concerns about their island's status. Thus did Puerto Rican migrants define their rights as citizens of the mainland in the thirties.

Puerto Rican New Yorkers persisted in their assertions of a New Deal–inflected rights discourse even as they failed to achieve the recognition they sought in local and national politics. Although he was backed by both the Republican and American Labor Parties during his 1939 reelection campaign, García Rivera lost his bid for a second term in the State Assembly, a major blow.[124] Unlike the results of African American activists' demands for rights, which were backed by a far-reaching urban constituency that grew steadily, in number and in power, throughout the World War II era—leading to increasing attention by government officials to those demands—

Puerto Ricans' political challenges of the era would be contained, their demands for rights as local citizens and sovereignty for Puerto Rico effectively ignored.

This failure can be attributed partly to the demographic fact that Puerto Ricans lacked the numerical force, even by 1940, to ensure the attention of Democratic Party leaders. But two more important reasons explain their marginalization in New York politics in the 1930s. First, Puerto Ricans' protests against New Deal liberals' actions on the island were forceful enough, threatening the triumphal version of late-thirties liberalism, that Puerto Ricans were edged out of what would come to be defined, later, as "the New Deal coalition," the collaboration of liberal politicians with formerly disempowered groups (most notably African Americans and unionized workers) who sought recognition as equal citizens. As liberal Democrats pulled back from President Roosevelt's promise for the island—of "not merely immediate relief, but permanent reconstruction"—and as they disengaged from the issue of island sovereignty, Puerto Ricans pointed to cracks in the façade of New Deal liberalism.[125] (Indeed, while the president had been active in the planning of the Puerto Rican recovery in 1933 and 1934, by the end of the decade he admitted to having no idea what was going on there: when Rexford Tugwell went to the island in 1941, the president instructed him, "Tell me . . . whether we have got rid of the slums; and whether there is any place on the island to get a safe drink of water." Tugwell reported that El Fanguito, San Juan's most notorious slum, had expanded exponentially since the early years of the Depression.)[126]

*Colonia* activists called attention to liberals' commitment to "freedom and democracy" elsewhere in the world that had yet to be extended to the island of Puerto Rico. In making these claims, migrants were not just elaborating a Puerto Rican, diasporic version of a nascent New Deal language of rights. They were articulating, as well, a critique of liberalism in practice in the local and international arenas. Reflecting on the turn of the new year in 1940, Bernardo Vega wrote that he noticed "ideological changes" in the *colonia*, especially the increase in the number of "staunch advocates of national independence" among his left-leaning compatriots. When Marcantonio gave voice to these views in Congress—he asserted, for instance, that the problem with the PRRA was not corruption but "our ruthless imperialism" that had "strangled the economic life of the country"—his critiques were met with silence.[127]

The other cause of migrants' political marginalization was the fact that political elites still regarded Puerto Ricans in general with the same presumption of their incapacity as citizens that had prevailed at the turn of the century. In congressional debates over the continued funding of the PRRA in 1940, for instance, representatives referred to the "stench" of mismanagement in the agency and to the "gross lack of qualification" and "crookedness" of its officials, whom representatives accused of "stealing." The one defender of the island agency, aside from Marcantonio, concluded his case for a smaller budget cut by asserting that "these little Latin brothers of ours down there . . . need our attention and warrant our care."[128] The still-powerful discourse of Puerto Ricans' incapacity remained firmly rooted both in their "mongrel" racial origins ("these little Latin brothers" failed to fit into U.S. racial categories) and in their identity as colonial citizens: people who lacked the proper knowledge of and commitment to political independence—a tautology indeed—to be deemed true citizens of the nation.

Liberals thus betrayed their unwillingness to recognize mainland Puerto Ricans as a constituency. Puerto Ricans paid a price for their association with Marcantonio, who would within a few years be marked "red." And agitation about island independence, never part of the American public's consciousness to begin with, was easily edged out of the headlines by the shadow of war in Europe. By the early forties, Puerto Rican activists in New York comprised a shrinking set of voices, drowned out in the patriotic commotion of a nation at war; so by the start of the mass migration from Puerto Rico at the end of World War II, Puerto Ricans' particular version of a New Deal rights discourse had been all but redacted from political memory. Amid wave after wave of media vilification of the new migrants after the war, and obsessive public discussion of New York's "Puerto Rican problem," even migrants' liberal defenders of the era sometimes referred to them as "passive" and politically "apathetic," treating them primarily as victims rather than as collaborators. Puerto Ricans, a heterogeneous group possessed of a rich history of political engagement in the city, became virtually invisible as historical actors in New York.

Chapter Four

# How to Represent the Postwar Migration

The Liberal Establishment, the Puerto Rican Left, and the "Puerto Rican Problem"

Before the spring of 1940, most New Yorkers outside of East Harlem or Red Hook in Brooklyn knew little of the existence of the city's rapidly growing population of Puerto Ricans, which had reached about 61,500.[1] Some may have noticed that there were more "Spanish" men shining shoes in Times Square; a few, taking note of a dark-skinned busboy or hotel maid with an accent, may have recalled Eleanor Roosevelt's alarming comments, in the mid-thirties, about the number of Puerto Ricans allegedly suffering from tuberculosis. There was little publicity about the report of Puerto Rican children's IQ test results in 1935, the first published academic study of Puerto Rican migrants in New York, whose pessimistic conclusions about New York's newest group of foreigners got a few paragraphs in the tabloids. Sociologist Lawrence Chenault published a survey of New York's Puerto Rican population in 1938, but it reached only a narrow academic audience and some practitioners in the still-growing field of social work. Even among the region's political elite, only a few were aware of the fact that these foreigners were also U.S. citizens and could not be managed by restrictive legislation. Congressman Thomas Jenkins from Ohio, chair of the Committee on Immigration and Naturalization, had asked his colleagues ominously in 1931: "How many know that the people of Porto Rico, including those in the New York colony, are already citizens? Who knows how long it will be when these new elements shall choose to elect three or four members to the House of Representatives from their group?"[2]

A member of New York City's Chamber of Commerce raised a similar call of alarm about Puerto Ricans' citizenship status in 1935. Following the Harlem riots, Charles Brown Jr., vice president of a Wall Street real estate firm, complained to Mayor La Guardia's office about the role of Puerto Ricans in that upheaval. Brown informed the mayor that in fact Puerto Ricans had been "flooding" into Harlem since the mid-twenties and warned that "this class presents a problem . . . which nobody knows how to handle."

> We find that a tremendous number of [them] are on "relief" of some kind or other. They do not learn to speak English. Apparently their morals are undesirable and they seem to be altogether a pretty nearly hopeless group.
>
> I bring this up because I understand that there is no bar to the immigration of these people. I do not think most people realize how many there are in the city and what a burden they are to the community . . . and in my opinion they are a source of danger from propaganda and from their inability to mix with other elements in the city.[3]

The comments about the Puerto Rican migration in the thirties reflected the range of deficits by which Puerto Ricans were alleged to threaten white American society: biological and intellectual inferiority, incapacity as workers, dependency on relief, susceptibility to disease, and political gullibility. For those who were aware of Puerto Ricans' political status, migrants' potential to participate as citizens was the most threatening aspect of their presence in the city.

As news of war in Europe dominated the U.S. media and concerns about fascism and the "fifth column" inspired Americans to build coalitions at home to face the threat of novel enemies abroad, Charles Hewitt, a writer for the monthly magazine *Scribner's Commentator*, warned New Yorkers to wake up to the threat of the creeping wave of migrants from Puerto Rico in 1940. Hewitt began his incendiary article, "Welcome: Paupers and Crime— Porto Rico's Shocking Gift to the United States," with an apocryphal anecdote about a small boat that had docked in New York the previous month carrying "Porto Ricans," "technically U.S. citizens . . . [who] were exempt from the rigorous physical, political and economic examinations applied to all other immigrants." "Of these 18 Porto Rican men and women," Hewitt informed his readers,

> Ten will be on relief in the minimum period.
> Six will save enough relief money to get one of his relatives up here to go on relief in his turn.
> One has active tuberculosis, and one more will come down with it within the year.
> Two are suffering from malaria.
> Six are thoroughly infected with hookworm.

Three have active syphilis.

All were unemployed back in Puerto Rico.

All will live in the most abjectly poor section of New York's
Harlem—or on the notorious Red Hook waterfront in Brooklyn, two of
the most disease and crime ridden slums in Eastern America.

Two will marry negroes, or live with them.

One of the women will have a child before she knows enough of the
English language or American customs to get any formal aid.

One will be mixed up in the dope business, or commit a sex-crime.

All will find their best chance to work in the "sweat-shop" trades, at
$5–7 a week—although the young girls may do better at prostitution,
particularly if they are under 20 years.[4]

Hewitt called this litany a "statistical history of Porto Rico's refugees" in
the United States and warned his readers that such evidence "holds out
a sentence of early death and subsidized pauperhood" for Puerto Rican
migrants. But even more threatening than this burdensome fate, Hewitt
suggested, was the "one vital immunity" that the European counterparts
of these migrants did not possess: "No Porto Rican may be deported—no
matter how shocking nor how repeated his crimes, nor how many years the
American government must pay his board and keep."[5] This was a nearly
verbatim repetition of Rep. Thomas Jenkins's and Charles Brown's warn-
ings about Puerto Ricans in the thirties, that they were most threatening as
foreigners primarily because their migration could not be stopped.

During World War II, members of Congress quietly addressed a different dimension of what a few commentators were beginning to call the
"Puerto Rican problem." The question of the island's status had been revived as a political issue for the United States amid the growing tide of
decolonization movements during World War II—the war that the Allies
were fighting in the name of freedom and democracy. The relatively few
congressional representatives and senators who listened to testimony regarding Puerto Rico or actually voted on bills related to the island were
more likely motivated by an interest in limiting the New Deal programs being carried out on the island than in participating in debates about Puerto
Rico's sovereignty. By 1947, when the postwar boom inspired a migration
that nearly doubled the city's Puerto Rican population in two years, the
"Puerto Rican problem" was once again popularly understood to be one
created by the island's people rather than its unresolved political status.
The media engaged in a relentless assault on Puerto Ricans, an avalanche

of negative press whose basic outlines were little different from what Irish and Russian and Italian immigrants had experienced in the first years of their settlement in New York. What was distinct, though, was how representations of Puerto Rican identity in the media and popular culture of the 1940s and 1950s served not just to undermine migrants' standing as potential employees or as potential leaseholders in Harlem tenements. Those representations also functioned to depoliticize the presence of migrants whose New York compatriots had marched through Harlem, just a few years before, denouncing U.S. policy in its largest remaining colonial outpost.[6]

As it became more common for observers like Jenkins, Brown, and Hewitt to take note of Puerto Ricans' special status as U.S. citizens, the arguments about the political danger migrants posed became more specific, and subtly but powerfully distinguished anti–Puerto Rican representations of that era from the classic anti-immigrant discourse in which they were rooted. The negative press about Puerto Ricans in the postwar decade also recalled the dimensions of the "racial incapacity" argument of the early debates about extending U.S. citizenship to Puerto Ricans while obscuring the conflicts about empire and colonial governance of the U.S. citizenry that underlay the relationship of migrants to their host country. Puerto Ricans' liberal defenders in New York tended to sidestep the migration's political dimensions as much as their opponents did. Particularly since many of them were in the midst of forging political bonds with their liberal counterparts in the island's Popular Democratic Party (the Partido Popular Democrático, or PPD) in order to launch the island's industrial development program, called Operation Bootstrap, they were no more inclined than Puerto Ricans' detractors to draw attention to the *longue durée* politics of the migration.

In New York, groups of Puerto Rican activists worked hard to keep the politics of the status question at the center of their responses to the negative press, but it was an uphill battle. Wartime patriotic discourses were still a powerful force, even among many politicized Puerto Ricans, and a notable number of migrant activists were being incorporated into the liberal networks surrounding the PPD—which in turn saw migration as a solution to island problems rather than as a symptom of its unresolved colonial relationship to the United States. Finally, the intensification of the cold war in these years meant that any critics of the U.S. government were likely to be vilified as unreliable citizens and marked as susceptible to the dangerous influence of communism and Puerto Rican nationalism.[7] (Two high-profile attacks by Puerto Rican nationalists on the U.S. government, in 1950 and 1954, would underscore the continuing and violent resentment of some migrants concerning the United States' role in Puerto Rico, and seemed to prove the threat posed by politicized Puerto Ricans on the mainland.) By 1957, Puerto Ricans appeared to other New Yorkers, still, to be a dangerous addition to the citizenry of the metropolis, expanding slums, exacerbating crime, overburdening the schools, flocking to the welfare office, and also, potentially, posing a continuing threat as an anti-American political force. That year, the representation of New York Puerto Ricans in *West Side Story* captured their identity as problematic strangers, presenting it in a political vacuum that made the colonial context of Puerto Rico disappear completely.

## Defining and Debating the "Puerto Rican Problem"

### A Rehearsal, 1940

Hewitt's venom sparked a predictable backlash from the *colonia*. Irate letters from *La Prensa* readers, crying libel and misinformation, filled the op-ed page for weeks, and the paper's editors wrote furiously about the feebleness of Hewitt's facts and the injustice of his interpretations. Within two weeks of the article's publication, *colonia* activists had convened representatives of over fifty Puerto Rican and Latino organizations in the city—working-class and elite, as well as Republican, Democratic, Nationalist, and nonpartisan civic and cultural groups—to head up the new "Puerto Rican Protest Committee." At a public meeting attended by hundreds, committee members planned an investigation to refute "every part" of the article and send a petition to the magazine's publisher. They also would enlist the aid of liberal publications ( *The Nation* and *The New Republic*) and island as well as local politicians, including Vito Marcantonio, Oscar García Rivera, and State Representative Sol Bloom. Erasmo Vando, a leftist writer, spearheaded the creation of a new weekly newspaper, *Brújula* ("Compass"), which ran for less than two months and devoted most of its pages to issues related to the furor over Hewitt's article.[8]

Under pressure to respond to the outcry, Hewitt wrote letters of apology to the Protest Committee and to the more elite Latin American Cultural Organization. He began by saying that his article had been written "to help, not to offend, the Puerto Ricans." He explained that "the reaction of any American who reads the article is not one of scorn towards the Puerto Ricans." Rather, the reader would ask himself "how it could be that he did not know before about the intolerable conditions and devastation of a group of American citizens?" In fact, he said, in the very week of the article's publication, three social workers had called him saying, "'Thank God someone has finally given some publicity to the anguish of the Puerto Ricans.'" And already, claimed Hewitt, Americans' interest in Puerto Rico had been piqued enough that *Scribner's* editors had suggested that he write a series of additional articles on unlikely topics—unlikely because they were so controversial—including the Ponce massacre, the imprisonment of Albizu Campos, and the impoverishment of the island under various U.S. governorships. Finally, Hewitt apologized elaborately for having insulted the honor of Puerto Rican women: "I deplore in particular that the material about prostitution has been interpreted as a general insult to the Puerto Rican woman . . . . There are prostitutes of all races. I have heard that the boldest in New York belong to my own race, the Anglo Saxon." Protesters scoffed at Hewitt's attempt to placate them. Erasmo Vando's retort in *Brújula* tersely called Hewitt's reply "not satisfactory."[9]

Although apparently few non–Puerto Ricans reacted to the article and the flurry of protest that it generated, Leonard Covello, an East Harlem educator, activist, and principal of the neighborhood's progressive and multiracial Benjamin Franklin High School, energetically took up the cause of Puerto Ricans' defense. Covello had spoken out against a series of infamous "IQ tests" conducted on Puerto Rican children in 1935, and he was quick to act as an ally to *colonia* residents again in 1940 during the furor over the *Scribner's* article. In the days after the publication of Hewitt's article, Covello called an "emergency meeting" of the East Harlem Committee for Racial Cooperation, a group started by him and his colleagues as part of their creation of the integrated progressive school.[10] The committee pointed out that "our Puerto Rican people are suffering from the same type of prejudice to which all minority groups are subjected to [*sic*] when they first come to this country." The implication was that if Puerto Ricans were "just like other immigrants," the problems they seemed to bring with them would soon be resolved, and migrants would quickly become contributing members of city life, just as early-twentieth-century immigrants had.[11] But debates in Congress at the same time showed how untrue this interpretation was. Puerto Ricans, with their colonial relationship to the United States and their mixed-race origins, were distinctly unlike their European predecessors.

## The "Puerto Rican Problem" in the U.S. Congress, 1940–46

At the turn of the twentieth century, members of the U.S. Congress certainly had been aware of the depth of the problem presented by the U.S. colonization of the island. Countless debates over how to define this "territory" and its legal relationship to the United States were recorded not only in the *Congressional Record* but also in major legal journals throughout the early years of the century.[12] These issues were put to rest, at least officially, with the passage of the Jones Act in 1917, and resurfaced only briefly in Congress when Senator Millard Tydings proposed his retaliatory independence bill in 1936. During World War II, however, federal lawmakers were forced to contend with an increasingly troubling "Puerto Rican problem," as Senator Tydings called the various issues surrounding the island's sovereignty and political status in 1943.[13] The "Puerto Rican problem" became a useful shorthand to describe the increasing number of discussions among politicians, policymakers, and journalists about how to approach the unresolved colonial relationship between the United States and Puerto Rico. Several books written about the problem of Puerto Rico in this period, with titles like *Dynamite on Our Doorstep* and *The Puerto Rican Paradox*, testified to the political intensity of the issue.[14]

The problem of Puerto Rico's sovereignty became an escalating if little-publicized political problem for the United States during the war for several reasons. Rexford Tugwell, in his memoir of his years as Puerto Rico's governor during the 1940s, *The Stricken Land*, recalled that by 1939, Puerto Rico had been identified by lawmakers as both "an important location in the grand strategy which must govern our defense" and as "something of a testing place for American professions of democracy."[15] Since the United States was fighting for liberty abroad, many observers assumed the nation should also strive—anew—to guarantee liberty in its own hemisphere. The nation's continuing failure to address this disconnect in the realm of domestic race relations spurred black civil rights activists to inaugurate a "Double V" campaign during the war, promoting victory abroad and victory for racial justice at home. And domestic pressure was not the only problem. The United States allegedly supported the scores of anticolonial movements that were gathering steam around the world, as the Allies fought for democracy against their Axis enemies in Europe, Asia, and Africa, so wouldn't the United States also have to grant self-determination to *its* colony?

Roosevelt administration officials were beginning to map out some policy changes to address Puerto Rico's sovereignty, but they equivocated on the extent of those changes. The two members of Roosevelt's brain trust who most closely managed Puerto Rican affairs, Secretary of the Interior Harold Ickes and the island's governor Tugwell, had begun to promote the idea of native elections for Puerto Rico's governors, which Roosevelt heartily supported. Privately, they hoped that the election of a native governor would be enough to quell the demands for outright independence.[16] Publicly, however, their rhetoric was expansive—and, it turned out, quite misleading. "The principles for which we are now fighting," Roosevelt proclaimed, "require that we should recognize the right of all our citizens—whether continental or overseas—to the greatest possible degree of home rule."[17] Ickes made an even stronger proclamation on the issue on July 4, 1942, as he commended Puerto Ricans for their wartime sacrifices: "It doesn't matter who the Governor is. . . . When the war ends, the people of Puerto Rico will be free."[18]

A heterogeneous group of Puerto Rican independence activists met in New York in 1943, inspired by these promises and seeking to capitalize on what seemed to be a most opportune moment for radical change. "There exists in the government of the United States a favorable atmosphere for the solution of the status of Puerto Rico, expressed by President FDR himself, and in the . . . form of legislation by Senator Tydings . . . and [other legislation] by Representative Vito Marcantonio," they proclaimed.[19] Once again, Marcantonio followed Tydings's bill with one of his own, adding his acerbic commentary on the realpolitik beneath the merely discursive idealism of U.S. politics: "Whereas in the present global war of survival of the United States against the Axis enemy, the leadership of the United States is impaired by her failure in the case of Puerto Rico to give living content to the principles embodied in the Atlantic Charter, the Declaration of Havana, and other pronouncements of American conferences and leaders guaranteeing the rights of small nations in the Western hemisphere."[20] Predictably, Marcantonio's independence bill received even less attention from his colleagues than had the Tydings bill. Most members of Congress had displayed a persistent and historic indifference to the situation in Puerto Rico. The few representatives who participated in debates on the island cared far more about controlling spending in Puerto Rico—and, now, taking a stand on the incipient cold war—than about the island's political fate. Governor Tugwell had a number of vocal enemies in Congress in the early forties, and if they talked about Puerto Rico at all on the House floor, it was not to address the sovereignty aspect of the Puerto Rican problem. They spent most of their time accusing Tugwell and his colleagues of overseeing "the most expensive planning board under the American flag" and promoting "supergovernment."[21]

In 1946, Jesús T. Piñero was appointed Puerto Rico's first native governor in its 450 years of colonial history. In 1947, the U.S. Congress amended the Jones Act so that thereafter the governor would be "elected by the other citizens of the Island," paving the way for the populist PPD leader Luis Muñoz Marín's election and inauguration the following year.[22] These developments did little to satisfy those who had hoped—indeed, assumed, as Bernardo Vega recalled—that "with the war's end . . . the issue of sovereignty would be speedily resolved."[23] When it became clear just after the war that this resolution was nowhere on the horizon, a coalition of leftist and anti-imperialist groups gathered in New York for a Conference on Puerto Rico's Right to Freedom. In his closing remarks, a Puerto Rican leader of the AFL's Bakery and Confectionery Workers took the measure of the postwar decolonization struggles, and accused North Americans of willful ignorance of their country's colonial control over Puerto Rico. U.S. citizens, he said, decried "British imperialism in India, French imperialism in Indonesia, but they know very little about what the American imperialists are doing in . . . Puerto Rico." The conference passed a resolution demanding "that the United States immediately recognize Puerto Rico's right to self-determination, including independence."[24] Within a year, though, the growing wave of migration from the island to New York City had produced an abrupt shift in the discourse about Puerto Rico. No longer was the "Puerto Rican problem" an issue of colonialism and sovereignty—a political problem, for which the United States sought to escape responsibility. Now, the "Puerto Rican problem" was confined to conflicts surrounding migration—a social problem that could readily be blamed on the migrants themselves.

## The Postwar Migration and the New "Puerto Rican Problem," 1947–48

By 1946, as Americans adjusted to the shift from wartime scarcity to a booming postwar economy, thousands of new Puerto Rican migrants came streaming into New York's ports and airports, lured by abundant industrial jobs and the promise of escape from Puerto Rico's poverty. In step with the wave of newcomers, the press embarked on a new campaign to warn New Yorkers of the dangers of a postwar "Puerto Rican influx."[25] The *New York Times* matter-of-factly reported that the "influx of Puerto Ricans drives up relief costs" and said "officials worried" about the impact of the migrant wave.[26] The tabloid *New York World-Telegram* recounted with great zeal the escalating problems of "perhaps the greatest mass migration in modern history—from poverty-stricken Puerto Rico to lush America, land of hope." The tenor of its articles on the migration in 1947 was alternately mildly sympathetic—toward the migrants who came to New York out of desperation, because they "can't stand starving" on the island—and relentlessly sensationalistic: Puerto Ricans "poured into" East Harlem, sleeping in shifts in apartments housing up to "23 in four rooms"; they swamped the city's schools, creating a "problem in a problem" and burdening teachers with the needs of children from "broken up homes"; they arrived with few skills, landing quickly on relief and causing "crime [to] fester in bulging tenements"; they suffered from venereal disease and tuberculosis, which exacerbated their plight.[27]

Activists in East Harlem responded to the tidal wave of insults with a coordinated defense campaign. Representatives of various Puerto Rican organizations joined together in new coalitions, and individual migrants—and even some islanders—wrote letter after letter to local newspapers. The most common point, in response to the charge that "all Puerto Ricans are on relief," was that "the vast majority" of migrants worked whenever they could, often at low-paying jobs under terrible conditions. Middle-class members of the *colonia* also objected to the claim that all migrants were poor. "We are doctors, lawyers, dentists, businessmen and industrialists . . . and three or four thousand [of us] work for the Federal government," wrote one man. *La Prensa* ran a series during the fall highlighting the accomplishments of Puerto Ricans who occupied prestigious posts in academia and in other professions in New York City as well as the stories of those who had risen from penniless migrant to successful *comerciante* in El Barrio and those who fought for the United States in World War II.[28] A common refrain in migrants' responses to the media assault was that Puerto Ricans were no different from any other immigrant group and that they should not be singled out as a "problem" in this nation of immigrants. The owner of a *colonia* travel agency told a reporter, "A long time back, everybody was beefing about the Irish when they came over. Then they got themselves a Mayor and a Senator and some Congressmen, and people quit bothering about them. Then came the Jews, and they started kicking them about. Next came the Italians, and they got guys like La Guardia and Marcantonio, and they let up on them. But us? We got nobody, so they pick on us. But just you wait—after a while we'll get some guys, and they'll let up on us too. That's the way it goes."[29] Ten years after the brief political success of García Rivera, many Puerto Ricans in New York may have been unaware

Figure 11. Librarian and community activist Pura Belpré leading story hour at Casita María, early 1940s. Lillian López collection, Archives of the Puerto Rican Diaspora, Centro de Estudios Puertorriqueños, Hunter College, CUNY.

of the many "guys" in the thirties whose active engagement in politics had faded during the Second World War and the early cold war.[30]

Among non–Puerto Rican liberals, the most common trope to defend Puerto Ricans against the media assault was to compare their experience to that of previous immigrant groups: the Irish, the Italians, and the Jews had all weathered the storm of xenophobia and discrimination and had gone on to achieve status as real citizens of the city and the nation. Leonard Covello became Puerto Ricans' most important ally in East Harlem, participating in many of the rallies and meetings organized by *colonia* leaders, conducting educational workshops at Benjamin Franklin High School, and writing scores of letters to the press. Covello had begun his career as a community activist defending his own people, the Italians of East Harlem; and as his neighborhood and his school became increasingly populated by Puerto Ricans, he extended his mission of tolerance and "intercultural democracy" to the new migrants as well.[31] While a range of social service professionals, city officials, and social scientists woke up rather abruptly to the so-called Puerto Rican problem in 1947 and scrambled to respond, Covello had already been working on the "adjustment" of Puerto Rican migrants for over a decade. He instituted a special English-language program for the Puerto

Rican students at Benjamin Franklin (an all-boys school) in the late thirties, oversaw the formation of a "Club Borinquén," and started a Spanish-
language parents' group as well. He organized numerous community conferences to address issues like the "civic and educational needs" of Puerto
Ricans in New York.[32] When tensions erupted in 1939 between Puerto Rican and Italian boys in the surrounding neighborhood, Covello organized a
community conference, conducted an "intercultural questionnaire" about
students' racial and ethnic attitudes, and made speeches about tolerance
that emphasized how Puerto Ricans were victims of the same tensions over
ethnic succession that had plagued the Jewish and Italian immigrants who
preceded them.[33] The problems of Puerto Ricans in the United States were,
Covello argued over and over, "no different than the experience of any
other . . . immigrant who leaves his home to settle in a new environment."[34]

Other liberals sympathetic to the plight of Puerto Rican migrants—of
whom there were many in New York's social service and "intercultural"
circles—drew on the same idea, hearkening back to the "nation of immigrants" ideal that liberals in the Progressive era had used to defend the reviled newcomers of their own time. In an address to the American Statistical Association's conference on "the Puerto Rican Population of New York
City" several years later, Clarence Senior elaborated on the place of Puerto
Rican migrants in a "city of immigrants," using the same formulation that
many other liberals relied on: "The interest in Puerto Ricans as migrants *per
se* is heightened by the fact that they are now recapitulating the past history of other waves of immigrants, and they are facing the same social and
economic problems as the earlier immigrants," he told his audience, warning them of the dangers of "our ethnocentrism."[35] His warning implied the
threat of serious consequences; but, in suggesting that the experience of
Puerto Ricans in the United States was a familiar story, Senior's conclusion
also seemed geared toward keeping fears about the "Puerto Rican problem" contained.

Most centrist liberal groups took the same approach, including the New
York office of the Puerto Rican Department of Labor's Migration Division,
an expansion of the thirties' Office of Employment and Identification that
now provided a range of social services for migrants. The Migration Division, whose New York headquarters was staffed largely by Puerto Rican
migrants but was directed from afar by a mix of North American researchers and island officials, represented a melding of island and New York liberal perspectives, and strenuously avoided—publicly, at least—any of the
political questions raised by the migration of Puerto Ricans to the United

States. As part of its public relations effort to counter the negative press about migrants, the office produced a pamphlet called "Attitudes toward Immigrants Old and New." The pamphlet reproduced a series of slanderous quotes about immigrants dating from the nineteenth century as a kind of cautionary tale, reminding its readers that anti-immigrant prejudice had always cropped up in the American media and that it always traded on spurious claims and unfair exaggerations regarding the newcomers' cleanliness, education, and morality.[36] Some Puerto Rican leaders advocated a stronger response, though. Ruperto Ruiz, head of a left-leaning social service agency called the Spanish-American Youth Bureau, suggested that Puerto Ricans follow the lead of African Americans in terms of media relations: "Much of the progress of the colored Continental people today," he said, was "due to the constant 'hammering' of their press . . . [to] demand respect for them." The Puerto Rican media "[has] yet to learn their full lesson on how to serve fully their educational function as an agent of the community and of the Spanish-speaking people and culture," he warned.[37]

Others critiqued the just-like-other-immigrants trope for its failure to acknowledge the racial differences between Puerto Rican migrants and their European predecessors in New York. Colón repeatedly raised such points.[38] Dr. Kenneth Clark, the African American psychologist who would later play a key role as expert witness in the 1954 *Brown v. The Board of Education* case, told a *New York Amsterdam News* reporter in 1952 that although "'we are a nation of immigrants,' and all immigrants have been stereotyped and discriminated against, 'every minority has had the privilege of moving upward—if it is white. . . . The reality of the United States is that assimilation is blocked by skin color.'" Clark criticized the limitations of Puerto Ricans' defenders' rather vague focus on "prejudice." He also said they failed to identify or respond to the specifically racial elements of the hostile discourse about Puerto Ricans, which was in fact suffused with racist imagery and assumptions. During the first few years of the mass migration, the *Amsterdam News* had paid little attention to the Puerto Ricans living in El Barrio, only a few blocks to the east of its offices, but in 1950 it ran a series that looked systematically at Puerto Ricans as "neighbors and fellow sufferers in Harlem," emphasizing Negroes' and Puerto Ricans' shared experience. "So here the two groups are washed up together in 'greater' Harlem still remaining aloof, nationalistic and prejudiced and at the same time enduring identical hardships," began one. The articles challenged prejudices current among black Harlemites, like the notion that Puerto Ricans "[stole] jobs from Negroes and members of other minority groups" and "lazily enjoy . . .

the luxury of taxpayers' money on home relief." Most interesting was the series's commentary on Puerto Ricans' vexed racial identity in New York. Reporter Randolphe White focused on Puerto Ricans' "resentment of being classed as Negro . . . though many of them are according to the criteria of what is Negro in America."[39] This was an implicit suggestion that perhaps Puerto Ricans should give up trying to buck their "inferior status," as he termed it, and follow the lead of African American leaders who were increasingly successful in gaining empowerment through local politics; and it was an argument that an increasing number of Puerto Rican leaders would take up by the mid-fifties.

## The "Puerto Rican Problem" and the Puerto Rican Left

Even more notable than the absence of discussion about race in the typical liberal defense of Puerto Rican migrants was the failure to acknowledge the politics of the migration. Defending Puerto Ricans as a group by arguing that they were "just like other immigrants" helped to situate anti–Puerto Rican discourse within a genealogy of American nativism dating back to the nineteenth century; and certainly there were elements of the old nativism animating this new, postwar version. But this was a weak basis for a counterdiscourse in that it failed to point to the sources of the postwar Puerto Rican migration that were rooted in U.S. colonialism on the island: how economic dislocation on the island had been wrought by the increase in sugar monoculture, then depression, and then, ultimately, by postwar industrialization itself. This liberals' response to the "Puerto Rican problem" failed to reshape the debate, leaving participants to spar over the failures and virtues of the migrants themselves rather than focusing on the structural and political factors that pushed Puerto Ricans out of their island and pulled them toward the metropole.[40] Thus did liberals help clinch the definition of the Puerto Rican problem as a problem of migrants themselves rather than a political problem resulting from U.S. imperial policy.

Members of the Puerto Rican Left—which had shrunk both in real numbers and, to a more obvious degree, proportionally since 1947 (the migrant population was growing by more than thirty thousand per year in the late forties and up to fifty-three thousand a year in the early fifties)—noted the limitations of liberals' bland rebuttals. As they responded to what Bernardo Vega called the "ongoing smear campaign" of 1947, they sought to bring the politics behind the migration to the center of the debate.[41] Casting Puerto Ricans as "just like other immigrants," these critics said, failed to address the sharpest edge of the anti–Puerto Rican discourse, the insinuation that Puerto Ricans were most dangerous because they could not, like other immigrants, be excluded. In a proposal to assemble and publish an almanac of the *colonia* that would emphasize its "positive side" instead of just the "negative factors," Jesús Colón pointed out—sounding much like Leonard Covello—that those who harshly judged Puerto Ricans in New York failed to recognize that they were the newest group of "immigrants" in the city. But he added an incisive description of the migration's genesis: "They have not come here by choice but were forced by the miserable and oppressive conditions imposed by the stupid colonial regime under which our country suffers."[42]

Because of the Left's reduced size and power, the kind of sharp-edged political critique that defined leftist migrants' voice throughout the late forties and early fifties was scarcely heard. Just after the *New York World-Telegram* printed the last article in its "Puerto Rican Influx" series, in late 1947, a handful of Puerto Rican organizations, led by two of the Hispanic lodges of the International Workers' Order (IWO), picketed the offices for what Nationalist Pilar Pacheco called this "cheap and opportunistic journalism." Members of other leftist groups in Harlem, including the black Communist leader Ben Davis and, of course, East Harlem's representative Vito Marcantonio, joined them. *La Prensa* reported that several hundred protesters gathered outside the *World-Telegram*'s offices despite rain and cold. Picketers' placards, written in both Spanish and English, informed passersby that Puerto Ricans were patriots and supporters of the American democratic government and that slandering them amounted to "Hitlerism." Slogans read:

"125,000 Puerto Ricans served in the American armed forces."
"Puerto Ricans did not wait to be drafted, they enlisted voluntarily."
"Freedom to lie and slander—this is not one of the Four Freedoms for which Puerto Ricans fought."
"Goebbels believed in racial superiority—America does not want superior races."
"Defending the rights of minorities is defending democracy."

Leaders of the National Maritime Union of the CIO, acting in solidarity with Puerto Rican protesters, called the recent media attacks an "American version of Nazism," "not isolated incidents but . . . part of the present pattern of whipping up hysteria against minority groups."[43]

Defenders of the Puerto Rican community also used the issue of Puerto

Rican participation in U.S. wars and the symbol of Puerto Rican veterans
to amplify instances of unjust treatment of Puerto Ricans in New York. Bernardo Vega asserted, for instance, that one of the reasons for Washington's
attention to "the demands raised on behalf of Puerto Rico" just after World
War II was the release of figures on wartime casualties by state and territory, showing that only Hawaii had a higher proportion of men wounded
or killed than Puerto Rico.[44] Puerto Rican participation in the war, which
amounted to more than fifty thousand soldiers and a just a handful of officers (the majority of both residing on the island), inspired Puerto Rican
leaders in New York to revisit some of the continuing complaints of World
War I veterans, mostly concerning the failures of the state to extend veterans' pensions to them and their families. However, Puerto Rican World
War II veterans in New York worried primarily about their ability to benefit from the G.I. Bill, particularly because of the time limit placed on the
training benefits, about which a number of them wrote to their congressional representative, Vito Marcantonio. On the mainland, Puerto Ricans
expressed a modest amount of pride in the island's Sixty-fifth Infantry, but
there was little discussion in New York of migrants who were veterans, and
virtually no coverage of them in the New York dailies. La Prensa rarely covered veterans' issues either. Most of the talk about Puerto Rican veterans
emerged, then, in the rhetoric of community activists who used the issue of
Puerto Ricans' wartime sacrifices for the United States to underscore the
injustice of their treatment in the metropole.

Leftist organizing to challenge the anti–Puerto Rican discourse continued throughout the years 1947 and 1948. The New York IWO lodges
to which Jesus Colón was connected held frequent meetings and wrote
scores of memos on strategic responses to the media attacks. Only a very
few non–Puerto Ricans, meanwhile, affirmed this more politicized version
of the community's defense. One was a leader of the Society for Ethical
Culture who reminded his audience, in a 1948 speech broadcast on the radio, that these new migrants came "not from the old world but from the
new," their presence in the United States a direct result of the American
acquisition of Puerto Rico after the Spanish-Cuban-American War. Furthermore, he said, U.S. economic policy on the island, and the ascendancy
of the American sugar companies, had created a climate in which it was
impossible for islanders to live, and so began the "influx" of Puerto Ricans
to New York. "Ministering to the Puerto Ricans in New York," a bulletin
of the New York City Mission Society, referred similarly to "landlessness,
unemployment, and overpopulation" in Puerto Rico as causes for the mi-

gration. Vito Marcantonio participated in many pro–Puerto Rican events, of course, and Jesus Colón recalled that "Marc" convened a conference in 1948 "of all Puerto Rican organizations and prominent people, to organize them in a very broad front." Colón and José Ramos López, a young Puerto Rican attorney from the Bronx who ran that year on the American Labor Party ticket, formed a "policy commission" to address the problems of migrants. Noting the diversity of the organization, in terms of its members' political and professional connections as well as their nationalities, Colón said, "There are great potentialities." "But," he concluded, "we have not got the means."[45]

Colón's lament was vague, only hinting at why, given the sharp critiques these activists formulated, the politics of U.S. imperialism in Puerto Rico was not a more powerful strain of the *colonia*'s response to the anti–Puerto Rican discourse of the late 1940s. One major reason was that the prewar migrant Left had developed an increasingly singular focus on antifascist organizing by the late thirties, leaving little energy for local politics, and this pattern persisted after the war. Spanish-speaking radicals had been animated and united by their support for the republican forces in the Spanish Civil War since 1936; and by 1940, as fascism threatened to spread through Europe, leftists in the *colonia* were staging regular events like the "Smash Hitler and Franco Rally," sponsored by the Comités Femeninos Unidos in Harlem.[46] As Bernardo Vega recalled, "The war absorbed the attention of everyone, and the Puerto Rican community in New York concentrated most of its energies on the war effort. For my part, I too was disposed to do all that was in my power to contribute—pardon the hackneyed expression—however little, to the defeat of fascism."[47] Indeed, Vega, who spearheaded countless community and labor organizing efforts during the thirties, spent the war years working long hours as a translator for the postal service as part of its wartime censorship efforts. Many other Puerto Ricans, including leftist activists, participated in various aspects of civilian defense work and reserved little energy for engaging in local conflicts.[48]

The focus on wartime American patriotism and antifascism meant that politically active migrants pulled back from their previous engagement in "the politics of here," the local politics of the migrant community's place in the city. Their distraction from local-level concerns was one of the reasons that the weaker response of liberals seemed to fill the void when the media assaults began in 1947. IWO leaders in the mid-forties claimed that they continued their efforts to "link . . . the daily problems affecting the Puerto Ricans in the United States . . . with the question of independence for

Puerto Rico." But the group now defined Puerto Ricans' "daily problems" as "the winning of the war, the reelection of President Roosevelt, price control, [and] discrimination," issues (except for the last) only remotely related to the everyday preoccupations of migrants.[49] This trend was certainly not unique to the *colonia*: leftists and liberals around the country tempered their dissent and their oppositional political action on many domestic issues during the war, embracing instead a politics of unity and mainstream antifascist discourse. The shift was particularly notable among immigrant and ethnic activists, who felt even greater pressure to demonstrate their loyalty; historian George Sánchez notes that Mexican Americans' labor militancy was significantly curtailed for precisely these reasons.[50] For Puerto Rican migrants in New York, the decision to focus on wartime unity would constrain the oppositional force of their political voice after the war.

The war focus distracted activist migrants not just from domestic issues but also, to an extent, from Puerto Rican independence politics. Members of the Hispanic lodges of the IWO reported during the war that Nationalist action had been largely superseded by "the present task[s] of all people living in the United States today, which are: the winning of the war and the re-election of President Roosevelt with a progressive Congress of Marcantonios' [*sic*] and Clayton Powells' [*sic*]."[51] Although Puerto Ricans in the IWO asserted that their organizational work emphasized connections among local, island, and international politics, it was overwhelmingly the latter set of issues on which their lodges focused during the war. The affiliated lodges of the Hispanic Section of the IWO issued a resolution on Puerto Rican independence in 1944, asserting that "[an] important relationship to the Puerto Ricans . . . exists between the winning of the war, the election of President Roosevelt, the extension and fight for democracy with other groups here and in Puerto Rico and the important issue of winning independence for Puerto Rico."[52] But they largely abandoned hard-line political action on independence in this era, and finally, by the end of the war, they withdrew their support of the Nationalist Party. This dominant sector of the Puerto Rican migrant Left now formally distinguished its more moderate *independentista* position from that of the *nacionalistas*, thus alienating Nationalist migrants from the heterogeneous coalitions Puerto Rican activists had forged during the late 1930s.[53]

The political fragmentation of the Puerto Rican Left during the war explains, to an extent, why those who tried to emphasize the political dimensions of the migration found themselves unable to speak louder—or at least more convincingly—than the journalists who pandered to the public's taste for racially charged scapegoating. But equally important in diminishing the force of the Left's response to the "Puerto Rican problem" was the red-baiting of *colonia* leftist leaders during these early cold war years. This was a clear message from the media and from local mainstream politicians that there would be a cost to continuing anti-imperialist critiques of the United States. Colón had been called in for a "voluntary appearance" before an FBI committee in 1944 and interrogated about his ties not only to the Communist Party and the International Workers' Order but also to various Puerto Rican Nationalist groups. Antonia Denis, the lone female political leader among Puerto Rican Democrats in Brooklyn, also was reportedly "called to the Democratic political carpet[,] . . . accused of letting herself be used by the communists," in the early fifties.[54] Colón had certainly participated actively in a number of Communist organizations in New York; Denis, firmly anchored in the Democratic machine, most likely had not. In her case, officials' suspicions were based more on assumptions about Puerto Rican leaders' political milieu than on their actual affiliations in New York. They presumed that Puerto Rican activists, already left-leaning, had an "affinity" for Communism, and that their Nationalist sympathies would be readily fueled by the specter of Communism's advance across Latin America.

It was not just the *colonia*'s leadership that was targeted in this early red scare. In addition to the publicity about Puerto Ricans' poverty, ill health, racial mixing, and general moral degeneracy, several journalists were adding a new, more sinister suggestion to the established discourse of danger: that poor Puerto Rican migrants might fall victim to, or were already affiliated with, the Communist Party in the United States. A *New York World-Telegram* editorial, "Welfare, Reds, Puerto Ricans," warned of such connections. It asserted a rising incidence of "cheaters" in the city's Welfare Department, blaming the putative trend on the alleged fact that "key supervisory positions" in the department were "controlled by the Communist-dominated CIO United Public Workers of America." And, wrote the editor, Puerto Ricans, as citizens and potential voters, were "of deep interest to Communists," especially in Marcantonio-dominated East Harlem. A later article in the magazine *American*—one that appeared in 1949, the year that China fell to Communism and the Soviets tested their first nuclear bomb—explained that Puerto Ricans' "misery" made them "highly susceptible to radical ideas" and loyal to Marcantonio, a suspected Communist. According to the article, city officials predicted that by 1960 New York would be home to over a million Puerto Rican migrants. "If that turns out to be the case," its author warned, "and they vote as overwhelmingly for extreme left-wing leaders as they do now, they could prove a powerful and . . . sinister political force." The implication was that it was in the city's self-interest to fix the problems that had inspired "a great Communist-breeding slum to grow up in the heart of our largest city."[55]

Like the other aspects of the anti–Puerto Rican discourse, this red-baiting sounded much like attacks on Jews and other Eastern European immigrants in the early twentieth century who were also targeted as political radicals. The prospect of Puerto Rican radicals' political influence, however, was even more threatening since they could not be deported as seditious aliens. It was in this context of heightened cold war hysteria in 1949 that a coalition of New York and PPD liberals would wrest control of the "Puerto Rican problem" discourse from the Left, turning it into a tool for their respective agendas of liberal ascendancy in New York and economic development in Puerto Rico. Fixing the problem of Puerto Ricans' "dependency," in both senses—migrants in New York dependent on government handouts, and economic and political institutions on the island dependent on their U.S. counterparts—became a central focus of the liberal coalition that came to Puerto Ricans' defense in 1949.

### The "Puerto Rican Problem" and the Liberal Machine

During the summer of 1947, at the height of the media hype about New York's "Puerto Rican problem," Mayor William O'Dwyer gave a press conference following a meeting with President Harry Truman in which he asserted that "there is no Puerto Rican problem." And, he said, if there were such a problem, "I don't know what I could do about it," adding that he had not even discussed the matter of the Puerto Rican migration with President Truman. Yet, only three days later, O'Dwyer held a meeting in New York with Puerto Rico's governor, Jesús Piñero, to discuss the living conditions of Puerto Rican migrants there.[56] Planners in Puerto Rico, and some North American social scientists, were beginning to put pressure on both the Puerto Rican and U.S. governments to provide formal, coordinated assistance to the growing population of migrants in New York. Piñero backed the creation of an Emigration Advisory Council in San Juan during the summer of 1947. Six months later, policymakers in both places facilitated the creation of a Bureau of Employment and Migration in New York (later known as the "Migration Division") that would expand on the existing Office of Employment and Identification, offering a full range of social services to new migrants.[57]

In the fall of 1949, just weeks before his bid for reelection, O'Dwyer formally announced his own administration's plans to address the problems of the Puerto Rican migration wave. The focal point would be a Mayor's Advisory Committee on Puerto Rican Affairs (MACPRA), which, notably, he had first called the Advisory Committee on the Puerto Rican Problem. The MACPRA, composed of forty-six members from public and private welfare agencies and educational and philanthropic organizations, was charged with formulating a program "for constructive, and comprehensive improvement" of the migrant community, "a group of citizens whose overwhelming majority consisted of self-supporting hard-working individuals making a contribution to the city's well-being."[58] The MACPRA would be a cooperative effort between Puerto Rican and Manhattan liberals to establish services and networks to help the struggling migrants. Fifteen of the original forty-six members of the committee were Puerto Rican, and four additional members were of other Latin American descent. (When the committee expanded to seventy-five members in the early fifties, at least twenty of the thirty-two Hispanic members were Puerto Rican.) O'Dwyer appointed Raymond Hilliard, commissioner of the city's Department of Welfare, as head of the committee.[59]

Critics of O'Dwyer complained that he had allowed his political ally Manuel Cabranes, director of the Migration Division office, to make all the recommendations for appointments. Jesús Colón argued that O'Dwyer's political motivations caused him to ignore the important expertise and experience of many other Puerto Rican leaders in the city—leftist leaders, he meant. "The question is," wrote Colón, "'Were they appointed in order to line them up on the side of the present City Administration and/or to favor publicity for the Director of the Office of the Government of Puerto Rico in New York?'"[60] Vito Marcantonio, who was running against O'Dwyer in the mayoral race that year, did not hesitate to point out the campaign-season timing of the establishment of the MACPRA. "Your latest maneuver is a campaign device to make the people forget your gross negligence towards our citizens of Puerto Rican origin," he said.[61] Just after the committee's creation was announced, O'Dwyer gained the backing of major *colonia* Democratic leaders Laura Santiago and Dr. José Cesteros and, more important, both San Juan's mayor, Felisa Rincón de Gautier, and the populist leader who had just become the island's first elected governor, Luis Muñoz Marín.[62] When Mayor Rincón de Gautier paid Mayor O'Dwyer a visit in

October, O'Dwyer said to her, setting the tone for the spin control that was a central goal of the committee: "Let us stop talking about a Puerto Rican problem. Let us talk about a gift an overcrowded island is offering us."[63]

One of the most important areas of the committee's accomplishments concerned welfare, both reducing the number of migrants who relied on city and federal relief programs and challenging the public's perception of Puerto Ricans as "welfare cheats." The number of Puerto Rican migrants receiving welfare assistance had been a focal point of the media assault since 1947. Welfare was an easy target, especially since at that time the city Department of Welfare did not record the race or nationality of its clients; those who criticized the Puerto Rican migration could continue to exaggerate migrants' dependency on public assistance using unclear data as evidence. The hysteria about Puerto Ricans and welfare was part of a broader concern in the late forties and early fifties about the growth of welfare dependency in the nation. Media attention to welfare focused mostly on welfare fraud, committed by "welfare cheats" and "chiselers" of all races and exemplified by the "woman in mink" who allegedly collected relief while living in a New York hotel where she stashed over sixty thousand dollars in cash.[64] Commissioner Hilliard's 1949 report determined that about 10 percent of Puerto Ricans collected welfare benefits, compared to the citywide average of 4.2 percent.[65]

Hilliard focused on two strategies to reduce Puerto Ricans' reliance on welfare. First, he asked the mayor to suspend the Welfare Department's three-year minimum residency requirement for social workers, so that it could hire fifty Puerto Rican social workers to better serve the migrant population of welfare clients. Within two years, Hilliard reported, the Welfare Department's Puerto Rican staff rose from 20 to 250, most of them professionally trained. Second, by the spring of 1950, the MACPRA had determined that one of the critical elements in improving the conditions of Puerto Rican migrants in New York was to ease the pressure for migration by ameliorating the economic conditions on the island; and the best means to achieve this goal, said the committee, was to extend federal welfare benefits to Puerto Rico. In April, the MACPRA made a formal recommendation to Congress to change the federal Social Security law so that benefits like Aid to Dependent Children and Old Age Insurance would be payable to Puerto Rican islanders. Before this change in the provision of federal benefits, noncontributory federal welfare benefits were not available to Puerto Ricans.[66] Welfare Commissioner Henry McCarthy declared in 1952 that Puerto Ricans had made "faster progress than any other immigrant group."

He considered the rate of Puerto Ricans on public assistance—about 9 percent that year, down from more than 10 percent in 1949, compared to a citywide rate of about 4 percent—to be "not high" given the "language barrier and the fact that they are the latest immigrant group and the largest to come here in many years." A year later, McCarthy estimated that Puerto Ricans, by that point 4.7 percent of the city's population, constituted only 7.5 percent of the city's relief rolls.[67] The committee, in its 1953 report, wrote that in 1949, "listening to [Puerto Ricans'] critics, one would have believed that every Puerto Rican was a Communist, a criminal, and on relief."[68]

Appearing to respond effectively to the most high-profile social problem of his first term as New York's mayor, O'Dwyer had handily won his reelection bid in 1949. The MACPRA not only focused on improving the public image of New York's Puerto Ricans, it also sought to reshape the representation of Puerto Rico's connection to the United States, showing the island to be increasingly less dependent on the United States. Rather than focusing exclusively on the dangers of the Puerto Rican migration to New York, now, the media began trumpeting the possibilities of this "showcase of democracy in the Caribbean." Early in 1950, *Newsweek* ran a feature article on the island's ambitious development program: "Once America's poor relation, Puerto Rico is making a determined bid for economic health," declared the magazine.[69] It also praised Puerto Ricans' increasing autonomy in the form of Public Law 600, which would be signed by President Truman on July 4, 1950, and would give Puerto Ricans the power to write their own constitution. (The U.S. Congress retained veto power over the document, however).[70] The week after Truman signed the law, the *Washington Post* editorial page trumpeted this moment of "Puerto Rican Progress," asserting that with the new law, "the American example of responsible stewardship toward dependent territories was carried forward in noteworthy fashion." Two years later, when the new Puerto Rican constitution took effect, the island inaugurated the "*Estado Libre Asociado*," or "Commonwealth," of Puerto Rico, and a *Post* editorial concluded, smugly, that "a more effective riposte to Soviet yelpings about American imperialism could scarcely be presented to the world."[71] Governor Muñoz Marín was at least as sanguine. The next year, when islanders ratified their new constitution, Muñoz declared that now "the United States of America ends every trace and vestige of the colonial system in Puerto Rico."[72]

Yet there were many critics, aside from Nationalists, who disagreed with these interpretations of the political meaning of the commonwealth. Academic observers who stood outside of the PPD–New York liberal alliance tended to be skeptical of the political promises of Muñoz Marín's "third way." An article in a political science journal in 1953 referred to Puerto Rico, still, as a "dependent area" that remained "a political and economic liability" for the United States and "proved increasingly embarrassing to the US in the forum of world opinion." In fact, the author asserted, the actual discussions in Congress about the new status, involving Muñoz Marín, resident commissioner Fernós Isérn, and their congressional supporters, had been "far more modest in nature" than the way they represented the issues to the public. Indeed, a Senate report on the proposed new law just a month before its passage admitted that it "would not change Puerto Rico's fundamental political, social, and economic relationship to the United States."[73] When migrant leftists like Jesús Colón and Bernardo Vega referred to Puerto Rico's new constitution as "perfumed colonialism," they were, in fact, capturing creatively the judgment they shared with mainstream academic observers and members of the U.S. Senate.

Nationalists, meanwhile, exploded in outrage over what they saw as Muñoz Marín's plan to make permanent Puerto Rico's dependent relationship to the United States. They had seen Muñoz Marín as their primary antagonist since his party formally renounced its independence platform in 1944. Now, within a couple of months of the passage of Public Law 600, island Nationalists staged coordinated attacks on public buildings in a handful of Puerto Rican towns and attempted to storm the Governor's Palace as well. Island news sources reported that at least twenty-eight people, most of them Nationalist rebels, died in the conflicts. PPD officials and the island's mainstream press at first called the events a "nationalist revolution," even as they claimed, by the end of the first day of attacks, that a "numerically insignificant" group was involved and that police had the situation under control. Several days later, Muñoz Marín retracted the "revolution" label, calling the Nationalists "fanatics who want to impose their will by means of terror." In typical cold warrior terms, Muñoz Marín asserted as well that the Nationalists had been spurred by "communist agitators."[74]

Several days later, two Nationalists attempted to assassinate President Truman at Blair House in Washington, DC. One, Griselio Torresola, a resident of East Harlem, was shot dead by Secret Service agents, and the other, Oscar Collazo, who lived in the Bronx, was wounded.[75] Whereas the Nationalist uprising in Puerto Rico had gotten little attention from the U.S. press, the assassination attempt presented a new challenge for the public relations work of the MACPRA, which immediately condemned the attacks, as did the leaders of most of the major Puerto Rican organizations in the city (excluding the Nationalist groups, of course).[76] Noting the immediate public relations fallout from the assassination attempt, *El Diario* editors lamented that the "Puerto Rican citizens of New York" had just begun to recover from the negative press of the late forties and prove their value to the city. New York liberals rushed to defend the group, trying to separate the largely "moderate" New York community from the island extremists. "Neither New Yorkers nor American citizens should judge the more than two million loyal Puerto Ricans for the absurd actions of two nationalist fanatics," said state senator Alfred Santangelo, up for reelection in the Harlem-Yorkville district. Harris Present, counsel for both the Spanish-American Youth Bureau and the Puerto Rican Employees Association, opened his speech at a convention of Puerto Rican organizations with the same observation. "My suggestion," he continued, "is that politics be left at home and that the Puerto Rican population unify its efforts in New York irrespective of race, political opinion, or religious conviction."[77]

The assassination attempt inspired a heightened sense of unity between New York liberals involved in migrant affairs and the many Puerto Rican New Yorkers who supported Muñoz Marín and the PPD. The fallout of the crisis also linked the PPD leadership even more closely with its liberal allies in New York. With Albizu Campos arrested and held once again in federal custody, liberals and PPD leaders were confident that they had reduced the threat of allegedly Communist-influenced Nationalist agitation on the island, in New York, and even throughout the Americas. Indeed, a wordy *El Diario* headline announced, "It is believed in Washington that the attack against the Pres. may cause repercussions in the continent; The fear is that elections in Guatemala may be influenced." The following day, the paper reported on an incident in Havana, Cuba, in which police dispersed a demonstration of students who said they were inspired by events in Puerto Rico.[78] The strengthening alliance between New York liberals and PPD leaders and planners—fueled by a shared fear of radicalism—would also serve to bolster the image of the developmentalist program Operation Bootstrap. At the 1953 Conference on Migration in San Juan, attended by Migration Division leaders and various New York liberals, commonwealth officials took pains to champion the "splendid strides" being made "in raising the levels of living in Puerto Rico"—not only a cheer for a newly autonomous island government and for Operation Bootstrap but also, more to the point, a renunciation of the island's dependency on the United States.[79] The implication was that if the Puerto Rican government had gained a degree of independence from the U.S. government, then migrants would, by extension, also become both less economically dependent and less susceptible to political extremism.

This certainly was the image of Puerto Ricans that New York's mainstream media was beginning to tout by 1954, a year after the peak of migration. In 1951, journalist Babby Quintero had written a series of articles for *La Prensa* called *"inmigrantes y pandilleros,"* an impressionistic view of the lives of recent newcomers in New York City whose title was a clever play on words: *pandillero* could mean "member of a gang," as in "hoodlum," or it could mean "member of *the* gang," as in "someone who belongs"—in this case, belonged in the *"gran metrópoli,"* New York. Behind Quintero's facile assertion that New York was a "melting pot . . . that offers equal opportunities to all citizens" lay the reality that the popular perception of Puerto Rican migrants was more often as "gang members" than "members of the gang." Yet the MACPRA and other liberal advocates had managed to chip away substantially at this image. By the mid-fifties, mainstream press coverage about Puerto Ricans in New York had shifted noticeably. Now journalists, rather than focusing on the burden that migrants placed on city services, wrote most often about how city programs and officials were managing to help Puerto Ricans in need, headlining the small celebrations as well as the big dreams of El Barrio residents.[80] The contextualization and the tone of much of the media attention was now often sympathetic, emphasizing, for instance, how migrants struggled with "barriers of language and discrimination" and how many Puerto Rican children found "school life hard" because of homesickness and trouble with English.[81] Journalists began writing more in-depth profiles of migrants and their struggles, imbuing these human-interest stories with a sensitivity about migrants' experiences that underscored the structural nature of their problems—with housing, unemployment, and job discrimination, for example—as well as the subjective quality of their suffering.[82]

The focus of social services related to Puerto Ricans also had changed. In addition to discussing, studying, and solving migrants' problems, many initiatives now emphasized the facilitation of "understanding" between New Yorkers and the Puerto Rican newcomers. The United Parents Association of the Board of Education organized a series of "Goodwill workshops" in 1953 designed to challenge stereotypes about Puerto Rican children and their families.[83] The Urban League and the Migration Division cosponsored a "study trip" to Puerto Rico in 1954, to provide affiliates with the chance to learn firsthand about migrants' homeland. The American Jewish Committee and the Council of Spanish-American Organizations collaborated on a pamphlet for educators and civic and religious leaders designed to arm its audience with not only "basic facts" about Puerto Ricans but also a clear understanding of "what *not* to say," a list of injunctions that included "*don't* refer to a Puerto Rican as an immigrant"; "*don't* forget that when a Puerto Rican migrates to the mainland, he has all the rights and privileges of every other first-class citizen"; and "*don't* create a Puerto Rican stereotype based on the lower working classes."[84] Educators, rather than worrying over the dire state of the "Puerto Rican problem" in the schools, as many had done in the late forties, now wrote about the complexity of Puerto Ricans' "acculturation." One City College professor of education declared that "the newcomers offer a stimulating challenge to the teacher" and asserted smugly that, in the case of Puerto Ricans, "[the schools] have been able to avoid many of the blunders made with earlier minority groups in the crude process of so-called Americanization."[85]

The media had become decidedly upbeat about political prospects of the migrant community. "The City Fathers Love the Puerto Ricans—at the Polls," declared a *New York Post* article in 1953. A conservative estimate put "the Spanish vote" at one hundred thousand, meaning not only that candidates were taking seriously their campaigns in Puerto Rican neighborhoods but also that party leaders were beginning to consider backing Puerto Rican candidates—suggesting, potentially, a major increase in migrants' political power in New York.[86] The Spanish-language daily *El Diario de Nueva York*, founded in 1948, commissioned a survey in 1955 of the "Spanish market" in New York in order to attract advertisers to its growing paper. The survey pamphlet trumpeted the growing population of Puerto Ricans, its "spread" to Queens and the Bronx, and the large size of Puerto Rican families and their expanding consumer needs. It concluded, "With a population already surpassing that of Boston, Mass., with a purchasing power rapidly approaching that of the average New York family, this vast and surging development of New York's Spanish-speaking market is vitally influencing the entire retail complexion of New York City."[87]

Employers, too, were turning their attention to the benefits rather than the liabilities of Puerto Ricans as workers. A 1956 feature on Puerto Rican manufacturing workers in the magazine *America Continental* praised the rising skill levels among Puerto Ricans employed on the mainland, quoting supervisors and managers from various industries with comments like "Mr. George B. Curl, Employment Department Supervisor, is extremely satisfied with the group, rates them superior in cleanliness, very good in punctuality, very good in productivity, and states that he intends to hire more."[88] Historian Carmen Whalen notes that the enthusiastic embrace of Puerto Rican workers in the mid-fifties was intensified by the cold war, which inspired "a patriotic tone to the hiring of citizens, including Puerto Ricans." During a moment in the national culture when the idea of hiring foreign workers was regarded as both unpatriotic and potentially dangerous, liberals argued that migrants from a U.S.-dominated island were a safe and responsible choice for employers.[89]

The shift in media coverage of Puerto Ricans, and their own efforts to burnish their image in the city, did not mean that they were no longer reviled by the public. No matter how many statistics showed that most Puerto Ricans were not on relief, for instance, resentful New Yorkers persisted in thinking otherwise. An anonymous letter to Leonard Covello, who headed the Education Sub-committee of the MACPRA, offered a set of reasons "as to why I do not like Puerto Ricans": "I'll tell you why. First, it is too darn easy for them to get on relief. Just how easy, you can find out for yourself by taking a ride with any taxi driver. He will tell you that the first place a Puerto Rican goes is directly to a relief office, direct from the plane."[90] One informant in a West Side neighborhood study expressed the same assumptions about Puerto Ricans. "They arrive . . . [and] in a week's time they are on relief. Children get free lunch. They have T.V. sets. Why not investigate where the money comes from?" he demanded. Another man quoted in the study pointed out that "the color of the migrant is different today." Their racial marking, he suggested, put them in a separate category, and they could not be expected to follow the path of steady achievement forged by earlier European immigrants.[91]

Nor were all in New York's liberal establishment convinced of the improved image of Puerto Ricans—or of the effectiveness of the MACPRA in salvaging that image. Some of the MACPRA's early supporters and collaborators had grown impatient with what they saw as the committee's ineffectiveness. The Protestant Council of New York charged that after four years of subcommittee investigations and "blocking by some of the commissioner members . . . and sometimes distortion of committee activities by political ambitions, some of the Puerto Rican leaders and committee members feel that accomplishments have been so few as to question the value of continuing the organization."[92] Although Robert Wagner, the Democratic winner of the 1953 mayoral race, pledged more financial and administrative support than his predecessor to the MACPRA, he disbanded the committee in 1955, promising that instead Puerto Rican leaders would be given a prominent place in the newly created City Commission on Intergroup Relations.[93] Puerto Rican leaders who remained outside the MACPRA and Migration Division circle heartily supported Wagner's move. Harris Present, a liberal activist and counsel to the Spanish-American Youth Bureau, wrote the New York Times to explain that the demise of the MACPRA was a good thing for Puerto Ricans, since "from this point on all problems concerning Puerto Ricans and other minority groups would be handled in their proper frame of reference—namely, a commission that will view these problems in terms of their interrelationship to the city as a whole."[94]

In 1955, when Wagner retired the MACPRA, it was still a distinct challenge to convince the public to see the problems of Puerto Ricans in such structural terms. And, of course, it was generally the most marginalized activists in the colonia, now, who argued that "these problems" had deeper roots in a society whose colonial status was largely unacknowledged in the metropole. Neither Wagner nor other New York and island liberals publicly linked the disbanding of the MACPRA to the Nationalists' most violent and high-profile protest on the mainland the year before, but there must have been a connection. In 1954, on the anniversary of both the signing of the Jones Act and the extension of U.S. citizenship to Puerto Ricans, a group of four Nationalists had entered the gallery of the United States Congress with guns and opened fire, wounding five representatives. A New York Times editorial the next day warned against "libel on the friendly Puerto Rican people" and admonished that "it would be a grave injustice today to indict Puerto Rico for the foul deed of a few demented citizens." Good citizens should remain on guard: "We live in a period of high nervous tension, an explosive era in which sparks are continually flying."[95] Puerto Rican nationalism, a movement whose explosiveness seemed powerful enough to add sparks to other powder kegs across Latin America (PPD officials regularly accused island Nationalists of colluding with socialist leaders in Guatemala and Bolivia in the early fifties), still haunted the cold war imagination in the United States. In spite of the elevated image of Puerto Ricans in New York, tensions generated by Puerto Rico as a "problem for the United States" continued to shape the experience not just of "a few demented citizens" but of all Puerto Ricans there.[96]

## West Side Story and the Politics of Representation

With the mayor's Puerto Rican advocacy group disbanded, and the memory of the violent Nationalist strike in Washington still recent, members of the elite Federación de Sociedades Hispanas met in late 1955 to plan the first Hispanic Parade in New York. They cited the parades in the Irish and Italian communities as models, saying that Spanish speakers in New York also needed a means to display their strength and unity. After two moderately successful years of the Hispanic Parade, a group of Puerto Ricans began lobbying to change the parade from a "Hispanic" event to a "Puerto Rican" one, a move that opened up bitter controversy. Puerto Rican leftist and Nationalist activists argued that their national community needed to pull together and call attention to its particular struggles, accusing the defenders of the pan-Hispanic parade (including Puerto Rican leaders like Oscar García Rivera, Antonia Denis, and Luisa Quintero) of *"antipuertorriqueñismo."* Although the challengers did not wrest control of the planning, they did succeed in changing the event's name. The Puerto Rican Parade became an enduring symbol of community pride.[97]

The fractious negotiations that changed the Hispanic Parade to, eventually, the Puerto Rican Day Parade took place just weeks after the opening of a new musical featuring Puerto Ricans. *West Side Story* hit Broadway in September 1957 and charmed audiences with its Romeo-and-Juliet story of

Figure 12. The first Hispanic Parade, 1956. After contentious debate, the name of the event was changed to the Puerto Rican Parade in the late 1950s; by the early 1960s, it was called the Puerto Rican Day Parade. Justo A. Martí photographic collection, Archives of the Puerto Rican Diaspora, Centro de Estudios Puertorriqueños, Hunter College, CUNY.

forbidden love between a Puerto Rican girl and an Italian American boy in New York. The show had been conceived in 1949, by Arthur Laurents, the show's writer, and Leonard Bernstein, its director, as "East Side Story," the tale of a tragic romance between a Jewish girl and an Italian American boy. However, as the media in Los Angeles, where Laurents and Bernstein were working at the time, began headlining the rise in gang fights and juvenile delinquency among Chicano youth there, the pair decided to design a more contemporary version of the old immigrant story. Framing the plot around a Puerto Rican instead of a Jewish girl, they felt, would add "color" to the musical. They shifted the story from the Lower East Side to the West Side—to Hell's Kitchen, in fact, a poor Midtown neighborhood that would be demolished just a few years later to make way for Lincoln Center and its associated urban renewal projects.[98] Especially after the Broadway musical was turned into a film that won ten Academy Awards in 1961, an enduring image of the Puerto Rican in New York was etched into the national imagination.

In fact, it was a split image, manufactured from a combination of "good immigrant" and "dangerous other" stereotypes. (Literature scholar Roberto Márquez, a teenager in El Barrio in the late fifties, described his 1957 self as "an already temperamentally suspicious spik and spade intelligent enough to feel insulted by the gossamer counterfeit of *West Side Story*.")[99] Typical liberal interpretations of the postwar Puerto Rican migration were most prominent in *West Side Story*: its setting and characters, built on classic imagery of American immigration and ethnic conflict transplanted from the early-twentieth-century Lower East Side to the mid-century West Side, suggested that Puerto Ricans were struggling just like previous immigrant groups. In "América," one of the show's most famous songs, the tragic heroine Anita sang passionately about her desire to achieve the American dream—just like other immigrants. She was portrayed not just as a dreamer but as a striver, willing to work hard and follow the rules to "make it" "in *América*."

On the other hand, *West Side Story* traded on the image of the dark and foreign Puerto Rican migrant who, despite striving for the dreams of America, brought intractable social problems to the city. Anita's version of life in Puerto Rico—"You ugly island / Island of tropic diseases / . . . Always the population growing / And the money owing"—confirmed that it was a place to be fled, a source of the very kind of "refugees" that Hewitt had warned New Yorkers about in 1940. Their racial otherness was as much a part of *West Side Story* as it had been a part of Hewitt's and other journalists' sensationalizing; and it was now, unlike in the thirties, portrayed as something distinct from Negro darkness. Journalist Christopher Rand published a book on El Barrio the same year that *West Side Story* made its debut, and in trying to make sense of Puerto Ricans' racial identity in a New York context, he wrote: "I have heard that a relatively small percentage of Puerto Rico's dark inhabitants—as against its light ones—are coming to New York, but this too is hard to verify. If you walk through East Harlem you get the impression that a *large* percent of dark Puerto Ricans have come up, but then East Harlem is a ghetto, from which the dark ones can escape less easily than the light."[100] And although the show offered a dose of liberal sympathy for those who, like Anita, tried to succeed in the United States, the more dominant symbols were those of the knife-wielding Puerto Rican youth who was inescapably drawn to delinquency and violence. The young Puerto Rican men in the play were portrayed as even more predatory than their "native" gang counterparts, shifty foreigners who would satisfy their hunger for power by violent means. As one of the Italian American Jets put it, their rivals in the Puerto Rican Sharks "bite hard . . . and we must stop them now."[101] Although local politics played no part in the story

Figure 13. Anita Vélez Mitchell as Anita in *West Side Story* in a Lambertville, New Jersey, production in the early 1960s. Erasmo Vando papers, Archives of the Puerto Rican Diaspora, Centro de Estudios Puertorriqueños, Hunter College, CUNY.

line, the idea of "stopping" the volatile Jets resonated with the fifties' sense of urgency about stopping the dangerous Puerto Rican radicals who were certainly anti-American and possibly also red.

Like the liberal discourses that informed it, the show's version of the postwar Puerto Rican experience silenced any suggestion of the political underpinnings of the migration. The "terrible island" that Anita sang about in her paean to America was terrible, presumably, because its backward people couldn't harness progress and modernity—not because, as many Puerto Rican activists argued, half a century of colonial rule had contributed to economic dependency and the fragmentation of the island's political sector.[102] Although Puerto Rican and American liberals had managed to whittle away at the damaging imagery of the anti–Puerto Rican campaigns of the postwar period, *West Side Story* illustrated the power of those images to set Puerto Ricans apart from the mainstream and to silence or at least obscure their claims for recognition as a group with legitimate demands on their liberal democratic society.

In his analysis of American colonialism in Puerto Rico at the turn of the century, historian Gervasio Luis García argues that "in the absence of other evidence, the representation (the discourse or the pictures) is privileged over other human activities. If we do not endeavor to compare what is said with what exists, the discursive realities will monopolize our attention, and the non-discursive realities will be forgotten or passed over as insignificant."[103] Certain nondiscursive realities of Puerto Rican New York in the fifties—the still-active if diminished Left; the noncommunist and nonviolent *independentistas*; the racially varied population with heterogeneous political views living in a vibrant if impoverished community—were certainly passed over. They were often, also, deliberately distorted. In a vignette in Dan Wakefield's 1959 book *Island in the City*, the most sensitive and complex of the many journalistic portraits of Puerto Rican New Yorkers in the fifties, a photographer from a New York daily is sent to East Harlem to take pictures of Puerto Rican children "playing in the garbage." But it was Sunday, and he soon realized that "the children were scrubbed and dressed in their finest clothes." The photographer, worried about fulfilling his assignment, "ran to a garbage can, yanked off the lid, and motioned to the silent, staring children. 'Hey kids—c'mere—over here! Let's play.'"[104] Ten years after the postwar migration began, stories about the human fallout of the Puerto Rican problem still sold newspapers, but only if the nondiscursive reality of the island's political economy—the background of the migration—was stricken from the story.

Chapter Five

# How to Study the
# Postwar Migrant

Social Science, Puerto Ricans, and Social Problems

|||||||||||||||||||||||||||||||||||||||||||||||||||||||||||||||||||||||||||||||||||||||||||||||||||||||||||||||||||||||||

In his 1958 portrait of El Barrio, journalist Christopher Rand described
a New York City Health Department worker's complaint about the major challenge he faced in conducting successful public health campaigns
in Puerto Rican neighborhoods: "They hadn't yet developed community
groups through which this could be done." "And," Rand continued, "other
city officials told me that no minority group had grown strong in New York
until it had raised up its own leaders. . . . The Puerto Ricans, it seems, are
not 'joiners' by tradition, and so they have a hard time fitting into this pattern of ours."[1] Although the worst of the vilification campaigns against
Puerto Ricans had subsided by this point, and at least a few of New York's
power brokers had begun to acknowledge the potential value of Puerto
Rican workers and voters in the city, Rand's description of Puerto Rican
communities shows that they were still largely invisible as social and political actors in the city. They were recognized not as active citizens but as
pliable subjects who could, if properly refashioned through education and
social services, fit into the city's social and economic framework—and into
the developmentalist goals of island leaders.

An increasing number of centrist liberal Puerto Rican leaders, part of
a new coalition of liberals and social scientists on the island and in New
York, were willing to cooperate with this refashioning agenda in the fifties.
They mistook their own sense of inclusion for the possibility that Puerto
Ricans in general would be acknowledged as equal citizens in mainland
society. Members of the liberal-PPD (Partido Popular Democrático) coalition refused to sanction any political action that challenged their vision of
Puerto Rican development, which depended on managing the migration to
New York.[2] Puerto Rican political action in New York that failed to fit into
this relatively narrow agenda was marginalized, its proponents threatened
and red-baited during the fifties. Representations of Puerto Ricans in the
late forties and early fifties had already reinforced a depoliticized vision of

the migration, sweeping arguments about colonialism under the rug. The growing interest of social scientists in Puerto Ricans reinforced this depoliticization, implicitly casting migrants as weak citizens who could not be taken seriously as political actors in New York.

By the late fifties, this dynamic had created the appearance of justice being done on behalf of Puerto Ricans in the realm of social service and education—and to an extent, at least on the surface, in the labor movement as well—but economic and political "full partnership" were more elusive than ever for the vast majority of Puerto Ricans in New York. In fact, it was in the fifties that their subordination in these realms became entrenched, as urban renewal and deindustrialization devastated the already ailing Puerto Rican communities and delivered them to a fate that liberals like Clarence Senior could pretend, from their academic offices and city hall meeting rooms, was still vaguely hopeful. Joseph Montserrat, head of the Migration Division throughout the fifties, later recalled that in that decade, "Puerto Ricans suddenly came to be in fashion," the subject of endless official reports and academic studies by liberal experts. From his vantage point within the liberal establishment, this looked like a good thing. But an alternate reading of the story, more likely the way many Puerto Ricans in the city experienced their fashionability, was better expressed by novelist Ralph Ellison, writing about the similar plight of African Americans in a later introduction to his 1947 book *The Invisible Man*: "High visibility . . . actually rendered one *un*visible."[3]

## A New Alliance between Island and Mainland Liberals

In a famous speech delivered in Barranquitas, Puerto Rico, in 1951, Luis Muñoz Marín recounted the story of the 1940 triumph of the PPD, a narrative framed around what was by then a familiar account of his party's move away from nationalism. Muñoz Marín explained that the PPD secured the support of the Puerto Rican people by at last managing to sidestep the "emotional confusion" generated by independence politics. The revelation, he said, came from listening to the Puerto Rican people themselves while on the campaign trail and seeing at last how politicians' singular emphasis on the status issue was hindering the progress of economic development that the *patria* so desperately needed. Thereafter, Muñoz Marín said, he understood that "economic freedom, real freedom, full freedom" could be secured only by "separating the economic from the political problem of Puerto Rico."[4] This ideal of separating development from politics would become foundational to the PPD's defining agenda, "Manos a la Obra" ("Operation Bootstrap"). It would also come to define the shared ideals that bound PPD leaders so closely to their liberal supporters in the United States, all of them embracing what historian Michael Lapp described as "the putatively non-ideological pragmatism of much contemporary American thought."[5] Of course, their fiction did not hide the fact that this largely state-sponsored development was highly politicized, and many in the U.S. Congress criticized it as "supergovernment" and noted its similarity to socialism.[6]

Rexford G. Tugwell, appointed governor of Puerto Rico by President Roosevelt in 1941, had vigorously promoted this vision of development and pushed the mainland liberals in his circle to follow. Tugwell was an authentic and unreconstructed New Dealer who saw no conflict between his ideas about state-sponsored economic reform on the one hand and, on the other, the cold war world that was taking shape during his tenure as governor. He also, despite his focus on alleviating Puerto Rico's poverty, claimed that he was "surprised to find," upon his arrival on the island, "that Puerto Ricans felt themselves badly treated by the United States."[7] Muñoz Marín, determined to rid his party of "divisive" anticolonialist discourse even before its renunciation of independence in 1944, was willing to overlook Tugwell's hubris on this score, and in the early forties forged a powerful collaboration with Tugwell that would help cement the dominance of the PPD for the next three decades. Central to the PPD's developmentalist program was the creation of a network of social science experts and political allies who would advance their policy recommendations. Muñoz Marín and members of his inner circle, particularly University of Puerto Rico chancellor Jaime Benítez, formalized this network in 1945 when they created the new Social Science Research Center (Centro de Investigaciones Sociales, or CIS) within the university's School of Social Science. Lapp, citing the work of literature scholar Arcadio Díaz Quiñones, asserts that this move turned the University of Puerto Rico into "a chief purveyor of the ideology of modernization and the primary training ground of functionaries of the new order."[8]

The ascendant PPD and its corps of experts—the "modernizing elite"—did, indeed, formulate a new order in policy terms.[9] While economic development and the amelioration of poverty dominated the PPD platform and its political discourse, there was a corollary element of the agenda that the CIS pursued somewhat more quietly: population control. Island leaders and their mainland supporters shared the conviction that the island's "overpopulation" was the most serious hindrance to economic progress. The notion of overpopulation was not exactly new in the 1950s. Tugwell wrote in his 1947 memoir of his time in Puerto Rico, *The Stricken Land*, that President Roosevelt had begun advocating population control measures for the island as early as 1934. During a planning meeting on Puerto Rico that spring, the president had insisted that "the frightening increase of the population had to be stopped. . . . There were too many of them and it was better to stop them at the source than to connive at the high death rate."[10] Clarence Senior, a young social scientist in training who was recruited to be the director of the CIS just after completing a master's degree in history in the United States, embraced the issue of population control wholeheartedly. In fact, Senior's focus on migration as the solution to Puerto Rico's population problem would become the signature agenda of his career as a social scientist. In an article he wrote for a leading U.S. social science journal, Senior made this clumsy pronouncement about the centrality of migration to Puerto Rico's development dilemmas: "It is the only means, short of widespread death, of directly reducing the present population."[11]

Migration in general was becoming a popular subfield among U.S. social scientists by about 1940, and during his tenure as director of the CIS, from 1945 to 1951, most of Senior's own research and writing focused on how to promote and manage the out-migration of Puerto Ricans to reduce the island's population.[12] He achieved greater acknowledgment of this agenda when he returned to the United States in 1951 to take on the directorship of a new comprehensive service agency for migrants, the Migration Division of the Puerto Rican Department of Labor. The Migration Division, designed to help migrants with housing, employment, education, health, and all other issues related to "adjustment," was partly a result of Senior's own advocacy. Since late 1946, he and Resident Commissioner Jesús Piñero had urged the Puerto Rican government to back a full-service organization to help what promised to be a growing tide of migrants to the United States following World War II. An Emigration Advisory Council met in San Juan during the summer of 1947, and by the end of that year, island and mainland policymakers had collaborated to open the Bureau of Employment and Migration.[13] The Puerto Rican government had established a smaller office to provide similar but much more limited services to migrants back in 1930; the Office of Employment and Identification dispensed identification cards and employment referrals but little else. With the postwar migration, however, Senior and his colleagues at the CIS predicted more difficulties than before. "The voluntary migration of substantial groups often gives rise to personal problems for the migrant and friction in his new community," he warned.[14]

Regulating contract labor was a central goal of the Migration Division when it first opened. During the labor shortages of the immediate postwar period, the island was a "happy hunting ground for private, fee-charging recruiting agencies," many of which exploited the Puerto Ricans who signed contracts to work in the United States. In 1947, the Puerto Rican legislature outlawed contract-labor fees on the island. Increasingly, then, Migration Division staff focused on providing assistance not just with the basics of housing, income, food, and clothing but also with various social and bureaucratic aspects of "adjustment" for migrants. While the city schools faced most of the adjustment issues of migrant children, the Migration Division created scores of programs for adults throughout the early 1950s, including English classes and vocational training as well as "housekeeping" and "budgets and finances."[15] Early detractors of the Migration Division—an unlikely pairing of xenophobic Americans and Puerto Rican Nationalists who opposed any institution affiliated with the PPD—accused the agency of encouraging Puerto Rican migration, to which Senior replied vaguely that "the official policy is that generally the government neither encourages nor discourages such migration."[16]

This criticism of the Migration Division and its PPD allies was one that would surface over and over, and it illustrates just one dimension of the

Figure 14. Migration Division voter registration drive, 1958. Labor activist Gilberto Gerena Valentín is standing behind those seated at the table, at center and wearing glasses. Records of the Offices of the Government of Puerto Rico in the United States, Archives of the Puerto Rican Diaspora, Centro de Estudios Puertorriqueños, Hunter College, CUNY.

fiction that Puerto Rican economic development—and one of its central mechanisms, migration—could proceed in a context that was "beyond politics." But the leadership at the CIS, at the new Migration Division, and in New York's liberal establishment continued to insist that their collaboration had no political goals attached to it despite the myriad political agendas that could be reinforced by their relationships. Jesús Colón had already criticized O'Dwyer ignoring the input of leftist Puerto Rican leaders in the city;[17] and this moment of cooperation between New York's liberal Democratic machine and the PPD was more ironic given *colonia* journalist Erasmo Vando's recent accusation that Muñoz Marín ignored his constituency in New York. "The Partido Popular Democrático, whose slogan is *"Pan, Tierra, y Libertad"* [Bread, Land, and Liberty], has done laudable work thus far," said Vando. "Why is the island legislature not interested in the problems of the decrepit Eighth District?" Puerto Rico was divided into seven voting districts, so Vando was implying that New York migrants comprised a key constituency to which Muñoz Marín and his party should pay attention.[18]

Through the Mayor's Advisory Committee on Puerto Rican Affairs (MACPRA), mayoral politics became bound up both with the selling of Operation Bootstrap (which Representative Vito Marcantonio derided as "Operation Booby Trap") and with the campaign to redefine the island's status as a "commonwealth" rather than a colony.[19] So this collaboration furthered a more abstract and unspoken political agenda as well: sweeping the critiques about colonialism and imperialism under the rug by making the migration about the island-specific problems of poverty and overpopulation rather than about the role the United States played in the development of these problems. Puerto Ricans arriving in New York in these years were readily incorporated into the social service machine that was being built around them. Encouraged to see the possibilities for their empowerment through the aid of the Migration Division, an organization with explicitly modernizationist and assimilationist goals, these migrants were less likely than their predecessors in the thirties to engage in political action that might involve criticism of the United States as a colonial power.

## A New Subject of Social Science

In the early years of the cold war, social science had begun a rapid ascent to a new status in the academy, offering tools with which to explain—and, according to many of its practitioners, control—human problems.[20] Social science research could provide the data on which to build an enormously ambitious development scheme like Operation Bootstrap, and it could certainly help solve the public relations catastrophe that Puerto Rican migrants were facing in New York. "While the commotion [of 1947] was at its height, somebody suggested to Governor Jesus T. Piñero of Puerto Rico that some grand gesture of concern on the part of the island's government might help pacify the papers," wrote anthropologist John Murra flippantly in 1950. "Somebody" was actually Clarence Senior, along with his collaborators on migration research at the CIS. The insular government announced that it had offered a thirty thousand–dollar research grant to a team at Columbia University's Bureau of Applied Social Research to study Puerto Rican migrants in New York. The project's lead researcher would be C. Wright Mills, who was just over thirty at the time and a rising star in his field, and he would be assisted by his Columbia colleague Rose Kohn Goldsen and by Clarence Senior, who was still directing the CIS.[21] When news of the commissioned study was announced by the Puerto Rican government in August of 1947, the Spanish-American Youth Bureau's president Ruperto Ruiz wrote to Governor Piñero with a complaint: he reminded the governor that they had had a meeting in 1945 to discuss the "serious" conditions among Puerto Ricans in New York, and that the governor had promised to provide financial assistance and to push for Spanish-speaking social workers to serve migrants. Ruiz claimed that Piñero had failed to follow through on these promises. Resentful about the exclusion of Puerto Rican social service providers from the project, he argued that the New York Welfare Council's 1947 study was adequate and that further funds should be devoted to action rather than research.[22]

The book published at the conclusion of Mills, Goldsen, and Senior's study in 1950, *The Puerto Rican Journey: New York's Newest Migrants*, would become the standard-bearer for subsequent efforts to study the "adaptation" and "adjustment" of Puerto Rican migrants in New York City. Before the Columbia study, only one academic monograph had been published on Puerto Rican migrants, sociologist Lawrence Chenault's 1938 book *The Puerto Rican Migrant in New York City*, also from Columbia University Press. This book was a lonely forerunner of liberal social scientists' postwar interest in Puerto Rican migrants, and remarkably, Mills and his collaborators failed even to cite it. Chenault had aimed to elucidate the "social effects of migration," examining how Puerto Ricans fared in housing, employment, health, and "social adjustment," and most of the book read like any early-twentieth-century study of the problems of an immigrant group in the United States. Chenault avoided discussion of Puerto Rico's political

status except to point out, in a veiled reference to *colonia* agitations following the 1937 Ponce massacre, that "to the extent that [the Puerto Rican] . . .
retains the attitudes which result from . . . an aroused nationalism among
his people, this problem of assimilation will be made more difficult."[23] Over
a decade later, Mills and his collaborators also skirted the political issues
surrounding the migration, although they did note in their introduction
that "dissatisfaction with the island's ambiguous political status is a source
of bitter feeling towards the United States among many Puerto Ricans"
and that some migrants also felt bitterness about "the gap between United
States principles and United States practice on the island."[24]

By the time the Columbia study was completed in 1950, social service
agencies and education officials in New York had produced scores of surveys and reports on Puerto Ricans. *The Puerto Rican Journey* stood apart,
however, not just because it was based on interview data that conformed
to the highest social scientific standards but also because Mills and his collaborators did not actually purport to solve the problems of the Puerto
Rican migrant. The authors described, instead, a nuanced and narrative
approach to their subject:

> We try to tell who the migrants are and why they came; how they
> compare with their compatriots who remain at home; what their jour-
> ney to the continent means in their occupational and income as well
> as life stories; what kind of social world they inhabit in New York, and
> how that world compares with the kind of world New York has been
> for previous migrants; what seem to be their solidarities and their con-
> flicts with other ethnic and racial groups in the city of New York; what
> is meant by "adaptation" for a group at this level of living, and how the
> Puerto Ricans are involved in this process in the middle of the twentieth
> century.[25]

This sensitive and scholarly discussion of the book hardly fit with the way
its publisher, Harper and Brothers, chose to advertise it in the *New York
Times* soon after its release: "Every New Yorker should read this book. It
turns a revealing spotlight on a disturbing corner of your city—'Spanish
Harlem'—where Americanization is retarded, where we confront urgent social problems. School teachers, political and civic leaders, social
agencies—all public-spirited citizens: here is essential light on a little-
understood group of Americans who sit in your classroom, vote for or
against you at the polls—or come to you for help."[26]

Following the publication of the Columbia study's preliminary findings in June 1948, *La Prensa* praised the study for providing the data to discredit "old erroneous concepts regarding migration." A series of articles highlighted those conclusions that countered most directly the negative stereotypes about Puerto Ricans in New York: that most migrants (74 percent of men, 38 percent of women) left the island in search of better work, not because they were unemployed; that the income, education, and skill levels of those leaving the island were actually higher than those who stayed—and that migrants were not, then, "the dregs" of Puerto Rican society; that migrants were not living "ten or fifteen persons huddled in one small apartment," as many of the tabloid journalists claimed; and that most migrants did not depend on welfare for their survival in New York (only about 12 percent of the more than eleven hundred households surveyed depended on some form of relief).[27] In sum, the migrants were "better fitted than stationary islanders for the struggle on the continent."[28]

*La Prensa* also highlighted the study's findings about the racial composition of migrants—erroneously. Mills, Senior, and Goldsen categorized 64 percent of their sample as "white," 16 percent "intermediate," and 20 percent "Negro," while the newspaper reported these figures as 68 percent "white," 15 percent "intermediate," and 5 percent "of the colored race." The error was particularly notable in that it literally erased from public view the majority of black Puerto Ricans, by subtracting most of their estimated number from the tally printed in the article. Compared to the 1940 U.S. Census figures on the racial composition of the island's population—76.5 percent white, 23.5 percent nonwhite (the Spanish term the census bureau used was *de color*)—the study's actual data countered the claims of those who said that the New York migrants constituted a "Negro exodus" from the island. The authors did not discuss their method of racial classification, but in their appendix listing the interview questions that all interviewers used in collecting data, they included the rubric that interviewers filled out regarding the racial identity of the interviewee and that resembled Puerto Ricans' own phenotypic schema to determine race:[29]

| SKIN | HAIR | LIPS | NOSE |
|---|---|---|---|
| __white | __kinky | __thick | __narrow-thin |
| __tan | __wavy | __medium | __medium |
| __brown | __straight | __thin | __broad-fleshy |
| __black[30] | | | |

Presumably—although they did not explain their methods—the researchers assigned numbers to each item in the rubric and calculated an average

score that they then translated into a racial category, "white," "intermediate," or "Negro." Mills, Senior, and Goldsen were as silent about the implications of their racial data as they were about their methodology of collecting it. Ira Reid, an African American sociologist who published the first
academic study of African-descended immigrants in the United States, set
forth in his review of *The Puerto Rican Journey* a convincing and dishearten-
ing hypothesis about Puerto Ricans' racial identity, one that the book's authors seemed afraid to make—and that many before him had made: "These
colored Puerto Ricans have less incentive and less opportunity to follow the
pattern of Americanization than any other immigrants America has known.
Only so long as they continue to remain conspicuously different from the
American Negro can they improve their status in America."[31]

When C. Wright Mills died young in the early sixties, a colleague ad-
miringly described him as "an authentic voice of an authentic liberalism,"
a voice, the colleague explained, that was flexible enough to provide ever
more precise descriptions of a changing world. This was a gloss of Mills's
political leanings that ignored his affinity for Marxism; his last two books
in particular—*Listen, Yankee!* on the relation between Cuban Marxism and
U.S. imperialism after the 1959 revolution, and *The Marxists*, a "primer on
marxisms"—reflected his intellectual stretch well beyond the liberalism of
his era. *The Puerto Rican Journey*, though, was a product of Mills's earlier career.[32] It was an important book, respectable for its accuracy and descrip-
tiveness, but it was a book whose conclusions were clouded by the hopeful
haze of postwar liberalism and by the optimistic agenda of its sponsors in
the PPD and the CIS, especially coauthor Clarence Senior. Emerging as it
did from the web of connections linking island and mainland liberals, *The
Puerto Rican Journey* failed, in the end, to comment on the political complexity of the migration's origins or the grimness of migrants' prospects, especially to the extent that they were limited by racism. For the book's primary
author in particular, the man who would become one of the foremost critics
of the cold war and of U.S. imperialist policy on Cuba, it was a remarkable
silence.

Nothing showcased the powerful collaborations of the liberals interested in Puerto Rican development and the Puerto Rican migration—or
highlighted their optimism about their agendas—like the 1953 issue of the
*Annals of the American Academy of Political and Social Science*, one of the premier
social science journals of the era. Titled "Puerto Rico: A Study in Democratic Development," the issue brought together powerful players beyond
just the leaders of the CIS and their early collaborators in New York. It was

coedited by Yale political scientist Henry Wells and Millard Hansen, who had been appointed director of the CIS when Senior left to head the Migration Division office in New York in 1948. The collection of articles encapsulated the participants' more or less unified perspectives on the answers to Puerto Rico's "democratic development," and as such the journal issue stands as a monument to the ascendancy of this liberal coalition at the moment of Puerto Rico's rebirth—or so it seemed to its supporters—as a commonwealth. The unity of the growing circle of Bootstrappers notwithstanding, the *Annals* articles actually spoke to two partially distinct subgroups: those whose primary concern was the political and economic vitality of the island in its new incarnation and those whose primary concern was the "management" of the migration process and of the migrants themselves. Muñoz Marín's famous Barranquitas speech, reprinted under the title "Development through Democracy," was the pièce de résistance for the former group, offering the final word, it seemed, on pushing the postwar developmentalist agenda beyond politics. Other political specialists expounded similar arguments, the North Americans in particular reinforcing the depoliticization of the relationship between the island and the mainland. Millard Hansen, in a discussion of "Training and Research in Puerto Rico," defined the Commonwealth of Puerto Rico as "a frontier state on the border between North and South America," adding that, "as Governor Muñoz Marín said in December 1950: Puerto Rico is a Latin American country consisting of good citizens of the United States."[33]

Just after the appearance of the *Annals* issue cemented the impression of a united front among policymakers on Puerto Rican problems, the Migration Division and the New York City Welfare Department staged a major conference in San Juan on the Puerto Rican migration to New York. It was attended by hundreds of PPD leaders, social scientists, and New York City social workers and government officials, convened to discuss strategies for solving the problems of the three hundred thousand or so migrants who had arrived in New York since 1946. Housing was at the top of the agenda, particularly the problem of protecting migrants from exploitative landlords.[34] Whereas the *Annals* contributors had argued convincingly for the nonpolitical nature of their work, participants at the 1953 Migration Conference could not hide the impact of the migration on city and island politics alike. Some emphasis on the political was intentional. Mayor of San Juan Felisa Rincón de Gautier, in her remarks at the close of the conference, suggested that migrants could protect themselves better in the United States if they could secure recognition from the major political parties. She added several veiled jabs about Vito Marcantonio's influence on the migrants, who had been, she said, "misled and induced to back such political movements headed by subversive leaders which tended to create the impression that the Puerto Ricans in New York were behind subversive movements." She went on to say that Mayor Impellitteri had thanked her and her sister, Josefina Rincón Marrero, the city manager of San Juan, for their "healthy influence" on the migrants, and for helping to "disassociate [them] from a political situation which was damaging to their best interests."[35]

On the other hand, the Puerto Rican government representatives at the conference issued a statement that "the Government of Puerto Rico is not now, and will not be in the future, involved in the political struggles of the parties and groups in any community on the continent." Of course this claim was disingenuous, since the governor and the mayor of San Juan had themselves been "involved in the political struggles of the parties" in New York during the 1949 mayoral race.[36] Nevertheless, participants seemed to agree that the overall tenor of the meeting was optimistic and collaborative. One attendee, a director at New York's Department of Welfare, recalled that the meeting filled its participants with a singular sense of purpose, concluding that "under the impact of the spirit of reform, Puerto Rico has become a truly exciting laboratory for social and economic experimentation." The conference was such a success that the Migration Division hosted several others throughout the fifties, hoping to draw an ever wider circle of experts to work in the "laboratory" of Puerto Rico and its migrant communities in New York.[37]

### "Puerto Ricans Suddenly Came to Be in Fashion"

The "spirit of reform" that animated research on Puerto Rico and Puerto Ricans in the late forties and fifties generated important but not always clear connections between social scientists and the staffs of the growing social service sector dealing with Puerto Rican migrants. But since much of the social science research relating to Puerto Ricans in this period dealt with island issues—The Puerto Rican Journey was the major exception until the mid-fifties—social workers and educators in New York organized quickly to fill the void, conducting their own surveys and research to aid in their work with migrants in New York. Bolstered by academic work on the importance of the migration to island development (for instance, the January 1953 Annals issue was cited numerous times at the social service–oriented Migration Conference in San Juan several months later), and by the flurry of interest in their client base, the cadre of educators and social workers who served Puerto Ricans grew exponentially in the early years of the postwar migration. It was not just the Puerto Rican migration swelling their ranks. Inspired by the varied impulses that informed the social philosophy of twentieth-century liberalism, rooted in the values of cultural pluralism born in the nativist 1920s, then cemented by a cold war–era desire to correct social problems in the style of the Marshall Plan, a powerful new social service "machine" emerged in New York. That machine incorporated a sprawling network of educators, service providers, and bureaucrats who worked on various dimensions of Puerto Ricans' "adjustment problems." With the Migration Division office an increasingly important link in this network, the growing social service machine at first looked like a new field of opportunity for Puerto Ricans seeking employment outside the manufacturing sector and recognition outside the boundaries of electoral politics. However, for most Puerto Ricans, the social service sector would not prove to be an avenue of group empowerment: although Puerto Ricans "suddenly came to be in fashion," as Migration Division head Joseph Montserrat later put it, it turned out they had little say in the development of those organizations.[38]

Even before the first wave of negative press about Puerto Ricans appeared in 1947, before the Columbia study was organized, in part, to counter that publicity, educators at the New York City Board of Education had decided to assess the needs of the migrant children and the impact of their presence on the city's public institutions. Schools had been coping with the influx of Puerto Rican children in the schools, many of whom did not speak English. Leonard Covello, the well-known community activist and principal of the Benjamin Franklin High School in East Harlem, had led the way with the programs he developed for Puerto Rican students beginning in the late thirties. Inspired by Covello's work, the Board of Education set up a committee of assistant superintendents to survey Puerto Rican students and their teachers with the goal of assembling a set of programming recommendations to meet the needs of the migrant children.

A few years later, in 1947, the New York City Board of Education published a comprehensive study of Puerto Rican children in the schools, the first in what would become an extensive body of research to monitor the progress of the city's Puerto Rican students. The report advised a number of practical changes, like adding special classes for the new students and extra medical services to treat common problems like malnutrition. It also recommended the creation of teachers' orientation courses in Puerto Rican culture and conversational Spanish. The most notable result of the study was the school board's creation of a new position, "substitute auxiliary teacher" (SAT), to be filled by Spanish speakers (mostly Puerto Rican) to serve as an intermediary between teachers and Puerto Rican families. Ten "SATs" were appointed by 1949, and the number had doubled four years later.[39] The authors of the "Program of Education" also took pains to address the larger context of Puerto Rican children's arrival in New York schools, reminding its readers that "although the Puerto Rican is an American citizen, the adjustment he must make in this city is like that of immigrants in this country from a foreign land."[40]

School officials' concerns inspired other city officials to pay attention to the younger migrants, as opposed to simply focusing on the needs of their adult relatives. When Mayor O'Dwyer convened the Mayor's Advisory Committee on Puerto Rican Affairs (MACPRA), the educational needs of migrant youth were a central concern.[41] In 1951, when the MACPRA's Subcommittee on Education, Recreation and Parks, chaired by William Jansen, superintendent of schools, surveyed city schools' efforts to integrate Puerto Rican children, it reiterated in more boosterish tones many of the points of the Board of Education's 1947 report: it hailed the successes of the substitute auxiliary teacher (SAT) program and affirmed the need for more bilingual teachers, the need to involve parents in the schools, and the need to better orient teachers of Puerto Rican students. New York's social service establishment was only a few months behind the school board in beginning to investigate its Puerto Rican client population, a process overseen by the representatives of several city departments and a handful of community agencies that comprised New York's Welfare Council. (The Welfare Council had actually established a "Puerto Rican Community Committee" in 1930 to assemble data on "the problem of the needy Puerto Rican" in New York during the Depression, but the committee was disbanded in 1934 due to lack of funds and the advent of federal-level relief.)[42] When the Welfare Council appointed a "Committee on American Citizens of Puerto Rican Extraction Living in New York City" in January 1947, members determined that the committee should not "engage in research" per se—which would cost too much—but should more quickly develop "recommendations for practical action to remedy the admittedly bad situation."[43]

In its 1948 report, the Committee on Puerto Ricans emphasized English-language instruction, to improve employability for adults; schooling for children, as an "assimilation tool"; and improvements in housing. Two conclusions of the committee gained the most attention from the press, especially *La Prensa*: first, that previous estimates of the migrant population had been exaggerated, in some cases by a factor of two or more, and second, that only 16 of the 112 families in the block study were dependent on relief—proving false "the widespread assumption . . . that most Puerto Ricans were on relief." The committee estimated (on the basis of its block survey in East Harlem) that about 230,000 Puerto Ricans lived in New York by the end of 1947, a fraction of the figure of 600,000 that the *New York Times* had printed in August of that year. In its concluding summary, the committee made an effort to situate New York's "Puerto Rican problem" in a broader perspective, asserting that "fundamentally [it is] the local manifestation of a nation-wide problem in which are involved on the one hand, the over-crowding of cities . . . and on the other hand, the unsolved economy of an island possession of the United States." It was the responsibility of the federal government to deal with both issues, by helping to ameliorate the post-war housing shortage and by "improving the standard of living for Puerto Rico." This was a rare acknowledgment of the colonial politics behind the migration, and not surprisingly, the *New York Times*'s coverage of the report ignored these points. It highlighted, instead, the committee's suggestion that, because New York had reached the "saturation point" in housing, it was critical that social service networks and the island and mainland governments cooperate to begin diverting migrants to destinations other than New York City.[44]

The Migration Division was, in fact, quietly engaged in such a project. Occasionally, when it seemed warranted by negative publicity about Puerto Ricans flocking to New York, the office would draft a press release about its work with migrants in other cities. However, the organization's leadership was much more interested in publicizing its bridge building between island and mainland experts on issues like education. One of the most popular and well-known efforts of this kind originated with the work of Robert Speer, chair of early childhood and elementary education at New York University, in 1948. Speer collaborated with Leonard Covello, Emilio Guerra (another Benjamin Franklin faculty member who, like Covello, occasionally taught at New York University), and Luisa Frías de Hempel, a director of education programming at the Migration Division, to develop an experimental program called the "Workshop–Field Study." For two decades, the program allowed New York City teachers to spend six weeks in Puerto Rico to foster "a deep-seated understanding of the circumstances under which the Puerto Rican children grew up."[45] After he became head of the Migration Division's New York office in 1951, Clarence Senior led the New York orientation for the teachers, using his newly published book *The Puerto Rican Journey* as the main text. Participants later commented about the enormous impression the trip made on them. Many of them also fortified their connections to various liberal networks relating to Puerto Ricans, including the Instituto de Puerto Rico, the Puerto Rican Public Relations Committee, and the Urban League.[46]

By the mid-fifties, the challenges posed by the Puerto Rican migration to educational institutions in New York had become a popular topic in many education-related publications in the city, and several regional journals also began publishing articles on Puerto Ricans. Some of this writing, like a series of articles in the Board of Education's *Curriculum and Materials*, aimed to provide another venue for practical information for teachers concerning their new Puerto Rican students.[47] Much of the literature published in liberal educational journals in the fifties cast Puerto Rican children as typical immigrants and analyzed their plight from a liberal-assimilationist point of view, like an article on special classes for Puerto Rican migrant pupils that began, "The public school . . . has an important function: that of teaching immigrant children the vernacular together with the values and customs of the new culture." A number of New York educators had begun writing articles for the school board's monthly publication, *High Points*, sympathetic in tone, full of praise for Operation Bootstrap, and intent on placing the children's problems in a larger social context.[48]

A variety of social service agencies joined the education experts in studying Puerto Ricans in the early fifties. The Boys' Athletic League, the Protestant Council of the City of New York, Catholic Charities, and the Brooklyn Council for Social Planning had all hosted conferences and produced reports on their Puerto Rican clients by the early fifties.[49] These organizations, following the liberal social service model of figures like Covello and the members of the Welfare Council, approached the subject of Puerto Rican migrants and their problems as a familiar issue of social acceptance of "foreign" populations, emphasizing as well some of the structural features—housing and English-language proficiency, for example—of migrants' "adjustment." But among the myriad social service organizations in New York that began to focus on Puerto Ricans in the postwar years, only a small number were Puerto Rican–led groups. The Spanish-American Youth Bureau, founded in 1943 by Ruperto Ruiz, boasted a range of services, support networks, and advocacy work geared toward helping Puerto Rican families to make the most of New York's educational opportunities. Casita

María, the East Harlem settlement house established in 1934, was another Puerto Rican–run organization that was a major source of support for the community.[50]

The problem for Puerto Ricans' empowerment in the expanding social service world was not just that Puerto Rican–run organizations were few in number. More important, these grassroots agencies—some of them, like Casita María, pillars of institutional strength in their communities—were excluded from the city's major social service networks. For instance, in spite of the important role it played in improving relations between Puerto Rican families and the schools, no Board of Education report ever acknowledged the Spanish-American Youth Bureau, and in spite of his ties to Leonard Covello and other non–Puerto Rican education activists, Ruiz was not among the dozen or so Puerto Ricans invited to participate in the Mayor's Advisory Committee on Puerto Rican Affairs. Nor were any representatives from Casita María. Jesús Colón noted that the most important "pro–Puerto Rican initiative" in the early fifties, organized in his home borough by the Brooklyn Council for Social Planning, included thirty-nine members but not a single Puerto Rican. The irony of the Brooklyn Council's emphasis on "encouraging Puerto Ricans to take leadership in programs designed to assist their own group," along with a focus on improving Puerto Ricans' access to schooling, decent housing, and English instruction, would not have escaped the notice of Colón and other activists in his community.[51]

In the fifties, Puerto Ricans indeed "came to be in fashion," as Joseph Montserrat put it, among social scientists and social work professionals in New York. The attention paid to migrants and their problems did increase knowledge about Puerto Ricans and improved the quality of services available to them. It also produced new opportunities for Puerto Ricans themselves to work in this exploding service sector. This is what Montserrat, as head of the New York office of the Migration Division, saw happening. But it was primarily members of the Migration Division leadership who were invited to "represent" the Puerto Rican community by groups like the MACPRA or the Brooklyn Council of Social Planning (if any Puerto Ricans at all were asked to participate), while smaller grassroots Puerto Rican social service providers were overlooked or ignored completely. It was a trend Ruperto Ruiz had foreshadowed when he accused Governor Piñero in 1947 of excluding *colonia* activists from the nascent coalitions organizing to serve Puerto Rican migrants in New York.[52] Had he been asked about his Puerto Rican neighbors in Harlem during one of the interviews he gave when *The Invisible Man* was published in 1947, Ralph Ellison might have predicted this:

the mass of Puerto Ricans in New York were not, in the end, empowered by their new visibility.

## Electoral Politics, Unions, and the Paradox of Puerto Rican Invisibility in the Fifties

A study published in 1957 by a group at New York University's Graduate School of Public Administration and Social Service concluded that, ten years after the first "influx" of migrants to New York, Puerto Ricans as a group were continuing to struggle with poor health and limited access to health care, dilapidated housing and discrimination in the housing market, inadequate English instruction in the schools, and heavy reliance on welfare services. The researchers warned that "the problems of serving these new New Yorkers and of integrating them into the community are likely to increase in the near future."[53] Puerto Rican community leaders and activists did not need an NYU study to tell them this. Alongside the range of social service solutions that looked so promising to many in the mid-fifties, it was clear that Puerto Ricans would have to make a renewed push for political empowerment in the city. This would be problematic, however, in the context of their high visibility as a "problem" in the city. By the 1950s, social science and social work networks had become more important for Puerto Ricans, in both symbolic and concrete ways, than the political networks they had struggled to create in the 1930s.

According to the *New York Post*, the "city fathers" began wooing Puerto Ricans for their votes in the early fifties, but they certainly were not interested in backing Puerto Rican candidates.[54] By 1956, there was still only one elected Puerto Rican representative in the city, Felipe Torres, of the Bronx Fourth Assembly District—the first Puerto Rican in the state government since the end of García Rivera's two-year term in the state assembly in 1940. No Puerto Rican was appointed to any municipal post until Mayor Robert Wagner named Manuel Gómez a municipal magistrate in 1957. Many *colonia* leaders expressed deep pessimism about the prospect of improvements for Puerto Ricans in housing, employment, schooling, and health without political representation or "complete voting rights," as one group put it.[55] A Puerto Rican candidate for the New York State Assembly, campaigning in a heavily Puerto Rican district in Brooklyn, appealed to voters with a grim prognosis if they failed to achieve greater recognition in politics: "We Puerto Rican people face bitter discrimination in our jobs, in housing and in our daily lives. . . . We are a growing community. Our present Assemblyman . . . has ignored the desperate needs of the people of his district. It is time that we had someone from our own people to speak for us and to represent us in the government."⁵⁶

It was a warning repeated over and over by Puerto Rican candidates throughout the fifties, a number of whom ran on the American Labor Party (ALP) ticket. When Jesús Colón and his fellow leftist and labor leader José Giboyeaux campaigned in 1953 for state senate and state assembly, respectively, they asserted that "a vote for Jesús Colón and José Giboyeaux is a vote for . . . treatment as first class citizens." The political rhetoric of mainstream office seekers was not very different from that of their leftist counterparts. The nonpartisan Spanish Voters Association echoed the same warning in 1955: "The denial of political representation hampers our efforts in the struggle for jobs, for more and better schools, for better attention in the hospitals, for better housing, against discrimination, for the problems of our youth who now have so few opportunities in the civic, social and cultural life of the City."⁵⁷

There was basic agreement across the political spectrum about the urgent need for Puerto Ricans to break into New York politics, echoing the calls of community leaders in the late twenties and early thirties. But only Puerto Rican liberals—allies of Muñoz Marín in the city's Democratic mayoral administrations of the fifties, including affiliates of the Migration Division—were optimistic. At a 1956 meeting of the Council of Spanish-American Organizations, held at Covello's Benjamin Franklin High School, "securing political recognition" was a major theme, and the panel chaired by Joseph Montserrat considered the possibilities of registering one hundred thousand Spanish-speaking voters in time for the upcoming presidential election. This was an exceedingly ambitious program, considering that most estimates of registered Spanish-speaking voters in all five boroughs in the mid-fifties fell below forty thousand.⁵⁸ Leftists in the Puerto Rican community, on the other hand, saw an uphill fight against marginalization and active exclusion by mainstream political leaders. This was especially true after the sudden death in 1954 of East Harlem's popular representative Vito Marcantonio, who had been a radical supporter of Puerto Rican migrants and Puerto Rican independence since he first took office in 1935. Ralph Medina, Marcantonio's Puerto Rican top lieutenant and protégé (who narrowly lost a bid for a state assembly seat in 1949 and one for city council in 1950), told journalist Dan Wakefield in 1957 that "most of the Puerto Ricans who were registered and brought into politics by Marcantonio's organization merely gave up when 'Marc' and his organization died."

Some of them, he said, went on to actively support the Democratic Party but "not enough to matter."[59]

Jesús Colón and his ALP allies argued that low voter registration among Puerto Ricans—an estimated 35,000 in the 1952 presidential elections, out of a population that could yield around 250,000 voters—had less to do with "apathy" and more to do with the hindrance created by the English-only literacy test, which remained in place until outlawed by the 1965 Voting Rights Act. (A New York State election law dictated that a literacy test be given to all potential voters who could not provide a diploma to prove that they had attended an elementary school in which English was the primary language of instruction; many Puerto Rican migrants alleged that their diplomas were not honored. After 1965, Puerto Ricans not literate in English could register by showing evidence of having completed at least six years of schooling.)[60] They also accused the Republican state legislature of gerrymandering the districts in which most Puerto Ricans lived in East Harlem and the Bronx so that only one out of approximately eight such districts actually obtained a Puerto Rican majority, hindering both their traditional support of Democratic candidates and their ability to lobby for backing for Puerto Rican candidates from any party.[61]

Puerto Rican ALP supporters also worried that Puerto Rican political recognition in New York was hindered by "increasingly close ties between the ruling government party of Muñoz Marín in Puerto Rico and the Democratic Party in the US," since that powerful alliance effectively silenced political views that challenged its agenda. In the same vein, a representative of the Puerto Rican Independence Party (PIP) told his colleagues in the island legislature in 1957 that Puerto Ricans in the United States were "virtually abandoned" by mainstream politicians who were "deaf" to their needs and that the Migration Division leadership was likewise failing the community, adhering to "the philosophy of the ostrich" (that is, burying their heads in the sand) when it came to strategies for empowering migrants. El Diario reported this accusation of centrist politicians and the Migration Division office on the same page that it printed a plea for "Puerto Rican unity" by Felisa Rincón de Gautier, San Juan's mayor and powerful ally of Muñoz Marín. During a visit to New York, Rincón advised a "non-political" form of organization to help the migrant community—a prescription that sounded identical to the mission of the Migration Division. Even while acknowledging the continuing struggles of Puerto Rican migrants in New York, liberal leaders like Montserrat and Rincón upheld the PPD party line about the benefits of migration to all and insisted that migrants could look ahead to a promising future. In Rincón's parting speech to Puerto Rican New Yorkers—on the very day that *West Side Story* premiered in New York, coincidentally—she reminded her compatriots that "no place in the world offers you better opportunities for progress than those that you have in New York and in the rest of this nation."[62] In the background, pushed aside by the boosters of Operation Bootstrap, was a less appealing message, one that emphasized the failures of a mass migration from colony to metropole, the suffering of the migrants, and the "deaf politicians" who preferred not to acknowledge them as full members of society, as equal citizens.

To the extent that hopeful liberals and skeptical radicals agreed on the goal of expanding political recognition for Puerto Ricans, they also shared an increasing interest in building alliances with African American groups by the early fifties. Finding common cause with African Americans was nothing new, of course—Puerto Ricans had struggled since the early thirties to balance the benefits of a strategic alliance with their black American neighbors with the costs of associating with another debased minority group. But whereas even many radical Puerto Ricans had leaned toward maintaining distance from blacks in the thirties, now the equation looked different. During and just after the tumultuous war years, blacks in the United States had made substantial gains in their own struggles for political recognition, symbolized especially by their successful pressuring of President Truman to desegregate the military. These were victories that Puerto Rican leaders observed closely. They also, at this point, tended to talk much less frequently about the threat of being identified as Negro. This was partly due to the fact that Puerto Ricans were developing, for better or worse, a racial identity in the United States that was distinct from African Americans. But it also stemmed from the sense that being perceived as Negro seemed less socially damaging in an era when African Americans were achieving political empowerment to a degree that was noticeable even before the beginning of a mass movement for civil rights by the end of the fifties. So it was not surprising or controversial in the least when, for instance, an Urban League officer participated in the 1952 New York University Workshop–Field Study in Puerto Rico and then arranged for a Migration Division representative to attend the national Urban League conference later that year. That connection resulted in a number of collaborations throughout the fifties, including an Urban League–sponsored trip to Puerto Rico and the first "Conference on the Problems of Negroes and Puerto Ricans in New York State," sponsored by the Urban League, the Migration Division, the NAACP, and the Council of Spanish-American Organizations.[63]

A simultaneous forging of alliances was happening at the community level in Harlem, bringing together local leaders, many of them leftists, who were not necessarily connected to major organizations like the Migration Division and the Urban League. The 1954 election season was a particularly intense period of "unity" discourse in Harlem. The Harlem Affairs Committee sponsored a forum to debate the question "Can Negroes and Puerto-Ricans Unite for Mutual Progress?" The Harlem office of the Communist Party printed pamphlets (written by Jesús Colón) entitled "The Struggle for Puerto Rican Representation, and for Negro–Puerto Rican Unity," and the leftist Comité de Unidad Hispana issued "an appeal for unity," proclaiming "unqualified support to the demands of the Negro people for political representation" and noting that "our problems in housing, in jobs, and many others are the same." Jesús Colón, who was running for the state senate that year, gave a campaign speech on the American Labor Party's weekly radio show in which he expounded on the similarity of Negro and Puerto Rican problems. This was just months after the *Brown v. The Board of Education* decision, and Colón declared that, "as a Puerto Rican, I have been deeply moved by the great fight the Negro people are making for integration in politics . . . for reasons which both the Negro and Puerto Rican people have in common." He also highlighted the failures of the major parties' alleged efforts to represent Puerto Ricans, asserting that in spite of their visibility as a "problem" in the city, "it is as though 500,000 Puerto Rican citizens did not exist."[64]

But just as alliances between the two groups were becoming the rule rather than the exception in the communities they shared, competition between Puerto Ricans and African Americans in the local political arena began to derail their spirit of cooperation. When Harlem's powerful U.S. congressional representative Adam Clayton Powell Jr. made what his loyal Puerto Rican constituents saw as an about-face to support the rising African American political star Hulan Jack for borough president in 1957, they were furious. "Puerto Rican and Negro gains should not be made at each other's expense," declared Jesús Colón, pointedly ignoring the intensified pressures for realpolitik in a district with so few resources to share. Colón argued that the structuring of Harlem's districts resulted not only in the weakening of the Puerto Rican voting majority but also in "divisive tendencies" between African Americans and Puerto Ricans. Indeed, the two groups now vied to convince the Democratic Party to back their "own" candidates in local elections; Puerto Ricans, the less powerful of the two constituencies, expressed growing resentment about African Americans' longer list of candidates and incumbents during voting season.[65] After this schism in the nascent black–Puerto Rican alliance, the two groups' political leaders seemed unable to regain the unifying momentum they had achieved by 1956. Issues like police brutality and housing continued to inspire co-operation at the grassroots level, but increasingly, conflicts caused by the scarcity of political clout in their poor districts divided them.

Labor politics was another arena in which Puerto Ricans and African Americans found themselves thrown together by virtue of their common struggles in the mid-fifties, and it seemed for some time that this might be another opportunity for cooperation. Herbert Hill, labor secretary of the NAACP, wrote and spoke frequently on the widespread exploitation of Puerto Ricans in the garment industry. For some months, when New York dailies' headlines focused on the exploitation of Puerto Rican workers in "racket" unions, and when the powerful and putatively liberal International Ladies Garment Workers Union (ILGWU) was pushed to acknowledge its role in their exploitation, it also seemed that union politics might offer Puerto Ricans a more concrete form of recognition and empowerment than electoral politics. But less than a decade later, when Herbert Hill testified before Congress about the racial practices of the ILGWU—after years of intense publicity surrounding the exploitation of Puerto Rican and Afri-can American workers in the union—he described steady wage losses for unskilled and semiskilled garment workers, an ever-increasing number of whom were Puerto Rican, and no gains in leadership positions for black or Puerto Rican union members. When charged with systematically hinder-ing the advancement of the union's black and Puerto Rican members in the early sixties, ILGWU officials insisted, "We are not an employment agency."[66] As with their stymied efforts in electoral politics, Puerto Ricans found that increasing their visibility in the union sector did not result in any measurable gains.

The horizon looked brighter for Puerto Rican garment workers in late 1955, after *El Diario* reporter José Lumen Román (who would run for city council, unsuccessfully, in 1957) broke the story of a group of Puerto Ri-can workers in two leather goods factories who fought back against the "backdoor" contracts—contracts made between employer and union without the workers' consent—that forced them to join a local of the AFL-CIO Retail Clerks International. When the workers began picketing the shops, their employers sought an injunction. Although their case was dis-missed by the New York State Supreme Court (the Association of Catholic Trade Unionists [ACTU] provided legal counsel to the workers), the strike was broken when the city Welfare Department sent destitute job seekers, many of them Puerto Rican, through the picket lines. After reading about the case in *El Diario*, scores of Puerto Rican workers began contacting the ACTU with complaints about the various practices of illicit "racket" unions. Eventually the ACTU estimated that one hundred thousand Puerto Rican workers in the city were being exploited by such unions. The AFL-CIO had set up an Advisory Committee on Puerto Rican Affairs (the name of which was later changed to the "Committee to End the Exploitation of Puerto Ricans and Other Minority Groups") a couple of years before, in response to pressure from the Migration Division, though it was considered to be "largely ineffectual" even after the mounting publicity over the racket unions.[67] The ILGWU showed more concern for Puerto Rican workers than any other "respectable" union, in part because Puerto Ricans consti-tuted a huge majority in the garment industry—as Jesús Colón observed, "Most Spanish-speaking families have at least one garment worker"—and in part because it defined itself as liberal and antiracist. (*The New Yorker*'s Christopher Rand said the ILGWU was "flat out against discrimination of any sort now, partly in reaction to Hitler's racist theories, which shocked their members in the 'thirties and 'forties.")[68]

But many liberal unions were being pulled in an opposing direction by the mid-fifties. Faced with the beginnings of the garment industry's migra-tion to suburbs and exurbs, where overhead costs were lower and profits higher, leaders of unions like the ILGWU compromised on wages and work standards in order to convince shop owners to keep their business in the city, "solv[ing] the problems of employers at the expense of impoverished garment workers."[69] That also meant abandoning any real commitment to nondiscrimination. During his unsuccessful campaign for a city council seat in 1957, *El Diario* journalist José Lumen Román—the first Puerto Rican to run for this post—asserted that only with the election of more working-class Puerto Rican leaders would the community be able to prevent the exploitation of workers "because we don't count with representatives in the city government."[70] Indeed, Joseph Montserrat's attitude toward labor activists during that very campaign all but proved Lumen Román's point. When a conflict arose between Joseph Montserrat and labor activist José Pérez over a union endorsement, arising from Pérez's alleged use of Migra-tion Division letterhead, Montserrat sent a telegram to the ACTU secre-tary proclaiming that "this office does not welcome meetings of unionized workers, nor does it permit the use of its letterhead for such events." A month later, when AFL-CIO head George Meany renounced the continuing exploitation of Puerto Rican workers by racket unions, he was told by a Migration Division representative that "Puerto Rican workers looking for work do not want to be sent to union shops"—and it was unclear whether this was the Migration Division's bias or an actual reflection of Puerto Ricans' mistrust of unions in the city.[71]

The new recognition of their conflicts with the city's unions was, in fact, bringing Puerto Rican workers together, and throughout 1956–58, they staged a number of notable strikes that got the attention of union officials and employers alike. And George Meany made some symbolic efforts on behalf of Puerto Ricans during the 1957 campaign season.[72] Sixty-three percent of Spanish-speaking households had a union member in 1959, according to a report cited by Clarence Senior in 1961. But Puerto Ricans' distrust of union leaders, including those of the liberal ILGWU, was a major stumbling block to achieving industry-wide gains. During a wildcat strike by ILGWU local 62, the mostly Puerto Rican workers at the Q-T Knitwear Company in Brooklyn carried placards that read, "We're tired of industrial peace. We want industrial justice." They were, then, protesting not just against their bosses' unjust treatment but also, as one reporter noted, "against [their] own union."[73]

Of course, the ILGWU defended its record on representing its Puerto Rican workers. At the same time, Montserrat was insisting that the Migration Division had no formal ties with Puerto Rican union activists. Other liberal observers, like Clarence Senior, erased the conflicts altogether, repeating the fictive notion that Puerto Ricans were "making solid gains" at little cost in the labor market. Senior reserved special praise for a 1958 initiative called "Operation Rapport," designed by the New York State Department of Labor and the Migration Division to help union officials understand their Puerto Rican constituents through "studying" them and in some cases visiting Puerto Rico. He was also sanguine about the power of unions as "civic organizations," since Puerto Ricans could use them to encourage political participation.[74] But neither Senior's optimism about Puerto Rican workers, nor Montserrat's claim that unions were "unnecessary" for them, could stand up very well to the kind of evidence that Herbert Hill laid out before Congress a couple of years later. Manufacturing "rapport" and praising workers for their "civic" activity did nothing to help them combat sharp declines in wages, Hill demonstrated.[75] And it is important to note that even critics of the liberal union practices in the late fifties, including Wakefield, Lumen Román, and Hill, failed to address the fact that Puerto Rican garment workers as a group were doubly invisible in this period, since a majority of them were women.[76]

## A New Nadir

While most manufacturing industries in New York faced increasing uncertainty, good reports continued coming in from Puerto Rico regarding its Bootstrap-based development throughout the fifties. For Puerto Ricans in New York, though, the economic outlook was grim indeed by the end of the decade. The struggles of Puerto Ricans in the garment industry and in other industrial sectors were only part of the story. The problem of housing had plagued many Puerto Rican migrants from the moment of their arrival in New York, even before the postwar mass migration; after new federal housing legislation in 1954 spurred a wave of "urban renewal" in New York, Puerto Ricans as a group experienced dislocation to a degree unprecedented in the city's history.[77] At the same time, juvenile delinquency had become a new and almost daily source of scandalous headlines in New York, often with Puerto Rican youth as their subjects. Gangs and youth violence were very visible problems in Puerto Rican communities, especially by the late fifties. At the end of the summer of 1959, the problem of juvenile violence was already dominating the pages of *El Diario* when the city's most dramatic juvenile crime of the decade took place. A Puerto Rican boy named Salvador Agrón, dubbed "the Capeman" in the English-language press, "Drácula" in the Spanish papers, stabbed two white teenage boys to death in a Hell's Kitchen playground, apparently without provocation (and the victims were "straight," not members of a gang).[78] For weeks, the incident occupied headlines in numerous New York dailies, where the "Drácula" story overshadowed another drama unfolding in the Puerto Rican community: the fight against the scheduled demolition of a dozen blocks on the West Side, which would affect up to ten thousand low-income families, most of them Puerto Rican. *El Diario* fit in its coverage of the West Side urban redevelopment plan alongside its stories about the "Drácula" murders, a vivid reminder to Puerto Rican readers about how their simultaneous visibility and invisibility operated to limit the possibilities for their empowerment.[79]

Securing decent housing was an old struggle for Puerto Ricans. In the late thirties, members of the Harlem Legislative Conference, including Vito Marcantonio, Oscar García Rivera, Leonard Covello, and Joseph

Figure 15. Salvador Agrón and Antonio Hernández, arrested for the murders of two other teenagers, Anthony Krzesinski and Robert Young Jr., September 2, 1959. Agrón became known as "the Capeman" ("Drácula" in Spanish) because he was wearing a black cape at the time of the murders. Al Fenn, Time & Life Pictures / Getty Images.

Montserrat, had organized a lobbying campaign in support of a proposed housing project in East Harlem, to be built on nine square blocks east of First Avenue and north of 102nd Street. During the war, the New York Housing Authority received hundreds of letters from applicants to the housing project, about 25 percent of them Puerto Rican. They were people hoping that their current housing would be considered "substandard" enough to make it onto the list of tenants for the new projects. At this point, the coalition of radical and liberal activists talked about "low rent housing" and "slum clearance" as initiatives that would be helpful, rather than discriminatory and damaging, to the city's poor.[80] Their discussion of the planned improvements in housing for the poor also implied their assumption that the process would include input from Harlem residents themselves.

By the mid-fifties, however, it was clear that the housing issue in Harlem resided firmly in the realm of liberals who tended toward paternalistic attitudes about the poor. When Charles Abrams, head of the New York State Commission against Discrimination, returned from a world tour as part of the United Nations Housing Mission in 1954, he commented, sympathetically if dramatically, that Puerto Ricans in Harlem lived in conditions worse than any he saw on his trip.[81] Other liberals working on housing were adept at taking the earlier goals of grassroots housing activists and shifting them to depoliticize the problem, most often by holding the victims of the problem responsible for their own suffering. The Mayor's Committee for Better Housing warned in a 1955 report that "as long as Puerto Ricans are content to live under conditions that to our modern civic conscience educated to higher housing standards appear to be intolerable, there will be such demand for cheap housing that the old law tenements will remain as a very undesirable part of our city housing supply."[82] Bernice Rogers, deputy commissioner of housing in New York, asserted that the problem of housing was "more one of citizenship than merely housing maintenance." She collaborated with city school administrators to set up an essay contest on "What I Have Done to Make My Home and Neighborhood More Livable," part of a new "Program of Housing Education and Citizenship."[83]

The fifties' incarnation of slum clearance—called "urban redevelopment" by now, and dubbed "Negro removal" or "spic removal" by many African Americans and Puerto Ricans—had begun in earnest by this point.[84] The most extensive and controversial urban redevelopment plan of the decade was the one to create a new arts complex at Lincoln Square on Manhattan's West Side. The actual condemning of the designated twelve square blocks was preceded by the precipitous raising of rents during the summer of 1957. Harris Present, counsel for the Spanish-American Youth Bureau, represented the residents of the condemned buildings in a suit against the city to try to stop the sale of the land. Present lost the case, and the newly incorporated Lincoln Center for the Performing Arts gave $150 to $550 "relocation bonuses" to residents who agreed to move voluntarily.[85] In its coverage of these events—which coincided with the premier of *West Side Story*, set in the same neighborhood that was now slated for demolition—the *New York Times* failed to mention that most of the six or seven thousand affected residents were Puerto Rican. The actual demolitions were scheduled by early September 1959, and the announcement of this phase of the redevelopment plan coincided exactly with the furor over the Capeman murders. During the next several years, as the redevelopment plan was to be extended north along the West Side, residents organized several groups to combat it or to push the city to execute it in a way that would be less damaging to their communities.[86]

Whereas most New Yorkers were blind to Puerto Ricans' role in the housing and labor dramas that were unfolding in the last years of the fifties, they missed no opportunity to point fingers at the Puerto Rican community when it came to blaming someone for the era's most visible juvenile crime. The Capeman murders confirmed white New Yorkers' worst fears about Puerto Rican youth, and they presented Puerto Rican leaders with the realization of their worst nightmare of anti–Puerto Rican publicity. One reason that the crime became such a cause célèbre was that the perpetrators of the violence were members of several West Side gangs, while their victims were "straight," not connected to youth gangs. They were, by all appearances, innocent targets of seemingly senseless gang violence, which struck a chord with middle-class New Yorkers already obsessed with the apparent senselessness of youth violence. Delinquency rates, measured through juvenile arrest counts, had peaked in the United States in 1943, declined in the first years after the war, then began rising again by 1949. In 1957, across the nation, more than twenty-three in one thousand children aged ten to seventeen appeared before juvenile court for alleged delinquency, nearly double the 1948 rate of about twelve per thousand.[87] In New York, black and Puerto Rican youth were scapegoated as the most dangerous and irredeemable delinquents.

Liberal social scientists had tried occasionally to counter such allegations with empirical evidence. The first real research on Puerto Ricans and delinquency appeared in 1949, based on sociologist Erwin Schepses's examination of the admission records of the New York State Training School for boys. While Schepses concluded that the percentage of Puerto Rican inmates was "much higher" than their share of the population of New York City, he also found that, compared to a control group of non–Puerto Rican boys at the training school, the Puerto Ricans displayed delinquent behavior of a less serious nature and performed substantially better than the control group in tests of nonverbal or "performance" IQ—despite reports of greater deprivation in their home lives.[88] (Schepses did not cite research published by Sophia Robinson in the thirties, which argued that court records could not provide a reliable means of assessing the "criminal element" in a given ethnic group, since "cultural factors"—that is, racism or ethnic prejudice—often determined who got arrested in the first place.)[89] Several years later, a Board of Education tally of court referrals among Puerto Rican and non–Puerto Rican children, aged six to fifteen, showed Puerto Rican children to be "offenders" at a slightly lower rate than their non–Puerto Rican peers. More illuminating than the overall numbers was the comparison of actual offenses: Puerto Rican child offenders were overrepresented in the categories "stealing," "marriage applications," and "narcotics" but underrepresented in "sex delinquency," "neglect," "holdup," "assault," and "gang fights." Puerto Rican leaders argued repeatedly that juvenile delinquency was a temporary problem resulting from postwar social changes, one that was not unique to Puerto Ricans. Migration Division head Joseph Montserrat quipped that juvenile delinquency was "just second-generationitis."[90]

Montserrat would not be so flippant when the problem exploded again in the summer of 1959. El Diario played into the drama, running countless stories like "victims of juvenile gangs symbolize the failure of community," "'Gang' says: We want to be good, but nobody helps us . . . ," and "juvenile gangsters live in a world apart and almost have their own language." The stories were accompanied by photographs of brokenhearted mothers of lawless youth, "their faces bathed in tears."[91] Thousands of individual Puerto Ricans gathered with representatives of over 160 Puerto Rican organizations in meetings, press conferences, and community forums throughout East Harlem and across New York City in the weeks following the murders, to outline strategies to combat the double plague of delinquency and prejudice.[92] New York's tabloids and even the Washington Post noted the community's efforts in editorials that commented on the injustice of putting a Puerto Rican face on youth violence. Clarence Senior would later comment, in his patronizing way, that "they explained their program to the other citizens of New York in full-page ads in all the daily newspapers, under the title 'We, Too, Fight Delinquency.' It is believed to be the first time a newcomer group ever took such a step."[93]

Other juvenile murders that year had involved "square" or "straight" victims of gang members and attained far less notoriety than this one that featured a Puerto Rican perpetrator. The Capeman murders inspired accusations from the public that gang members were being "coddled" by city officials who were reluctant to punish them adequately—a debate only one step removed from the recurrent accusation by hostile observers that Puerto Rican migrants in general were "coddled" by the city welfare bureaucracy, allowed to collect welfare checks as soon as they arrived. It was an elision of the basically separate problems of juvenile delinquency and welfare dependency, and some city officials allowed that "Puerto Ricans do take more than their share of public assistance," while others firmly defended the "get-tough" approach of the police on juvenile delinquency.[94] There were actually four gang killings that week, and Harlem city councilman Earl Brown said that record "ought to convince us that we cannot cope successfully with the juvenile delinquency problem by dealing with juvenile gangs as if each one were a separate nation entitled to all the rights and privileges which a sovereign power enjoys." This comment referred to the New York City Youth Board's strategy of placing "street workers" in a gang's territory, where they would try to "convert" individual gang members or convince whole gangs to "go social," but it also sounded like a roundabout reference to some of his Puerto Rican rivals in the district, some of whom sought to keep the independence of their homeland, a "separate nation," on the political agenda.[95] A Brooklyn judge, Samuel Lie-bowitz, used the Capeman case to try to argue that Mayor Wagner should discourage Puerto Ricans from migrating to New York: since Puerto Rican youth comprised 22 percent of juvenile delinquency cases, he said, and only 7 percent of the population, they represented what was clearly a net negative influence on the city.[96]

The Reverend Joseph Fitzpatrick, a liberal sociologist and staunch defender of Puerto Ricans, made a case for more historical perspective on delinquency in a lecture he gave to his Fordham students a month after the Capeman murders. He told his audience how accusations of criminality and epidemic gang violence had been thrown at all previous immigrant groups in New York, quoting at length various mayors, United States legislators, and Catholic bishops and archbishops on the moral failings and insidious vice of Irish immigrants. Fitzpatrick argued that there had never been, in fact, any "good old days"—crime and violence had been far worse in the nineteenth and early twentieth centuries, he said, than in the 1950s.[97] Later in September, when Joseph Montserrat testified before the U.S. Senate Subcommittee to Investigate Juvenile Delinquency, he pointed to "poverty, insecurity, ignorance, prejudice and discrimination, living in slums, and substandard wages" as the "major causes" of juvenile crime. In the same testimony, Montserrat mentioned a proposal before the subcommittee to raise the barriers to migration and for residency requirements for public assistance—a backlash against the presumed "coddling" of Puerto Ricans. "We [at the Migration Division] take issue with such proposals," he said. "They reflect a shocking lack of knowledge about migration and public assistance, and a disregard for rights of citizens." Montserrat went on to argue that the committee was not adquately aware that "juvenile delinquency is inextricably linked with broader problems such as nation-wide population shifts, housing conditions, opportunities for education and employment, and economic development."[98] For many New Yorkers, of course, those links were invisible. The only salient fact about the murders remained that the Capeman was the embodiment of the dark-skinned, violent delinquent and the youthful symbol of the city's ongoing Puerto Rican problem.

When Clarence Senior published a book on Puerto Ricans in the United States in 1960, an impressionistic and boosterish survey that he called "a candid picture of the largest immigrating group in the nation today," he gave it the sanguine subtitle *Strangers—Then Neighbors*. It was an elaboration on liberals' bland trope that Puerto Ricans were "just like other immigrants," bound to adjust and assimilate more or less like their predecessors. Senior's vague arguments and scantily documented evidence pointed out improvements in migrants' health, education, employment, housing, and "integration into the larger community," attempting to show that indeed Puerto Ricans had been incorporated as members of equal standing in American society.[99] Migrants may have experienced some measurable gains during the fifties, but the common features of Puerto Rican life in New York City in the late fifties—continuing marginalization in politics, exploitation by employers and unions, persistent impoverishment compounded by new "slum clearance" programs, stereotyping as "welfare cheats," scapegoating of Puerto Rican youth—belied Senior's putatively scholarly claims. (His praise for Operation Bootstrap, turning the migrants' homeland into a "showcase for democracy," would also turn out to be off the mark, as economic reports after the mid-sixties showed.)[100] Thus did Senior insist on the fait accompli of Puerto Ricans' inclusion in a liberal vision of postwar society, on the incorporation of Puerto Ricans into an orderly, basically egalitarian society where complaints and critiques could be smoothed over by studies that would demonstrate how "valuable" Puerto Ricans were and how much they were "improving."

But the particular modes of that inclusion functioned to turn Puerto Rican visibility in this era—what Ralph Ellison called "high visibility" and some recent scholars have referred to as "surplus visibility"—into an entrenched *in*visibility in the political and civic life of the city. Or, as Michel Foucault put it in his well-known study of the technological development of modern prisons, "Visibility is a trap."[101] Leaders like Muñoz Marín and Joseph Montserrat, along with other key actors in the CIS and the Migration Division, were determined in the fifties to elevate Puerto Ricans to a place that would fit with the social vision of postwar liberals. Their approach, however, involved the unwitting subjection of Puerto Rican migrants by offering them up as objects of study rather than collaborating with leaders and members of the grassroots organizations that predated the Migration

Division. Not unintentionally, the "Bootstrap" liberals on the island and in New York also silenced dissenters, the erstwhile "subjects in communication" who sought to describe a different reality for their fellow Puerto Ricans in New York. Many of the liberals who considered themselves to be Puerto Ricans' greatest boosters thus contributed to their invisibility in New York, and compounded their disempowerment not by calling them apathetic or incapable of producing effective leaders, but by refusing to acknowledge the colonial roots of the Puerto Rican migration.

The focus on Puerto Ricans as objects of social scientific study continued into the sixties. Much of the work produced in that era, like Senior's, was attentive to the struggles of Puerto Ricans in New York and critical of the treatment they encountered there.[102] However, only a couple of the many book-length studies of Puerto Rican migrants' lives—anthropologist Elena Padilla's *Up from Puerto Rico* and journalist Dan Wakefield's *Island in the City*—treated them in nuanced and complex ways that acknowledged the full range of Puerto Ricans' social and political engagement in New York. Aside from these two exceptional books, even the most sympathetic social science and journalistic writing on Puerto Ricans followed the pattern of treating their subjects as significant and visible historical actors while refusing to recognize their capacity to participate as "full partners" in social and political fields. Oscar Handlin's discussion of Puerto Ricans and their socioeconomic stagnation in his 1959 book *The Newcomers* paid close attention to the structural disadvantages they faced, like discrimination in housing and employment. But Handlin's research was glaringly thin in many places, leading him to reproduce in spades the stereotypes about Puerto Ricans' political apathy, their lack of "associational life," and the "tragically rare" instances of Puerto Ricans who were "willing and able to exercise creative leadership."[103]

The regularity with which even liberal scholars engaged in such willful misrecognition of Puerto Rican activism helps explain the pervasive popular images of Puerto Ricans as gang members and welfare cheats. While Puerto Rican communities remained visible for their many problems, Puerto Rican activists outside the liberal establishment—those involved in labor and housing activism, collaboration with African Americans on the Left, or organizing for the American Labor Party, for instance—were largely invisible in their varied efforts at solving those problems. By the late fifties, however, a new generation of young activists would manage to establish a rich and durable "associational life" even as Handlin described its absence. Not only would they succeed in making themselves, and many of their compatriots, "subjects in communication" rather than "objects of information"; they also initiated a shift in Puerto Ricans' discourse about their political identity that would find a clear voice by the mid-sixties, creating space for mainstream and radical activists alike to make claims that challenged the limitations of liberal citizenship.

# *"Juan Q. Citizen,"*
# *Aspirantes, and Young Lords*

## Youth Activism in a New World

In 1951, a group of Puerto Rican students from Benjamin Franklin High School (BFHS) in East Harlem wrote a plaintive letter to *El Diario* asking the editors to publicize a series of attacks they were suffering at school. The students reported that members of Italian gangs at Franklin were targeting Puerto Rican boys, stealing their lunch money, and beating them up to the point that several, they said, had left the school in fear. "We believe that we have the right to study without being harassed by anyone," the students wrote, "since we are American citizens and our parents pay taxes just like [the Italians] do." A couple of months later, *El Diario* reported again on gang attacks against Puerto Ricans at Franklin, naming the Red Wings as the perpetrators and remarking on the principal's handling of the conflicts internally.[1] Leonard Covello, who had steered Franklin through a number of previous anti–Puerto Rican incidents as principal of the progressive and multiethnic high school since he founded it in 1934, made no public statements about the harassment. He did, however, speak on the issue to the school's Club Borinquén, which he had helped organize in the late thirties following the first wave of ethnic conflict between Puerto Rican and Italian youth in East Harlem. In their discussion of the injustice of these attacks, both the students and Covello framed the problem as one of the denial of individual rights in a liberal framework. That is, their status as citizens should protect the students from discrimination at the very least, giving them the freedom to study and thereby, they implied, the opportunity to become even better citizens.

For the Puerto Rican students, this was a new kind of assertion, expressive of the second generation's efforts both to gain a foothold in the city's social landscape and to demand their individual rights as aspiring members of the mainstream. In terms of relations with the Italian community, on the other hand, their lament was old news: members of both communities testified to the Italians' anti–Puerto Rican sentiment dating back to their first contact in the twenties. The first youth conflict between Puerto Ricans and Italians covered in the press, an incident that took place in 1938, had not directly involved any Franklin students, according to reports, but the school community got caught up in the feuds between rival groups across "the line" that separated the Italian and Puerto Rican sections of East Harlem, fueds that were, according to reports, exacerbated when a bunch of the Italian boys accused El Barrio's beloved congressional representative, Vito Marcantonio, of being a "spic lover."[2] Covello's advocacy on the part of Puerto Ricans in 1938 won him much admiration from the *colonia*. But it also generated some furious reactions from non–Puerto Rican community members, the majority of whom were Italian and many of whom resented having to send their sons to one of the city's few desegregated schools. One letter, signed only with a crudely drawn skull and crossbones, presented Covello with a "WARNING. No damn lousy Spics are allowed in Franklin. . . . This is your last warning. The next time we will use more *drastic* measures." Undeterred, Covello conducted an "intercultural questionnaire" about students' racial and ethnic attitudes and made speeches about tolerance, emphasizing how Puerto Ricans were victims of the same tensions over ethnic succession that had plagued the Jewish and Italian immigrants who preceded them.[3]

Ten years later, with the postwar migration from Puerto Rico still escalating, Italian Americans all over East Harlem expressed resentment about the changes in their community, as did New Yorkers throughout the city who feared the "dangerous influx." Puerto Rican youth continued to bear a heavy burden of the anti–Puerto Rican fury on the streets. Throughout the 1950s, Puerto Ricans under the age of twenty-five comprised New York's most rapidly expanding demographic group, so they were ready targets of the public's anxiety about a postwar world in flux. Widespread fears about young Puerto Ricans and their fitness as American citizens had developed alongside the national obsession with youth, especially those with dark skin, that dominated the media in the decade following the "zoot suit" riots in 1943 and a spike in gang activity and youth homicides in the same decade.[4] While Covello and some of his progressive colleagues had been working to counter the vilification of poor youth since the thirties, their efforts on behalf of the growing Puerto Rican population touched only a small fraction of the city's migrants. A larger number of Puerto Rican children and families were drawn into New York's education and social service institutions via the more dominant liberal agendas that would, by the mid-fifties, describe the ideal new migrant as "Juan Q. Citizen." Adult migrants *social reform agenda*

were barraged with messages from the Migration Division and other social service agencies about voting and learning English, as well as about comportment in the workplace and proper standards of dress and housekeeping, and younger Puerto Ricans were targeted by liberal educators who hoped to provide the most promising students with the tools to embark on middle-class lives. The Puerto Rican students at Franklin who publicized their experience of discrimination in 1951 would have heard dozens of versions, sometimes indistinguishable from one another, of these progressive and liberal messages directed at youth.[5]

Shortly after the gang harassment incidents at Benjamin Franklin, in a conformist cold war milieu that intensified nationwide fears about juvenile delinquency, a growing number of Puerto Rican youth leaders began to take the reins from their white liberal allies, defining themselves as the future leaders of their community. They worked to create a new image of Puerto Rican youth, plotting a path of selective assimilation—and navigating around obstacles like *West Side Story*'s gang stereotypes or the publicity surrounding the Capeman murders—to be recognized as equal members of postwar American society. Theirs was not a direct challenge to the assimilationist ideal of turning the Puerto Rican migrant into "Juan Q. Citizen," although it was an assertion of their power to articulate the ideals of American citizenship for themselves.

Gradually, over the course of the fifties, this first generation of young Puerto Rican leaders began to emphasize demands for recognition as a group alongside more standard claims for individual rights. And, by the early sixties, many of the young mainstream leaders began to challenge the political and institutional assumptions of the social liberals who supported them, for the first time making colonialism part of the mainstream conversation about Puerto Rican advancement in New York.[6] With deindustrialization as a stark backdrop of the community's struggles in the sixties, along with new debates about its "culture of poverty" and then the radicalization of the African American civil rights movement, politicized young Puerto Ricans began to challenge the moderate, liberal approach of the older second generation and embrace a more radical agenda that would shift the balance of Puerto Rican activism in New York by 1970. During the decade in which some began to talk about Puerto Ricans' struggles in the United States in terms of "recognition" instead of simply in terms of equality as citizens, young activists made a definitive contribution to the language of their community's various political claims. Rather than asking for recognition in a liberal discourse of inclusion-as-equals, militant youth and even some of their more mainstream counterparts framed their demands for recognition in American society in more challenging terms, insisting on the legitimacy of their claims for sovereignty—"self-determination" and "liberation"—both for Puerto Ricans in the metropole and for their homeland itself.[7]

## "Education for Citizenship" in El Barrio

In 1936, the year that Dr. Clairette Armstrong and Dr. Edith Achilles published their IQ study of Puerto Rican children, there were approximately eleven thousand Puerto Ricans enrolled in New York City schools. A decade later, at the beginning of the massive migration of islanders to New York, there were about twenty-five thousand. Even then, few New Yorkers, including many city officials, were aware that the city already housed a sizable Puerto Rican community. Leonard Covello was one of the few non-Hispanics who was interested in the growing population of Puerto Ricans before the late 1940s. He had commented on their rising enrollments at BFHS by 1935, but it was the controversy over Puerto Rican children's intelligence that called his attention to their problems as reviled immigrants and confirmed for Covello the importance of the pluralist program of citizenship education at his school. Covello called his educational philosophy "intercultural democracy," which he and other progressive educators developed in the thirties amid the broader intellectual embrace of cultural pluralism. New York's cosmopolitan intelligentsia both inspired and legitimized the turn to pluralism in progressive education by the early 1930s; in this milieu, it had become axiomatic that the "melting pot" was a flawed metaphor, no longer a useful guide in the incorporation of immigrants.[8]

In a 1941 radio interview with Gilberto Concepción, of the East Harlem Educational and Research Bureau, Covello highlighted the importance of a holistic, community-based approach to educating young people according to the principles of cultural pluralism: "These young people may be Americanized through the schools, they may receive all the formal education which comes of intimate association with fellows and young people of other racial stocks. [But] it is the informal, intimate association with fellows, the absorption of attitudes and ways of conduct and thought and action, . . . that is after all, the real education. The education must be a carryover of the community into the school and from the school into the community."[9] His point resonated with the lessons American progressives were gleaning from the World War II era about the violent rise of Nazism in Europe and the continuing violence of racial conflict at home. Social problems, they argued, emerged from broad social and historical forces and could not be eradicated solely from within the protected social environment of the school.[10] However, in spite of Covello's optimistic agenda, BFHS—one of the only intentionally integrated schools in New York in that era—was not immune to the impact of social conflict in the surrounding neighborhood. The most widely publicized racial incident at Benjamin Franklin took place in 1945, a series of so-called student riots (only minor disturbances according to some observers) that lasted for two days and were definitively quelled only, according to the *New York Times*, when four hundred police officers settled in to patrol the neighborhood night and day. Although the original conflict reportedly began as a classroom fight between an Italian American boy and an African American boy, Covello said the incidents were instigated by a "vicious hoodlum element" outside the school that "would vent their race hatred by using violence against our colored students."[11] In a larger frame, the 1945 "clash" at Franklin signified the intensification of racial conflict during the war as well as the nation's sense of impending doom about the future of American youth—fears that were fed by events like the zoot suit riots in Los Angeles in 1943 and more generally by the spike in juvenile delinquency during the war. Across the country, concerned educators had begun to develop programs to promote "good citizenship" as a strategy to reverse the path of wayward youth after the war.[12]

At the local level, the incident at Franklin exposed the overweening optimism of Covello and other progressive educators' "intercultural democracy" program, weaknesses that East Harlem's skeptical whites in particular found unsurprising.[13] Covello received more than a dozen angry letters after the conflict, most of them from white parents complaining about the dangers confronted by their children at Franklin, where, as one Italian American mother put it, "their lives are [put] in peril by this negro element who are beyond control in their viciousness towards the White Race."[14] A few of the letters avoided explicitly racial language, but to the same effect, like the one from a father named Ralph De Donato: "I take pride in stating that my son has been reared in strict adherence to the traditions of well bred people, and has been trained to carry to school a pen and pencil, rather than an ice pick or a razor."[15] Another letter, different in tone, admonished Covello for downplaying the role of "the economic conditions among the people of [Harlem]," echoing interpretations of the Harlem riot ten years earlier. L. F. Coles, who had in fact given a statement to police following the 1935 riot, wrote: "I agree with you that we must teach the groups to understand each other and to appreciate the contribution made by each other. The police did not arrest any of the white students as you may know, but arrested and man-handled many of the colored students. Of course the colored people will resent this for a long time to come. You did not say anything about that."[16] Though he did not identify his race, Coles was African American, the only nonwhite Harlemite to write to Covello about the student conflict.[17] He was also the only observer who suggested the impact of the incident on the people whom he and Covello agreed were the victims, "the colored people." As with the Harlem riot, Puerto Rican students at Franklin were invisible participants in this drama in the event's newspaper coverage and in white residents' verbal attacks on the "nigger element" in the neighborhood. Their role as suffering, struggling members of the community, people who also experienced violent discrimination, disappeared in the framing of the incident as a black-white conflict.

Meanwhile, young Puerto Ricans were simultaneously becoming more visible as potential juvenile delinquents. In the thirties, experts had worried over the delinquent tendencies of the European immigrant second generation primarily. But by 1945, debate about delinquency focused on its dangerous prevalence among all youth, although in cities like New York and Los Angeles, it was especially the darker ones that worried experts and the white public.[18] While many liberals were already arguing for the need to counter delinquency among youth with "education for citizenship," the nascent cold war made the issue doubly urgent.[19] Sociologist Henry Thurston, who had published a number of books on delinquency since the 1920s, warned in the late forties: "Even if we could succeed in the complete prevention of juvenile delinquency, which I once called bad citizenship, we should still be only at the threshold of our main problem of education of youth in good citizenship, on . . . which the progress . . . of our American democracy depend[s]."[20]

The National Education Association (NEA) was concerned enough about the link between delinquency and citizenship to organize an annual National Conference on Citizenship throughout the first decade of the cold war.[21] At the opening of the 1949 conference in New York City, in a speech full of canned pedagogical rhetoric, the NEA's president admonished the audience to work toward educating responsible voters. Her opening anecdote was anything but predictable, however, and had little obvious connection to a talk on "the role of public schools in developing American citizens." Mabel Studebaker described to her listeners the inauguration of the first native Puerto Rican governor, Luis Muñoz Marín, which she had attended

on the island just a few months before. It was "faith in the democratic process," she said, that inspired "poor farmers from the hills" to line up in droves
to vote—just the kind of faith that educators needed to instill in the nation's
youth. There was a certain irony to her rhetorical strategy that was, no
doubt, unintentional: the keynote speaker at an event driven by triumphant
liberal nationalism holding up the United States' only colonial citizens as
a shining example of democratic engagement.[22] On the other hand, it was
probably not unintentional that Studebaker celebrated Puerto Ricans' fine
citizenship at a point in the late forties when Puerto Rican youth were presumed to be the most dangerous citizens in New York City.

Indeed, at the moment Studebaker was delivering her speech, East
Harlem was still straining to accommodate the massive migration from
Puerto Rico, and Leonard Covello and his cohort of progressive educators
and activists found that the sparkling ideals of "tolerance" had faded to
almost nothing. Overshadowed by postwar conformism and paranoia, and
by the problems of educating a group of poor, disoriented children, most
of whom did not speak English upon arrival in New York, the hope that
Puerto Rican children would be "appreciated" without having to assimilate fully seemed naïve. Even in the view of many progressives, intercultural
democracy programs now seemed both less effective and less necessary
than bilingual teachers and parent education. Inspired by Covello's work at
Benjamin Franklin, New York's Board of Education published a committee
report in 1947 on Puerto Rican children's adjustment problems and the
impact of the "undesirable socio-economic influences" in their communities. Above all, the committee asserted, "with the Puerto Rican pupil . . . the
most important objective of education is the development of good citizenship." But they saw this as a "real challenge," because of the prevalence of
broken homes and the behavioral problems that often resulted from such
situations. The school board's approach to educating Puerto Ricans in the
postwar years had come a long way from its "Americanizing" notions thirty
years before, which the report's authors remarked on sanctimoniously:
"There is a danger in confusing good citizenship with 100% conformity.
In this process [of adaptation], an attitude of respect and appreciation for
other cultures and other races is encouraged."[23] Nevertheless, the prepon-
derance of educators' reports and policymaking in this era would continue
to focus on coping with "the usual delinquencies," with an implicit presumption about Puerto Ricans' particular susceptibility to them.

While the postwar emphasis on rehabilitating delinquents and training
citizens to fight the cold war dominated the city's education agenda, Cov-

ello and Benjamin Franklin faculty quietly if less optimistically persisted in their intercultural programming and bolstered support of Puerto Rican students, whose numbers increased every year between 1947 and 1955. By the time the first big wave of postwar migrants began settling in East Harlem in 1946, Covello and other BFHS staff had modified most aspects of the school programming to include issues concerning Puerto Rican children and their families. Club Borinquén continued to sponsor regular dances and cultural events, and by 1948, it had established the annual "Latin American Festival," which quickly attracted high-profile artists, writers, and performers from El Barrio, who donated their time "for the aid of the poor Puerto Rican student."[24] Covello was probably one of the few principals who actually used some of the educational films created by the Migration Division, like *A Girl from Puerto Rico*, which the accompanying literature described as "portray[ing] the difficulties of a Puerto Rican girl who is snubbed by a classmate on her first day of school. The film shows the reaction of other students and the progressive measures suggested by them and the teacher to make the girl feel more at home." The Migration Division suggested that teachers use Puerto Rico as the subject of a social studies unit. "Student interest and understanding are increased and, through Puerto Rican music and dances, a friendlier atmosphere is created," one of its pamphlets read, echoing the intercultural education ideas of Covello, who would retire from Franklin and become the education director at the Migration Division in 1956.[25] His progressive advocacy notwithstanding, Covello never rejected traditional postwar educational ideals. He noted proudly, for instance, that "we are interested in preparing these [Puerto Rican] boys for active participation and useful citizenship in the U.S."[26]

Their agenda was not limited to Franklin. Partly due to Covello's advocacy on the issue, by 1951 there were ten bilingual teachers in the handful of schools with the highest Puerto Rican concentration.[27] Of course this was inadequate: a Mayor's Advisory Committee on Puerto Rican Affairs (MACPRA) report from that year insisted that "the need for teachers who can speak Spanish is urgent. If . . . increased proportionately to the Puerto Rican school population, we should need approximately 1000 real Spanish-speaking teachers." As early as 1936, following the controversy over Puerto Rican children's IQ scores, Covello also argued that the standard IQ testing practices in the United States were not valid for "foreign-born" children, including Puerto Rican migrants. In 1947, Covello was still demanding that current tests of academic achievement and mental ability for Puerto Rican students should be reevaluated, and "appropriate instruments of

measurement should be developed for [them]." By 1951, with input from
Covello, the MACPRA recommended that tests should be given in Spanish and "standardized according to our knowledge of their background in
Puerto Rico and the emerging cultural pattern in their new environment";
or, alternatively, "non-language tests" should be given to determine grade
level and aptitude.[28] It also recommended that a full-time staff person be
hired to "cope . . . with the Puerto Rican orientation and assistance program." This report made it clear that assimilation of Puerto Ricans was the
goal, but with an explicit call for cultural sensitivity and inclusiveness: "The
Puerto Rican parent must be made to feel that his child is being accepted
with the same status as that of the Continental child . . . that his home life is
not being held up to criticism."[29]

During these first years of New York's anti–Puerto Rican backlash,
Leonard Covello was second only to Vito Marcantonio in terms of actively
fostering the "mutual respect" that so many white liberals talked about.
Covello addressed other New York City school principals on what he saw
as their obligation to the city's Puerto Rican families: "The post war world
requires of citizens and teachers more than mere understanding of their
neighbors—immediate or distant. It demands, in addition, an understanding, mutual respect, and a mutual sharing of our cultures. [We have] an opportunity for gaining such an understanding of our fellow Americans—the
*Puerto Ricans.*"[30] During the summer of 1947, Covello traveled to Puerto
Rico to deliver a series of lectures at the University of Puerto Rico and
to meet with colleagues there about a proposed training program for
Puerto Rican teachers on the island to prepare them to work with migrant
students in New York. During the ten-day tour of the island, Covello visited
twenty or so towns in a quest to "get to know" the island from which so
many of his students had emigrated, hand-delivering scores of letters written by Benjamin Franklin students to their friends and family.[31] Upon his
return, the *New York Herald Tribune* praised the principal who "walked the
walk" of progressive educators. As far away as Pittsburgh, the *Courier* proclaimed, "There's a Far Brighter Story about New York's Puerto Ricans,"
touting the school's "fine program for Puerto Ricans," which offered a "new
approach" to educating "foreign youth."[32]

It was no surprise that the nuances of Covello's work, his progressive
and pluralist approach to "education for citizenship" that challenged the
orthodoxies of traditional assimilationism, were absent from the discussion of what he was actually attempting to do in East Harlem. Although
his vision of Puerto Ricans as "just like other immigrants" was in many re-

spects similar to the liberal social service ideal of training the migrant to become "Juan Q. Citizen," Covello's advocacy on behalf of Puerto Rican youth—as in the case of the aggrieved students in 1951, among countless others—helped foster their leadership skills independent of the social service establishment. Ultimately, this generation of young leaders would contribute substantially to the challenging of the old liberal orthodoxies via new discourses of group rights in the 1960s.

### Aspiration: "New Leaders in New York"

In 1952, the Mayor's Advisory Committee on Puerto Rican Affairs established a scholarship fund for Puerto Rican students, explaining its primary goal as "to promote maximum integration of our citizens of Puerto Rican background into the general New York citizenry in the shortest possible time."[33] Their publicity materials did not actually use the "Juan Q. Citizen" phrase that the Migration Division included in at least one of its pamphlets in that era, but the idea was the same: assimilation facilitated by a shared national citizenship. In its first year, the scholarship provided ten students with $300 toward the cost of college. By 1955, the program had expanded enough to offer nineteen students a grant of $500. (In 1955, the State University of New York [SUNY] colleges cost about $450 per year, and private colleges in the region ranged from $800 to $1,000.)[34] Emphasizing that the scholarship was about more than just educational achievement, a 1953 press release explained the committee's vision of the "next steps" of the scholarship fund: housing; "integration," focusing especially on English-language proficiency; "mutual understanding" and civility; employment; and building a Puerto Rican leadership base in New York.[35]

Around the same time, the Riverside Neighborhood Assembly, a liberal organization on the Upper West Side, established a more experimental leadership program, involving exchanges of promising youth between Manhattan and Puerto Rico. Upon their return, the "Goodwill Ambassadors" would write a weekly newsletter on issues in the Puerto Rican community and speak to New York–area youth groups about their experiences on the island. The program was described by the *Herald Tribune* as an "anti-bias plan," though its less publicized goal was to encourage Puerto Rican children to become community leaders, in part by providing them with extra educational support.[36] The Board of Education's experimental "Higher Horizons" program was part of the same constellation of initiatives geared toward supporting minority children, and it received praise from Puerto

Rican educational activists. Unlike other programs that focused on training participants in practices of "good citizenship," which proliferated in the
first decade after the war, Higher Horizons provided for educational enrichment broadly conceived: more guidance counselors, remedial reading
and math teachers, and specialty teachers in its target schools, as well as
trips to the opera, the theater, and science laboratories.[37]

The advocacy of liberals like Covello and the members of MACPRA was
only a small part of the story of efforts to change educational outcomes
for—and the public image of—Puerto Rican youth in the fifties. Early in
the decade, young migrants themselves, including a small but growing cohort of college students, sought to strengthen their community and take
control of the negative discourses about Puerto Ricans in New York by
creating youth-based leadership initiatives and youth-run community organizing campaigns. Certainly the public's focus on juvenile delinquency
helped galvanize Puerto Rican youth to promote their own agenda of "civic
pride" for Puerto Ricans by the mid-fifties. But the force of youth activism
had more to do with demographic change in the Puerto Rican community.
Second and third generations were now attending high schools and colleges, and growing numbers of Puerto Rican youth were inspired to build
networks and create alliances with existing community organizations to
promote their own agendas for change. This was a common pattern among
immigrant youth, one that historian George Sánchez traces in Los Angeles
among the Chicano youth whose parents settled in the city in large numbers before the First World War and who created their first educational
and self-help organization by 1934.[38]

Among the new generation of young Puerto Rican leaders in the 1950s,
Antonia Pantoja would become the best known, although, as a migrant herself who arrived in New York in her twenties, her background was different
from that of many of the second-generation members of her cohort. Soon
after her arrival in the city near the end of World War II, Pantoja fell in with
a multiethnic group of artists and radicals, lived downtown, and briefly attended the radical Jefferson School for a course on the "Marxist Interpretation of the History of Puerto Rico," a set of formative experiences more
cosmopolitan than those of many of her contemporaries who spent their
youth in New York's *barrios*. What Pantoja did share with the other young
leaders of her generation, many of them students and activists at a number of New York's high schools and colleges, was a sense of anger at the
discrimination and exclusion experienced by the people of her community
and a determination to challenge the anti–Puerto Rican status quo.

Pantoja had been a youth worker at a community center, a job that was a point of entry for many young activists by the early sixties.[39] She then became one of the leaders of the first formally organized, youth-led Puerto Rican organization in New York, the Hispanic Young Adult Association (HYAA), while she was an undergraduate at Hunter College in the early 1950s. HYAA's goal was to create a forum to bring together the energies of an emerging cohort of activist Puerto Rican youth. One of its central objectives was to influence the images of Puerto Ricans circulating in New York, images that HYAA felt were being "managed" somewhat ineffectively by liberals in the Migration Division and in the city's educational and social service establishment.[40] A growing and increasingly divisive debate emerged within HYAA's leadership between, on the one hand, a moderate, liberal, and nonpolitical response to elevating the community through its youth, and, on the other hand, a more politicized faction that sought to call attention to the ways in which existing institutions and city officials were failing to meet the needs of the Puerto Rican community, and young Puerto Ricans in particular. "We described this approach as one of community development instead of 'firefighting,'" recalled Pantoja.[41]

This split was partly responsible for the emergence, out of HYAA, of the Puerto Rican Association for Community Affairs (PRACA), in 1956. Pantoja recalled that the motivation for the change in the organization's name came from a desire to make the organization explicitly a Puerto Rican one, a group that would proudly assert its Puerto Rican identity rather than retaining the more vaguely assimilationist label "Hispanic." Though not officially organized to serve youth, PRACA was led by young Puerto Rican professionals and activists.[42] Shortly after the creation of PRACA, Pantoja, who had gotten a master's degree in social work from New York University, was offered a staff position on the new Commission on Intergroup Relations. Her mentor there, Dr. Frank Horne, encouraged her in the creation of the Puerto Rican Forum, a larger and more powerful organization than PRACA. Pantoja modeled the Forum after a similar group that Horne had founded for young African Americans in the South and designed it to support both general institution building in the Puerto Rican community and the fostering of young leaders who would initiate Puerto Rican–run programs.[43] Many of the participants in these groups described them as modeled after "uplift" and "community defense" groups like the NAACP.[44]

Although this movement of youth activists was well under way before the Capeman murders in 1959, the incident, and the renewed flood of anti–Puerto Rican vitriol that followed, inspired a new flurry of organizing by young leaders focusing primarily on educational issues. A group calling itself the Hispanic Association Pro–Higher Education (HAPHE), founded in 1959, sponsored the first in a series of annual conferences for Puerto Rican youth that met throughout the sixties. The second Puerto Rican Youth Conference, in 1960, articulated a goal that still echoed with the Puerto Rican community's trauma following the Capeman incident: "to set a positive image to counter 'pathology and fear' to show the Puerto Rican as ambitious, with a desire and increasing ability to climb upwards, as have all past newcomers to the city." Indeed, the conference report's summary of audience responses to the panel presentations—which covered a wide range of issues, including housing, city politics, and island culture as well as problems of educational achievement—reflected this focus. Although the attendance at the conferences was primarily Puerto Rican, HAPHE held the events at high-profile institutions like the Dalton School, Hunter College, and Columbia University, a sign both of the youth leadership movement's increasing visibility in the city and of its determination to be included as a participant in the city's mainstream educational establishment.[45]

In 1961, members of the Puerto Rican Forum's board of directors created a youth organization that Pantoja had envisioned, she recalled, since the mid-fifties, "an instrument to develop leaders from among our youth." They named the organization Aspira, from the verb "to aspire," and Pantoja says that she and her collaborators planned Aspira as a movement, not a service agency, and structured it around "clubs" that would allow youth to set their own agendas and designate their own leadership. Aspira began as a movement, indeed, but not a radical or even an unconventional one; it was based on a premise of maximizing "professional and technical talent in the community," as a group of leftist researchers described it in the 1970s.[46] Though often accused—especially by Puerto Rican activists in the late sixties and early seventies—of promoting a conservative or assimilationist agenda, Aspira served as an early model of cultural pride and community autonomy that would become central to Puerto Rican community organizing in the sixties. Its programs, emphasizing educational skills and achievement and access to higher education, were indeed more moderate than radical, but its firm commitment to a Puerto Rican–run leadership structure (as opposed to collaboration with non–Puerto Rican social service professionals) and to the teaching of Puerto Rican history and culture marked Aspira as a challenger of the status quo within New York's social service networks.[47]

Pantoja would later describe Aspira's relationship to the Puerto Rican

Figure 16. Antonia Pantoja, founder of Aspira, 1960s. Antonia Pantoja papers, Archives of the Puerto Rican Diaspora, Centro de Estudios Puertorriqueños, Hunter College, CUNY.

social service sector, dominated by the Migration Division, as an uneasy one. She acknowledged that the Office of the Commonwealth "believed that their mission was to help the community solve its problems" but said that it "was equally concerned with maintaining a position of control over New York Puerto Ricans and keeping the leadership in the hands of the government of Puerto Rico." Moreover, she remembered its approach to community as one limited by racism: "The leadership of the [Migration Division] office espoused integration and assimilation, but I knew that only those of us who were white-skinned had any hope of this kind of acceptance." José Morales, another participant in the leadership movement of the early sixties, described a related split among some leaders of both the Forum and Aspira, one whose fault lines followed the tensions Pantoja described with the Migration Division. It was an explicitly political schism: leftist *independentistas* in the group accused their more moderate colleagues—those who supported the work of the Migration Division—of being *"perfumados,"* those who supported the "perfumed colonialism" of the commonwealth relationship.[48]

The shadow of colonial politics was visible even to some of the young Aspirantes, framing their sense of their own educational horizons in the United States. David Pérez, who became a Young Lord in 1969, argued that one problem for Puerto Rican children in North American schools in that era was that "language becomes a reward and punishment system" for those who did not necessarily learn English at home. It was this kind of experience that motivated many Aspirante leaders, along with other Puerto Ricans, to pursue bilingual education beyond the limited structure of the late-forties' SAT program. (And in 1974, Aspira filed a lawsuit against the New York City Board of Education, charging that teaching non-English-speaking children in a language they did not understand violated their constitutional rights.) Gradually, Aspirantes' critical stance about Puerto Ricans' educational experience led to more aggressive positions on the teaching of Puerto Rican history and culture, pushed forward by activists later in the sixties. Pérez described the experiences behind the demands that resulted, finally, in the creation of Puerto Rican studies courses in New York high schools and colleges: "Puerto Ricans are taught three things: Puerto Rico is small and the United States is big; Puerto Rico is poor and the United States is rich; Puerto Rico is weak and the United States is strong."[49] In spite of its identity by the late sixties as a moderate and even "assimilationist" organization, Aspira's young members considered it their mission to challenge this prevailing orthodoxy concerning Puerto Rico and its people. It was not just about demanding individual rights for young Puerto Ricans to achieve "respect" in American society. More important, and increasingly, their struggle was about insisting on group justice—an argument for recognition that Jesús Colón, ahead of his time, was making already in the mid-fifties: "The community is struggling to express itself more forcefully, to unite itself, to gain recognition and the rights it is entitled to, in the city at large."[50]

### Puerto Rican Youth in a Declining City

When the Board of Education named its new middle school enrichment program "Higher Horizons" in 1956, the presumption was that the many Puerto Rican students it served could look forward to greater opportunity and material gains in the near future. Although for some young Puerto Ricans—those who benefited from new bilingual teachers, social service support for their families, and the strong start of grassroots youth organizations like HYAA—the late fifties and early sixties did look brighter, most Puerto Rican children lived in households in which poverty and insecurity still outweighed opportunity. The average Puerto Rican child in 1960 would have had a parent who worked as a factory operative, probably in the garment industry, and if that parent was a man employed full-time, he made just over five thousand dollars a year, 30 percent less than his white male counterpart in the same industry. If that parent was a woman employed full-time in a garment factory, she made barely more than half the salary of her male coworkers. Even if the child's mother were lucky enough to land a clerical position in a midtown accounting office or insurance company, she would still make 35 percent less than the average white male factory operative.[51]

And it got worse over the course of the sixties. Puerto Ricans' family earnings dropped from 71 percent of the national average in 1959 to 59 percent by 1974.[52] In 1967, 33 percent of Puerto Ricans were receiving welfare benefits, up from 29.5 percent in 1959. The regional director of the state Bureau of Labor Statistics told journalist Pete Hamell in 1968 that 36.9 percent of East Harlem's Puerto Rican population reported unemployment or underemployment, compared with about 30 percent of African Americans in the neighborhood.[53] These figures belied sociologist Clarence Senior's assertion in the mid-sixties that Puerto Ricans were "climbing the economic ladder." This was a conclusion he arrived at via a facile contortion: comparing 1960 census data on median family income for Puerto Ricans in New York to that of median family income in Puerto Rico and sidestepping any comparison to whites or blacks in New York or to Puerto Rican migrants in the fifties.[54] The impact of deindustrialization and their still-poor educational attainment were stark facts for most Puerto Ricans in New York and meant that material security was even further out of their reach than it had been a decade earlier.

Race- and culture-based discrimination were critical factors in Puerto Ricans' income and employment disadvantages. In 1964, the Hispanic American Labor Council protested the "rank discrimination" still experienced by Puerto Ricans in labor unions, in spite of the push for equity by black and Puerto Rican labor activists since the late fifties.[55] NAACP labor lawyer Herbert Hill cited a 1964 report whose title summed up its importance for the Puerto Rican community: "Most Garment Worker Paychecks Are Below Johnson Poverty Level." Average hourly wage levels for majority Puerto Rican unions had declined substantially.[56] Complaints by black and Puerto Rican members of the ILGWU sounded the same in the sixties as they had a decade before: in 1967, labor activist Gilberto Gerena Valentín pushed the mayor's office to study the same problems of exploitative wages, discriminatory leadership, and racketeer and ghost unions that had plagued Puerto Rican union workers in 1957.[57] Compounding the impact of discrimination was the problem of deindustrialization, the flight of factory-based industries from the city by the early sixties. According to some scholars of this period, like sociologist Clara Rodríguez, it was the Puerto Rican migration itself that had allowed New York City to hold on to the garment industry as long as it did, since other industries had begun leaving the city several years earlier. Rodríguez explains that "without this source of cheap labor, many more firms would have left the city; those that stayed would have had to reduce their production." The discriminatory labor practices to which garment factory owners and union leaders subjected their Puerto Rican workers allowed owners to stave off the economic pain of relocating or shutting down. "In this sense," Rodríguez asserts, "New York's claim to be the garment capital of the world rests upon Puerto Rican shoulders." The average Puerto Rican worker's lack of options made the growing instability in the garment industry catastrophic for her community. Whereas nearly one-quarter of African Americans in New York were employed in local or state government by 1970, only 12 percent of Puerto Ricans were able to secure government jobs. By 1970, more than 50 percent of Puerto Rican families were living in poverty.[58]

Puerto Rican New Yorkers did not need the State Department of Labor or the Bureau of the Census to tell them how things were going on the ground. It was clear that their compatriots were losing the slight income gains they had made in the fifties, and losing the tenuous security and faint hopes for advancement they had nourished just a few years before. The early signs of these socioeconomic losses were alarming but not surprising, and they helped confirm the sense of mission that was already driving activists. Housing was still a persistent problem at the top of the agenda of many Puerto Rican community leaders in this decade, but it was education that became the real focal point. By 1960, with the implications of the *Brown* decision reverberating throughout northern cities, the politics of school integration mobilized parents and activists alike in New York. That year, residents of African American and Puerto Rican communities in Brooklyn, the Bronx, and Manhattan began pushing the Board of Education to site new schools in mixed-race areas or on the borders of more segregated neighborhoods, to encourage racial integration.[59] Puerto Rican and African American parents and community leaders also pushed for transfers of students in areas where they sought the desegregation of existing schools. Following the threat of a strike at the mostly black Junior High School 258 in Bedford-Stuyvesant, the superintendent of schools responded by instituting an "open enrollment" policy and encouraging parents to enroll their children in schools where "they will have a greater op-portunity to study with children of different ethnic backgrounds."[60]

Activists and parents used the school boycott as a tool to force the school board's hand on desegregation. Some observers hypothesized, however, that desegregation in itself did not animate Puerto Ricans—whose communities were "integrated already, biologically and socially"—as it did black Americans. Joseph Fitzpatrick, a Fordham sociologist, noted in 1968 that Puerto Ricans were "bewildered about their relationship to the civil rights movement" because of their multiracial group identity, and had retreated from their participation in the fight for black-white desegregation by the mid-sixties. Though Fitzpatrick's assertion was too broad to be fully accurate, it did explain part of the motivation behind the creation of organizations like the National Association of Puerto Rican Civil Rights by 1965, which focused on equity issues specific to Puerto Ricans, like abolishing the English-only literacy test for voting.[61] A more pressing issue than integration in the early sixties was the lack of any Puerto Rican, or even Hispanic, presence on the Board of Education. Puerto Rican children comprised almost 16 percent of the city's public school population in 1961, and they were the majority or near majority in over a dozen schools in both Manhattan and the Bronx, and in a handful of schools in Brooklyn. Lamenting that "there is no group so completely voiceless" in the city, the Puerto Rican Bar Association petitioned the mayor to appoint a school board member to ensure that the Puerto Rican community would "see [their] role changed from that of a voiceless subject of sociological thesis [sic] and studies, to that of equal citizens with a share in the policy making of a system so vital to themselves." Puerto Rican education activists managed a more symbolic but still powerful victory in 1964, when longtime Brooklyn activist Ramón Colón spearheaded an effort to build a new elementary school named for Puerto Rican Brooklyn's beloved community leader Carlos Tapia.[62]

By the mid-sixties, activists working on education issues were also asking why so many black and Puerto Rican students were being pushed into vocational training schools instead of academic high schools. This was not a new question—working-class parents and some liberals had objected to such "tracking" since the early twentieth century—but by 1965 African Americans and Puerto Ricans were suggesting that the failures of vocational education and a declining economy exposed the weaknesses, and perhaps the empty rhetoric, of President Lyndon Johnson's new War on Poverty.[63] At an antipoverty conference early in 1965, Michael Harrington, whose 1962 book *The Other America* had painted a shocking portrait of poverty amid prosperity in the United States, joined Aspira's Antonia Pantoja in arguing that the War on Poverty needed to focus on youth and "rock the boat" in order to "prepare a child of the poor to fight his way out of poverty," as Pantoja put it. Both criticized the tendency to steer poor teenagers toward vocational high schools, from which few graduated; indeed, one 1963 study cited by the *New York Amsterdam News* reported that over 80 percent of Puerto Rican students who graduated from New York public high schools in 1963 received their diplomas from vocational programs.[64] As Harrington told his audience, without a "real" War on Poverty that would provide jobs for the unemployed youth, "you . . . take young people, teach and train them and then put them back on the streets."[65]

Its critics notwithstanding, by 1965 money flowing through Johnson's War on Poverty initiatives supported a proliferation of new grassroots organizations in New York's poor neighborhoods. In 1964, seeing the success of a coalition of antipoverty groups in central Harlem, HARYOU-ACT, the Puerto Rican Forum applied to the Office of Economic Opportunity to fund a comprehensive, citywide agency that would promote, integrate, and supervise a system of projects designed to assist the Puerto Ricans in New York. The Puerto Rican Community Development Project (PRCDP) won a half-million-dollar grant from the city to distribute among twenty-five hometown clubs and other civic groups participating in a coordinated self-help initiative, and a multimillion-dollar grant from the federal government. Although one outcome of the PRCDP was increased tensions among factions of the activists and political leaders involved in its planning, they did continue to agree that the city was shortchanging Puerto Rican organizations as well as the Puerto Rican people.[66]

The unity of their discontent was publicized in the spring of 1967, when Mayor John Lindsay's office coordinated a conference with the awkward title "Puerto Ricans Confront Problems of the Complex Urban Society: A Design for Change." Lindsay invited over fifty activists, scholars, social service workers, and bureaucrats, nearly all of them Puerto Rican, to discuss the full range of problems facing the Puerto Rican community in New York, from housing and employment to educational attainment and delivery of social services. The most notable comments at the conference came from Gilberto Gerena Valentín, the longtime labor activist who became the head of the increasingly visible Puerto Rican Council of Hometown Organizations in the early 1960s and by 1965 headed the new National Association of Puerto Rican Civil Rights. Gerena Valentín spoke forcefully on the city's failures to adequately represent Puerto Ricans in its key institutions, pointing out that "there is no representation of our community in the Mayor's Cabinet, yet we comprise 12% of the City's population. . . . There is not a single Puerto Rican as a full paid commissioner." The other key problem Gerena Valentín identified was the literal and symbolic disfranchisement of monolingual Spanish-speaking Puerto Ricans. He insisted that they be included in the political process by offering civil service forms, tests, and applications in Spanish, "just as tax forms are in Spanish to extract our taxes."[67] A more concrete outcome of the conference was the commitment by the city to build a new public housing development at West Ninety-third Street and Amsterdam Avenue, which would be named in honor of the Puerto Rican writer and *independentista* Eugenia María de Hostos.[68]

To the extent that Puerto Rican activists and community leaders saw their work as insurance against the explosion of poor urbanites' resentments—as in the 1964 riots, which happened in mostly African American neighborhoods—they did not succeed. In the summer of 1967, just a few months after the mayor's "Design for Change" conference, and weeks after the Puerto Rican Day parade (whose theme that year was "War on Poverty"), El Barrio exploded.[69] This was its first full-scale riot, and the spark was the fatal shooting by police of a twenty-five-year-old Puerto Rican man who had allegedly stabbed another man. Journalist Peter Kihss, who had covered issues in Puerto Rican neighborhoods for the *New York Times* throughout the sixties, opened his description of the events with the question that many outside the community were asking: "Why did New York City's Puerto Ricans erupt into violence when they had endured ghetto conditions for so many years and had struggled to rise above them without such disorders before?"

The following day, Mayor Lindsay assembled a group of forty Puerto Rican leaders. As Kihss's question suggested, there was no singular cause to which the community leaders could attribute the riot. Instead, the most essential insight of the meeting at Gracie Mansion—though it may have been lost on many of the participants—came from the reports of a young community worker who was not an official invitee of the mayor. Arnold Segarra addressed the conference, emphasizing the need for "more meaningful dialogue" between East Harlem youth and both police and antipoverty workers. "Tell a kid you're putting $1 million [into the community], and he says, 'That's got nothing to do with me.'" Meeting attendees decided on the spot to assign Segarra, already an employee of the city's Human Resources Administration, to form a youth council. Kihss interviewed another young man, Aníbal Solivan, a former vice president of MEND (the Massive

Economic Neighborhood Development program) involved in several Community Action Program–funded organizations, who more pointedly than Segarra criticized the participants in the Gracie Mansion conference for being removed from El Barrio's problems on the ground: "That's the established power structure of the community. None of those cats was there during the weekend. They're not in the streets when they're needed. They don't relate."[70]

Two months after the riots, Puerto Rican writer Piri Thomas, whose notorious memoir *Down These Mean Streets* appeared in May that year, testified before the National Advisory Commission on Civil Disorders. Thomas posed a series of questions that sounded merely rhetorical only because his real interlocutors, his *barrio* neighbors, were not present:

> Did you ever stand on street corners and look the other way, at the world of *muchos ricos* [sic] and think, I ain't got a damn? Did you ever count the garbage that flowed down dirty streets, or dig in the back yards who in their glory were a garbage dump's dream? Did you ever stand on rooftops and watch night time cover the bad below? Did you ever put your hand around your throat and feel your pulse beat say, "I do belong and there's not gonna be nobody can tell me, I'm wrong?"[71]

In trying to explain why East Harlem had exploded, Thomas had little interest in the local politics of the riot, in the resentments over who controlled antipoverty funds and at what distance from the streets. His interpretation had more to do with what he might have called the existential pain of the rioters, a larger framework for understanding the "why now" question: for how many years can a group of people be told, in a thousand ways, "you're wrong" before they explode? In this sense, Thomas's reading of the riot and the beating pulse of El Barrio was not just about class and the impossibility of Puerto Ricans' belonging to "the world of *muchos ricos.*" It was also about Puerto Rican New Yorkers' ambivalence and anger about the various forms of exclusion they experienced in the United States—the consistent rejection of their claims for recognition as people who "belonged" and whose status as citizens promised some measure of sovereignty, over both their community and their island nation.

Just before the riot, the Puerto Rican writer and *independentista* César Andreu Iglesias had published a long review of Oscar Lewis's 1965 anthropological study *La Vida: A Puerto Rican Family in the Culture of Poverty,* about a poor Puerto Rican family whose members lived in and between two notorious slums, East Harlem and La Perla in San Juan. While acknowledging the damage the book would do to Puerto Ricans' image in the United States—a complaint detailed by Migration Division director Joseph Montserrat and other civic leaders in a tense meeting with Oscar Lewis that spring—Iglesias praised the accuracy of Lewis's "photographic" portrait of poverty. He argued that the debates about whether or not a "culture of poverty" existed among Puerto Ricans missed the mark, since they tended to focus on spurious measures of development and whether Puerto Rico was seen as either "falling behind" the fifty U.S. states or pushing ahead of other Latin American nations.[72] Andreu Iglesias deemed this conversation diversionary. The "key to the riddle" of the intransigence of Puerto Rican poverty was not the domino effect of weak morals or even, less damning, the weight of the cultural forms (unstable family units, or prostitution as "*la vida*" for many women and girls) that poverty created. The key, said Andreu Iglesias, was imperialism, and the complicity of those who believed the "empty propaganda" that programs like Operation Bootstrap could solve the problems of a dependent society like Puerto Rico.[73] According to Andreu Iglesias, *La Vida* had "awakened *inquietud*" not so much because it made Puerto Ricans look bad but because it revealed an animating truth: the official story that the Commonwealth of Puerto Rico was barreling ahead in its social and economic development was a lie.

Echoing Piri Thomas's suggestion in his postriot testimony, Andreu Iglesias insisted that poverty itself was only part of the struggle for Puerto Ricans. The lack of sovereignty, the lack of freedom to address their island's problems independently of the United States, was the real key to the riddle. More significant than the material failures they had accumulated during the sixties was Puerto Ricans' intensifying sense of disempowerment—"failures of recognition," as some theorists would later explain such experience—that created motivations for widespread radicalization in the New York *barrios*.[74] More accessible versions of these interpretations were being worked into the political vernacular of Puerto Rican youth even as Thomas and Andreu Iglesias were speaking them. Young radicals would thus hammer another nail into Juan Q. Citizen's coffin and, echoing Nationalist Pilar Pacheco's words thirty years earlier, demand recognition of the "free and sovereign" Puerto Rican in his stead.

## Puerto Rican Youth and Island Nationalism

Left-leaning Puerto Ricans like Andreu Iglesias and Piri Thomas were only the better known among thousands of activists who were determined to make a connection between the liberal antipoverty agenda in the United States and a new nationalist vision for Puerto Rico by the late 1960s. The sixties' Puerto Rican nationalist movement still identified itself with Pedro Albizu Campos's Nationalist Party of the 1930s, but now it was also defined by the increasing militancy of young radicals who were animated by the Cuban revolution, by decolonization struggles across Africa and southeast Asia, and by their opposition to the United States' war in Vietnam. In defining the field of struggle in this way, young Puerto Rican *independentistas* connected themselves to a complex network of radicals in the United States and to a worldwide network of radicalism beyond. In 1961, Jean Paul Sartre had written, in his preface to Frantz Fanon's iconic book *The Wretched of the Earth*, that the Europe of the colonial past was "at death's door." "And," he continued, "that super-European monstrosity, North America? Chatter, chatter: liberty, equality, fraternity, love, honor, patriotism, and what have you."[75] This cynicism is what young leaders of the fledgling Students for a Democratic Society articulated that year in their Port Huron Statement, and it was what most other politicized youth were saying in some form by the mid-1960s—especially the Puerto Rican, Chicano, and African American activists who sought to hold their liberal democratic society accountable for its violent exclusions and oppressions of so-called minority peoples. Long after the 1960s were over, literary critic Fredric Jameson described those years as the period in which "all these [Third World] natives and . . . those inner colonized of the first world . . . became human beings," autonomous subjects at last—at least in terms of their demands for recognition if not in terms of the reception of those demands by the state or the national mainstream.[76]

The politicized "inner colonized" of New York's *barrios*, whose families had come from an actual colony, now seized on every opportunity to link their local experience of oppression to the larger problem of colonialism. They were inspired by university students and other young activists generating a new nationalist surge on the island and also by what they saw as the failures of the traditional Puerto Rican nationalist movement. Disaffected members of the Puerto Rican Independence Party (PIP) and other young *independentistas* had created the radical Pro-Independence Movement (Movimiento Pro Independencia, or MPI) just weeks after Fidel Castro took Havana in 1959. The MPI would dominate independence politics in Puerto Rico throughout the sixties (and would transform into the Puerto Rican Socialist Party [PSP] by 1971). Rejecting electoral politics with even more vehemence than their predecessors in the thirties, MPI activists and affiliated student groups organized countless peaceful demonstrations as well as violent actions, particularly attacks on North American–owned businesses and homes—such as when an offshoot of the MPI, calling itself Armed Commandos for the Liberation, sent a volley of rocks into Harlem congressman Adam Clayton Powell's vacation house at Condado Beach in 1967, after he announced his support for the plebiscite that would allow Puerto Ricans to vote on the status question, which *independentistas* dubbed the "colonial plebiscite."[77]

The island's nationalist leaders of the sixties believed, more firmly than the Nationalist Party's founders in the thirties, that the goals of sovereignty and independence for Puerto Rico could not be pursued effectively without a substantial collaboration with activists in New York. Attempting to legitimize itself via the political memory of their parents' generation in the New York *barrio*, the MPI promoted itself there as the "Misión Vito Marcantonio" and established a network of committees and offices in New York that sponsored regular events in the city throughout the sixties. The MPI admonitions against mobilizing "pity, pity for the poor" (the words of MPI head César Andreu Iglesias) echoed what Piri Thomas and other Puerto Rican New York activists were saying about poverty being the straw man of New York Puerto Ricans' oppression. Instead, MPI leaders crafted political messages that would be relevant to their New York audience: "When Puerto Rico is liberated, what will be the status of the Puerto Rican in New York?"[78] They prodded their compatriots with what would become the signature slogans of the radical Puerto Rican movement in New York: "Wake up, *Boricua*, defend what is yours" and "¡Pa'lante, pa'lante! [Move forward, move forward!]."[79] (Nevertheless, members of the Young Lords Party, along with other activists, noted in the early seventies that the MPI "had not been able to raise itself as a significantly strong force among the Puerto Rican people in the U.S." before the Lords took up a more explicit nationalist agenda in 1970, more firmly connecting the island-based group with its constituency in the diaspora.)[80]

The MPI worked hard to publicize protests leading up to the planned 1967 plebiscite. The U.S. Congress and the Puerto Rican legislature had established a Status Commission in 1963 to test whether the "compact" between the island government and the U.S. Congress, under the commonwealth arrangement, was working to the satisfaction of the Puerto Rican people.[81] Nationalists' refusal to participate in the vote, scheduled for April 1967, stemmed from their increasingly militant abstention from what they referred to as "colonial elections." They also argued that the plebiscite represented an effort by the U.S. government to make the commonwealth look like a voluntary political relationship. The nationalist protesters waged an extensive media campaign. The Cuban paper *Granma* interviewed the *independentista* intellectual Manuel Maldonado-Denis about the boycott, and a group called the Congreso Puertorriqueño Anticolonialista took out a two-page ad in the *New York Times*, accusing the United States of staging the plebiscite to "avoid a United Nations inquiry on the case of Puerto Rico."[82]

About a year before the vote, politicians on the island and in New York began arguing over the question of whether Puerto Ricans in New York would be allowed to participate. Bronx borough president Herman Badillo came out against New York Puerto Ricans' participation, while the editors of *El Diario–La Prensa* supported it, saying that "the future of Puerto Rico does not belong to half the Puerto Ricans. It belongs to all and should be decided by all."[83] Journalist José Lumen Román (who had run unsuccessfully for city council in 1957) wrote a forceful endorsement of New Yorkers' participation for the island's largest nationalist paper, *El Imparcial*. Lumen Román argued that Puerto Ricans in New York, who "go to sleep thinking of and wake up dreaming about Puerto Rico," maintained direct ties to the island's future through their remittances and must therefore have a say in the outcome of the plebiscite. In the end, Puerto Rican New Yorkers did not participate in the vote, though reportedly some Puerto Ricans born on the island returned home to cast a ballot.[84]

The outcome of the vote was unsurprising. Votes for the commonwealth option won out at 60 percent of the total, statehood got almost 39 percent, and independence less than 2 percent of the votes. MPI leaders claimed that the actual support for independence was exponentially larger than the vote demonstrated, that the official results failed to represent the real political preferences of Puerto Ricans because the MPI had successfully convinced so many supporters of independence to stay away from the polls. In fact, they went so far as to assert that the 35 percent of the electorate that abstained from the vote represented a full 35 percent in support of independence, a seriously flawed claim given that the normal rate of abstention in island elections was about 30 percent.[85] Perhaps not anticipating the extent of nationalist protest, the plebiscite's planners had scheduled the vote for the fifty-year anniversary of the Jones Act, the 1917 law that extended U.S. citizenship to Puerto Ricans. A variety of celebrations in New York marked this "gold anniversary," each one an opportunity for nationalist activists to protest both the plebiscite itself and the colonial relationship with the United States. While the president of the Puerto Rican Senate was ad-

Figure 17. Puerto Rico's governor Luis Muñoz Marín (*left*) with Averell Harriman, a U.S. ambassador (*center*), and Senator Jacob Javits (*right*) celebrating the tenth anniversary of the Commonwealth of Puerto Rico at the offices of the Migration Division in Manhattan, 1962. Records of the Offices of the Government of Puerto Rico in the United States, Archives of the Puerto Rican Diaspora, Centro de Estudios Puertorriqueños, Hunter College, CUNY.

dressing hundreds of celebrants at the Park Sheraton in Manhattan, insisting that American citizenship offered "equality to all" and that there was only one "class" among U.S. citizens, protesters outside were making different arguments. They chanted slogans like "American citizenship no, independence yes," "Muñoz Marín is a traitor," "To Hell with the Plebiscite," and "American citizenship forces Puerto Ricans to die in Vietnam."[86]

Opposition to the war in Vietnam, particularly the draft, was increasingly central to the radical *independentista* agenda by the mid-sixties. It especially animated young radicals in New York, who borrowed many of their antiwar critiques not from more proximate groups like SDS but from island nationalists. The MPI and other groups staged numerous marches and protests in Puerto Rico starting in 1965 in support of members of the independence movement who refused to register for the draft, and coordinated similar efforts in New York, including a three-day hunger strike by protesters in front of the United Nations building. Recognizing that it would help cement their ties to New York activists beyond the city's *barrios*, nationalist radicals from the island explicitly framed their antiwar discourse in a way that would insinuate Puerto Rican sovereignty into the agenda of radical organizations—nearly all of which also opposed the war—in the United States. Nationalists argued that, just as the draft yoked young men on the island in a violent relationship with the colonial power, so did it implicate all American youth in the larger imperialist system. (For instance, when Puerto Rico's governor Luis Ferré was given a Freedom Award by the Order of Lafayette in 1969 for "distinguished leadership in fighting Communism," protesters proclaimed to their New York audience that "we concede to Ferré's right to this prize because he has handed Puerto Rican youth over on a silver platter, to North American imperialism, to be utilized as cannon fodder for the criminal aggression waged against the heroic people of Viet Nam [sic]."")[87] As one *independentista* group put it, in a flyer circulated among youth organizations in New York, "The same forces that are attempting to stifle the struggle for Puerto Rican Independence are aiming at the militarization and intellectual castration of the youth of the US."[88]

Many African American radicals welcomed the backing of the antiwar *independentistas*, and before long the support was flowing both ways. Stokely Carmichael, leader of the Student Nonviolent Coordinating Committee (SNCC), traveled to Puerto Rico in January 1967 for an antiwar demonstration, invited by MPI leader Juan Mari Bras. At the march, reportedly ten thousand strong, young Puerto Ricans carried banners that read, "We support Black Power in the United States." Stokely Carmichael—himself a Caribbean immigrant who had moved from Trinidad to the Bronx in 1952 at the age of ten—addressed the marchers directly with a fiery speech about the broad scope of their common cause: "There is an intimate relationship between our movement for black power and your movement for independence. Our people is a colony within the United States, in the same form that Puerto Ricans are a colony outside the continental United States. Brothers, we see our struggle allied with the movements for national liberation of the people of Asia, Africa, and Latin America, especially the struggle against North American oppression."[89]

Before his departure, Carmichael signed a pact with Mari Bras pledging coordinated action between SNCC and the MPI to address their shared concerns beyond stopping the war: "the struggle for political and economic control, better living conditions, and education" for African Americans and Puerto Ricans in the United States. Mari Bras told Carmichael that he had ordered members of the MPI's New York branch to "lend all their support in every possible way to the black movement in the U.S."[90] Then, in the weeks before the 1967 plebiscite on Puerto Rico's status, *independentistas* from the island and New York and other young radicals staged a "Teach-In on Puerto Rico" at Columbia University, featuring Puerto Rican leaders like MPI member Juan Angel Silén, together with H. Rap Brown of SNCC and SDS founder Tom Hayden. It was modeled after a similar event held in Chicago earlier in the year, planned by the Puerto Rican group Federación de Universitarios Pro Independencia, which reportedly had drawn three hundred attendees from ninety universities in the United States.[91] Three weeks after the Columbia teach-in, Stokely Carmichael met with Juan Mari Bras again, this time in Havana, at a meeting with other radical leaders in the hemisphere. Puerto Rican independence had entered the pantheon of radical causes in the United States, united, according to their proponents, by the destructive power of U.S. imperialism.

What radical *independentistas* had accomplished by the late sixties was more than just the publicizing of their agenda beyond the island. They also forged important alliances with other activists, black nationalists as well as the increasingly militant Puerto Rican youth in New York, that expanded activists' vision beyond their own particular causes. Most narratives of the heterogeneous terrain of sixties radicalism presume that Black Power was the progenitor of radical politics in the United States, a singular force in the radicalization of other identity-based activist groups—Chicanos, Asian Americans, Puerto Ricans, feminists, gay liberationists.[92] In fact, the long history of radical nationalism and anti-imperialism in twentieth-century Latin America, which formed the ideological roots of both Puerto Rican and Chicano nationalists, was also essential in shaping black nationalists' ideas by the mid-sixties. A more specific borrowing from the Latin American left was the theory of "internal colonialism." The genealogy of this idea was not linear—it had traveled along the intellectual trajectories of decolonization and dependency theory critiques in Africa and Latin America, respectively, since the late fifties at least. But it was a critical framework that Puerto Rican nationalist groups were developing well before Black Panther Eldridge Cleaver appropriated it in the mid-sixties to argue that African Americans in the United States were a subject people, disempowered and exploited much like an actually colonized people. It was an echo of what the MPI claimed in 1962, for instance, during a protest at the United Nations building against police brutality and the imprisonment of Puerto Rican nationalists; its leaflets described the victimization of African Americans and U.S. Puerto Ricans at the hands of "the empire that oppresses us."[93]

### Young Militants in New York's *Barrios*

In 1970, a leftist journalist reflected on what he called the turning point in El Barrio around 1965: "While the dust from the first pro-independence explosions was settling, more and more Puerto Ricans, especially the young, were beginning to see . . . the bitter fact that their island was and is the only classic colony in the American experience."[94] As a growing number of Puerto Rican college students in the mid-sixties mobilized to change this "bitter fact," they began to form nationalist-oriented organizations like the Puerto Rican Student Union and the Sociedad Albizu Campos. Island nationalists, for all their success connecting with Black Power leaders, in fact had been less effective at shaping the politics of young Puerto Ricans in New York. One reason for this was that working-class Puerto Ricans tended to be suspicious of what they saw as the historic racism and class pretensions of nationalist groups, including the MPI.[95] Also, because the politicization of the younger generation in New York was so deeply influenced by their local context—weaving together a diasporic version of nationalist ideals that was inclusive and antiracist with a radical grassroots antipoverty agenda—many young activists saw island nationalists' agenda as too narrowly focused on Puerto Rican politics.

Unlike their island counterparts, many of whom situated themselves in a century-long tradition of nationalism defined largely by elite intellectuals, the politicized New York Puerto Rican youth of the 1960s were better described as "revolutionaries-in-waiting," "ready to explode at the moment they began to grasp the depth of their oppression and its origins in a colonial system," as Michael Harrington wrote in his 1967 review of *La Vida*. Harrington actually meant to challenge the accuracy of such notions about the poor and the oppressed, popularized by anticolonial radicals like Fanon. But in fact many young Puerto Ricans in New York were describing themselves in just those terms on the eve of the full explosion of radical activism in El Barrio and the Lower East Side by 1969.[96]

By the mid-sixties, even the less radical young Puerto Ricans in New York were rejecting the "Juan Q. Citizen" ideal that seemed to them to define the previous generation's presumptions about how to achieve inclusion. At the sixth annual Puerto Rican Youth Conference, held in 1964 at Columbia University, members of mainstream youth groups like Aspira articulated forceful messages about demanding rights and fighting oppression, framed in ways similar to those of their African American counterparts.[97] Puerto Rican youth were expressing the same frustration with moderate activism that had caused the civil rights movement's young avant-garde to repudiate its elder leaders by the mid-sixties. In the words of the NAACP's Herbert Hill, black youth no longer pinned their hopes on collaborations with "the vague arrangement of groups assembled under the worn banner of 'liberalism,' a liberalism that has been in retreat and decline for over a generation."[98] Young Puerto Ricans were assembling in storefronts and back rooms and tenement apartments all around El Barrio and the Lower East Side, plotting not to "work hard" to participate in the American society that already existed but to re-create that society altogether. Groups like the Independent Committee in Support of Mobilization for Youth and Social Progress—which would later change its name to the Real Great Society, a multiethnic and multiracial group of radicals working on the Lower East Side—called for a *real* War on Poverty" that would guarantee them their rights, they said, to better housing, employment, and better schooling.[99] Tensions emerged between organizations that drew on the plentiful new federal, city, and state antipoverty funds and those that rejected the approach of the "poverty pimps," as younger, more radical activists called those who were "removed from the community" and sought, in the words of Pablo Guzmán, to "keep the savages down" as they bickered over the spoils of the War on Poverty.[100] While established leaders worked on organizing Puerto Ricans to participate in the planned Poor People's March in Washington in 1968, members of groups like the Sociedad Albizu Campos and the Real Great Society were envisioning bigger moves like revamping CUNY's curriculum and staging massive, citywide rent strikes.[101]

Their potential collaborators in New York's poor neighborhoods were young and increasingly volatile. In 1968, the median age among Puerto Ricans in New York was 19, compared to 38.6 years for whites.[102] After a nine-year decline in net migration from Puerto Rico, the number of Puerto Ricans migrating to and staying in New York increased substantially in 1965 and spiked in 1966, staying high through the end of the sixties. The *New York Times* reported on the new trend in migration with some alarm in 1966, noting that the "Caribbean gaiety and garishness" typical of Puerto Rican newcomers was now being superceded by political "ferment" and a "characteristic Latin dissension" in community politics.[103] Indeed, virtually every possible radicalizing influence on Puerto Rican activists was intensifying after 1965: the war in Vietnam, Black Power actions, the U.S. invasion of the Dominican Republic, and ongoing decolonization struggles in Africa and Southeast Asia. Their Chicano counterparts in the western United States, dubbed the "invisible minority" by *Newsweek* in 1966, were mobilized by the same forces and formulating the same kinds of political demands as Puerto Ricans in New York.[104] It was less than a year after the *Times*'s ominous report that El Barrio exploded in rioting, marking a turning point and a real acceleration in what had been a gradual trend in radical community organizing up to that point. (A year earlier in Chicago, where there was also a very young and quickly growing Puerto Rican population, rioting in the largest Puerto Rican neighborhood had also accelerated the politicization of many youth groups.) One African American minister had written just before the 1967 riot, in the *New York Amsterdam News*, about the "rising and justifiable militancy in the Puerto Rican community and a demand for a fair share of the city's services and resources."[105]

Finding themselves in noticeable numbers on college campuses also contributed to the young Puerto Ricans' radicalization. The SEEK (Search for Education, Elevation, and Knowledge) program, instituted in 1965, provided academic assistance to many young people who were the first in their families to attend college.[106] It also, according to many activists' recollections, separated them from their white classmates at CUNY.[107] Activist Iris Morales recalled, about the group of students in SEEK in its first years, that "we were marginalized, and we tended to stick together united by common experiences of poverty and racial oppression." Many of these students had been influenced by Black Power ideology; several of the Young Lords' early leaders had attended SNCC and Black Panther meetings, or other African American student groups, often while still in high school, before starting their own radical Puerto Rican organizations. Some explained their interest as simply being drawn to what was available in terms of activist groups. "I found there was nothing else for me to relate to then," said Iris Morales, who would become the Young Lords' deputy minister of education. "I saw things in terms of black and white, and given that choice, it was very clear to me that my choice was black not white." Others were unambivalent about their racial identity, coming to see themselves as Afro–Puerto Ricans. Pablo "Yoruba" Guzmán, later a member of the Lords' central committee, said that "before people called me a spic, they called me a nigger."[108]

These students not only stuck together, they also crafted an increasingly clear agenda as activists. In 1967, around the same time as the riot in El Barrio, Puerto Rican college students formed two organizations that would become central to the radical movement by the end of the decade. The first was the citywide Puerto Rican Student Union (PRSU), which evolved out of a collaboration of smaller groups of Puerto Rican students on individual CUNY campuses, like City College's Puerto Ricans Involved in Student

Action (PRISA), formed in the spring of 1966. The second, the Sociedad Albizu Campos (begun at State University of New York–Old Westbury), was named to honor the founder of the Puerto Rican Nationalist Party, who died in 1965, and focused on a combination of nationalist and local community issues. Members of both groups, after meeting for over a year, devoted increasing attention to the goal of creating Puerto Rican studies courses. In general, activists wanted to see greater acknowledgment of Puerto Rican issues on their campuses as well as a commitment to teaching Puerto Rican history and culture. Their organizing led to scores of protests and a handful of takeovers at various CUNY campuses in April 1969, many of them undertaken in conjunction with African American radicals.[109]

Less than a month before the takeovers, a busload of the New York student activists attended a national Latino youth conference in Denver called the Crusade for Justice. One of the high-profile attendees was a charismatic young Puerto Rican from Chicago, Cha Cha Jiménez, who was in the process of leading his street gang, the Young Lords, to abandon its hoodlum identity in favor of political action. Back in New York, some members of the PRSU and the Sociedad Albizu Campos, along with other nonstudent activists, became intrigued by the Young Lords' model and arranged to take a trip to Chicago to meet with Jiménez. They identified closely with his vision of radical community development and were impressed by the Chicago Young Lords' collaboration with local chapters of the Black Panthers and the Young Patriots, a militant organization of poor white youth with roots in Appalachia (who together formed the Rainbow Coalition). Within a month or so, the Sociedad Albizu Campos leaders decided to turn their organization and a couple of smaller groups into a New York chapter of the Young Lords. Young Lord Mickey Meléndez later wrote of their inspirations that year, 1969, that "it was a world of revolution"—Sandinistas in Nicaragua, Tupamaros in Uruguay, Torrijos in Panama, Mexican students at Tlateloco, Catholic bishops supporting liberation theology in Medellín, student rebels in Paris, nationalists throughout Africa—"and we did not want to be left out." In July, at a demonstration in Tompkins Square Park on the Lower East Side commemorating Fidel Castro's first revolutionary attack in July 1953 and his successful one in 1959, future Young Lord leader Felipe Luciano took the microphone. He introduced the newly named Young Lords to the crowd and told them that the Lords were in New York "to serve and protect the best interests of the Puerto Rican community." "Without an office, platform, or program," recalled Meléndez, "we went back to El Barrio to start the revolution."[110]

The Young Lords would become the most visible of the scores of radical Puerto Rican organizations in the late sixties and early seventies. After their first high-profile action in the summer of 1969 in East Harlem, a "garbage offensive," barricading several East Harlem blocks to protest the city's consistent failure to collect trash in the neighborhood, the Young Lords commanded the attention of the media and city officials. They were described by an admiring journalist as the "vanguard . . . of an awakening of a Puerto Rican political consciousness and cultural pride," by critics as "the fifth column in the service of Castro and Moscow."[111] They were indeed a novel force in New York's *barrios,* but they and many of their admirers mistook their brand of activism for something entirely new. One former member recalled the Young Lords as "the first true symbol of community protection" for Puerto Ricans in the ghetto neighborhoods in which the Lords worked, an assertion that illustrated both a disinterest in the accomplishments of the more mainstream activists who were the Lords' contemporaries as well as a lack of knowledge of their predecessors.[112] Carlos Tapia represented the same trusted source of services and protections in Brooklyn in the twenties and early thirties; Vito Marcantonio certainly had been a "symbol of protection" in El Barrio in the late thirties and throughout the forties; even in the fifties, there were the less comprehensive but still central sources of community support like Casita María and the Civic Orientation Office.[113]

It was true, however, that the Lords took "community protection" to a more militant degree than any previous bunch of activists. Their next major action involved the takeover of the First Spanish Methodist Church in East Harlem, where the Lords planned to set up a free breakfast program, clothing drives, health services, and Puerto Rican history classes. The group had approached the church leadership several times during the fall of 1969, asking to use the church's vacant facilities for their programs on weekdays, but were refused. One Sunday after worship, in late December, they barricaded the building and set to work establishing the "People's Church," serving several thousand East Harlem residents during the eleven days they managed to keep the police at bay in spite of a court order commanding them to leave by January 2. Hundreds of hungry children came to the church for breakfast each morning, sporting buttons proclaiming "Puerto Rican Power." The Young Lords asserted that they were enacting the will of the community; "by then Spanish Harlem was loyal to the Lords," wrote Pablo Guzmán later. They finally left the church peacefully on January 7 after 105 of them were arrested, and faced contempt charges for having ignored the court injunction. Young Lords chairman Felipe Luciano, as he was escorted from the church, told the media, "The people have spoken. What can I say but power to the people." Former Bronx borough president Herman Badillo mediated on the Lords' behalf, convincing the church's reverend Dr. Humberto Carranza—a Cuban refugee who said he was repulsed by the Lords' revolutionary ideology—to drop the charges.[114]

Thereafter, the Young Lords Organization (YLO) continued with what it called "serve the people" programs, including activities like needle exchanges and a pathbreaking anti-lead campaign. It also grew quickly. Within a few months of the People's Church action, branches of the Lords were established in Newark and in the Bronx, and by August 1970, the group recognized another branch in Philadelphia and the New York leaders renamed the organization the Young Lords Party (YLP).[115] In September, the Lords hosted a youth conference at Columbia to promote the liberation of Puerto Rico, which they said was attended by about a thousand high school and college students. In December of that year, Pablo Guzmán, minister of information, took what he called an informal tally of the Lords' membership in New York and counted over a thousand.[116]

Some *barrio* residents were put off by the Young Lords' Black Power salute and their militants' uniforms. Iris Morales recalled that one of their methods of collecting food for the breakfast program—"it wasn't like there were any grants for the Young Lords"—involved going to local grocery stores and simply demanding donations. "You put on your beret, that helped," she said.[117] But relations with the community were often positive. Although many of their actions were of more symbolic than practical value, the Young Lords were mostly fighting for things that mattered to "the people" in general, problems that more moderate activists had been trying to solve in El Barrio for decades. After several months of working with activists trying to improve services at the dilapidated and dysfunctional Lincoln Hospital in the South Bronx, for instance, the YLP staged a one-day takeover of Lincoln in the spring of 1970, transferring acute-care patients to other hospitals, hoisting a Puerto Rican flag on the roof, and, according the Lords, running the hospital with the help of a "reenergized staff."[118] Their high-profile seizure of the hospital partly obscured a longer history of strikes by the hospital workers themselves, organized by the late sixties as the Health Revolutionary Unity Movement. It also overshadowed previous protests by moderate community leaders—as when Migration Division chief Joseph Montserrat, black labor leader A. Philip Randolph, and writer James Baldwin collaborated on a letter to the New York Times to condemn "the second-class citizenship status and sweatshop wages of all minority group workers in our city." The 1970 takeover was a militant assault on the realities of second-class citizenship, executed with the Lords' signature style, and it succeeded in getting the attention of city officials who ultimately (in 1976) rebuilt the hospital, though not without bitter conflict among the militants, the hospital board, and many of its doctors.[119]

*Newsweek* covered the goings-on in El Barrio in 1970, observing that "most Puerto Ricans—even those impressed by the bravado and machismo of the Young Lords—support the militant reformism of the advocacy planners rather than the violence prescribed by the revolutionaries. But even the most moderate admit this could change abruptly. 'We've gone through the stage of apathy, we're now at the stage of resentment,' and if nothing is done to improve things dramatically, 'we're going to be at the state of "Burn, baby, burn,"' says Lindsay staff member Amalaia Bentanzos."[120] The Puerto Rican staffer's reference to the explosive anger of African American neighborhoods—which in some places were intertwined geographically with the Puerto Rican *barrios*—played on the tensions that continued to mark the relationship between American and Puerto Rican radicalism into the seventies.[121] If whole *barrios* in New York took up the call to "burn, baby, burn" instead of "*¡Despierta, Boricua!*" would they be protesting as Puerto Ricans or simply as another group of poor and dark-skinned victims of oppression in the United States? And would the difference matter to most Puerto Rican New Yorkers? Some observers noted continuing hostility between the groups during the Young Lords' era, especially amid a series of riots in the South Bronx in 1968, about which Fordham sociologist Joseph Fitzpatrick wrote that spring that "at the present time there is great open hostility between Puerto Ricans and Black citizens, particularly about control over public schools and anti-poverty programs." But Juan González told a *New York Amsterdam News* reporter (who captured the quote in his headline) that "Puerto Rican [and] Black strife" was a "hoax." Indeed, at the level of radical activism, ties between African American and Puerto Rican youth were stronger than they had ever been by 1970. Young Lords and other Puerto Rican militants organized and socialized not just with Black Panthers members, some of whom had mentored the Puerto Rican leaders early on, but also with militant black cultural leaders like Amiri Baraka and the Last Poets.[122]

It was in their dramatic protest against police brutality, another issue with a long history of community response, that the Lords first got close to a public display of "revolutionary violence," in the fall of 1970. When YLP member Julio Roldán was picked up for loitering on a stoop in El

Barrio ("remember, this was 1970," explained Guzmán), he was locked up overnight in "the Tombs" and, according to police, hung himself in his cell that night. The Lords were convinced that Roldán's suicide had been staged by police to cover up the fact that they had beaten him to death. Their assumption was based on the general pattern of police brutality in their community, though it was unclear whether the Young Lords knew about the specific history of protests against staged "prisoner hangings," which Gilberto Gerena Valentín and the National Association for Puerto Rican Civil Rights had led just five years earlier.[123] After a funeral procession for Roldán with two thousand marchers, the Young Lords spontaneously took over the First Spanish Methodist Church again, this time with guns. While community members flocked to the Young Lords' service programs again, police surrounded the church, determined to arrest members whenever they emerged on charges of illegal gun possession. In the end, all of the occupying Lords managed to escape arrest, either because Mayor John Lindsay decided to sidestep another high-profile confrontation with the increasingly popular militants, or because—as the more dramatic version goes—the YLP's wily minister of defense, David Pérez, dismantled the guns and packed them out under the skirts and coats of "las viejitas," old ladies, as they left the church. Some of the Lords worried that the violence symbolized by their weapons during the Second People's Church takeover might scare off potential participants in the march the Lords were planning for the end of October, a protest at the United Nations building to mark the anniversary of the start of the 1950 nationalist uprising in Puerto Rico. But the intensifying nationalist spirit in the community carried them; even the New York Times counted ten thousand participants at the U.N. demonstration.[124]

Within two years of that march, the original Young Lords Party was coming apart. The leadership had struggled over the question of whether to open a branch in Puerto Rico, a move they finally made in 1971. The Lords had come to describe New York Puerto Ricans' relationship to the island as the "divided nation theory," with one-third of the Puerto Rican nation living in the United States and two-thirds on the island.[125] Puerto Rican islanders were not as receptive to the Lords' approach to political change as central committee members had hoped they would be. Critics in Puerto Rico called them extremists and opportunists, and many others, affiliated with one or another of the island's established nationalist organizations, either resented the "Americans'" presumptuousness—coming to the island to tell Puerto Ricans how to liberate themselves—or simply didn't care what

Figure 18. Rally to free Puerto Rican nationalist political prisoners, early 1970s. Máximo Colón photographic collection, Archives of the Puerto Rican Diaspora, Centro de Estudios Puertorriqueños, Hunter College, CUNY.

the Lords were doing. "That's when we first lost it," said Iris Morales. "We closed down, we stopped a lot of our door to door activities, which . . . were the vibrancy of the organization." Pablo Guzmán described the move as a "disastrous, ill-conceived" decision.[126]

It was not just the move to open a branch in Puerto Rico that pulled the Lords' energy away from El Barrio; at the same time, bitter disputes over degrees of political orthodoxy were dividing members of the central committee. New leadership by late 1971 was increasingly emphasizing Maoist forms of ideological purity at the expense of connecting with the needs and goals of the community. Most former members also believe that the Lords were infiltrated by CIA informants who successfully pitted members against one another.[127] Many members who stuck with the organization into 1972 went on to found the Puerto Rican Revolutionary Workers Party, representing the radical Maoist bent of the more recent leadership and largely abandoning the island nationalist component of its ideology. Others got involved with the new Puerto Rican Socialist Party, which was founded in New York in early 1971 by leaders of the MPI and would become a defining organization of El Barrio in the seventies. Whatever the many reasons for its decline, the dissolution of the Young Lords signaled a transition in New York's *barrios*. Some described it as the end of an era of new hope, an ending mourned not just by former Young Lords but by the many people in the larger Puerto Rican community whose private struggles for recognition had been voiced by the young militants.

## Claims for Recognition, Old and New

Historian Johanna Fernández has argued that the Lords' lasting impact stemmed as much from their ability to articulate what she calls a "theory of oppression," linking the everyday suffering of people in the ghetto to understandings of power relations in the particular context of the capitalist and democratic liberal United States, as from their signature political actions or their grassroots organizing.[128] The same could be said, to a degree at least, of many of the radical Puerto Rican groups working in the *barrios* in the late sixties and early seventies, including El Comité, the Real Great Society, and the PSP. Puerto Rican nationalism was one of the animating ideological forces of the members who had begun meeting as the Sociedad Albizu Campos, but, as one Young Lord later recalled, "a lot of us didn't understand the nationalist component of what we were doing at first."[129] Many of the New York militants, unlike their MPI counterparts, interpreted issues of independence and sovereignty in general terms, often as symbols for local power relations and the oppression of Puerto Ricans in New York rather than as true nationalist orthodoxy. From the beginning, for instance, the Lords described themselves primarily as socialists, announcing in their "Thirteen Point Program" in late 1969 that "we oppose capitalists and alliances with traitors." They went on to assail the liberal reformism that they saw as the greatest stumbling block for their vision of socialist justice for Puerto Ricans: "Puerto Rican rulers, or puppets of the oppressor, do not help our people. They are paid by the system to lead our people down blind alleys, just like the thousands of poverty pimps who keep our communities peaceful for business, or the street workers who keep gangs divided and blowing each other away. We want a society where people socialistically control their labor. VENCEREMOS!"[130]

Their heterodox Marxism led the Lords to incorporate ideological approaches like Cuban socialism and also, increasingly, Maoist communism.[131] Or, at least, Mao's "Little Red Book" was a central element of the curriculum of the Lords' ministry of education. Its appeal to these young critics of American society was concrete, and obvious, and extended to many other radicals, including the Black Panthers in particular. Mao's assertion that "the people's democratic dictatorship needs the leadership of the working class" captured both the major goal and the central identity of the Lords' political vision; his admonition that every Communist "grasp the truth [that] 'Political power grows out of the barrel of a gun'" justified their most aggressive tactics; and his trenchant and extensive critiques of First World imperialism resonated with youth who had cut their political teeth on their own diaspora's anticolonial nationalism.[132] The old ladies who willingly (or perhaps apocryphally) carried the Lords' guns out of the Second People's Church had no interest in Mao and probably opposed communism, but they cared about a local version of justice that its most visible proponents said was connected to Mao. They probably felt no allegiance to Che or to Fidel, but they did have an affinity for the notion that they were caught up in an exploitative economic system and a society that failed to treat them as equals. This was the brilliance of the young radicals' connection to *el pueblo*, the Lords' in particular. They articulated a connection between abstract problems like colonialism and racism on the one hand and, on the other, the particular manifestations of those problems in people's lives: economic displacement, epidemic garbage, poisonous ghetto housing, failing schools. Such a practical and mostly undidactic "theory of oppression" served not only to animate their own programs but also to draw in people in their communities who cared less than the radicals about international politics or even their native country's colonial past.

In fact, in weaving together an internationalist critique of capitalism and imperialism with a mission to "serve and protect the best interests of the community," these groups were doing just what the *colonia*'s leftist activists in the thirties had done. The Young Lords' berets and guns, their protest slogans, and the words of their Thirteen Point Program all represented their aspiration for revolution in the sixties, but it was a version of revolution that was actually quite familiar to Jesús Colón, Bernardo Vega, and their radical internationalist working-class compatriots. The idea of the laboring classes winning power over the capitalists and imperialists, traditional socialist revolution, was part (number eight) of the Lords' Thirteen Point Program. But in the confounding way of political genealogies—so often marked by generational ruptures and ideological blind spots—the Young Lords for the most part knew nothing of the very similar political critiques articulated by activists just slightly older than their parents. When Young Lord Iris Morales was interviewed in the 1980s by Columbia University's oral history archivist Ron Grele, Grele asked her, "What was your take on the Old Left?

Figure 19. Marchers honor community leader Carlos Tapia at the Puerto Rican Day Parade, 1961. Justo Martí collection, Archives of the Puerto Rican Diaspora, Centro de Estudios Puertorriqueños, Hunter College, CUNY.

Had you met anyone in the Puerto Rican community from the Old Left?" Morales answered, "No. No. No. It was almost . . . starting all over again. I may have met people and not known it. But what I was conscious of was like, 'This was it,' what we were doing was it."[133] Pablo Guzmán and many other sixties radicals argued that the New Left, including the Young Lords, "disdained" the old left because of its affiliation with the U.S. Communist Party (CPUSA), which was seen as having sold out to capitalism after Stalin's death in 1953.[134]

Many other young Puerto Rican activists did not reject the first-generation old left as much as they simply failed to see the congruence of their projects: using an internationalist frame, arguments about sovereignty, and a noncapitalist vision of justice in the nation to push for social and political change. The first point of the Lords' Thirteen Point Program, asserting that "we want self-determination for Puerto Ricans, liberation on the island and inside the United States," was an open-ended revolutionary vision, one that interpreted both individual and national sovereignty ("self-determination") as synonymous with liberation from oppression at the level of society and state. But it was also a vision whose goals of self-determination and liberation represented a specific demand for recognition as equals, and it suggested that the recognition of the Puerto Rican "minority" in the mainland's society and polity depended on the recognition of the island as a sovereign nation.

It was in this sense, this diasporic and anticolonial way of demanding recognition, that the Lords most resembled their predecessors of the Puerto Rican old left in the thirties. Erasmo Vando, Jesús Colón, Bernardo Vega, and others had continually connected the failures of island sovereignty to the denial of rights for Puerto Ricans on the mainland—or, as Vando admonished his compatriots more positively in 1936, "Protect and defend Liberty, the inalienable right of each citizen . . . to disseminate and defend his ideas, within the exercise of our rights," whether on the island or in the United States.[135] Members of the old left may have relied more heavily on the language of liberalism to make their claims, but the challenge they presented to the metropole's liberal democracy was similar to the way the Young Lords and others framed the problem three decades on. The young militants expanded the discourse by demanding *group* recognition, leaving aside the liberal language of individual rights that the thirties' activists had drawn on. One of the ironies of the distance between the old and young radicals was that, all along, Jesús Colón, still an active leftist, was collecting reams of documentary minutiae about young radicals in the sixties and early seventies, preserving records of their activities more systematically than the radicals themselves. (The FBI's files on the Lords, however, are certainly more complete than those kept by Colón.) As Andrés Torres argues, the sixties represented "another cycle of militancy rather than a new state of mind."[136]

During the years of the Young Lords' rise and fall, more mainstream Puerto Rican activists and politicians had been trying to cope with the needs of their community in their own ways in the context of a growing fiscal crisis in New York. Herman Badillo was the most successful Puerto Rican politician in the mainstream in this era, narrowly losing the Democratic primary election for mayor in 1969 and winning a seat to represent his Bronx district in the U.S. Congress in 1970.[137] Within a few months, his rival Ramón Vélez challenged his congressional seat and won the support of *El Diario–La Prensa*. Puerto Ricans whose political leanings fell somewhere between Badillo or Vélez on the one hand and the young militants on the other formed groups like the People's Action Party, aiming to organize the community's anger about its worsening conditions to lobby mainstream politicians. Another heterogeneous bunch of activists, ranging from mainstream to radical—which included leaders of the NAACP and the Real Great Society, Gerena Valentín representing the Puerto Rican Community Conference, and Ramon Colón representing the Brooklyn Democratic machine—formed a loose coalition in 1970 to petition New York's governor Nelson Rockefeller to abolish the Council on Human Relations, which they charged was doing a shamefully inadequate job of following through on the governor's promises of jobs and decent housing for minority communities.[138] Residents of Puerto Rican communities all over New York, many of whom had never before participated in grassroots politics and may never even have voted, got involved in various levels of community action through hundreds of organizations that spanned a broad range of the political spectrum left of center. Most of these activists, more mainstream than the Lords or the militant students or the hard-line *independentistas*, would have rejected the label "radical," but together—including, even, Democratic "hacks" like Vélez and the "dean of mainland Puerto Rican politicians," Badillo—made up what was coming to be called the Puerto Rican movement.[139]

Many radicals who participated in the Puerto Rican movement and who wrote about their experiences, either at the time or later, focused on the political and ideological divisions among Puerto Rican leaders in the late sixties and early seventies, conflicts that Pablo Guzmán referred to as "the battle between reform liberals and revolutionary activists for preeminence among barrio hearts and minds."[140] These ideological divisions between, on the one hand, "poverty pimps," social workers, Democratic machine members, and mainstream Aspirantes and, on the other, radical activists and militant nationalists were real and in many cases extreme. The former rejected the radicals' agenda of "national liberation," while the latter scorned the moderates' interest in electoral politics and "accommodationist" strategies for social change. But much of the history of the thousands of young Puerto Rican activists in this era is lost if it is analyzed only through its ruptures. Puerto Rican activists in the sixties, no matter their institutional affiliations or ideological positions, occupied the same social terrain in the same national political context, even if they disagreed sharply about the boundaries of that terrain and the best routes for navigating it. They also shared a commitment to a forceful challenge to the status quo. The Young Lords and their successors in other radical Puerto Rican groups, along with their progenitors and their less radical contemporaries, were indeed divided, sometimes bitterly, but they formed a sphere of activism marked by many interconnections. When activist Carmen Rivera reflected on her experience in the PSP in the mid-1970s, for instance, she called it "the perfect extension of the learning process I had begun in Aspira." This was an uncommon assertion, but it reflected a certain dimension of the actual experience of many of Rivera's contemporaries: the mainstream organizations of the sixties, especially those that served youth, were not necessarily enemies of radicalism.[141]

In fact, for many Puerto Rican activists of this era, moderate political views were a function not of hostility toward the Left and its answers but of their own generational constraints. Many members of this older generation admired the young radicals even as they remained deeply connected to the "uplift" institutions they had been building and investing in since the early fifties. In their recollections about the sixties, older activists like Antonia Pantoja and José Morales consistently invoked the work of the Young Lords and other young radicals with great respect.[142] Pantoja, Morales, and other members of their cohort had begun their careers as activists in a radically different time, as the "1.5 generation," or the first wave of a second generation suffused with a sense of possibility about their future, during an era whose economy was still, outside the *barrios* at least, looking hopeful. It was also an era during which the metaphor of "Operation Bootstrap"—achieving economic security through hard work—had some influence over all but the most dissident Puerto Ricans (communists and *independentistas*, for the most part) in the United States. Members of this generation of youth came of age before the failures of the ILGWU campaigns, before the factories started leaving New York, before the second generation saw their parents not just working hard at two jobs each but losing those jobs, before the garbage was piled up chest-high on 112th Street—and before the Vietnam War, the expansion of anticolonial struggles around the world, and the Cuban revolution galvanized anti-imperialists and nationalists across the region, including Puerto Rico. Instead of the liberal "uplift" models of the fifties, Puerto Rican teenagers in the mid-sixties were influenced by the explosive energy of urban riots, the power of the Black Panthers' militant organization, and the magnetic popularity of Mao's "Little Red Book."

In the late seventies, the collective of activist Puerto Rican studies scholars at the infant Center for Puerto Rican Studies described the ideological conflicts in the sixties' Puerto Rican New York as "the seesawing struggle between formulas for controlled social reform organized from the top and the sustained protest and demand for autonomy constantly renewed by new leaders and new organizations arising directly from within the community."[143] Many members of organizations like the Puerto Rican Forum were indeed "accommodationist," more interested in "handling poverty as a business" than in radically changing the power dynamics that kept their communities locked in poverty. But radicals like Catarino Garza, of the Socialist Workers' Party, overstate the case when they argue, as he did in 1977, that the unitary purpose of mainstream "bourgeois" Puerto Rican organizations in the sixties was "to derail the rising protest of the ghettos."[144] The reality on the ground was that the relationships between people who subscribed to "two rival formulas for attacking poverty" were porous, not limited absolutely by the competing camps they occupied. Nearly all of them—the National Association for Puerto Rican Civil Rights, the PRCDC, Aspira, the Lords, El Comité—were moving away from making claims primarily for individual rights, rooted in the traditional language of liberalism. Instead, they were making arguments, in diverse ways, for group recognition in American society.

Although even hard-line nationalists like PSP leader Alfredo López were willing to concede that most Puerto Ricans were never concerned with "the highest stage of nationalism," the heterogeneous energies of the Puerto Rican movement, broadly defined, were animated by a new nationalist spirit during the late sixties and early seventies. "Nationalism has hit the Puerto Rican community like a club on the head," he wrote hopefully in 1973. "It is in everybody's mind. You can't board a subway train without seeing Puerto Ricans with *la bandera* sewn to their jackets. You can't walk the streets of a Puerto Rican community without seeing at least one button, beret, or flag on every block."[145] Historian Carmen Whalen recounts, in a similar vein, the story of a young man who helped organize his high school's Aspira club around 1970. Juan Ramos remembered that, although "'Aspira was very conservative then,'" he and his friends succeeded in naming their club Albizu Campos. "'Before you know it,'" he recalled, "'all the Aspira clubs changed their names.'"[146]

The symbols of nationalism circulating in Puerto Rican *barrios* called forth a range of possible political meanings, some more concrete than others. The most enduring of these, without a doubt, was sovereignty. Sovereignty was an idea protean enough to represent the conflicting hopes of each political faction within Puerto Rico's status debate, as well as, for instance, the goals of Puerto Ricans participating in the school-based "community control" movement in 1968. In an even more general sense, sovereignty reflected the still-hopeful aspiration of poor and marginalized Puerto Rican New Yorkers to assert some authority over their own lives in the city of which they were, if only officially, citizens. Thus did national-ism's insistence on sovereignty give meaning to a collective demand for recognition for Puerto Ricans in the United States, articulated primarily though not entirely by youth, and now, finally, acknowledged (if not fully answered) by the national mainstream. In 1951, aggrieved students had ap-pealed simply to their status as American citizens, and their parents' cre-dentials as taxpayers, to defend their rights to an education free from vio-lence and discrimination. Two decades later, Puerto Rican youth (some of them graduates of Benjamin Franklin) had helped shift the discourse from a language of individual liberal rights to a language of global recognition on the basis of justice.[147]

# From Colonial Citizen
# to Nuyorican

In describing the middle years of the seventies, the years that marked the
return of Richard Nixon, an invigorated New Right, and COINTELPRO,
and that followed the demise of several of the high-profile radical Puerto
Rican organizations born in the sixties, former Young Lord Pablo Guzmán
quoted singer and social critic Gil Scott Heron: it was "Winter in America."[1]
This was especially true for the poor and otherwise marginalized groups
in the nation, a point so obvious to the members of the History Task Force
at the Center for Puerto Rican Studies in the late seventies that they criticized other scholars for broadcasting over and over the "stale news of the
stagnation of the poor."[2] It was this period in the New York *barrios* that
confirmed the legacy of the Puerto Rican postwar migration as "the Puerto
Rican tragedy," as historian Mike Davis put it, something that, arriving in
their footsteps, all other Latinos seek to avoid.[3] It was also a moment when
the U.S. State Department once again qualified relations with Puerto Rico
as a "problem," the failures of Operation Bootstrap having turned the island from the developmentalists' sparkling showcase of the Caribbean to
a hothouse for anti-American radicals, a political nightmare once again
for the United States.[4] On the mainland, though, radicals like New York
socialist Catarino Garza lamented that Puerto Ricans there had lost their
political focus and were unable to meet the challenge of demanding another hearing on the question of "self-determination." Liberal institutions
like the U.S. Commission on Civil Rights were less likely, now, to be corrected by louder dissident voices from the *barrio*'s left when they made mild
pronouncements such as this one: "Puerto Ricans ask that they be given an
opportunity to participate on an equal footing with their fellow citizens. . . .
It is incumbent upon government at all levels to guarantee that their rights
are not denied."[5]

In New York, "into this vacuum," wrote Guzmán, came a new wave of
reformist politicians who shifted the center of El Barrio's political culture

away from the radical challenges of the previous decade. Most visible were elected leaders like Herman Badillo and Ramón Vélez, who worked along-side many former "poverty pimps" and even, according to Guzmán, some ex-militants who helped legitimize the use of the sixties' nationalist rhetoric to connect with voters in a generally less politicized polity.[6] Puerto Ricans were also, suddenly, becoming invisible again by the mid-seventies. Na-tionalists' ongoing protests against the incarceration of political prisoners dropped off the radar screen of the popular media. Even the high-profile action of hanging a Puerto Rican flag on the Statue of Liberty in 1977 was buried on page 30 of the *New York Times*.[7] In the background, getting even less attention from the press or the public, other activists in various sec-tors of the community continued with their own political projects. Puerto Rican parents, working with Chinese and African American neighbors in their Lower East Side school district, briefly won control of their school board and succeeded in setting the educational agenda in their commu-nity.[8] The Puerto Rican Legal Defense and Education Fund, established in 1972, won a number of lawsuits dealing with issues like bilingual teachers in public schools, bilingual ballots for voters, and housing and employment

Figure 20. The Puerto Rican flag flying from the crown of the Statue of Liberty, part of a protest by the Committee to Free the Five Puerto Rican Nationalists, 1977. Neal Boenzi for the *New York Times*, Redux Pictures.

discrimination.⁹ In spite of newer *barrio* politicians' failures to "capture the popular imagination" as the radicals had, and in spite of the overall decline in coordinated grassroots activism, the *despertar boricua*—the "Puerto Rican awakening"—maintained a strong pulse.

One of its signs of life was a thriving movement of cultural nationalism in the arts, perhaps less flamboyant than the Lords but no less animated, a vanguard of artists and writers who described themselves as "Nuyorican." The beginnings of this cultural movement had grown up alongside the radical organizations of the late sixties and were influenced by and connected to the Black Arts movement. Members of the Nuyorican movement tended to define themselves as both artists and political activists; Felipe Luciano, for instance, first chairman of the Young Lords' central committee, was a member of the militant group of musicians called the Last Poets before he became a Lord. The first widely circulated use of the term *Nuyorican* had originated with the poet Jaime Carrero in his 1964 *Jet Neorriqueño: Neo-Rican Jetliner*, a book of poems in Spanish and English. It was the reappropriation of a term of opprobrium—much like *Chicano* and *Dominican-york*—to advance what became a force of cultural nationalist pride, first in Loisaida (the Lower East Side) and then in all the city's *barrios*.¹⁰ Amid the political fragmentation of Puerto Rican activism after the early seventies, the Nuyorican movement offered the possibility of cultural unity and collaboration, pushing forward the *despertar boricua* in a different language than that of the political organizations preceding it. "The Nuyorican poet fights with words," wrote poet Miguel Algarín in 1975.¹¹

The artist- and writer-activists who called themselves Nuyoricans embraced a cultural nationalist politics that was more heterodoxical and less rigid than that promoted by leaders of groups like the Young Lords or El Comité. Algarín argued that this flexibility was a strength of the movement he helped form: "A Young Lords Party member ran into Chino García, once leader of the Real Great Society, and said, 'Your politics stink,' and Chino replied, 'I think your politics are okay.' Both organizations are Nuyorican born. . . . Nuyorican poets are more like Chino García: as the poets redefine their language, Chino redefines his politics, thus both deal with what is."¹² Dealing with "what is" expressed the broader political imagination of Nuyoricans but suggested as well a sense of continuity with the more rigid politics of the movement with which it originated. "They [Nuyorican poets] are at home in a place where their needs for social and human recognition go unsatisfied. And so they have opted to create, within their inner-city frontiers, their own society with its own music, language, ethics, politics," wrote literature scholar Eugene Mohr.[13] In 1974, Piñero's *Short Eyes*, set in the prison world from which he had just emerged, garnered acclaim from arts institutions outside those inner-city frontiers when it won the New York Drama Critics Circle Award for best American play. It was no small irony that Piñero's play was then produced at Lincoln Center, barely fifteen years after the construction of Lincoln Center had destroyed a poor Puerto Rican community like the one where Piñero grew up. Piñero and other Nuyorican artists experimented with their own creative visions of righting the "injustices of recognition" committed against their New York compatriots. In conducting their struggles for justice outside the formally political arena, Nuyorican activists sought to shift the site of their political agency beyond the limitations of the nation-state.[14]

Writing from a distance of only a few years, in 1983, sociologist Manuel Castells argued in *The City and the Grassroots* that the vision of his generation's social movements had been to transform urban structures and cultural spaces. Indeed, in their disparate ways, different factions of the Puerto Rican movement retained their visions of transformation across a decade that looked, to grassroots activists, bleaker by the year. More centrist community leaders fought in the arenas of status quo *barrio* politics, competing for local funding and voter support, while the Nuyorican artists in their midst argued daily with the status quo on street corners and in the new galleries and performance spaces they created on shoestring budgets.[15] Radical political activists may not have given up their goals, but, having ceased to lead a coherent movement by the mid-seventies, they did relinquish the expectation that they would really transform the city this time around. It was a fourth group of Puerto Rican activists, many of whose members had direct ties to the youth organizations of the late sixties, that took the grassroots movement into the academy to do the work of transforming the intellectual terrain—an agenda that became as important to them as transforming the city directly. They, like Nuyorican artists, claimed recognition in spheres beyond the strictly political, inserting themselves as participants, and insisting on equality, within fields of intellectual inquiry.

The most important contribution of these scholars as a group was their determination to point directly at the continuing injustices of colonialism to explain why Puerto Ricans had failed to achieve recognition as equals in the United States. In doing so, Puerto Rican intellectuals in this era made interpretive links that social theorist Juan Flores has argued are crucial to any analysis rooted in the theory of recognition: connecting the origins of social conflict to "a broad theory of geopolitical and social power capable of registering differential kinds and conditions of relationality."[16] In that sense, groups like the History Task Force contributed to the academy ideas that built on various late-sixties' articulations of recognition in grassroots discourse. By the late seventies, however, the goal was an epistemological shift as much as a structural shift regarding the place of Puerto Ricans in the United States. Few scholars outside of ethnic studies were listening, though; or if they were listening, all they heard was, at first, "identity politics." Distant from the concerns of mainstream philosophers and political theorists—not to mention practitioners in the new interdisciplinary field of cultural studies—Puerto Rican intellectuals' analysis of colonialism and its connection to the failures of recognition that Puerto Ricans experienced in the United States remained entirely disconnected from the theoretical debates about recognition emerging during the 1980s.[17]

Although still often marginalized in the academy, Puerto Rican scholars by the late eighties had begun to fortify their projects by collaborating across the national boundaries that divided various fields in Latino ethnic studies. Together, they created broader agendas for the study of Latinos in the United States at a time when the so-called culture wars had generated a more open conversation about how power was distributed within institutions like the university. The idea of cultural citizenship that anthropologist Renato Rosaldo proposed in the early nineties reflected the expansive vision of Latino studies as a field: to situate and analyze Latinos as social and political actors in frameworks beyond the usual binaries. Rather than categorizing people in polarizing ways—as citizen or noncitizen (which often meant "illegal alien"); black or white; migrant or settled; middle-class and "assimilated" or poor and marginal—scholars like Rosaldo proposed ways to interpret their experience more fluidly. This analytical innovation reflected ideas emerging from other areas of the intellectual spectrum at around the same time, especially the refinement of concepts like globalization and transnationalism.[18]

It was in this context that new questions about citizenship emerged, probing both its praxis and the limitations of its traditional meanings. And now, in the twenty-first century, a growing number of political scientists, historians, sociologists, and anthropologists are connecting those questions to the theory of recognition in order to analyze social conflicts around the world. In addition to broadening the geographic scope of empirical studies of struggles for recognition—scholars working in Turkey, East Asia, Central Africa, western Europe, the Balkans, Mexico, and South America are drawing on this relational theory—authors of recent studies show less reluctance than those of the previous two decades to link failures of recognition to imbalances of geopolitical and social power.[19] This is particularly true of scholars working in postcolonial societies, where conflicts over recognition remain, as Fanon predicted in the 1960s, central to the critique of colonial oppression and its aftermath.

This book's conclusions about the expansive goals of Puerto Ricans' claims for recognition have much in common with the findings of scholars working on similar themes in other regions, but they also point to a frequent weakness of some of these studies, which tend to use the idea of recognition in its simplest form, usually "political recognition." Relying on this limited definition of recognition suggests that the challenges posed by social actors would be satisfied by the achievement of "equal citizenship," measured by the attainment of certain promised rights and protections. This presumption is problematic for several reasons. Not only would attaining the goal of equal or "first-class" citizenship not satisfy another key dimension of claims for recognition, namely the acknowledgment of and respect for a distinctive group identity within the surrounding society, but more important, in many instances, this is simply not possible: the Puerto Rican case, and other similar ones, demonstrate that fully "equal citizenship" remains largely unattainable for groups that are ethnically or racially marked within the majority society. And when scholars characterize conflicts like that of the Zapatistas in Mexico as struggles primarily about "recognition by the state" or "recognition as equal citizens," they sidestep the claimants' more significant challenges to rework historically unequal power relations within the nation and to broaden the normative political narratives that describe the relationships among members of the nation. As one Zapatista put it, "For us, autonomy is the heart and soul of our resistance. It is a new way of doing politics. It is part of the construction of democracy, justice, and dignity."[20] This statement, I would argue, is a claim rooted in the sovereignty and rights promised by liberal ideology. But also embedded in it is a powerful demand for recognition framed much like that of Puerto Rican activists in the twentieth century: they wanted recognition *beyond* citizenship, a recognition that promises not just formal equality within the state but also the "respect" and "dignity" that come from real equality.

This book has traced the outlines of an evolving political identity among Puerto Rican New Yorkers in the twentieth century, following debates over the meaning of key ideas like "citizenship" and "sovereignty" and the distances they traveled in Puerto Ricans' political imagination from 1917 to the early 1970s. Residents of the twenties' *colonia* were colonial citizens, recent arrivals to the metropole without a clear political identity as a group beyond that of the striving immigrant. Although socialist ideology was common among the largely skilled working-class migrants, their ideas about how they fit into the United States' liberal democracy were still in flux. By the end of the thirties, Puerto Ricans in New York had become self-conscious members of a flawed democracy, demanding recognition in a limited way as citizens and claiming the rights promised by that status. On the eve of World War II, they were beginning to situate those demands within a critique of liberalism in the United States, the history of which, they had begun to argue, was marked by racist foundations and colonial relationships. Throughout the early cold war, the activist community in New York was split, many adopting the liberal party line in support of the triumphant postwar state and of the new Puerto Rican commonwealth, keeping their distance from anti-imperialist critiques of the United States, while others continued with their political dissent but kept a low profile, lamenting the broken spirit of New York's Puerto Rican Left in the era of McCarthyism.

Then, in the late fifties, after nearly two decades of marginalization of Puerto Rican *independentistas*, an increasingly radical youth movement adopted community organizing strategies that paralleled those of Puerto Rican leftists in the 1930s and began weaving together—once again— nationalist ideology and "the politics of here."[21] Unlike the thirties' radicals, though, most of whom started with the politics of independence and anti-imperialism and added to that a community-based activism, the young radicals of the sixties began their careers with quotidian and concrete issues— garbage strikes, rent strikes, university and hospital takeovers—and along the way crafted their heterodoxical politics that included Puerto Rican nationalism and Maoism as well as some vestiges of U.S. democratic liberalism. They demanded recognition not just as citizens whose legal status earned them equality but as members of a group whose colonial ties to the United States had created, in the first place, their historic experience of denied rights. Young Puerto Rican radicals of the late sixties and early seventies accomplished something substantial and lasting for Puerto Rican New Yorkers, even though much of their politics was at best incomprehensible to members of their parents' generation and to many of the more moderate community leaders just a decade older. The radical activists destabilized the "Juan Q. Citizen" ideal of the fifties' social service establishment, and they chipped away at the expository fiction of Puerto Rican passivity and political apathy. ("As far as the Puerto Ricans are concerned," wrote historian Oscar Handlin in 1959—a few pages before he regretfully noted their weak "associational life" and lack of "creative leadership"—"there seems to be a growing consciousness of, and pride in, their group identity.")[22] More important, they amplified the interconnectedness between, on the one hand, the respect for "difference" that defined what would soon become known as "identity politics" and, on the other hand, the call for redistributive justice that was the hallmark of radicalism in the late sixties and seventies.

Catarino Garza, who grew up in the South Bronx in the sixties and, in 1977, ran for mayor as a candidate of the Socialist Workers' Party, explained then that his vision of "the struggle for freedom" involved the following goals: the release of Puerto Rican political prisoners, Puerto Rican independence, bilingual-bicultural education, community control of schools, protection against police brutality, affirmative action, and protection against discrimination in employment.[23] In fact, none of these demands were specifically socialist. They represented, rather, claims for recognition of the legitimacy of Puerto Ricans' political vision, focused on cultural sovereignty and social justice—claims rooted not just in U.S. democratic liberalism but also in the increasingly popular ideology of human rights. Alongside such militant claims for recognition, older arguments about the failure of U.S. citizenship to deliver on promises of equality continued to circulate and remained a focal point of political action, especially after the fragmentation of the young radical generation in the early seventies. In 1974, for instance, the recently established Puerto Rican Legal Defense Fund lent its gravitas to a complaint that had been repeated countless times in the previous half century, that "Puerto Ricans are granted citizenship by law but its privileges are often denied in fact."[24]

What the sixties' generation had managed to do was to extend the power of that complaint. Those activists articulated, like their Black Power counterparts, what historian Manning Marable has called "a new dream of freedom, *not* social acceptance and upward mobility within the centers of corporate power."[25] They also asked their own versions of a question later posed by political theorist Wendy Brown, about the failures of justice that marked liberal democracies in the twentieth century: "How do we live in these broken narratives, when nothing has taken their place?"[26] Participants in the Puerto Rican movement answered this question—trying to craft new narratives from the broken ones—by making broad demands for recognition that resonated across the decades. In doing so, they brought full circle the political discourses combining citizenship rights, economic justice, antidiscrimination, and anti-imperialism deployed by *colonia* leaders more than three decades earlier. The struggle for recognition is indeed the common thread that links the diverse claims of the many Puerto Ricans in this story—women and men; nationalists and Democrats; liberals and communists; working-class and elite; and the many in between—whose dreams of freedom spanned the better part of a century.

# Notes

## Locations of Archival Collections

Brooklyn Public Library
  Brooklyn Council for Social Planning papers
Centro de Estudios Puertorriqueños
  Pura Belpré papers
  Jesús Colón papers
  Erasmo Vando papers
  Costureras Project
  A la izquierda collection
  Pioneros Project
New York City Municipal Archives
  John Hylan papers
  Fiorello La Guardia papers
  John Lindsay papers
  WPA files
New York Public Library
  Vito Marcantonio papers
Historical Society of Pennsylvania / Balch Institute
  Leonard Covello papers

## Introduction

1. Until 1898, Puerto Ricans were Spanish colonial subjects; between 1900 and 1917, they were U.S. nationals; after 1917, they were United States citizens. Those who rejected U.S. citizenship—almost three hundred Puerto Ricans did so—could choose Spanish citizenship or adopt the ambiguous status of "Puerto Rican citizens"; either way, they lost many of their civil rights, including the right to vote. Truman Clark, *Puerto Rico and the United States, 1917–1933* (Pittsburgh: University of Pittsburgh Press, 1975), 25–27. Mari Bras won confirmation that he could vote in Puerto Rican elections as a "Puerto Rican citizen" after a decision in his favor in the case *Miriam J. Ramírez de Ferrer v. Juan Mari Bras*, heard by the Puerto Rican Supreme Court in 1997. Ramírez de Ferrer was president of Puerto Ricans in Civic Action, an organization that lobbies for Puerto Rican statehood. "Small Gain in Big Fight to Liberate Puerto Rico," *New York Times*, Dec. 17, 1995, 31; "A New Debate on the Fate (and State) of Puerto Rico," *New York Times*, Mar. 30, 1998, 1. See also Christina Duffy Burnett, "'They Say I Am Not an American': The Noncitizen National and the Law of American Empire," *Virginia Journal of International Law* 48 (2008):

659–718. Although, as a commonwealth (or *"estado libre asociado"* ["associated free state"], as its status is called in Spanish), Puerto Rico is not an independent nation-state, I refer to the island as a "nation" since it is indeed an "imagined political community" in the sense in which Benedict Anderson defines the term *nation*. Anderson, *Imagined Communities: Reflections on the Origin and Spread of Nationalism* (London: Verso, 1983), 6–7.

**2.** A *tabaquero* is a cigarmaker. A "national" is "a person who, though not a citizen, owes permanent allegiance to the state and is entitled to its protection." Quoted from G. Hackworth, *Digest of International Law* 1 (1942), cited by José A. Cabranes in *Citizenship and the American Empire: Notes on the Legislative History of the United States Citizenship of Puerto Ricans* (New Haven, CT: Yale University Press, 1979), 6. As a Puerto Rican in 1916, Vega possessed, as he explained it, a "natural citizenship" that was not recognized outside of Puerto Rico. I call Vega an immigrant because his migration was a move between two distinct countries, although Puerto Rico was not, obviously, a nation-state. Bernardo Vega, *Memoirs of Bernardo Vega: A Contribution to the History of the Puerto Rican Community in New York*, edited by César Andreu Iglesias (New York: Monthly Review Press, 1984), 6.

**3.** Vega, *Memoirs*, 27.

**4.** Prior to the 1917 Jones Act, Puerto Rico had been governed by the 1900 Foraker Act, which established civilian rule following the U.S. military takeover of the island in 1898. The Jones Act created a new legislative structure and greater separation between the lawmaking and executive bodies of the island government. The citizenship provision of the Jones Act gave U.S. citizenship to all Puerto Ricans who did not officially reject it.

**5.** In 1930, the U.S. Bureau of the Census estimated the Puerto Rican population of New York City at 44,908, although many in the Spanish-speaking community believed that the numbers of migrants were much higher. See Ira Rosenwaike, *Population History of New York City* (Syracuse, NY: Syracuse University Press, 1972), 121; see also chapter 1. Christina Duffy Burnett and Burke Marshall, "Between the Foreign and the Domestic," in *Foreign in a Domestic Sense: Puerto Rico, American Expansion, and the Constitution*, edited by Christina Duffy Burnett and Burke Marshall (Durham, NC: Duke University Press, 2001), 13 and passim.

**6.** See, for instance, "Porto Ricans Are Citizens," *New York Times*, June 15, 1917, 8. (Some migrants used the Americanized spelling "Porto Rico" in this period.)

**7.** On the political and policy history of citizenship, see, for example, Rogers Brubaker, *Citizenship and Nationhood in France and Germany* (Cambridge, MA: Harvard University Press, 1992); Will Kymlicka and Wayne Norman, "Return of the Citizen: A Survey of Recent Work on Citizenship Theory," *Ethics* 104 (Jan. 1994): 352–81; Charles Tilly and Michael Hanagan, eds., *Extending Citizenship, Reconfiguring States* (New York: Rowman and Littlefield Publishers, 1999); Keith Faulks, *Citizenship* (New York: Routledge, 2000); Linda Bosniak, *The Citizen and the Alien: Dilemmas of Contemporary Membership* (Princeton, NJ: Princeton University Press, 2006); and Peter Spiro, *Beyond Citizenship: American Identity after Globalization* (New York: Oxford University Press, 2008). For work that treats the "practice" of citizenship, see Margaret Somers, "Citizenship and the Public Sphere: Law, Community, and

Political Culture in the Transition to Democracy," *American Sociological Review* 58 (1993): 587–620, and Somers, "Rights, Relationality, and Membership: Rethinking the Making and Meaning of Citizenship," *Law and Social Inquiry* 19 (Winter 1994): 63–112; Nick Ellison, "Towards a New Social Politics: Citizenship and Reflexivity in Late Modernity," *Sociology* 31 (Nov. 1997): 697–717; William Flores and Rina Benmayor, eds., *Latino Cultural Citizenship: Claiming Identity, Space, and Rights* (Boston: Beacon Press, 1997); Linda Kerber, "The Meaning of Citizenship," *Journal of American History* 84 (Dec. 1997): 833–54; Michel Laguerre, *Disaporic Citizenship: Haitian Americans in Transnational America* (New York: St. Martin's Press, 1998); Nicholas de Genova and Ana Ramos-Zayas, *Latino Crossings: Mexicans, Puerto Ricans, and the Politics of Race and Citizenship* (New York: Routledge, 2003); Mae Ngai, *Impossible Subjects: Illegal Aliens and the Making of Modern America* (Princeton, NJ: Princeton University Press, 2004); Mary Lewis, *Boundaries of the Republic: Migrant Rights and the Limits of Universalism in France, 1918–1940* (Palo Alto, CA: Stanford University Press, 2007); and Sam Erman, "Meanings of Citizenship in the U.S. Empire: Puerto Rico, Isabel González, and the Supreme Court, 1898–1905," *Journal of American Ethnic History* 27 (Summer 2008): 5–33.

**8.** See, for instance, Jesús Colón, "Manifiesto—a los españoles, puertorriqueños, cubanos, mexicanos y demás hispanos . . . ," 1939, and "The Growing Importance of the Puerto Rican Minority in N.Y.C.," [1955], Colón papers, series III, box 2, folder 1.

**9.** Colón, "Growing Importance of the Puerto Rican Minority." Charles Taylor, ed., *Multiculturalism: Examining the Politics of Recognition* (Princeton, NJ: Princeton University Press, 1994), 40. Johannes Fabian, "Remembering the Other: Knowledge and Recognition in the Exploration of Central Africa," *Critical Inquiry* 26 (Autumn 1999): 53. Rebecca Scott, *Degrees of Freedom* (Cambridge, MA: Harvard University Press, 2005), 256.

**10.** Jürgen Habermas, "Struggles for Recognition in the Democratic Constitutional State," in *Multiculturalism: Examining the Politics of Recognition*, edited by Charles Taylor (Princeton, NJ: Princeton University Press, 1994), 108.

**11.** Although I agree with Wendy Brown's skepticism about the integrity of ideas like "rights" and "sovereignty" as "sites of justice claims" within traditional liberalism, I also think that liberal rights and their promises of protection remain very real to people on the ground. Brown, *Politics Out of History* (Princeton, NJ: Princeton University Press, 2001), 3–5 and passim. In addition to my own evidence on this point, throughout this book, see Robert C. Smith, "Migrant Membership as an Instituted Process: Transnationalization, the State and the Extra-territorial Conduct of Mexican Politics," *International Migration Review* 37 (Summer 2003): 325.

**12.** On the history of the idea of human rights in the twentieth century, see Lynn Hunt, *Inventing Human Rights: A History* (New York: W. W. Norton, 2007), 200–208. Costas Douzinas writes about the connections between discourses of human rights and recognition in the sixties; Douzinas, "Identity, Recognition, Rights, or What Can Hegel Teach Us about Human Rights?" *Journal of Law and Society* 29, no. 3 (Sept. 2002): 386.

**13.** See Juan Perea, "Fulfilling Manifest Destiny: Conquest, Race, and the *Insular Cases*" (159 and passim), and Rogers Smith, "The Bitter Roots of Puerto Rican

Citizenship" (379 and passim), in Burnett and Marshall, *Foreign in a Domestic Sense*. Sam Erman notes that the contemporary discussion about U.S. citizenship vis-á-vis Filipinos was even more racist; Erman, "Meanings of Citizenship," 32. See also Jorge Duany, *Puerto Rican Nation on the Move: Identities on the Island and in the United States* (Chapel Hill: University of North Carolina Press, 2002), 50–56.

**14.** Cabranes, *Citizenship and the American Empire*, 481.

**15.** Vega, *Memoirs*, 28.

**16.** Matthew Frye Jacobson, *Barbarian Virtues: The United States Encounters Foreign Peoples at Home and Abroad, 1876–1917* (New York: Hill and Wang, 2000), 239–41.

**17.** "Government of Puerto Rico," *Congressional Record* 33, 56th Cong., 1st sess., Mar. 2, 1900, 2473–74, cited in Juan F. Perea, "Fulfilling Manifest Destiny: Conquest, Race, and the *Insular Cases*," in *Foreign in a Domestic Sense: Puerto Rico, American Expansion, and the Constitution*, edited by Christina Duffy Burnett and Burke Marshall (Durham, NC: Duke University Press, 2001), 162.

**18.** Luis Muñoz Marín, in "Civil Government for Porto Rico," *Congressional Record* 53, 64th Cong., 1st sess., May 5, 1916, 7472.

**19.** Paul Faulks, *Citizenship*, 75, cites Thomas, "Alien Citizenship: A Marxian Perspective on Citizenship and Democracy," in *After Marx*, edited by Terence Ball and James Farr (New York: Cambridge University Press, 1984), who says Marx saw citizenship in its liberal form as another "opium of the people" (a quote from one of Marx's earliest published essays, "On the Jewish Question").

**20.** Rogers Smith, *Civic Ideals: Conflicting Visions of Citizenship in U.S. History* (New Haven, CT: Yale University Press, 1997).

**21.** With the passage of the Jones Act in 1917, United States citizenship was conferred on Puerto Ricans in a form that legal scholar and judge José Cabranes refers to as "second-class," since Puerto Ricans on the island cannot vote in presidential elections, have only a nonvoting elected representative in the U.S. Congress, and do not pay federal taxes. This particular form of U.S. citizenship is explained in the 1922 legal decision *Balzac v. Porto Rico*, 258 U.S. 298 (1922). See José Cabranes, "Citizenship and the American Empire: Notes on the Legislative History of the United States Citizenship of Puerto Ricans," *University of Pennsylvania Law Review* 127 (Dec. 1978): 391–492, especially 403–4; and Smith, "Bitter Roots." When Puerto Ricans migrate to the continental United States, their citizenship becomes identical to that of other mainlanders.

**22.** "Los portorriqueños de Nueva York piden explicaciones a Sol Bloom," *La Prensa*, Apr. 28, 1925, 2; "Sol Bloom increpa a los portorriqueños que protestaron por sus declaraciones," *La Prensa*, May 8, 1925, 1.

**23.** Angelo Falcón, "A History of Puerto Rican Politics in N.Y.C., 1860s–1945," in *Puerto Rican Politics in Urban America*, edited by James Jennings and Monte Rivera (Westport, CT: Greenwood Press, 1985), 27. Letter from Victor Fiol Ramos, secretary of the Liga Puertorriqueña e Hispana, to the editor of the *New York Times*, Aug. 16, 1926, 8.

**24.** U.S. Congress, 71st Cong., 3rd sess., House Committee on Immigration and Naturalization, "Temporary Restriction of Immigration," report no. 2801, Feb. 17, 1931, 13.

**25.** María Más Pozo, "De nuestros lectores," *La Prensa*, Jan. 12, 1931, 6.

**26.** As Negrón-Muntaner and Grosfoguel argue, citing Immanuel Wallerstein, "The tactic of 'taking the old liberal ideology literally and demanding its universal fulfillment' is a form of parodic or mimetic politics." Frances Negrón-Muntaner and Ramón Grosfoguel, eds., *Puerto Rican Jam: Rethinking Colonialism and Nationalism* (Minneapolis: University of Minnesota Press, 1997), 32.

**27.** Political theorists define the "negative rights" of classical liberalism as the kind of rights that promise freedom from certain harms. "Positive rights," on the other hand, are rights that promise access to certain benefits; in twentieth-century American liberalism, these would be rights like the social insurance provisions of the New Deal.

**28.** Daniel Rodgers, *Contested Truths: Keywords in American Politics Since Independence* (Cambridge, MA: Harvard University Press, 1998), 217. Historian Lizbeth Cohen explores how workers, for example, developed a newly collective sense of rights during the Great Depression: "On the job and at the polls, working people throughout the country were speaking in a collective voice and having it heard." Cohen, *Making a New Deal: Industrial Workers in Chicago, 1919–1939* (Cambridge, MA: Harvard University Press, 1990), 3. Legal scholars tend to use a different definition of "rights talk," which most on the Left interpret as a generally negative trend toward excessive emphasis on individual rights. See, for example, Mary Ann Glendon, *Rights Talk: The Impoverishment of Political Discourse* (New York: Free Press, 1991).

**29.** Alan Brinkley writes that the latter days of the New Deal, combined with the social and political climate at the start of World War II, spurred a shift in American liberalism from "reform liberalism" to "rights-based liberalism." See Alan Brinkley, *The End of Reform: New Deal Liberalism in Recession and War* (New York: Alfred A. Knopf, 1995), 10–11, 164–70. Rodgers asserts that the ideas on which twentieth-century liberalism was based had been "radically transformed from below" but also seems to concur that the "era of rights-making more vigorous than ever before"—that is, the sixties—had its roots during World War II. Rodgers, *Contested Truths*, 217.

**30.** Puerto Ricans echoed arguments of African Americans both in the contemporary period and during Reconstruction. See, for example, Eric Foner, *The Story of American Freedom* (New York: W. W. Norton, 1998), 100–107, 208–10.

**31.** See, for example, Laguerre, *Diasporic Citizenship*, 8–13 and passim.

**32.** Rexford Guy Tugwell, *The Stricken Land: The Story of Puerto Rico* (New York: Doubleday, 1947), 42.

**33.** This phrase comes from Nancy Fraser's critique of Jürgen Habermas's idea of the public sphere in Fraser, "Rethinking the Public Sphere: A Contribution to the Critique of Actually Existing Democracy," *Social Text* 25–26 (1990): 56–80. On the changing discourses of liberalism in this period, see Gary Gerstle, "The Protean Character of American Liberalism," *AHR* 99 (Oct. 1994): 1043–73. See Pedro Malavet, *America's Colony: The Political and Cultural Conflict between the United States and Puerto Rico* (New York: New York University Press, 2004), 117–31, for an incisive discussion of the failures of American liberal citizenship for Puerto Rico and ideas for reforming it.

**34.** Phillip Gleason, "Minorities (Almost) All: The Minority Concept in American Social Thought," *American Quarterly* 43 (Sept. 1991): 398, 401. In the decade after the publication of Louis Wirth's essay "The Problem of Minority Groups," in *The Science of Man in the World Crisis*, edited by Ralph Linton (New York: Columbia University Press, 1945), according to Gleason, a dozen books on minorities and "race relations" and over a thousand scholarly articles were published.

**35.** Nancy Fraser and Axel Honneth, *Redistribution or Recognition? A Political-Philosophical Exchange* (New York: Verso, 2003), 10.

**36.** Taylor, *Multiculturalism*, 35–36. Or, as philosopher Paul Ricoeur has written, "Recognition means identifying each person as free and equal to every other person." Ricoeur, *The Course of Recognition* (Cambridge, MA: Harvard University Press, 2005), 197.

**37.** See Axel Honneth, *The Struggle for Recognition: The Moral Grammar of Social Conflicts* (Cambridge, MA: Polity Press, 1995), 161, for a note about Robert Park and Ernest Burgess's use of *recognition* in 1921. Anthropologist Johannes Fabian cites Fanon's statement about recognition as the anticolonialists' "topos"; Fabian, "Remembering the Other," *Critical Inquiry* 26 (Autumn 1999): 63.

**38.** Axel Honneth, *The Struggle for Recognition: The Moral Grammar of Social Conflict* (Cambridge, MA: MIT Press, 1966).

**39.** Frank Torres, secretary, Puerto Rican Bar Association, letter to Mayor Wagner, Aug. 1961, cited in "Puerto Ricans Seek School Board Say," *New York Amsterdam News*, Aug. 26, 1961, 16.

**40.** Peter Kihss, "Puerto Rican Story: A Sensitive People Erupt," *New York Times*, July 26, 1967, 20; "Negroes and Puerto Ricans Stage Bronx Revolution," *New York Amsterdam News*, Feb. 20, 1960, 1.

**41.** "A Silent Minority Starts to Speak Out," *U.S. News*, July 13, 1970, from Vertical File, "Puerto Ricans—Social Welfare," City Hall Library (hereafter CHL).

**42.** Hunt, *Inventing Human Rights*; also see, for example, Harri Englund and Frances Nyamnjoh, eds., *Rights and the Politics of Recognition in Africa* (London: Zed Books, 2004); and Obrad Savic, ed., *The Politics of Human Rights* (New York: Verso, 1999).

**43.** Thomas Jackson, *From Civil Rights to Human Rights: Martin Luther King, Jr., and the Struggle for Economic Justice* (Philadelphia: University of Pennsylvania Press, 2007). The parallel national body, the U.S. Commission on Civil Rights, never changed its name, however. The *New York Times* did not report on this change of name; the first article using the new agency title was "Rights Unit Sees Gains in Housing," *New York Times*, July 1, 1962, 169.

**44.** From a speech at the Militant Labor Forum in Palm Gardens, NY, Apr. 8, 1964. George Breitman, ed., *Malcolm Speaks: Selected Speeches and Statements* (New York: Pathfinder Press, 1965), 50–51.

**45.** The specific goal of these activists was the pardon and release from prison of the four Nationalists charged in a 1954 attack on the U.S. Congress. President Jimmy Carter ultimately pardoned them, and all four were released by 1979. "Four Who Got Clemency," *New York Times*, Sept. 7, 1979, B18; Francesco Ortiz Santini, "The National Security Council during the Carter Administration and the Liberation of the Puerto Rican Nationalists in 1979," *Centro Journal* 19, no. 2 (2007): 150–81.

**46.** Seminal books like the collectively written History Task Force's *Labor Migration under Capitalism: The Puerto Rican Experience* (New York: Monthly Review Press, 1979), and even Virginia Sánchez-Korrol's *From Colonia to Community: The History of Puerto Ricans in New York City, 1917–1948* (Westport, CT: Greenwood Press, 1983), were hardly read outside of the field for a decade or more. See also Kelvin Santiago-Valles's interesting discussion of the "traditionalist anticolonialist historiography" in Puerto Rico during the same period (and then the later "new historiography" that challenged it), Santiago-Valles, "The Discreet Charm of the Proletariat: Imagining Early-Twentieth-Century Puerto Ricans in the Past Twenty-five Years of Historical Inquiry," in *Puerto Rican Jam: Rethinking Colonialism and Nationalism*, edited by Frances Negrón-Muntaner and Ramón Grosfoguel (Minneapolis: University of Minnesota Press, 1997), 96. For a thorough discussion of the parallel marginalization of scholars in Chicano studies (mostly on the West Coast), see Renato Rosaldo, "Chicano Studies, 1970–1984," *Annual Review of Anthropology* 14 (1985): 405–27.

**47.** Lorrin Thomas, "What Happened to History in the Seventies? Beyond 'The Personal Is Political'" (International Women's Day keynote lecture, Rutgers University–Camden, Mar. 10, 2009). Linda Martín Alcoff, "Fraser on Redistribution, Recognition, and Identity," *European Journal of Political Theory* 6 (2007): 261, emphasis in the original; see also Alcoff, *Visible Identities: Race, Gender, and the Self* (New York: Oxford University Press, 2006).

**48.** See, for instance, Will Kymlicka, *Multicultural Citizenship: A Liberal Theory of Minority Rights* (New York: Oxford University Press, 1995), 18 and passim; and Iris Marion Young, *Inclusion and Democracy* (New York: Oxford University Press, 2000), 103–8 and passim.

**49.** Habermas in Taylor, *Multiculturalism*, 108, 110, 113.

**50.** Redistribution is essential to correcting "injustices of recognition," Fraser argues, because they are "rooted at once in the economic structure and the status order of society." Her "status model" of recognition mediates between the liberal and the communitarian by suggesting that injustices of recognition experienced by groups in the past be interpreted as failures to protect the rights of individual members of that group rather than as groupwide claims for special treatment. Fraser and Honneth, *Redistribution or Recognition?* 19, 33, and passim. Iris Marion Young, *Democracy and Inclusion* (New York: Oxford University Press, 2000), 107.

**51.** Kymlicka and Taylor, who are both Canadian, were the most prominent theorists writing about the French-Canadian example of recognition of difference in a particular society. The influence of their example is widespread: even theorists like Kwame Anthony Appiah, in *The Ethics of Identity* (Princeton, NJ: Princeton University Press), 99–105, and Axel Honneth, *Struggle for Recognition*, x, use the French-Canadian case as a primary example.

**52.** Renato Rosaldo, "Whose Cultural Studies?" *American Anthropologist* 96 (Sept. 1994): 527.

**53.** In the introduction to their book, William Flores and Rina Benmayor argue that the idea of cultural citizenship provides a clearer, more accurate theoretical framework for the real goals of Latinos, revising inaccurate or insufficient concepts like "multiculturalism, assimilation, acculturation, and even broad concepts of citizenship and social rights" that have been used to analyze the experiences and dilemmas of Latinos in the United States. Flores and Benmayor, eds., *Latino Cultural Citizenship: Claiming Identity, Space, and Rights* (Boston: Beacon Press, 1997), 8–9. Renato Rosaldo laid out his idea of cultural citizenship in a 1994 article, "Cultural Citizenship and Educational Democracy," *Cultural Anthropology* 9 (Aug. 1994): 402–11. For an example of the use of the cultural citizenship concept for non-Latino groups, see Sunaina Marr Maira, *Missing: Youth, Citizenship, and Empire after 9/11* (Durham, NC: Duke University Press, 2009). On Chicano activism that was critical of liberal citizenship, see, for example, Biliana Ambrecht and Harry Pachon, "Ethnic Political Mobilization in a Mexican American Community: An Exploratory Study of East Los Angeles, 1965–1972," *Western Political Quarterly* 27 (Sept. 1974): 500–519.

**54.** See, for example, George Sánchez, *Becoming Mexican American: Ethnicity, Culture, and Identity in Chicano Los Angeles, 1900–1945* (New York: Oxford University Press, 1993); David Gutiérrez, *Walls and Mirrors: Mexican Americans, Immigrants, and the Politics of Ethnicity* (Berkeley: University of California Press, 1995); Matt García, *A World of Its Own: Race, Labor, and Citrus in the Making of Greater Los Angeles* (Chapel Hill: University of North Carolina Press, 2001); and Carmen Whalen, *From Puerto Rico to Philadelphia: Puerto Rican Workers and Postwar Economies* (Philadelphia: Temple University Press, 2001).

**55.** Flores and Benmayor, *Latino Cultural Citizenship*, 14.

**56.** New scholarship on recognition in Latin American contexts includes: Lucy Taylor and Fiona Wilson, "The Messiness of Everyday Life: Exploring Key Themes in Latin American Citizenship Studies," introduction to special issue of the *Bulletin of Latin American Research* 23 (2004): 154–64; and Brett Trojan, "Ethnic Citizenship in Colombia: The Experience of the Regional Indigenous Council of the Caucus in Southwestern Colombia from 1970 to 1990," *LARR* 43 (2008): 166–91. Lisa Maya Knauer, "The Politics of Afrocuban Cultural Expression in New York City," *Journal of Ethnic and Migration Studies* 34 (Nov. 2008): 1257–81. For recent work on citizenship and recognition in other parts of the world, see Englund and Nyamnjoh, *Rights and the Politics of Recognition*; Savic, *Politics of Human Rights*; Renato Rosaldo, ed., *Cultural Citizenship in Island Southeast Asia: Nation and Belonging in the Hinterlands* (Berkeley: University of California Press, 2003); and Ewa Morawska, "The Recognition Politics of Polish Radio MultiKulti in Berlin," *Journal of Ethnic and Migration Studies* 34 (Nov. 2008): 1323–35. Some of this scholarship employs a rather limited use of the idea of recognition, cast more accurately as conventional politics of citizenship; however, all of it at least attempts to work beyond the framework of traditional citizenship. See discussion of this point in the epilogue.

**57.** Alcoff, "Fraser on Redistribution, Recognition, and Identity," 263.

**58.** The phrase "grammar of social conflict" is from Hegel; Axel Honneth uses it as a subtitle in his essay "Redistribution as Recognition: The Moral Grammar of Social Conflicts," in Honneth and Fraser, *Redistribution or Recognition?*

**59.** Craig Calhoun, *Critical Social Theory* (Cambridge, MA: Blackwell, 1995), 218, and Calhoun, "'New Social Movements' of the Early Nineteenth Century," *Social Science History* 17 (Autumn 1993): 385–427; Honneth, "Redistribution as Recognition," 133.

**60.** Gutmann, introduction, in Taylor, *Multiculturalism*, 17.
**61.** See, again, Alcoff's arguments for adjusting Fraser's propositions about recognition versus redistribution. Alcoff, "Fraser on Redistribution, Recognition, and Identity."
**62.** Gerstle, "Protean Character of American Liberalism"; Habermas, in Taylor, *Multiculturalism*, 108; Malavet, *America's Colony*, 117–26.
**63.** Brown, *Politics Out of History*, 14.


Chapter One

**1.** Jesús Colón, *The Way It Was and Other Writings* (Houston: Arte Público Press, 1993), 49.
**2.** On the early Spanish-speaking community in New York, see Bernardo Vega, *Memoirs of Bernardo Vega: A Contribution to the History of the Puerto Rican Community in New York*, edited by César Andreu Iglesias (New York: Monthly Review Press, 1984), 8–9 and passim; and Jesse Hoffnung-Garskof, "The Migrations of Arturo Schomburg: On Being *Antillano*, Negro, and Puerto Rican in New York," *Journal of American Ethnic History* 21 (Fall 2001): 9.
**3.** Colón, *Way It Was*, 84.
**4.** The size of the Puerto Rican *colonia* in this decade was difficult to ascertain and remains a slippery fact of demography primarily because, as citizens, Puerto Ricans entered the United States under the radar of official immigration figures. Moreover, as with many residents of poor and marginalized neighborhoods, the number of Puerto Ricans counted in both federal and local censuses was probably much lower than their actual numbers. See Virginia Sánchez-Korrol, "Survival of Puerto Rican Women in New York before World War II," in *Historical Perspectives on Puerto Rican Survival in the U.S.*, edited by Clara E. Rodríguez and Virginia Sánchez-Korrol (Princeton, NJ: Markus Wiener Publishers, 1996), 57–67; and R. A. Gómez, "Spanish Immigration to the United States," *Americas* 19 (July 1962): 59–78.
**5.** Vega, *Memoirs*, 107.
**6.** Contemporary estimates of the *colonia* population appear in the following documents: "El voto portorriqueño en Nueva York," *La Prensa*, Oct. 15, 1923, 4; "La organización del voto," *La Prensa*, Oct. 9, 1924, 4; "La colonia portorriqueña," *La Prensa*, Jan. 22, 1926, 4, was an editorial that remarked vaguely, "We are informed that about 40,000 Puerto Ricans live in New York"; and Porto Rican Brotherhood of America, "La colonia puertorriqueña," *Souvenir* pamphlet, May 1927, Vando papers, series III, box 13, folder 17. For estimates by the U.S. Bureau of the Census and the Research Bureau of the Welfare and Health Council of New York City, see Ira Rosenwaike, *Population History of New York City* (Syracuse, NY: Syracuse University Press, 1972), 121. Some migrants used the Americanized spelling "Porto Rico" in this period. Puerto Rico's first peacetime military governor under U.S. rule, Major General Brooke, ordered that the official spelling of the island be changed to this spelling for American English; "Porto Rico" remained the official spelling until 1932. James Dietz, *Economic History of Puerto Rico: Institutional Change and Capitalist Development* (Princeton, NJ: Princeton University Press, 1986), 85.

**7.** *Trigueño* means "wheat-colored," a description for light-skinned mulattoes. Chief Aguaybana was a leader of the Tainos, the native people of Puerto Rico. Jesús Colón, "La única manera—A los puertorriqueños en N.Y.," Mar. 30, 1923, Colón papers, series III, box 5, folder 8.

**8.** A reprint of a map prepared by the New York Urban League showing the racial/ethnic composition of Harlem in 1935 appears in Joseph P. Fitzpatrick, *Puerto Rican Americans: The Meaning of Migration to the Mainland* (Englewood Cliffs, NJ: Prentice-Hall, 1971), 54, as well as in two contemporary social science monographs: James Ford, Katherine Morrow, and G. Thompson, *Slums and Housing* (Cambridge, MA: Harvard University Press, 1936), 323; and Lawrence Chenault, *The Puerto Rican Migrant in New York City* (New York: Columbia University Press, 1938), 95. The neighborhood's demographics would have looked somewhat different ten years earlier, but anecdotal sources from the twenties describe Puerto Ricans' presence in Harlem in similar patterns.

**9.** Ramón Colón, *Carlos Tapia: A Puerto Rican Hero in New York* (New York: Vintage Press, 1976), 71.

**10.** Vega, *Memoirs*, 97. Linda Martín Alcoff writes that the term comes from the denigration of Spanish speakers who would say "No spic English" when addressed in English. Alcoff, "Latino/as, Asian Americans, and the Black-White Binary," *Journal of Ethics* 7 (Mar. 2003): 5–27.

**11.** Interview with Ramón Colón, conducted by Thomas Rivera, Apr. 30, 1973, Pioneros Project.

**12.** These figures come from the 20 percent sample I took from data on two election districts in the 1925 New York State manuscript census, which records residents' occupations and nationality as well as sex, race, age, and marital status.

**13.** Félix Cordillero, "De nuestros lectores," *La Prensa*, Jan. 4, 1924, 4. Historian Winston James asserts that it is "no accident that Puerto Rico's black leaders in New York came not from Manhattan but primarily from Brooklyn." James, *Holding Aloft the Banner of Ethiopia: Caribbean Radicalism in America, 1900–1933* (New York: Verso, 1998), 224. My sample of the 1925 New York State manuscript census bears out this assertion, although the very small number of residents categorized as "black" in the sample means that my findings are not statistically significant.

**14.** Hoffnung-Garskof, "Migrations of Arturo Schomburg," 9; Vega, *Memoirs*, 195–96.

**15.** The series of restrictive immigration laws passed during the early 1920s did not limit immigration from the Western Hemisphere, including, of course, Latin America.

**16.** "Diez mil obreros hispanos del mar va a la huelga hoy," *La Prensa*, Apr. 25, 1923, 1.

**17.** On *La Prensa*'s history, circulation, and readership, see Vega, *Memoirs*, 99; and WPA Federal Writers' Project, "Spanish Newspapers, Magazines, etc., in New York," Spanish Book, n.d., WPA files, reel 269, folder 1. The WPA Writers' Project members were working on a study of the Spanish-speaking population of New York informally known as the "Spanish Book." The project involved an extensive survey of many facets of the lives of New York's Spanish-speaking residents—

demographic information, organizations, churches, commerce, arts and culture, health—to be boiled down and included in a publication on New York City as part of the American Guide series.

**18.** "Nueva York celebra con grandes solemnidades hispanas hoy la memorable fiesta de la Raza," *La Prensa*, Oct. 12, 1923, 1. In Spanish, *hispano* could mean either "Spanish," as in "of Spain," or "of Spanish descent," understood as "of Latin America." For instance, when *La Prensa* marked the celebration of the *colonia*'s first "*Fiesta de la Raza*," citing "*la música hispana*" and "the joviality *del carácter hispano*," the adjective took on the implication "of Spain." In the language of the middle class, these meanings were often elided in references to Spanish speakers and their culture.

**19.** See Pedro Juan Labarthe, "De nuestros lectores," *La Prensa*, Jan. 8, 1931, 6; and interview with Pedro Cresente, conducted by B. Richardson, Apr. 13, 1975, Pioneros Project. Xavier College was a private Jesuit high school founded in the 1840s. Pedro Juan Labarthe, *The Son of Two Nations: The Private Life of a Columbia Student* (New York: Carranza and Co., 1931).

**20.** Interview with Pedro Cresente. Ángel Santana, "De nuestros lectores," *La Prensa*, Oct. 14, 1930, 6; D. Lorenzo Piñeiro Rivera, "De nuestros lectores," *La Prensa*, Oct. 17, 1930, 6. A Venezuelan reader, and director of the culturally conservative Federación Latinoamericano, followed these complaints with a lament about the "inexplicable" attitude of disdain that most other Latin Americans felt for Puerto Ricans because, as he explained it, they had never achieved independence from Spain. J. R. Gutiérrez, "De nuestros lectores," *La Prensa*, Sept. 26, 1930, 6–7.

**21.** See Jeffrey S. Gurock, *When Harlem Was Jewish, 1870–1930* (New York: Columbia University Press, 1979), and Robert Orsi, *Madonna of 115th Street: Faith and Ritual in Italian Harlem* (New Haven, CT: Yale University Press, 1985).

**22.** Interview with Lorenzo Homar, conducted by Rina Benmayor, Sept. 21, 1983, Costureras Project.

**23.** Interview with Louise Delgado, conducted by Rina Benmayor and Blanca Vázquez, Feb. 17, 1985, Costureras Project.

**24.** Interview with Mercedes Díaz, conducted by Bob Rosado, Apr. 11, 1974, Pioneros Project.

**25.** Interview with Félix Loperena, conducted by John Vásquez, Nov. 22, 1974, Pioneros Project. Ramón Rodríguez did not explain why only Irish immigrants, and not Italians, would resent this privilege. Interview with Ramón Rodríguez, conducted by John Vásquez, Oct. 29, 1974, Pioneros Project.

**26.** Interview with Juan Ramos, conducted by Mayda Cortiella, Oct. 21, 1974, Pioneros Project.

**27.** Interview with Clemente Torres, conducted by John Vásquez, Nov. 18, 1974, Pioneros Project.

**28.** Vega, *Memoirs*, 121. On the *marqueta*, see Virginia Sánchez-Korrol, *From Colonia to Community: The History of Puerto Ricans in New York City* (Berkeley: University of California Press, 1983), 63.

**29.** Interview with Ernesto Sepúlveda, conducted by John Vásquez, Nov. 6, 1974, Pioneros Project. Sepúlveda and Ramon Colón shared the recollection that migrants who arrived in New York before the "great migration" of the post–World

War II years were better educated, "more concerned about real progress," and generally more "responsible" than the migrants who came in the postwar wave. Interview with Ramón Colón, conducted by Pedro Rivera and Thomas Rivera, Apr. 30, 1973, Pioneros Project.

**30.** Interview with Vicente Luis Marrero, conducted by John Vásquez, June 24, 1974, Pioneros Project; interview with Gonzalo Plasencia, conducted by Jaime Barreto, Nov. 4, 1974, Pioneros Project; interview with María Rodríguez, conducted by Jaime Barreto, Nov. 15, 1974, Pioneros Project; and interview with Loperena.

**31.** Interview with Juan Ramos; Mercedes Hernández, "De nuestros lectores," *La Prensa*, Dec. 2, 1924, 4. On migrant women's work in the needle trades in this era, see Altagracia Ortiz, "*En la aguja y el pedal eché la hiel*: Puerto Rican Women in the Garment Industry in New York City, 1920–1980," in *Puerto Rican Women and Work: Bridges in Transnational Labor*, edited by Altagracia Ortiz, 55–81 (Philadelphia: Temple University Press, 1996); and Sánchez-Korrol, "Survival of Puerto Rican Women in New York," 59–60, 64–66.

**32.** Details on the labor participation of Puerto Rican migrants in this era are difficult to pin down; Virginia Sánchez-Korrol has estimated that 29 percent of women in "Spanish" Harlem in the 1920s worked outside the home. See Sánchez-Korrol, "Survival of Puerto Rican Women in New York," 58. Rates for men must have been considerably higher, although anecdotal sources also suggest high rates of unemployment even before the Depression; see, for instance, Vega, *Memoirs*, 117–20 and passim.

**33.** "Vida obrera: Por el interés de todos," *La Prensa*, Jan. 14, 1922, 4. One of the column's early contributors, M. Callejo, wrote a letter in January of 1922 titled "For the Interest of All," thanking "the gentlemen of *La Prensa*" for "kindly offering" the newspaper's space to workers.

**34.** Jesus Colón, of the Ateneo Obrero Hispano de Nueva York, to Gonzalo Rivera, editor of *El Pueblo*, Nov. 11, 1926, n.p.; Alianza Obrera Puertorriqueño de Nueva York, constitution (1926), Colón papers, series V, box 15, folder 1. The constitution of the Alianza Obrera Puertorriqueña in New York charged the "dominant class" with "converting entire populations into serfs and pariahs . . . like they've done in our beloved Puerto Rico."

**35.** On the early organizations of *tabaqueros* in particular, and the history they brought from the island, see Sánchez-Korrol, *From Colonia to Community*, 137–42.

**36.** See Vega, *Memoirs*, 93–96; César Ayala and Rafael Bernabe, *Puerto Rico in the American Century: A History since 1898* (Chapel Hill: University of North Carolina Press, 2007), 280.

**37.** Vega, *Memoirs*, 112, 126.

**38.** Ateneo Obrero Puertorriqueño de Nueva York, constitution (1923), Colón papers, series V, box 15, folder 5.

**39.** This June meeting of the Alianza Obrera was motivated by the Sol Bloom incident; see pages 47–49. L. Gómez García, "Vida obrera: La situación en Puerto Rico," *La Prensa*, June 10, 1925, 7; Vega, *Memoirs*, 37.

**40.** See "De nuestros lectores: La crisis de los tabaqueros," *La Prensa*, May 30, 1929, 6.

**41.** "Vida obrera: Planes de organización obrera," *La Prensa*, Feb. 21, 1927, 2, 5.

**42.** Historian Virginia Sánchez-Korrol writes that women were "well represented in the cigar making industry" in this period, although she does not provide an estimate of their rates of participation as workers. Sánchez-Korrol, "Survival of Puerto Rican Women in New York," 65.

**43.** "Vida obrera: Los trabajadores del tabaco en Nueva York, sus luchas e ideales," *La Prensa*, June 4, 1925, 6, 7.

**44.** "La heulga de tabaqueros de Pto. Rico tiene en la miseria de 12,000 personas," *La Prensa*, Jan. 20, 1927, 1.

**45.** Vega, *Memoirs*, 106–7; Ayala and Bernabe, *Puerto Rico in the American Century*, 66.

**46.** "Apreciaciones, por Jibarito," *El Caribe*, Oct. 6, 1923, n.p.

**47.** R. Arias del Valle, "Tribuna libre: Las madriñas de guerra," *La Prensa*, Feb. 13, 1925, 5; "El honor de las mujeres hispanas en Nueva York," editorial, *La Prensa*, Feb. 13, 1925, 4; Maximiano Ríos Ríos, "Tribuna libre: La escuela de la soledad," *La Prensa*, Apr. 27, 1925, 8.

**48.** It is not clear that it was only, or even primarily, the men in these associations who organized the *reinados*; women members of the clubs' auxiliaries seem to have played an important role in their organization. For a discussion of *"reinados"* among *obreras* in Latin America—specifically, millworkers in Colombia in the 1940s and 1950s—see, for example, Ann Farnsworth-Alvear, *Dulcinea in the Factory: Women, Men, Myths and Morals in Colombia's Industrial Experiment* (Durham, NC: Duke University Press, 2000), 171–76.

**49.** "Puerto Rico da otra candidata al Certamen de Simpatía de Obreritas," *La Prensa*, Mar. 27, 1926, 1. *"Obreritas"* were defined by the sponsors as "Spanish-speaking working girls" who were employed in workshops, factories, and shops in New York and who "earn a living honorably by manual labor." "El concurso de simpatía entre obreritas," *La Prensa*, Mar. 3, 1926, 4.

**50.** "Concurso de simpatía."

**51.** See Chenault, *Puerto Rican Migrant*, 146, 151–53; Fitzpatrick, *Puerto Rican Americans*, 115–16, 123–29; C. Wright Mills, Clarence Senior, and Rose Kohn Goldsen, *The Puerto Rican Journey: New York's Newest Migrants* (New York: Harper and Brothers Publishers, 1950), 110–14.

**52.** See Leonard Covello, "History of East Harlem," manuscript, n.d., 8–9, Covello papers, series VIII, box 79, folder 6; Chenault, *Puerto Rican Migrant*, 152; and WPA Federal Writers' Project, "Puerto Rican Colony in N.Y.," Spanish Book, WPA files, reel 269, folder 9.

**53.** See Fitzpatrick, *Puerto Rican Americans*, 121–22, 127–29. See also Antonio M. Stevens-Arroyo, "Puerto Rican Struggles in the Catholic Church," in *Historical Perspectives on Puerto Rican Survival in the U.S.*, edited by Clara E. Rodríguez and Virginia Sánchez-Korrol (Princeton, NJ: Markus Wiener Publishers, 1996), 153–66, although this chapter deals primarily with the postwar period; and Stevens-Arroyo,

"The Emergence of a Social Identity among Latino Catholics: An Appraisal," in *Hispanic Catholic Culture in the U.S.: Issues and Concerns*, edited by Jay P. Dolan and Allan Figueroa Deck, S.J. (Notre Dame, IN: University of Notre Dame Press, 1994), 77–130; and Jay P. Dolan and Jaime R. Vidal, eds., *Puerto Rican and Cuban Catholics in the U.S., 1900–1965* (Notre Dame, IN: University of Notre Dame Press, 1994).

54. Interview with Gloria Tejada, conducted by John Vásquez, June 24, 1974, Pioneros Project.

55. Fitzpatrick, *Puerto Rican Americans*, 124–25.

56. See Sánchez-Korrol, *From Colonia to Community*, 112, 159.

57. For discussion of how the Catholic Church mediated Italians' adjustment to life in New York City, see Robert Orsi, "The Religious Boundaries of an Inbetween People: Street *Feste* and the Problem of the Dark-Skinned Other in Italian Harlem, 1920–1990," *American Quarterly* 44 (Sept. 1992): 313–47, and Orsi, *Madonna of 115th Street: Faith and Ritual in Italian Harlem, 1880–1950* (New Haven, CT: Yale University Press, 1985).

58. Vega called it "the first serious effort to set up one unified grouping for the entire community" but noted that none of the elected leaders of the new organization represented the working-class Puerto Ricans in New York. Vega, *Memoirs*, 121.

59. Porto Rican Brotherhood of America, "La colonia puertorriqueña."

60. See, generally, Lawrence H. Fuchs, ed., *American Ethnic Politics* (New York: Harper & Row, 1968); Stanley Lieberson, *Ethnic Patterns in American Cities* (New York: Free Press of Glencoe, 1963); and Herbert J. Gans, *The Urban Villagers: A Study of the Second Generation Italians in the West End of Boston* (Boston: Center for Community Studies, 1962).

61. In fact, the Campbell bill of 1922 advanced the idea of a status called an "associated free state," or "*estado libre asociado.*" This answer to the "status question" was tabled for several decades but was finally adopted in 1952, after an 81 percent majority of Puerto Rican voters approved a constitution providing for such a relationship with the United States. See Dietz, *Economic History of Puerto Rico*, 161, 236–37; and Pedro A. Cabán, *Constructing a Colonial People: Puerto Rico and the United States, 1898–1932* (Boulder, CO: Westview Press, 1999), 219–20.

62. Truman R. Clark, *Puerto Rico and the United States, 1917–1933* (Pittsburgh: University of Pittsburgh Press, 1975), 8. This nondefinition of Puerto Rico's status between 1898 and 1917 allowed the United States full latitude in controlling the relationship between the two countries, especially vis-à-vis policies affecting tariffs, taxes, and citizenship. In 1899, Henry Curtis, a member of the Insular Commission, wrote that "time alone can demonstrate whether we shall ever want to make them [Puerto Rico and the Philippines] States. If we are not certain as to this, we should not make them Territories; for statehood follows territorial conditions." Henry G. Curtis, "The Status of Puerto Rico," *Forum* 28 (Dec. 1899), 408, quoted in Clark, *Puerto Rico and the United States*, 8.

63. After several splits and rebirths, the core of the Union Party re-formed in 1938 as the Popular Democratic Party, under the leadership of Muñoz Rivera's son, Luis Muñoz Marín, who would become Puerto Rico's first native elected governor in 1948. For a discussion of political parties and political culture in Puerto Rico in

this period, see Pedro Malavet, *America's Colony: The Political and Cultural Conflict between the United States and Puerto Rico* (New York: New York University Press, 2004), 57–66.

**64.** By 1920, the Socialist leadership's personal loyalty to the American Federation of Labor and Samuel Gompers was firm. In 1901, Gompers had intervened on Iglesias's behalf when the latter was charged with leading a Federación Libre de Trabajadores (FLT) strike deemed illegal under the still-prevailing Spanish law. Gompers was instrumental in convincing the U.S. Federal Court of Appeals to hear the case, and its decision in favor of Iglesias and the FLT laid the groundwork for a new, more progressive body of labor laws in Puerto Rico. These events also laid the groundwork for a fierce allegiance on the part of Puerto Rican workers to the U.S. labor movement and to the U.S. political system in general. See Vega, *Memoirs*, 92–94; and "Santiago Iglesias ataca con furia a sus detractores ante la Alianza Obrera," *La Prensa*, Jan. 19, 1913, 2. See also, generally, Miles Galvin, *The Organized Labor Movement in Puerto Rico* (Rutherford, NJ: Farleigh Dickinson University Press, 1979); Juan Angel Silén, *Apuntes para la historia del movimiento obrero puertorriqueño* (Río Piedras, PR: Ediciones Cultural, 1978); and Angel G. Quintero Rivera, *Workers' Struggles in Puerto Rico* (New York: Monthly Review Press, 1976).

**65.** Puerto Ricans did not win the right to elect their own governor until 1948; Luis Muñoz Marín served as governor from 1948 to 1964.

**66.** See comments of Representative James G. Strong (R-KS) in 67th Cong., 2nd sess., *Congressional Record* 62, part 1 (Mar. 17, 1922): 4040–44. These early discussions about an "associated free state" laid the groundwork for conceptualizing the *estado libre asociado*, or commonwealth, in the forties.

**67.** For an interesting discussion of Reily's controversial inaugural speech—and evidence that President Harding personally edited the speech to tone down its offenses to the Puerto Rican people—see Clark, *Puerto Rico and the United States*, 51–54. "Se combate al Ptdo. Unionista Portorriqueño," *La Prensa*, Jan. 18, 1923, 1.

**68.** Former Unionista José Coll y Cuchí served as the party's first president. The new Nationalist Party brought together disaffected Unionists, members of the Juventud Nacionalista, groups of *independentistas* who had organized across the island during the previous decade, and members of municipal nationalist clubs from across the island. Pedro Cabán, *Constructing a Colonial People: Puerto Rico and the United States, 1898–1932* (Boulder, CO: Westview Press, 1999), 220; José Trías Monge, *Puerto Rico: The Trials of the Oldest Colony in the World* (New Haven, CT: Yale University Press, 1997), 79–81; Ayala and Bernabe, *Puerto Rico in the American Century*, 58–59.

**69.** "La asociación nacionalista portorriqueña discutirá el proyecto de Estado Libre," *La Prensa*, Feb. 2, 1922, 1.

**70.** Vega, *Memoirs*, 114, 127–28.

**71.** Ibid., 203.

**72.** Roosevelt to Colonel Lafayette B. Gleason, Oct. 20, 1930, and Roosevelt to Dr. Hubert C. Herring, Dec. 5, 1931, Theodore Roosevelt Jr. papers, box 29, Library of Congress, cited in Clark, *Puerto Rico and the United States*, 76.

**73.** Flyer, Alianza Obrera Portorriqueña, n.d. [1923], Colón papers, series V, box 15, folder 1; and Vega, *Memoirs*, 129. Bernardo Vega—betraying his "proletarian" bias—deemed the *alianza* to be "the most important organization in the life of Puerto Ricans in New York." Vega, *Memoirs*, 11–12. Porto Rican Brotherhood of America, "Porto Rico en Nueva York," *Souvenir*, May 15, 1926, Vando papers, series III, box 2, folder 17.

**74.** "Se combate al Ptdo. Unionista Portorriqueño."

**75.** "La Liga Portorriqueña se alía con el partido demócrato nacional," *La Prensa*, Apr. 12, 1923, 1. "Liga Puertorriqueña de Nueva York, 1922," Vando papers, series III, box 2, folder 14.

**76.** "La unión política de los portorriqueños en Nueva York," editorial, *La Prensa*, Feb. 10, 1923, 4.

**77.** "El Club Democrático Portorriqueño de B'kln lucha practicamente por la unión," *La Prensa*, Apr. 24, 1923, 2. See also Vega, *Memoirs*, 129.

**78.** "El Club Democrático Portorriqueño," 1–2. See also Vega, *Memoirs*, 111, 129, for mention of the "Club Democrático Puertorriqueño," which Vega says was formed in 1918 by José Alonso and Joaquín Colón, to garner support for the Al Smith gubernatorial campaign of that year.

**79.** Flyer, Porto Rican Democratic Club de Brooklyn, n.d. [June 1923], Colón papers, series V, box 18, folder 1.

**80.** Colón, "La única manera."

**81.** There is no way to verify Vega's claim, since votes and registrants were not recorded by ethnic group. See Fred I. Greenstein, "The Changing Pattern of Urban Party Politics," *Annals of the American Academy of Political and Social Science* 353 (May 1964): 1–13; Elmer Cornwell Jr., "Bosses, Machines, and Ethnic Groups," in *American Ethnic Politics*, edited by Lawrence H. Fuchs (New York: Harper & Row, 1968).

**82.** "El Club Democrático Portorriqueño de B'kln." The PRDC spelled its name "Porto Rican" until the late 1920s.

**83.** Colón, *Carlos Tapia*, 46.

**84.** This is how migrant Clemente Torres described Tapia. Interview with Clemente Torres. Many migrants who remembered Tapia in interviews referred to his racial identity, calling him *"un negrito,"* a term of affection.

**85.** Interview with Félix Loperena.

**86.** Interview with Doña Gregoria Lausell, conducted by Ana Juarbe, Apr. 2, 1984, Costureras Project.

**87.** Interview with Doña Gloria Rodríguez, conducted by Ana Juarbe, Dec. 19, 1983, Costureras Project.

**88.** Interview with José Ramón Giboyeaux, conducted by Rina Benmayor and Blanca Vásquez, Mar. 12, 1984, Costureras Project.

**89.** Interview with Clemente Torres.

**90.** Colón, *Carlos Tapia*, 46. Colón puts "Puerto Rican" in quotes to emphasize his position as a supporter of statehood for the island—and attributes the same position to Tapia: that Puerto Ricans are actually "Americans" and should not necessarily be distinguished as a separate national group.

**91.** Joaquin Colón, *Pioneros Puertorriqueños en Nueva York, 1917–1947* (Houston: Arte Público Press, 2002), 45.

**92.** Between the 1900 Foraker Act (which replaced U.S. military rule with a U.S.-dominated civilian government) and the 1917 Jones Act, which provided for universal male suffrage, suffrage on the island was limited to men who could read and write in Spanish or English and who met a property requirement. This was actually a step backward from Spanish colonial rule: Puerto Ricans had lobbied for and won universal male suffrage from the Spanish Cortes by the end of the nineteenth century. Women did not win the vote in Puerto Rico until 1929. See Trías Monge, *Puerto Rico*, 42–43, 75; and Dietz, *Economic History of Puerto Rico*, 85, 97.

**93.** "Los portorriqueños deben inscribirse esta semana," *La Prensa*, Oct. 11, 1923, 4; "El voto portorriqueño en Nueva York," editorial, *La Prensa*, Oct. 15, 1923, 4; "La organización del voto," editorial, *La Prensa*, Oct. 9, 1924, 4; "Los 40,000 votos portorriqueños de aquí son una gran fuerza política," *La Prensa*, Mar. 8, 1927, 1. "Debe inscribirse enseguida," editorial, *La Prensa*, Sept. 27, 1927, 4; "¡Hay que inscribirse y votar!" editorial, *La Prensa*, Oct. 9, 1928, 4.

**94.** Interview with María Rodríguez, conducted by Jaime Barreto, Nov. 15, 1974, Pioneros Project.

**95.** This is according to Ramón Colón, *Carlos Tapia*, 44. The following is a list of clubs and incorporation dates based on Colón: Porto Rican Democratic Club, 1923 (First Assembly District); De Hostos and Guaybana Democratic Clubs, 1928–32 (First Assembly District, at 115 Johnson St.); Betances Democratic Club Inc., 1928 (Third Assembly District); Baldorioty Democratic Club Inc., 1932 (Fourth Assembly District, near the Navy Yard, and Sixth Assembly District, at Tompkins and Marcy Aves.); Guarionex Democratic Club Inc., 1929 (Fifteenth Assembly District, Greenpoint).

**96.** See Colón, *Carlos Tapia*, 44. On the numbers game in Harlem in this era, see Claude McKay, *Harlem: Negro Metropolis* (New York: Harcourt Brace Jovanovitch, 1968), 100–120; and Rufus Schatzberg, *Black Organized Crime in Harlem* (New York: Garland Publishing, 1993), 100–118. On patronage and the street-cleaning department, see Ira Katznelson, *Black Men, White Cities* (London: Oxford University Press, 1973), 79–85. My sample of Spanish-surnamed New Yorkers in the 1925 New York State manuscript census provides suggestive evidence of this disparity in employment levels between the Brooklyn and Manhattan sectors of the *colonia*: 36 percent of the Manhattan sample were categorized as unskilled laborers, 46 percent were skilled workers, and 15 percent worked in offices or owned shops. By comparison, 68 percent of the Brooklyn sample were unskilled laborers, 29 percent skilled workers, and fewer than 3 percent worked in offices or owned shops.

**97.** Interview with Juana Weber Rodríguez, conducted by John Vásquez, Oct. 25, 1974, Pioneros Project.

**98.** "Comité puertorriqueño de protesta," *La Prensa*, Dec. 10, 1924, 4; Vega, *Memoirs*, 111. Collazo was also one of the early members of the Cuban–Puerto Rican revolutionary organization Las Dos Antillas in the 1890s.

**99.** "La Alianza Obrera P.R. elige su junta directiva," *La Prensa*, Oct. 11, 1923, 1; Vega, *Memoirs*, 171.

**100.** Interview with Julio Hernández, conducted by Jaime Barreto, Dec. 1974;

interview with Pedro Cresente, conducted by B. Richardson, Apr. 13, 1975; interview with Doña María Fortún, conducted by J. Barreto, Dec. 18, 1974; interview with Julio Estepa, conducted by Jaime Barreto, Dec. 7, 1974, Pioneros Project.

**101.** La Prensa printed a section every day called "Para las damas" ("For the Ladies") that addressed issues of concern to mothers and homemakers, such as including an adequate amount of milk in children's diets, managing the sewing of clothes for new seasons, and so forth.

**102.** Ayala and Bernabe, Puerto Rico in the American Century, 59; Malavet, America's Colony, 64–65. "Porto Ricans Bring Plea to Congress," New York Times, Jan. 10, 1924, 8; "Coolidge Receives Porto Rican Delegates," New York Times, Jan. 24, 1924, 10.

**103.** Iglesias traveled to Washington as part of a commission sent by the Puerto Rican legislature (which included Representative Horace Mann Towner, head of the House Committee on Insular Affairs) to request a "statement of intention" from the U.S. government about the final status for Puerto Rico. Clark, Puerto Rico and the United States, 88.

**104.** On the Socialist Party's statehood platform, see Malavet, America's Colony, 62.

**105.** "Puerto Rico no quiere la independencia, dice Iglesias," La Prensa, Nov. 19, 1923, 1–2. In an editorial printed on the following day in La Prensa, the editor asserted that "the declaration [by Iglesias] is one of the most categorical and definitive that, on this matter, has been made to date." "Independencia y política en Puerto Rico," editorial, La Prensa, Nov. 20, 1923, 4.

**106.** This accusation that Iglesias was attempting to spread "Communist and Bolshevik propaganda" was obviously specious: most of Iglesias's critics from the Left accused him of being too centrist to be a true Socialist.

**107.** "Portorriqueños neoyorquinos acusan al senador Iglesias ante Washington," La Prensa, Jan. 2, 1924, 1–2.

**108.** "Grupos borinqueños de N.Y. rechazan los ataques a Iglesias y a la comisión," La Prensa, Jan. 14, 1924, 1. "Santiago Iglesias ataca con furia a sus detractores ante la Alianza Obrera," La Prensa, Jan. 19, 1924, 1–2. See also Vega, Memoirs, 132–34.

**109.** "Los portorriqueños de Nueva York piden explicaciones a Sol Bloom," La Prensa, Apr. 29, 1925, 2; "Un núcleo borinqueño trata de organizar políticamente a los electores hispanos," La Prensa, Oct. 22, 1925, 1.

**110.** "Los portorriqueños de Nueva York piden explicaciones"; "Sol Bloom increpa a los portorriqueños que protestaron por sus declaraciones," La Prensa, May 8, 1925, 1.

**111.** "Un núcleo borinqueño," 2; Vega, Memoirs, 140–41. According to Bernardo Vega, Joaquín Colón and José Alonso established New York's first Puerto Rican Democratic club during the 1918 presidential campaign (they backed Alfred Smith) in Brooklyn. The club Collazo led in Manhattan was created not long afterward. Vega, Memoirs, 111.

**112.** "Wants Governors Elected—Bloom Offers House Bill to Change Porto Rican Law," New York Times, May 15, 1926, 16.

**113.** "La zona portorriqueña de la 110 a la 116, teatro de intensa perturbación," *La Prensa*, July 28, 1926, 1.

**114.** Porto Rican Brotherhood of America, "Puerto Rico en Nueva York," in "Souvenir, Baile de las Flores," May 15, 1926, Vando papers, series III, box 2, folder 17.

**115.** "La zona portorriqueña," 2.

**116.** "Los desórdenes de la calle 116," editorial, *La Prensa*, July 29, 1926, 4; Porto Rican Brotherhood of America, "La colonia puertorriqueña," in "Souvenir," May 1927, Vando papers, series III, box 2, folder 17.

**117.** "Ask Police Protection—New York Porto Ricans Complain of Being Attacked," *New York Times*, July 30, 1926, 29; and "Trio Held as Police Block Harlem Riot," *New York Times*, July 27, 1926, 21.

**118.** "Se piden policías e inspectores de sanidad hispanos para Harlem," *La Prensa*, Sept. 6, 1927, 4. Colón, *Carlos Tapia*, 75. See also Sánchez-Korrol, *From Colonia to Community*, 68–69. Colón, *Carlos Tapia*, 76, also quoted in James, *Holding Aloft the Banner of Ethiopia*, 227.

**119.** "Prejuicios deprimentes e injustos," editorial, *La Prensa*, July 31, 1926, 4.

**120.** J. M. Vivaldi, "Los puertorriqueños no son extranjeros," in "Tribuna Libre," *La Prensa*, Aug. 6, 1926, 4. Emphasis in original.

**121.** "Liga Cívica Hispana en Nueva York," editorial, *La Prensa*, Aug. 5, 1926, 4; Porto Rican Brotherhood of America, "La Colonia Puertorriqueña;" "Form Latin League in Harlem Center," *New York Times*, Aug. 9, 1926, 5; "Cohesión hispana en Harlem," editorial, *La Prensa*, Aug. 10, 1926, 4; "Harlem Porto Ricans Unite to Prove Faith," *New York Times*, Aug. 16, 1926, 8; Liga Puertorriqueña e Hispana, "Programa y constitución," n.d. [1926], Colón papers, series V, box 2, folder 8. An article in *La Prensa* a year later reported an increase in the Liga's membership from 33 active members when it was formed in the fall of 1926 to 865 active, dues-paying members one year later. "Se piden policías e inspectores de sanidad." Angelo Falcón cites this quote in "A History of Puerto Rican Politics in N.Y.C., 1860s–1945," in *Puerto Rican Politics in Urban America*, edited by James Jennings and Monte Rivera (Westport, CT: Greenwood Press, 1985), 27.

**122.** Jesús Colón and several of the other organizers had been charter members of the Alianza Obrera Portorriqueña, whose founding in 1923 is discussed above.

**123.** The term *latino* appeared periodically in references to the Spanish-speaking *colonia* and its inhabitants in the early 1920s, primarily among its working-class inhabitants, while a number of elite Hispanophile writers expressed quite emphatically their dislike of the term *Latin America* and its permutations. Manuel García Peláez, "Misnaming Our Neighbors," *New York Times*, July 11, 1926, X8. In the new working-class weekly *Gráfico*, which Bernardo Vega bought and began editing in the spring of 1927, writers tended to use "*latino*" more often than "*hispano*" as a description of the members of their community, and it almost always appeared in quotation marks; Jesús Colón took this approach in his column "En neoyorkino," under the pseudonym "Míquis Tíquis," in *Gráfico*, issues Sept. 25, 1927, and Mar. 3, 1928, n.p. Colón papers, series III, box 10, folder 9. See Lorrin Thomas, "The Politics of

Naming: A Genealogy of *Latinismo* in New York City in the 1920s" (presentation, University of Pennsylvania, Philadelphia, Feb. 11, 2000).

**124.** Porto Rican Brotherhood of America, "La colonia puertorriqueña."

**125.** Ibid.

**126.** "Judíos y cristianos en Harlem," editorial, *La Prensa*, Aug. 12, 1927, 4.

**127.** "Los puertorriqueños de Harlem hacen frente a la oposición de la raza de color," *La Prensa*, May 4, 1928, 1; "Puertorriqueños y sirios en B'klyn se van a los manos," *La Prensa*, May 5, 1928, 1.

**128.** "Se piden policías e inspectores de sanidad"; "Un puertorriqueño, casi adolescente, es acusado de la muerte de un compañero," *La Prensa*, Apr. 6, 1928, 1; Vega, *Memoirs*, 54. Interview with Loperena.

**129.** "Puerto Rico pide que se les considere iguales a los demás 'American citizens,'" *La Prensa*, Mar. 21, 1924, 1. The resident commissioner of Puerto Rico was the island's nonvoting representative in Congress, a position created under more limited terms by the 1900 Foraker Act. "Apreciaciones, por Jíbarito."

**130.** George Sánchez, *Becoming Mexican American: Ethnicity, Culture, and Identity in Chicano Los Angeles, 1900–1945* (New York: Oxford University Press, 1993), 216–24; Clare Sheridan, "Contested Citizenship: National Identity and the Mexican Immigration Debates of the 1920s," *Journal of American Ethnic History* 21 (Spring 2002): 3–35.

**131.** For a general discussion of island politics in the period 1925–28, see Trías Monge, *Puerto Rico*, 82–83.

**132.** *Gráfico*, Mar. 27, 1927, 2, quoted in Sánchez-Korrol, *From Colonia to Community*, 73. On the other hand, Ramón Colón later argued unconvincingly (in reference to the 1920s and 1930s) that "unlike the other ethnic groups who came to New York before them, the Puerto Ricans did not have to begin by organizing themselves in fraternities or protective societies to defend themselves and be respected by other predatory elements. In New York, as American citizens, they could organize themselves politically and attain *political power* by using their American citizenship." Colón, *Carlos Tapia*, 43 (emphasis in original).

## Chapter Two

**1.** José C. González, "De nuestros lectores," *La Prensa*, Aug. 22, 1930, 4. González later became active in the Democratic Party in Brooklyn. See "Comité Demócrata de Boricuas Nueva York se reúne en Brooklyn," *El Diario*, Apr. 11, 1952, 4. Gilberto Gerena Valentín, a migrant who arrived from Puerto Rico in 1936 and became a prominent labor activist and community leader, also recalled, from his first job in a New York hotel, how work was divided both by nationality and by color, with little room for Puerto Ricans in the employment structure ("Housekeeping was blacks, cooks were Greeks and Italians, chefs were French") and that the "Europeans" were "quite racist, racist to the end. Racist in terms of the kinds of division . . . of labor, among the people in the kitchen." Interview, Sept. 10, 1980, conducted by Espi Martell, Costureras Project.

**2.** Puerto Ricans were not counted separately in census figures on unemployment for this decade; the categories were "Negro," "native white," "foreign-born white," and "other races." Census takers made their own judgments about the categories in which Puerto Ricans should be placed, which means that they were scattered throughout the aforementioned categories. See Cheryl Greenberg, *Or Does It Explode?* (New York: Oxford University Press, 1991), appendix II, for a thorough review of statistics on unemployment in the 1930s, tabulated by race.

**3.** Although the Mexican immigration to the western United States advanced more rapidly than the Puerto Rican migration, in absolute numbers, between 1930 and 1950, the Puerto Rican population of the United States experienced the largest proportional growth of any immigrant group, including Mexicans, in this period. The island-born population increased at least 500 percent from 1930 to 1950, from about 45,000 to more than a quarter of a million; meanwhile, rates of increase of all other foreign-born groups, except Mexicans, were declining. See U.S. Immigration and Naturalization Service, *1996 Statistical Yearbook of the Immigration and Naturalization Service* (Washington, DC: U.S. Government Printing Office, 1997), 27. Even in absolute numbers, the growth of the Puerto Rican population in New York rivaled or surpassed that of the five national groups whose immigration was highest in this period: Canadians, Mexicans, Italians, Germans, and British. See Reed Ueda, *Postwar Immigrant America: A Social History* (New York: Bedford / St. Martin's, 1994), 36 and passim; Oscar Handlin, *The Newcomers: Negroes and Puerto Ricans in a Changing Metropolis* (Cambridge, MA: Harvard University Press, 1965), 141−42; and U.S. Immigration and Naturalization Service, *1990 Statistical Yearbook of the Immigration and Naturalization Service* (Washington, DC: U.S. Government Printing Office, 1991), "Trends in Immigration" section, 24−27. The population of "foreign-born Negroes" in New York City grew from 30,400 in 1920 to 54,700 in 1930; by contrast, the Puerto Rican population grew from 7,300 in 1920 to 44,900 in 1930. Ira Rosenwaike, *Population History of New York City* (Syracuse, NY: Syracuse University Press, 1972), 121. For more data on the foreign-born Caribbean population in New York in the period 1920−30, see also Ira D. Reid, *The Negro Immigrant: His Background, Characteristics, and Social Adjustment, 1899−1937* (New York: AMS Press, 1970), table V, p. 237, and table XV, p. 248.

**4.** U.S. Congress, 71st Cong., 3rd sess., House Committee on Immigration and Naturalization, "Temporary Restriction of Immigration," report no. 2801, Feb. 17, 1931, 13.

**5.** There is a substantial and diverse literature on the nonwhite "other" racial identities ascribed to various immigrant groups in the United States in the twentieth century. See, for example, Ian F. Haney López, *White by Law: The Legal Construction of Race* (New York: New York University Press, 1996), and Haney López, "Race and Erasure: The Salience of Race to Latinos/as," in *The Latino/a Condition: A Critical Reader*, edited by Richard Delgado and Jean Stefancic (New York: New York University Press, 1998); Mae Ngai, "The Architecture of Race in American Immigration Law: A Reexamination of the Immigration Act of 1924," *Journal of American History* 86 (June 1999): 67−92, and Ngai, *Impossible Subjects: Illegal Aliens and the Making of Modern America* (Princeton, NJ: Princeton University Press, 2004); David Gutiérrez, *Walls and Mirrors: Mexican Americans, Mexican Immigrants, and the Politics of*

*Ethnicity* (Berkeley: University of California Press, 1995); Lisa Lowe, "Immigration, Citizenship, Racialization: Asian American Critique," in *Immigrant Acts: On Asian American Cultural Politics* (Durham, NC: Duke University Press, 1996); Claire Jean Kim, "The Racial Triangulation of Asian Americans," *Politics and Society* 27 (Mar. 1999): 105–38; and Eiichiro Azuma, *Between Two Empires: Race, History, and Transnationalism in Japanese America* (New York: Oxford University Press, 2005). Shaping the racial identities ascribed to nonwhite others in the early twentieth century were new racist discourses of imperialism, lumping the Cuban, Puerto Rican, and Filipino people over whom the United States ruled into crudely differentiated categories of "nigger," "savage," and so forth. See, for example, Angelo Ancheta, "Filipino Americans, Foreigner Discrimination, and the Lines of Racial Sovereignty," in *Positively No Filipinos Allowed: Building Communities and Discourse*, edited by Antonio Tiongson Jr., Edgardo Gutiérrez, and Ricardo Gutiérrez (Philadelphia: Temple University Press, 2006); and Nerissa Balce, "Filipino Bodies, Lynching, and the Language of Empire," in *Positively No Filipinos Allowed*. Balce cites W.E.B. DuBois's 1920 book *Darkwater* (1920; repr., New York: Washington Square Press, 2007), probably the first published book to explore the racist language of empire in the United States.

**6.** Ngai, "Architecture of Race," 69–70. See also, generally, Haney-López, *White by Law*.

**7.** Matthew Pratt Guterl, *The Color of Race in America, 1900–1940* (Cambridge, MA: Harvard University Press, 2001), 154–44; and Sharon M. Lee, "Racial Classification in the U.S. Census, 1890–1990," *Ethnic and Racial Studies* 16 (Jan. 1993): 77. On racial categories in the census more generally, see Clara Rodríguez, *Changing Race: Latinos, the Census, and the History of Ethnicity in the United States* (New York: New York University Press, 2000), and Melissa Nobles, *Shades of Citizenship: Race and the Census in Modern Politics* (Palo Alto, CA: Stanford University Press, 2000). It was also in 1930 that the state of Virginia adopted a new definition of a Negro person as someone with "one drop" of African blood. Since 1910, that label had applied to people who were at least one-sixteenth black (someone with one African American great-grandparent); and from 1785 until 1910, a Negro person had to be at least one-quarter African or African American. Gary Nash, "The Hidden History of Mestizo America," *Journal of American History* 82 (Dec. 1995): 950.

**8.** On the class composition of the early Puerto Rican community in New York, see generally Bernardo Vega, *Memoirs of Bernardo Vega: A Contribution to the History of the Puerto Rican Community in New York*, edited by César Andreu Iglesias (New York: Monthly Review Press, 1984), 105, 136–44, and passim; Virginia Sánchez-Korrol, *From Colonia to Community: The History of Puerto Ricans in New York City* (Berkeley: University of California Press, 1983), 53–77; Roberto P. Rodríguez-Morazzani, "Linking a Fractured Past: The World of the Puerto Rican Old Left," *CENTRO Journal of the Center for Puerto Rican Studies* 7 (Winter 1994–95): 20–30; and WPA Federal Writers' Project, "Life Histories," Spanish Book, WPA files, reel 269, folder 4.

**9.** See, for example, Harvard Sitkoff, *A New Deal for Blacks: The Emergence of Civil Rights as a National Issue* (New York: Oxford University Press, 1981); Ralph Bunche, *The Political Status of the Negro in the Age of FDR* (Chicago: University of Chicago

Press, 1973); Raymond Wolters, *Negroes and the Great Depression* (Westport, CT: Greenwood Publishing, 1970); Richard Dalfiume, "The 'Forgotten' Years of the Negro Revolution," *Journal of American History* 60 (June 1968): 90–106; Barbara Savage, *Broadcasting Freedom: Radio, War, and the Politics of Race, 1938–1948* (Chapel Hill: University of North Carolina Press, 1999); and Manning Marable, *Race, Reform, and Rebellion: The Second Reconstruction in Black America, 1945–1990* (Jackson: University Press of Mississippi, 1991), chapter 1. On the burgeoning interracial reform movements of the 1930s and 1940s, see also Patricia Sullivan, *Days of Hope: Race and Democracy in the New Deal Era* (Chapel Hill: University of North Carolina Press, 1990); Walter Jackson, *Gunnar Myrdal and America's Conscience: Social Engineering and Racial Liberalism, 1938–1987* (Chapel Hill: University of North Carolina Press, 1990); and John Egerton, *Speak Now against the Day: The Generation before the Civil Rights Movement in the South* (Chapel Hill: University of North Carolina Press, 1994). On anticolonialist activism for racial justice, see Penny Von Eschen, *Race against Empire: Black Americans and Anticolonialism, 1937–1957* (Ithaca, NY: Cornell University Press, 1997); and Winston James, *Holding Aloft the Banner of Ethiopia: Caribbean Radicalism in Early Twentieth Century America* (New York: Verso, 1998).

**10.** The description of African Americans as "citizens without rights" is historian Barbara Savage's, personal correspondence with the author, July 2003. Carey McWilliams, *Brothers under the Skin* (New York: Little, Brown, 1943), 216–17. See also, generally, Ramón Grosfoguel with Chloe Georas, "'Coloniality of Power' and Racial Dynamics," in *Colonial Subjects: Puerto Ricans in a Global Perspective*, edited by Ramón Grosfoguel (Berkeley: University of California Press, 2003), 144–73; and Jorge Duany, *Puerto Rican Nation on the Move: Identities on the Island and in the United States* (Chapel Hill: University of North Carolina Press, 2002), 236–60.

**11.** *La Prensa* printed many letters on the subject of discrimination against Puerto Ricans within New York's Spanish-speaking community. See Ángel Santana, "De nuestros lectores," *La Prensa*, Oct. 13, 1930, 6; D. Lorenzo Piñeiro Rivera, "De nuestros lectores," *La Prensa*, Oct. 17, 1930, 6; J. R. Gutiérrez, "De nuestros lectores," *La Prensa*, Sept. 26, 1930, 6–7; interview with Pedro Cresente, conducted by B. Richardson, Apr. 13, 1975, Pioneros Project.

**12.** Pedro Juan Labarthe, "De nuestros lectores," *La Prensa*, Jan. 8, 1931, 6.

**13.** "Newcomers in the Slums of East Harlem," *New York American*, Dec. 28, 1930.

**14.** María Más Pozo, "De nuestros lectores," *La Prensa*, Jan. 12, 1931, 6.

**15.** Fernando Arjona López, "De nuestros lectores," *La Prensa*, Jan. 26, 1931, 6; C. Cedeño Ferrer (writing from Aguadilla, PR), "De nuestros lectores," *La Prensa*, Jan. 30, 1931, 6.

**16.** Gabriel Rivera, "De nuestros lectores," *La Prensa*, Jan. 27, 1931, 6–7.

**17.** Researchers at the Tuskegee Institute in the 1930s determined that the number of lynchings in the South tripled during the first year of the Depression, from seven in 1929 (down from a high of twenty-three in 1926) to twenty-one in 1930. See Sitkoff, *New Deal for Blacks*, 268–69 and passim; Bunche, *Political Status of the Negro*, 116–17; and Wolters, *Negroes and the Great Depression*, 337–40. See also Mark

Naison, *Communists in Harlem during the Great Depression* (New York: Grove Press, 1985), 41–42, 200–201. Nationalists frequently responded to *La Prensa*'s stories and editorials on lynching throughout the 1920s and early 1930s.

**18.** María Más Pozo, "De nuestros lectores," *La Prensa*, Feb. 16, 1931, 6.

**19.** María Más Pozo, "De nuestros lectores," *La Prensa*, Oct. 3, 1930, 6.

**20.** Miriam Jiménez Román, "*Un hombre (negro) del pueblo:* José Celso Barbosa and the Puerto Rican 'Race' toward Whiteness," *Centro Journal* 8 (1996): 9–29.

**21.** See, for instance, Lucila Padrón interview, conducted by Rina Benmayor and Blanca Vázquez, Jan 12, 1984, Costureras Project; also see generally Tomás Blanco, *El prejuicio racial en Puerto Rico* (1942; repr., Río Piedras, PR: Ediciones Huracán, 1985).

**22.** María Más Pozo, "De nuestros lectores," *La Prensa*, Feb. 16, 1931, 6.

**23.** By the end of 1930, African American activists, along with a growing number of white collaborators, were beginning to organize a national campaign to publicize the rising incidence of lynching and to demand substantive legal and civic protections for African Americans. Sitkoff, *New Deal for Blacks*, 268–69 and passim; see also Bunche, *Political Status of the Negro*, 116–17; and Wolters, *Negroes and the Great Depression*, 337–40.

**24.** "Hoover Welcomed with Gratitude by Crowd in Porto Rico," *New York Times*, Mar. 23, 1931, 17.

**25.** Agapito Caraballo, "De nuestros lectores," *La Prensa*, May 6, 1931, 6.

**26.** Rafael M. Pontón, "De nuestros lectores," *La Prensa*, May 8, 1931, 6.

**27.** Josefa Muñoz Cruz, "De nuestros lectores," *La Prensa*, May 14, 1931, 6. Other relevant letters to *La Prensa* concerning Hoover's trip include those from Domingo Andújar, Apr. 6, 1931, 7; L. Piñero Rivera and Max Vázquez, Apr. 14, 1931, 6; and Marcelino Méndez Pidal, Apr. 24, 1931, 6.

**28.** By July 1931, *La Prensa* editors had stopped printing the "De nuestros lectores" column almost entirely.

**29.** "1 Slain, 3 Wounded in Uptown Race Riot," *New York Times*, July 16, 1931, 1. Interview with Louise Delgado, conducted by Rina Benmayor and Blanca Vázquez, Feb. 17, 1985, Costureras Project.

**30.** Club Azteca flyer, "Gran Baile . . . ," Oct. 15, 1932, Colón papers, reprinted (image no. 8) in Ruth Glasser, *My Music Is My Flag: Puerto Rican Musicians and Their New York Communities, 1917–1940* (Berkeley: University of California Press, 1995), n.p.

**31.** I was unable to find a copy of the article. *Literary Digest* was a very popular national magazine during the 1920s and 1930s, known especially for its influential monthly readers' polls. The magazine merged with *Time* in 1938. On the 1899 report *Our Islands and Their People*, see Jiménez Román, "*Un hombre (negro) del pueblo,*" 15, and Gervasio Luis García, "I Am the Other: Puerto Rico in the Eyes of North Americans, 1898," *Journal of American History* 87 (June 2000): 39–64.

**32.** Dr. Augusto Arce Álvarez, "De nuestros lectores," *La Prensa*, Feb. 6, 1934, 4.

**33.** M. Callejo, "De nuestros lectores," *La Prensa*, Feb. 9, 1934, 4. Callejo had also contributed to *La Prensa*'s "Vida obrera" (Workers' Life) column in 1922. See chapter 1, n. 33.

**34.** See, for example, Manuel Maldonado-Denis, *Puerto Rico: A Socio-historic Interpretation* (New York: Random House, 1972), 108, and Kal Wagenheim and Olga Jiménez de Wagenheim, eds., *The Puerto Ricans: A Documentary History* (Princeton, NJ: Markus Wiener Publishers, 1994), 123–24. Judge José Cabranes, the foremost legal scholar on Puerto Rican citizenship, disagrees with this interpretation, asserting that "there is no evidence . . . that the timing of the two actions by Congress [extending U.S. citizenship to Puerto Ricans and, a month later, declaring war on Germany] was anything but coincidental. . . . Indeed, the number of Puerto Ricans who served in the First World War appears to have been quite small." Cabranes, "Citizenship and the American Empire: Notes on the Legislative History of the United States Citizenship of Puerto Ricans," *University of Pennsylvania Law Review* 127 (Dec. 1978): 391–492.

**35.** Marcelino Méndez Pidal, "De nuestros lectores," *La Prensa*, Feb. 15, 1934, 7.

**36.** Osvaldo Maqueira Calvo, "De nuestros lectores," *La Prensa*, May 17, 1934, 4.

**37.** *La Prensa*'s editorial leadership, headed by Spanish-born editor in chief José Comprubí, remained the same throughout the thirties, so a change in the paper's editorial agenda was not the reason for the shift.

**38.** See, generally, Naison, *Communists in Harlem*; Frederick T. Griffiths, "Ralph Ellison, Richard Wright, and the Case of Angelo Herndon," *African American Review* 35 (Winter 2001): 615–36.

**39.** Michael Lapp, "Managing Migration: The Migration Division of Puerto Rico and Puerto Ricans in New York City, 1948–1968" (PhD diss., Johns Hopkins University, 1991), 36–38; WPA Federal Writers' Project, "Government of Puerto Rico Employment Office," Dec. 7, 1938, Spanish Book, WPA files, reel 269, folder 9; F. C. Berdecía, "De nuestros lectores," *La Prensa*, Feb. 8, 1930, 6; and José Vivaldi, "De nuestros lectores," *La Prensa*, Oct. 22, 1930, 6, reporting on the success of the employment service's first two months of operation.

**40.** Lapp, "Managing Migration," 151–52. Some migrants reported that such employment agencies sometimes refused to serve Puerto Ricans and sent them instead to the "Puerto Rican employment office," the OEI. M. Rivera González, "De nuestros lectores," *La Prensa*, Sept. 17, 1934, 4. Another migrant wrote that the employment office was "an obstacle presented to Puerto Ricans when they go to apply for jobs at one of the city-run employment offices, where they tell us, 'go to the Puerto Rican employment office.'" Also, he said, "Vivaldi's agency doesn't offer much because you have to have connections, and it's not well organized." J. Cabrera Hernández, "De nuestros lectores," *La Prensa*, June 7, 1935, 4.

**41.** "La identificación de puertorriqueños," editorial, *La Prensa*, July 28, 1930, 4. Migrants began talking about the criminalization of Puerto Ricans, due to other immigrants' false self-identification as Puerto Ricans and misapprehensions by police, in the mid- to late 1920s (see chapter 1). Gonzalo Placencia, who arrived in New York in 1929, said that "the police treated us badly here . . . by '36, '40, the police were like a Gestapo for the Puerto Rican" (interview, conducted by Jaime Barreto, Nov. 4, 1974, Pioneros Project). Juan Ramos arrived in 1926 and recalled that whenever police arrived on the scene of a street fight, "you would hear, 'me Puerto Rican, me Puerto Rican,' and I knew a lot of them . . . weren't Puerto Rican . . . so they would attribute the problem to Puerto Ricans" (interview, conducted by Mayda Cortiella, Oct. 21, 1974, Pioneros Project). See also interviews with Ramón Rodríguez, conducted by John Vásquez, Oct. 29, 1974; and Félix Loperena, conducted by John Vásquez, Nov. 22, 1974, Pioneros Project. A pamphlet of the Porto Rican Brotherhood of America in 1927 noted that "it is not uncommon to hear, each time that the echo of some criminal act resounds in the Hispanic districts, that the authors are Puerto Ricans, or 'Porto Ricans.'" Porto Rican Brotherhood of America, "La colonia puertorriqueña," May 1927, Vando papers, series III, box 2, folder 17.

**42.** J. Cabrera Hernández, "De nuestros lectores," *La Prensa*, June 7, 1935, 4.

**43.** All discussion of the identification cards is based on a sample I took of the approximately 30,500 ID card applications that comprise part of the Migration Division archive at the Centro de Estudios Puertorriqueños at Hunter College. My sampling technique involved coding groupings of 220–250 applications during roughly the same time period every two years from 1930 to 1949. (The actual span of months decreased as the concentration of applications per month rose, from an average of about 250 applications in four months during the 1930s to about 250 applications in one month during the 1940s.) I recorded the "complexion" label from each application, along with notes about whether the label was handwritten or typed; whether, if handwritten, the handwriting appeared to match that of the applicant's signature; and whether the labeling was corrected or in any way altered after the original label was assigned (either by the applicant or by the ID office employee). I then created a table showing the frequency of thirteen different commonly used complexion categories as well as a column to mark "other" categories and a column to mark labels that were crossed out or changed after the original complexion label was filled out.

**44.** See discussion of sampling technique in n. 43 above. The guidelines governing women's applications differed from those of men in several ways. First, if the female applicant were married, divorced, or widowed, she was required to give information about the nationality and place of residence of her husband (or her ex- or deceased husband); however, if the husband was not Puerto Rican, the applicant had to provide the same information about her father. Single women and all male applicants had to provide documentation of their nationality in the form of a birth certificate or baptismal record; or, in the absence of these documents, applicants had to provide either a notarized statement from the father or doctor/midwife present at the birth, or a certificate from an island official stating that the applicants had proved satisfactorily their birth in Puerto Rico and therefore their U.S. citizenship. For a contemporary description of the process of applying for identification cards, see "La identificación de los puertorriqueños de aquí, regulada por Gobnor. Roosevelt," *La Prensa*, July 25, 1930, 1. See also Lapp, "Managing Migration," 56.

**45.** See, for example, the following on racial classification in Latin America: Ginetta Candelario, *Black behind the Ears: Dominican Racial Identity from Museums to Beauty Shops* (Durham, NC: Duke University Press, 2007); Jorge Duany, "Reconstructing Racial Identity: Ethnicity, Color, and Class among Dominicans in the United States and Puerto Rico," *Latin American Perspectives* 25 (May 1998): 147–72; Jiménez Román, "Un hombre (negro) del pueblo"; Thomas Skidmore, "Bi-racial

U.S.A. vs. Multi-racial Brazil: Is the Contrast Still Valid?" *Journal of Latin American Studies* 25 (May 1993): 373–86; Richard Graham, ed., *The Idea of Race in Latin America, 1870–1940* (Austin: University of Texas Press, 1990).

**46.** Tomás Blanco, *El prejuicio racial en Puerto Rico* (1942; repr. Río Piedras, PR: Ediciones Huracán, 1985), 12; Maxine Gordon, "Race Patterns and Prejudice in Puerto Rico," *American Sociological Review* 14 (Apr. 1949): 298.

**47.** Interview with Carmelo Castro Martínez, conducted by Blanca Vázquez and Rina Benmayor, Dec. 21, 1983, Costureras Project.

**48.** Victor Clark, *Porto Rico and Its Problems* (Washington, DC: Brookings Institution, 1930), 8, 519.

**49.** Jiménez Román, "*Un hombre (negro) del pueblo*," 10. See, generally, "Introduction: Racial Nations," in *Race and Nation in Modern Latin America*, edited by Nancy Appelbaum, Anne Macpherson, and Karin Alejandra Rosemblatt (Chapel Hill: University of North Carolina Press, 2003). On racial ideology in Puerto Rico, see Maxine Gordon, "Race Patterns and Prejudice in Puerto Rico," *American Sociological Review* 14 (Apr. 1949): 294–301; Charles C. Rogler, "The Role of Semantics in the Study of Race Distance in Puerto Rico," *Social Forces* 22 (May 1944): 448–53; Joseph Fitzpatrick, "Attitudes of Puerto Ricans toward Color," *American Catholic Sociological Review* 20 (Autumn 1959): 219–33. The contradictory discourses of *mestizaje*, "race-lessness," and "racial democracy" exist in somewhat different forms in many other Latin American societies as well; see, for instance, Peter Wade, *Blackness and Race Mixture: The Dynamics of Racial Identity in Colombia* (Baltimore: Johns Hopkins University Press, 1993); Thomas Skidmore, *Black into White: Race and Nationality in Brazilian Thought* (1979; repr. Durham, NC: Duke University Press, 1992); and Winthrop Wright, *Café Con Leche: Race, Class, and National Image in Venezuela* (Austin: University of Texas Press, 1992). On contemporary racial discourse among Puerto Ricans in the United States, see also Clara Rodríguez, "Puerto Ricans: Between Black and White," in *Historical Perspectives on Puerto Rican Survival in the United States*, edited by Clara Rodríguez and Virginia Sánchez-Korrol (Princeton, NJ: Markus Wiener Publishers, 1996); and Nancy S. Landale and R. S. Oropesa, "White, Black, or Puerto Rican? Racial Self-Identification among Mainland and Island Puerto Ricans," *Social Forces* 81 (Sept. 2002): 231–54.

**50.** Interview with Doña Lucila Padrón, conducted by Ana Juarbe, Jan. 12, 1984, Costureras Project. Interview with Anita Vélez Mitchell, conducted by the author, July 22, 2000, New York City.

**51.** Blanco, *El prejuicio racial*, 62.

**52.** Quoted in Cabranes, "Citizenship and the American Empire," 98, from the Puerto Rican Reconstruction Administration in Cooperation with the Writers' Program of the Works Progress Administration, *Puerto Rico: A Guide to the Island of Borinquén*, 1940, 110. Maxine Gordon cites a similar quote by James Bryce in *American Commonwealth* 2 (1910): 555: "In Latin America, whoever is not black is white; in teutonic America, whoever is not white is black," Gordon, "Race Patterns," 295.

**53.** See Rodríguez, "Puerto Ricans: Between Black and White," and Gordon, "Race Patterns."

**54.** Clark, *Puerto Rico and Its Problems*, 8–9. See also "El informe del 'Brookings

Institution' y sus indicaciones extra-oficiales," *La Prensa*, May 26, 1930, 1; and Gordon, "Race Patterns," 299–300.

**55.** Interview with Pi Santos, conducted by Celia Álvarez, Aug. 30, 1983, Costureras Project.

**56.** Birth certificates were not standardized from town to town; some listed the race of the mother or of both parents, and some did not. The parents' (or, more often, the mother's) racial designation did not automatically define that of the child, since the ascription of racial identity in Puerto Rico often depended on criteria other than color itself.

**57.** Lapp, "Managing Migration," 151–52. Lapp cites an interview with Joseph Montserrat, director of a later incarnation of the Office of Employment and Identification, who recalled emphasizing to his employees the need for respectful treatment of their clients, many of whom were "darker skinned" and "less educated" than the office staff. Montserrat noted that these tensions between employees and clients had been an issue as well in the office's earlier days. Unfortunately, there are no data in the records of the Migration Division to corroborate this anecdotal evidence. See chapter 1 for a general discussion of issues of class and color in the *colonia* in the 1920s.

**58.** Lawrence Chenault, *The Puerto Rican Migrant in New York City* (New York: Columbia University Press, 1938), 151.

**59.** Nash, "Hidden History," 954; Lee, "Racial Classification in the U.S. Census," 77–79.

**60.** Greenberg, *Or Does It Explode?* 3; Robert Fogelson and Richard Rubenstein, eds., *The Complete Report of Mayor La Guardia's Commission on the Harlem Riot of March 19, 1935* (New York: Arno Press and the New York Times, 1969), 2–7. "Extract: Telephone Operator's Ambulance Call Report," Mar. 19, 1935, La Guardia papers, reel 76, folder 5. Greenberg does not mention that Rivera is Puerto Rican.

**61.** Fogelson and Rubenstein, *Complete Report*, 7.

**62.** Claude McKay, *Harlem: Negro Metropolis* (New York: Harcourt Brace Jovanovich, 1968), 206.

**63.** Fogelson and Rubenstein, *Complete Report*, 15.

**64.** Ibid., 8.

**65.** "Graves resultados de simple incidente," *La Prensa*, Mar. 21, 1935, 1; and Fogelson and Rubenstein, *Complete Report*, 10. "1 Dead, 7 Shot, 100 Hurt as Harlem Crowds Riot over Boy, 16, and Hearse," 1, and "Disturbance in Harlem," 6, *New York Herald-Tribune*, Mar. 20, 1935; and "Mayor Plans Own Riot Inquiry," *New York Sun*, Mar. 20, 1935, 1.

**66.** Fogelson and Rubenstein, *Complete Report*, 11.

**67.** Red-baiting was also an issue in the selection of members of the Mayor's Commission on Conditions in Harlem, established by Mayor Fiorello La Guardia in the days following the riot. The *Sun* pointed to the radical activities of black appointees A. Phillip Randolph, Countee Cullen, and Arthur Garfield Hays ("Four Indicted for Looting as Result of Riot," *New York Sun*, Mar. 22, 1935, 1).

**68.** See Reid, *Negro Immigrant*, 202–13 and passim; and, generally, Mary C. Waters, *Black Identities: West Indian Immigrant Dreams and American Realities* (Cambridge, MA: Harvard University Press, 1999).

**69.** McKay, *Harlem: Negro Metropolis*, 207.

**70.** "1 Dead, 7 Shot, 100 Hurt," 1, 9; "Police Shoot into Rioters; Kill Negro in Harlem Mob," *New York Times*, Mar. 20, 1935, 1; "Mayor Lays Riot to 'Vicious Group,'" *New York Times*, Mar. 21, 1935, 16; "Did Not Know He Caused Riot," *New York Sun*, Mar. 22, 1935, 21.

**71.** "Tropas para Harlem pedidas ayer; centenares de policías patrullaban anoche el barrio," *La Prensa*, Mar. 21, 1935, 1.

**72.** This was a reference to the church of Father Divine.

**73.** "Los 'motines' de Harlem," editorial, *La Prensa*, Mar. 21, 1935, 4.

**74.** "Numerosos establecimientos hispanos apedreados y saqueados por la turba," *La Prensa*, Mar. 22, 1935, 1–2.

**75.** "Tropas para Harlem pedidas."

**76.** "Rivera, causa involuntaria del choque racial de Harlem, deplora lo que sucedió," *La Prensa*, Mar. 22, 1935, 1.

**77.** Libertad Narváez, "De nuestros lectores," *La Prensa*, Apr. 2, 1935, 4.

**78.** Vega, *Memoirs*, 180.

**79.** Fogelson and Rubenstein, *Complete Report*, 122.

**80.** "Mayor Plans Own Riot Inquiry," *New York Sun*, Mar. 20, 1935, 1.

**81.** See population map, "Street Map Shows Distribution of Harlem's Population," accompanying article "Idleness, Harlem's Chief Threat," in *New York Sun*, Mar. 23, 1935, 23; and Welfare Council, *Population in Health Areas: New York City, 1930* (New York: Research Bureau, Welfare Council of New York City, 1930), 1.

**82.** Walter White, "Suggestions of Problems Which Might Be Investigated by the Commission Appointed by Mayor La Guardia . . . ," Mar. 26, 1935, La Guardia papers, reel 76, folder 5.

**83.** Jesús Flores, Unidad Obrera, Committee to Investigate Conditions in Harlem, Mar. 25, 1935, La Guardia papers, reel 77, folder 8.

**84.** Jesús Flores, el Comité Pro–Puerto Rico, to Committee to Investigate Conditions in Harlem, Mar. 25, 1935, La Guardia papers, reel 77, folder 8.

**85.** Antonio Rivera, Liga Puertorriqueña e Hispana, to Mayor Fiorello La Guardia, June 24, 1935, La Guardia papers, reel 77, folder 8.

**86.** Isabel O'Neill, Junta Liberal Puertorriqueña de Nueva York, to Mayor Fiorello La Guardia, June 24, 1935, La Guardia papers, reel 77, folder 8.

**87.** Rafael W. Carreras, "De nuestros lectores," *La Prensa*, June 26, 1935, 4. Other letters and articles on the "anti-Hispanic campaign" include J. M. García Casanova, "De nuestros lectores," *La Prensa*, June 13, 1935, 4; "El 'anti-hispanismo' en Washington Heights," editorial, *La Prensa*, June 13, 1935, 4; Richard F. Martin, "De nuestros lectores," *La Prensa*, July 2, 1935, 4; and Cosmo Alda Wahl, "De nuestros lectores," *La Prensa*, July 10, 1935, 4.

**88.** "Las condiciones de vida en Harlem bajo estudio," editorial, *La Prensa*, Dec. 13, 1937, 4.

**89.** Dr. Armstrong was affiliated with the Children's Court of the City of New

York, and Dr. Achilles was employed by the Psychological Corporation in New York City. See Vito Marcantonio, "Puerto Rican Children in New York Schools," 74th Cong., 2nd sess., *Congressional Record* 80, part 10 (June 19, 1936): 10310.

**90.** Quoted in Pedro A. Cebollero, assistant commissioner of education, San Juan, "Reactions of Puerto Rican Children in New York City to Psychological Tests: An Analysis of the Investigation Conducted by Messrs. Armstrong, Achilles, and Sacks under the Auspices of the Special Committee on Immigration and Naturalization of the New York State Chamber of Commerce" (San Juan: Bureau of Supplies, Printing, and Transportation, 1936), 11. I have not been able to find a copy of the actual report by Armstrong and Achilles. Extensive passages of the report are quoted in Marcantonio, "Puerto Rican Children in New York Schools"; in a *New York Sun* article, "Puerto Rican Pupils a Problem" (Jan. 6, 1936, n. p.); and in a typed page labeled "Summary" and "Conclusions" from Leonard Covello's files on the report, Covello papers, series VI, box 51, folder 15, and series X, box 115, folder 2.

**91.** Henry W. Thurston, *The Education of Youth as Citizens: Progressive Changes in Our Aims and Methods* (New York: Richard R. Smith, 1946), 37–38.

**92.** See Elazar Barkan, *The Retreat of Scientific Racism: Changing Concepts of Race in Great Britain and the United States between the World Wars* (New York: Cambridge University Press, 1993); Stephen Jay Gould, *The Mismeasure of Man* (New York: W. W. Norton, 1981); and David K. Yoo, "Testing Assumptions: IQ, Japanese Americans, and the Model Minority Myth in the 1920s and 1930s," in *Remapping Asian American History*, edited by Sucheng Chan (Lanham, MD: Altamira, 2003).

**93.** Historian George Sánchez cites similar interpretations of IQ tests done on Mexican children in California in the 1920s and 1930s (though he says the primary objective of those debates was to justify the segregation of Mexican children in separate schools). See Sánchez, *Becoming Mexican American: Ethnicity, Culture, and Identity in Chicano Los Angeles, 1900–1945* (New York: Oxford University Press, 1993), 259.

**94.** "Puerto Rican Pupils a Problem," *New York Sun*, Jan. 6, 1936, n.p., Covello papers, series VIII, box 74, folder 3.

**95.** Julio Garzón M., "Los 'monos' de Puerto Rico," *La Prensa*, Jan. 16, 1936, 6. I could find no reports on the IQ controversy in the *New York Amsterdam News*.

**96.** The chairman of the Spanish Welfare League, Pagán Tomei, described his organization as comprised of Puerto Rican students and intellectuals "of the lower middle class interested in sociology in general and the social welfare problem in particular," interview conducted in May 1936 with Pagán Tomei, by B. Conal of the Works Progress Administration's Federal Writers' Project. WPA Federal Writers' Project, "Spanish Welfare League," May 19, 1936, Spanish Book, WPA files, reel 269, folder 9.

**97.** Minutes of the Racial Committee Conference, Feb. 7, 1936, Covello papers, series VI, box 51, folder 15. See also "The Intelligence of Negro Children," editorial, *Opportunity* 5 (Mar. 1927): 66. As the principal of Benjamin Franklin, Leonard Covello himself organized the administration of intelligence tests to incoming students, but his methods remained consistent with the critiques generated by the Racial Committee: when Covello and other Benjamin Franklin educators administered the Henmon-Nelson Test of Mental Ability to incoming students in 1936, they did not divide the results of the students' performance by race or ethnic background. "Results Based on the Henmon-Nelson Tests of Mental Ability," Feb. 1936, Covello papers, series VI, box 48, folder 30.

**98.** The committee argued that the test procedures used by the investigators placed the Puerto Rican children at a disadvantage: they were given less time than the "control group" was given (twenty minutes as opposed to thirty) and had to respond to the questions in English, which for the majority of the children was their second language. "An Analysis of and Comments upon 'A Report of the Special Committee on Immigration and Naturalization of the Chamber of Commerce of the State of New York Dated December 31, 1935, Submitting a Study on Reactions of Puerto Rican Children in New York City to Psychological Tests,'" n.d., Covello papers, series VI, box 51, folder 15, and series X, box 115, folder 2.

**99.** Marcantonio used the text of this report, verbatim, in his presentation to Congress on the subject on June 19, 1936. The two had become friends after Covello served as Marcantonio's mentor while the latter was a student at DeWitt Clinton High School (Marcantonio later dubbed Covello "Pops"); over the years, they worked closely together on a variety of community issues and political campaigns. See Gerald Meyer, *Vito Marcantonio, Radical Politician, 1902–1954* (Albany: State University of New York Press, 1989), 11–13.

**100.** Vito Marcantonio, "Puerto Rican Children in New York Schools," speech to the U.S. House of Representatives, June 19, 1936, 74th Cong., 2nd sess., *Congressional Record* 80 (June 19, 1936): 10310.

**101.** Cebollero, "Reactions of Puerto Rican Children," 3. Cebollero explained: "An agitation now on foot to include Puerto Rico as a state in the Federal Union suggested that an investigation of the quality of immigration received from Puerto Rico would be a valuable contribution to our knowledge." As a *New York Times* article, "Mentality Report Angers San Juan," put it: "Inasmuch as a grant of statehood can never be rescinded, the investigation conducted by Dr. Armstrong and her associates certainly suggests that the proposition to incorporate Puerto Rico as a State in the federal Union should be held in abeyance," Feb. 11, 1936, 5.

**102.** Quotation from Rudolf Pintner, *Intelligence Testing* (New York: Henry Holt and Co., 1923), 345, cited in Cebollero, "Reactions of Puerto Rican Children," 5.

**103.** Chenault describes the report as the first published academic research on Puerto Ricans in the United States; in my research, I never came across any earlier published work (aside from journalism) on Puerto Ricans in the United States. Chenault, *Puerto Rican Migrant*, 38.

**104.** A number of New Yorkers, most of them African American or Hispanic residents of Harlem, wrote to Mayor La Guardia to express their concerns and resentments about the "crime wave." Letters to Mayor Fiorello La Guardia from: Dr. E. N. Bocanegra López, Nov. 7, 1941 (folder 1); Thomas J. Curtin, Nov. 7, 1941 (folder 1); Felipe S. Amezaga, secretary of the Hispano American Lodge, Nov. 14, 1941 (folder 3); and Douglas M. Payne, Oct. 15, 1942 (folder 10), La Guardia papers, reel 76. *La Prensa* also covered the incidents. See Augusto Kurland, "De Nuestros Lectores," *La Prensa*, Nov. 11, 1941, 2; and "Otra ola de atracos en Harlem," editorial, *La Prensa*, July 28, 1942, 4.

**105.** Philip Gleason cites Louis Wirth's essay "The Problem of Minority Groups" in *The Science of Man in the World Crisis*, edited by Ralph Linton (New York: Columbia University Press, 1945), 398, 401. Gleason also says that at the college level, a dozen books and over a thousand more or less scholarly articles on minorities and "race relations" appeared between 1948 and 1955. Gleason, "Minorities (Almost) All: The Minority Concept in American Social Thought," *American Quarterly* 43 (Sept. 1991): 392–424.

**106.** For a discussion of various aspects of the interracial reform movement of the 1930s and 1940s, see Patricia Sullivan, *Days of Hope: Race and Democracy in the New Deal Era* (Chapel Hill: University of North Carolina Press, 1996); Gary Gerstle, "The Protean Character of American Liberalism," *American Historical Review* 99 (July 1994): 15–23; Richard Steele, "War on Intolerance: The Reformulation of American Nationalism, 1939–41," *Journal of American Ethnic History* 9 (Fall 1989): 9–35; Richard Weiss, "Ethnicity and Reform: Minorities and the Ambiance of the Depression Years," *Journal of American History* 66 (Dec. 1979): 566–85; David Hollinger, "Ethnic Diversity, Cosmopolitanism, and the Emergence of the American Liberal Intelligentsia," *American Quarterly* 27 (May 1975): 133–51; and Richard Dalfiume, "'The Forgotten Years' of the Negro Revolution," *Journal of American History* 55 (June 1968): 90–106. See also Lorrin Thomas, "'What Have We Done—Except Talk?' Pluralism, Race, and Intercultural Democracy, 1925–1945" (paper, University of Pennsylvania, 1997). Although they actively sought inclusion in liberal Democratic politics in this era, Puerto Ricans were almost never included in these liberal coalitions. See chapter 3.

**107.** Rexford G. Tugwell, in *The Stricken Land: The Story of Puerto Rico* (New York: Doubleday, 1947), 69, called Puerto Rico "something of a testing place for American professions of democracy." See also Charles T. Goodsell, *Administration of a Revolution* (Cambridge, MA: Harvard University Press, 1965), 55–58; Andrés Torres, *Between Melting Pot and Mosaic: African Americans and Puerto Ricans in the New York Political Economy* (Philadelphia: Temple University Press, 1995), 27; and testimony of Vito Marcantonio, 78th Cong., 1st sess., *Congressional Record* 85, part 5 (June 17, 1943): 6028.

**108.** Cabranes, "Citizenship and the American Empire," 98, quoted from the *Encyclopedia Americana* (New York: Americana Corp., 1939), 410. Cabranes points out "the absurdity of trying to classify Puerto Rico's racially mixed population in terms of North American notions of race" (ibid., 98).

**109.** Following the transition to civilian rule by the United States in Puerto Rico in 1900, the Census Bureau began reporting each decade on the demographics of the island, using the categories "white," "black," and "mixed race." Census statistics showed the proportion of the "white" population of Puerto Rico to be growing every decade, from about 62 percent in 1900 to almost 80 percent in 1950. Arguing that "the absurdity of trying to classify Puerto Rico's racially mixed population in terms of North American notions of race" betrays an ideological agenda, legal historian José Cabranes cites the "'vanishing Negro' thesis" printed in the 1939 edition of the *Encyclopedia Americana*: "If this decrease should continue for a number of years, the black race would eventually disappear from Porto Rico. . . . This is the only island in all the West Indies where the white population is so overwhelmingly in the majority. . . . In 1910 the colored population was 34.5 percent of the whole; in 1920 it had declined to 27 percent." Cabranes, "Citizenship and the American Empire," 98, quoted from *Encyclopedia Americana* (1939), 410.

**110.** Oscar Handlin, *The Newcomers: Negroes and Puerto Ricans in a Changing Metropolis* (1959; repr., Cambridge, MA: Harvard University Press, 1965), 59.

**111.** For an example of a contemporary discussion of "passing" as Spanish, see Pedro Juan Labarthe, "De nuestros lectores," *La Prensa*, Jan. 8, 1931, 6.

**112.** Manuel Ríos Ocaña, "La raza de color de Puerto Rico y el Día de Lincoln," *La Prensa*, Feb. 14, 1940, 4; Luisa Dessus Cruz, "La contribución de la raza de color a la intelectualidad borinqueña," *La Prensa*, Feb. 22, 1940, 4. Dessus Cruz was presumably related to the poet Luis Felipe Dessus (1875–1920), whose poem she quoted, though I could not confirm this; my best guess, based on their names and his birth date, is that she was his daughter. See Jorge Luis Morales, *Poesía afroantillana y negrista* (Río Piedras, PR: Editorial UPR, 1981), 36.

## Chapter Three

**1.** WPA Federal Writers' Project, "Life Histories, Individual Case No. 9," José Pastrana, reporter, Apr. 18, 1939, Spanish Book, WPA files, reel 269, folder 4.

**2.** WPA Federal Writers' Project, "Life Histories, Individual Case No. 6," José Pastrana, reporter, Feb. 20, 1939, Spanish Book, WPA files, reel 269, folder 4.

**3.** See chapter 2, n. 2, on the difficulty of determining unemployment statistics for Puerto Ricans during the Depression. For examples of anecdotal evidence, see WPA Federal Writers' Project, "Life Histories, Individual Case No. 3," José Pastrana, reporter, Jan. 31, 1939, Spanish Book, WPA files, reel 269; and Dr. José R. Cruz, "¿Por qué emigramos?" in "De nuestros lectores," *La Prensa*, Oct. 18, 1930, 6.

**4.** U.S. Bureau of the Census, "Puerto Ricans in the Continental U.S.," 1950 *Census of Population*, Special Report P-E (Washington, DC: U.S. Government Printing Office, 1950), 4. (The total number of immigrants entering the United States dropped to a rate almost 85 percent lower than that of the five years preceding the Depression.)

**5.** María Más Pozo, "De nuestros lectores," *La Prensa*, Feb. 17, 1931, 6. The "special committee" of agencies cited in the *Evening Telegram* article was most likely the Porto Rican Community Committee (PRCC), established by the Welfare Council of New York City early in 1930. A Federal Writers' Project contributor to the "Spanish Book" in 1936 described the inspiration for the PRCC as follows: "The wretched condition of Porto Ricans in New York, the realization that little was known about them and their backgrounds, the fact that thousands were arriving in New York yearly to escape Porto Rico's poverty only to find themselves poverty stricken here, aroused the leaders of New York's welfare field." See WPA Federal Writers' Project, "Interview with Dr. Samuel Joseph of CCNY on Puerto Rican Survey," May 19, 1936, Spanish Book, WPA files, reel 269, folder 9. Gabriel Blanco, "De nuestros lectores," *La Prensa*, Aug. 4, 1930, 6; J. L. Olivero, "De nuestros lectores," *La Prensa*, Aug. 13, 1930, 6.

**6.** See Virginia Sánchez-Korrol, *From Colonia to Community: The History of Puerto Ricans in New York City* (Berkeley: University of California Press, 1983), 159; Sister Carmelita, interview with Pedro Rivera, May 12, 1973, Pioneros Project.

**7.** Repatriation was a major topic of debate among Hispanics of all nationalities in the early years of the Depression. See, for instance, "El 'desempleo' puertorriqueño," editorial, *La Prensa*, Oct. 3, 1931, 4; Carmen B. Córdova, "La repatriación de cubanos," in "De nuestros lectores," *La Prensa*, Sept. 1, 1930, 6; "Repatriaciones de hispanos," editorial, *La Prensa*, July 8, 1931, 4; "La repatriación de hispanos," editorial, *La Prensa*, Mar. 19, 1932, 4; "Las repatriaciones de hispanos," editorial, *La Prensa*, Aug. 19, 1932, 4. George Sánchez writes that, although federal and local authorities in California, along with the Mexican government, plotted the forcible repatriation of some Mexican immigrants (and even Mexican Americans who were naturalized or born in the United States) during the Depression—and pressured many others with threats of deportation—a great many Mexicans in Los Angeles actually chose to return or sought the aid of their consul in an effort to return to Mexico. See Sánchez, *Becoming Mexican American: Ethnicity, Culture, and Identity in Chicano Los Angeles, 1900-1945* (New York: Oxford University Press, 1993), chapter 10, "Where Is Home? The Dilemma of Repatriation," especially 214-17.

**8.** Altagracia Ortiz, "Puerto Rican Women in the Garment Industry," in *Puerto Rican Women and Work: Bridges in Transnational Labor*, edited by Altagracia Ortiz (Philadelphia: Temple University Press, 1996), 58-59. See also interviews with Gilberto Gerena Valentín (Sept. 1980), and with Espi Martell and Doña Emilia Giboyeaux (Aug. 1, 1984), by Ana Juarbe and Rina Benmayor, Costureras Project.

**9.** One migrant interviewed by a WPA field-worker said, for instance, that "as in Puerto Rico, I virtually live here practically isolated from the rest of the world. Am only preoccupied about my work and my family. . . . Am not interested in local or national politics. Have only voted twice." WPA Federal Writers' Project, "Life Histories, Individual Case No. 6," José Pastrana, reporter, Feb. 20, 1939, Spanish Book, WPA files, reel 269, folder 4.

**10.** Max Ríos Ocaña and Dr. D. Randolfo Marty, "De nuestros lectores," *La Prensa*, Jan. 10, 1939, 4, Jan. 18, 1939, 5, Feb. 17, 1939, 4, and Apr. 19, 1939, 5; "La Confederación Boricua cooperará en demandas beneficiosas para Pto. Rico," *La Prensa*, Apr. 27, 1939, 2. For a discussion of similar transnational politics later in the twentieth century, see Karen Richman, "A *Lavalas* at Home / A *Lavalas* for Home: Inflections of Transnationalism in the Discourse of Haitian President Aristide," in *Towards a Transnational Perspective on Migration: Race, Class, Ethnicity, and Nationalism Reconsidered*, edited by Nina Glick Schiller, Linda Basch, and Cristina Blanc-Szanton (New York: New York Academy of Sciences, 1992).

**11.** Bernardo Vega, *Memoirs of Bernardo Vega: A Contribution to the History of the Puerto Rican Community in New York*, edited by César Andreu Iglesias (New York: Monthly Review Press, 1984), 172.

**12.** Ibid., 171-72. See also Mark Naison, *Communists in Harlem during the Depression* (New York: Grove Press, 1983), although he does not talk specifically about Puerto Ricans.

**13.** The "Organizations" section of the WPA "Spanish Book" lists or describes scores of organizations—fraternal, political, labor, social, and cultural—that were founded by Puerto Ricans (and other Hispanics) during the 1930s. See WPA Federal Writers' Project, "Organizations," 1938, Spanish Book, WPA files, reel 269, folders 7 and 9.

**14.** See Chris McNickle, *To Be Mayor of New York: Ethnic Politics in the City* (New York: Columbia University Press, 1993), 13–21 and passim, for a discussion of the different expectations of the Democratic machine's Irish and Jewish constituents. McNickle argues that while Tammany won the Irish vote through the delivery of patronage and various kinds of "welfare benefits," including intervention in cases of eviction or arrest, Jews began voting for Democrats only when bosses demonstrated credible proof of their willingness to stand up for "moral" issues, especially opposition to anti-Semitism.

**15.** Enrique C. Rosario, "De nuestros lectores," *La Prensa*, Oct. 19, 1936, 8.

**16.** Felipe Sosa, "De nuestros lectores," *La Prensa*, Sept. 1, 1934, 4.

**17.** Rogers Smith, "Rights," in *A Companion to American Thought*, edited by Richard Wightman Fox and James T. Kloppenberg (Malden, MA: Blackwell Publishers, 1995), 596.

**18.** Daniel Rodgers, *Contested Truths: Keywords in American Politics since Independence* (Cambridge, MA: Harvard University Press, 1998), 217. Legal scholars tend to use a different definition of "rights talk," which most on the Left interpret as a generally negative trend toward excessive emphasis on individual rights. See, for example, Mary Ann Glendon, *Rights Talk: The Impoverishment of Political Discourse* (New York: Free Press, 1991), and Thomas Halper, *Positive Rights in a Republic of Talk* (Boston: Kluwer Academic Publishers, 2003). Some historians have used the term *rights talk* more loosely. Tom Sugrue argues that a New Deal–inspired rights revolution prompted distinct groups of Americans, including "African Americans, trade union members, and military veterans"—as well as racist white homeowners in Detroit—"to use rights talk to express their political discontent and their political vision." Sugrue, "Crabgrass-Roots Politics: Race, Rights, and the Reaction against Liberalism in the Urban North, 1940–1964," *Journal of American History* 82 (Sept. 1995): 564. Historian Alan Brinkley writes that the latter days of the New Deal, combined with the social and political climate at the start of World War II, spurred a shift in American liberalism from "reform liberalism" to "rights-based liberalism." See Alan Brinkley, *The End of Reform: New Deal Liberalism in Recession and War* (New York: Vintage Press, 1995), 10–11, 164–70.

**19.** Ira Katznelson, *City Trenches: Urban Politics and the Patterning of Class in the United States* (Chicago: University of Chicago Press, 1981), 65 and passim.

**20.** For example, a New York organization called the Bureau for Intercultural Education printed a pamphlet entitled "Agencies in the Field of Intercultural Education," which listed the following organizations based in New York: the American Civil Liberties Union, the American Film Center—Committee on Mass Education in Race Relations, the American Council on Race Relations, the American Jewish Committee, the American Jewish Congress, the Anti-Defamation League of B'nai B'rith, the Bureau for Intercultural Education, the Catholic Interracial Council, the Common Council for American Unity, the Council against Intolerance in America, the Council for Democracy, the East and West Association, the Federal Council of the Churches of Christ in America—Department of Race Relations, the Jewish Labor Committee, the League for Fair Play, the NAACP, the National CIO Committee to Abolish Racial Discrimination, the National Conference on Christians and Jews, and the National Urban League. Bureau for Intercultural Education, "Agencies in the Field of Intercultural Education," Covello papers, series VI, box 50, folder 11. See also Richard Dalfiume, "'The Forgotten Years' of the Negro Revolution," *Journal of American History* 55 (June 1968): 90–106; Richard Weiss, "Ethnicity and Reform: Minorities and the Ambience of the Depression Years," *Journal of American History* 66 (Dec. 1979): 566–85; and Richard W. Steele, "The War on Intolerance: The Reformulation of American Nationalism, 1939–1941," *Journal of American Ethnic History* 9 (Fall 1989): 9–35.

21. Ira Rosenwaike, *Population History of New York City* (Syracuse, NY: Syracuse University Press, 1972), 121.

22. Historical sociologist Margaret Somers has written extensively on the idea of citizenship not as a status but as "a set of institutionally embedded social practices," framed by expressions of expectations of the state. See, for example, Somers, "Citizenship and the Public Sphere: Law, Community, and Political Culture in the Transition to Democracy," *American Sociological Review* 58 (Oct. 1993): 587–620. Political scientist José Cruz, in his study of Puerto Rican politics in Hartford, Connecticut, since the 1960s, makes an interesting distinction between "power awareness," which he defines as "a sense of how political actors came to be favored in the polity," and "empowerment." José Cruz, *Identity and Power: Puerto Rican Politics and the Challenge of Ethnicity* (Philadelphia: Temple University Press, 1996), 12.

23. August Heckscher, *When La Guardia Was Mayor: New York's Legendary Years* (New York: W. W. Norton & Company, 1978), 26–30; McNickle, *To Be Mayor of New York*, 32–33.

24. Given the local dynamics of political reform, and the recent exposure of widespread corruption in Tammany Hall, La Guardia's victory did not amount to an upset; however, it did contradict a national trend of local Democratic election victories following on the coattails of FDR's new and immensely popular administration.

25. McNickle, *To Be Mayor of New York*, 5–19, 41–53.

26. "El Alcalde Walker, en nombre de la ciudad, apoya nuestra suscripción Pro–P. Rico," *La Prensa*, Jan. 1, 1930, 1. Probably Walker had learned from the hard experience of Tammany's Sol Bloom, the state congressional representative for East Harlem, that Puerto Rican voters played by the rules of the Tammany game and demanded respect and at least rhetorical support—even if they could not command the kind of substantive patronage that the more established immigrant groups had won. On the relationship between Rep. Sol Bloom and Puerto Ricans in East Harlem, see chapter 1, pp. 47–49.

27. Interview with Doña Gregoria Lausell, conducted by Ana Juarbe, Apr. 2, 1984, Costureras Project. A *La Prensa* reporter noted that "Mr. Luis Weber exhibited the brotherly unity and energy that exists among the Brooklyn groups, to unite volunteers," "O'Brien encomia la lealtad de los borinqueños," *La Prensa*, Nov. 1, 1933, 8.

See chapter 1, pp. 41–44, for a description of the role of Puerto Rican bosses in the Brooklyn *colonia*.

**28.** The "bigwigs" included borough president Henry Hesterberg, an alderman, a congressman, and several district leaders. "La campaña política local y los electores hispanos: Clubs puertorriqueños demócratas de Brooklyn definen su actitud política," *La Prensa*, Nov. 1, 1933, 6.

**29.** "O'Brien encomia la lealtad de los borinqueños."

**30.** Ibid.

**31.** "Instantáneas de la colonia," *La Prensa*, Oct. 26, 1933, 6.

**32.** "La campaña política local y los electores hispanos: Mujeres hispanas votantes pro McKee," *La Prensa*, Nov. 4, 1933, 2.

**33.** Vega, *Memoirs*, 198; "La vida obrera," *La Prensa*, May 23, 1925, 2.

**34.** "La campaña política local y los electores hispanos: Partido fusionista en el distrito 17," *La Prensa*, Nov. 4, 1933, 6.

**35.** The Communist Party, which had begun to gain a foothold in Harlem since the beginning of the Depression, nominated two Hispanic candidates to the party ticket. Pedro Uffre, secretary-general of the Industrial Union of Cigarworkers, ran for city council in District Seventeen, campaigning on the argument that the situation for Puerto Rican workers in New York was "disastrous" and that only the Communist Party would address these needs in El Barrio. "La campaña política local y los electores hispanos: Frente unido comunista," *La Prensa*, Nov. 4, 1933, 6. See also, generally, Naison, *Communists in Harlem*.

**36.** Most of these booster-leaders talked about "betterment" in cultural terms, making reference to refinements in language, music, and in a general public image that would add up to a much-needed respectability for Puerto Ricans.

**37.** "El momento político y los hispanos," *La Prensa*, Aug. 8, 1934, 1.

**38.** "El momento político y los hispanos," *La Prensa*, Aug. 10, 1934, 1; Pedro Rovira, "De nuestros lectores," *La Prensa*, Aug. 15, 1934, 4.

**39.** "El momento político y los hispanos," *La Prensa*, Aug. 9, 1934, 1; "El momento político y los hispanos," *La Prensa*, Aug. 4, 1934, 1.

**40.** "El momento político y los hispanos," *La Prensa*, July 30, 1934, 1; "Quayle promete su apoyo a la colonia boricua de B'klyn," *La Prensa*, Jan. 9, 1934, 1.

**41.** "El momento político y los hispanos," *La Prensa*, Aug. 13, 1934, 1.

**42.** "El momento político y los hispanos," *La Prensa*, July 31, 1934, 1; María Marín Reguero, "De nuestros lectores," *La Prensa*, Aug. 1, 1934, 4; "El momento político y los hispanos," *La Prensa*, Aug. 16, 1934, 1.

**43.** "Instantáneas de la colonia," *La Prensa*, Jan. 5, 1934, 2; Pedro San Miguel, "De nuestros lectores," *La Prensa*, Jan. 30, 1934, 4; Diego Flores, "De nuestros lectores," *La Prensa*, Aug. 2, 1934, 4.

**44.** Gumersindo Márquez, "De nuestros lectores," *La Prensa*, Aug. 20, 1934, 4. Márquez complained that "the only thing we have conquered after our long stay in this great city is the right to be victims."

**45.** Chris McNickle offers a concise and convincing summary of Tammany's relationships with the Irish and the Jews of New York City in the late nineteenth century, a dynamic of votes, patronage, and power that he dubs "ethnic arithmetic." McNickle says that Tammany first realized that a "Jewish vote" existed in the mayoral election of 1886; by 1900, Jewish voters had become important enough to the machine that its leaders were willing to nominate a Jew for the congressional seat of the Fourth District. It is interesting to note that, for all the cynicism among Puerto Ricans about Tammany's playing favorites with the Jews in Harlem, the two groups experienced a similar lag period between Tammany leaders' recognition of the importance of the group's vote and the leaders' concession to run a candidate from that group. See McNickle, *To Be Mayor of New York*, 5–19.

**46.** Felipe Sosa, "De nuestros lectores," *La Prensa*, Aug. 4, 1934, 4; María Marín Reguero, "De nuestros lectores," *La Prensa*, Aug. 1, 1934, 8.

**47.** "El momento político y los hispanos," *La Prensa*, Aug. 8, 1934, 1; "La campaña política local y los electores hispanos," *La Prensa*, Nov. 7, 1933, 2.

**48.** "Niégase entendido alguno entre los puertorriqueños y la raza de color," *La Prensa*, Aug. 3, 1934, 1.

**49.** "Candidaturas hispanas en Nueva York," editorial, *La Prensa*, Sept. 6, 1934, 4; "¡A unificar el voto puertorriqueño!" editorial, *La Prensa*, Sept. 17, 1934, 4; Gustavo Ramos, "De nuestros lectores," *La Prensa*, Aug. 10, 1934, 4.

**50.** Ramón Colón, "De nuestros lectores," *La Prensa*, Sept. 6, 1934, 4.

**51.** "Mayor Orders Inquiry in Reply to Dennigan," *New York Herald-Tribune*, Apr. 5, 1935, 1.

**52.** "El socorro a los hispanos," editorial, *La Prensa*, Feb. 8, 1932, 4. As a service to the community, the newspaper began to publish employment advertisements, free of charge, for Spanish-speaking employers and job seekers. Aside from this gesture, there was little that the paper could offer its readers other than weak admonishments that the *colonia* did possess the "resources, reserves, and possibilities" to sustain itself during this difficult time. "N.R.A. hispana espontánea," editorial, *La Prensa*, Aug. 8, 1933, 4.

**53.** Letter from Gumersindo Márquez, "De nuestros lectores," *La Prensa*, Aug. 20, 1934, 4, 8.

**54.** City of New York Board of Elections, *Annual Report*, 1932 (New York: Board of Elections of the City of New York).

**55.** "Instantáneas de la colonia," *La Prensa*, Nov. 6, 1933, 6.

**56.** Ruth Glasser, *My Music Is My Flag: Puerto Rican Musicians and Their New York Communities, 1917–1940* (Berkeley: University of California Press, 1995), 171, and Glasser, personal communication with the author, Aug. 11, 2005.

**57.** City of New York Board of Elections, *Annual Report*, 1933 and 1934 (New York: Board of Elections of the City of New York).

**58.** "Hodson Is Accused of Relief Politics," *New York Times*, Aug. 31, 1934, 1; "Los jefes del Home Relief en el este de Harlem están sembrando el terror," *La Prensa*, Aug. 31, 1934, 1.

**59.** "Hodson Is Accused of Relief Politics."

**60.** Carlita Gutiérrez, Viuda de Vélez, to Hon. Vito Marcantonio, Mar. 8, 1940; Porfirio Maldonado (Barrio Barrochales, PR) to Vito Marcantonio, June 27, 1939. Vito Marcantonio papers, box 4, reel 2.

**61.** "400,000 Families on City's Relief Rolls at a Cost of $201,000,000 for a

Year," *New York Times*, Aug. 27, 1934, 2. Of course, it was only naturalized foreign Spanish speakers who were eligible for government relief benefits.

**62.** "Una manifestación contra el 'H. Relief' en Harlem," *La Prensa*, Apr. 6, 1935, 1.

**63.** "7 Reds Found Guilty in Relief Office Riot," *New York Times*, Oct. 17, 1934, 17; "9 Held after Riot at Relief Bureau," *New York Times*, Jan. 30, 1935, 14.

**64.** "Negroes' Charges Denied by Corsi," *New York Times*, Apr. 28, 1935, 23; Naison, *Communists in Harlem*, 145–46.

**65.** Naison, *Communists in Harlem*, 98–103. "Unemployment Discrimination on Relief and Works Jobs in Harlem," testimony of James W. Ford, secretary of the Harlem Section of the Communist Party, before the Mayor's Commission on Conditions in Harlem, Apr. 13, 1935, La Guardia papers, reel 76, folder 8.

**66.** In his testimony before the Mayor's Commission, James Ford referred to HRB administrator Victor Suárez as a "Puerto Rican schoolteacher" who distributed relief and discriminated against Negroes, Apr. 13, 1935, La Guardia papers, reel 76, folder 8.

**67.** "Negro Discrimination in the E.H.R.B.," *Red H.R.B. Worker*, vol. 1, no. 1, May 1935, 6. (The paper's banner explained that it was "published by the Communist Party and the Young Communist League Workers in the Home Relief Bureaus in Harlem.") "Negroes' Charges Denied by Corsi."

**68.** Isabel O'Neill, Junta Liberal Puertorriqueña de Nueva York, to Mayor Fiorello La Guardia, June 24, 1935, La Guardia papers, reel 76, folder 8.

**69.** Net migration figures for Puerto Ricans entering the United States during the 1930s were low in comparison to later years, just under one thousand, according to sociologist Clarence Senior, but Depression-era migration was not insignificant in terms of its impact on the *colonia*: first, the number of migrants arriving in New York during the first few years of the Depression was probably higher, in fact, than in the later thirties (anecdotal sources indicate that desperate islanders still believed that the situation in New York would be better than it was on the island); and the average in-migration during the twenties was only about nineteen hundred, so the number of migrants entering the *colonia* in the thirties was still relatively significant. For figures on net annual migration averages, see Clarence Senior, *The Puerto Ricans: Strangers—Then Neighbors* (Chicago: Quadrangle Books, 1961), 39.

**70.** "Life Histories, Individual Case No. 7" (Apr. 18, 1939), "Life Histories, Individual Case No. 6" (Jan. 27, 1939), and "Life Histories, Individual Case No. 3" (Jan. 31, 1939), José Pastrana, reporter, Spanish Book, WPA files, reel 269, folder 4.

**71.** Sánchez, *Becoming Mexican American*, 261, citing Beatrice Griffith, *American Me* (Boston: Houghton Mifflin, 1948), 290.

**72.** "Island Is Inspired by Mrs. Roosevelt," *New York Times*, Mar. 18, 1934, IV, 8; Ruby Black, *Eleanor Roosevelt: A Biography* (New York: Duell, Sloane, and Pearce, 1940), 296–97.

**73.** "Sorprende a Mrs. Roosevelt la limpieza de las casas y la gente de P.R.," *La Prensa*, Mar. 14, 1934, 1.

**74.** "President's Wife Sees a New Order," *New York Times*, Apr. 10, 1934, 10; "Instantáneas de la colonia," *La Prensa*, Apr. 23, 1934, 2. Nélida Pérez discusses the controversy over Eleanor Roosevelt's speech in an article titled "Community at Risk: Puerto Ricans and Health, East Harlem, 1929–1940," Centro de Estudios Puertorriqueños, *Bulletin* 2 (Fall 1998): 19–20.

**75.** Antonio González, letter to the editor, *New York Times*, Apr. 13, 1934, 18. The telegram was from the Liga Puertorriqueña e Hispana, whose president at the time was Bernardo Vega. Bernardo Vega, "De nuestros lectores," *La Prensa*, Apr. 30, 1934, 4; see also Vega, *Memoirs*, 176. "Mrs. Roosevelt Warns School Girls Era of Unearned Privilege Is Over," *New York Times*, Apr. 19, 1934, 27.

**76.** Bernardo Vega, "De nuestros lectores," *La Prensa*, Apr. 30, 1934, 4. This last sentence is Vega's own translation and condensation of a part of his letter to *La Prensa* that is not fully legible in the original document; see Vega, *Memoirs*, 176.

**77.** Vega claims that up to six thousand Puerto Rican children were sent to such camps in this period. Vega, *Memoirs*, 177.

**78.** Ibid., 177–78; "MANIFIESTO a la colonia hispana en general," flyer of the United Front Committee against Discrimination of Puerto Ricans, Sept. 14, 1934, Colón papers, series V, box 16, folder 14.

**79.** Interview with José Ramón Giboyeaux, conducted by Rina Benmayor and Blanca Vázquez, Mar. 12, 1984, Costureras Project, 24.

**80.** Dietz, *Economic History of Puerto Rico*, 163–70; Blanca G. Silvestrini, *Los trabajadores puertorriqueños y el Partido Socialista, 1932–1940* (Río Piedras, PR: Editorial Universitaria, 1979), 66–72.

**81.** "La NRA nos trata como perros: Diez y seis personas vivimos con 50 centavos," *La Prensa*, Mar. 12, 1934, 1. Rexford Tugwell, a key administration adviser on Puerto Rican issues in the late thirties and early forties, then appointed governor in 1941, observed that during his spring 1934 trip to the island, "unemployment relief was just then spreading into Puerto Rico from the continent." Rexford Guy Tugwell, *The Stricken Land: The Story of Puerto Rico* (New York: Doubleday, 1947), 56.

**82.** Between the U.S. takeover of the island in 1898 and 1935, the amount of arable land converted to sugar production had increased almost 400 percent, and over two-thirds of this land was owned or controlled by four U.S. sugar corporations; during approximately that time period, the value of sugar exports increased about 1,000 percent. Moreover, although the Jones Act of 1917 included a clause that outlawed the creation of plantations larger than five hundred acres, more than 65 percent of the island's land devoted to sugar was held by plantations of more than five hundred acres. James L. Dietz, *Economic History of Puerto Rico: Institutional Change and Capitalist Development* (Princeton, NJ: Princeton University Press, 1986), 103–16, 148–51; César Ayala and Rafael Bernabe, *Puerto Rico in the American Century: A History since 1898* (Chapel Hill: University of North Carolina Press, 2007), 102.

**83.** Tugwell, *Stricken Land*, 5. See "El problema de P.R. será resuelto inmediatamente, dijo Antonio R. Barceló," *La Prensa*, Nov. 24, 1934, 1. On the demise of the PRRA, see Dietz, *Economic History of Puerto Rico*, 149–58. WPA Federal Writers' Project, "Puerto Rican Political Alignments in New York," Sept. 8, 1936, Spanish Book, WPA files, reel 269, folder 9.

**84.** "'Los borinqueños nos agradecen con asesinatos, odio,'" *La Prensa*, Feb. 25, 1936, 1.

**85.** See the following illustrations of the increasing popularity of Nationalist events, both leading up to and following the killing of the four Nationalists and the assassination of Riggs: "Gran mitín público, pro-presos nacionalistas de Puerto Rico," flyer by the Junta Nacionalista Puertorriqueña, Oct. 29, 1936, Vando papers, series III, box 2, folder 16; Carlos Vélez, presidente del Partido Nacionalista de Puerto Rico, Junta de Nueva York, to Sr. Presidente y Señores Miembros de la Vanguardia Puertorriqueña, regarding a "magno Congreso Pro-Convención Constituyente de la República de Puerto Rico," May 16, 1936, Colón papers, series II, box 2, folder 6; "Gran mitín de protesta," flyer by the Junta Nacionalista Puertorriqueña, Feb. 24, 1937, Vando papers, series III, box 2, folder 16; Vega, *Memoirs*, 180. There were also scores of letters from readers printed in *La Prensa*'s "De nuestros lectores" section between mid-March and late August 1936 illustrating the same trend; *La Prensa*'s politically moderate to conservative editors did also print a number of letters criticizing the growing levels of radical nationalism among *colonia* members or expressing generally moderate views on the question of the U.S. presence in Puerto Rico.

**86.** Letter from Luisa Salgado, "De nuestros lectores," *La Prensa*, Mar. 12, 1936, 4.

**87.** "Life Histories, Individual Case No. 6" (Jan. 27, 1939) and "Life Histories, Individual Case No. 9" (Apr. 18, 1939), José Pastrana, reporter, Spanish Book, WPA files, reel 269, folder 4.

**88.** "Albizu Campos fué arrestado," *La Prensa*, Mar. 6, 1936, 1; "Ickes ve 'seria' la campaña separatista de P.R.," *La Prensa*, May 15, 1936, 2; Dietz, *Economic History of Puerto Rico*, 168–70; Manuel Maldonado-Denis, *Puerto Rico: A Socio-Historical Perspective* (New York: Vintage Press, 1972), 124–25.

**89.** "Proposed Independence of Puerto Rico," 74th Cong., 2nd sess., *Congressional Record* 80, no. 6 (Apr. 23, 1936): 5925.

**90.** Ibid., 5926; José Trías Monge, *Puerto Rico: The Trials of the Oldest Colony in the World* (New Haven, CT: Yale University Press, 1997), 94–96.

**91.** "Senate Bill Gives Full Independence to Puerto Ricans," New york Times, Apr. 24, 1936, 1; Surendra Bhana, *The United States and the Development of the Puerto Rican Status Question* (Lawrence: University Press of Kansas), 18–23.

**92.** "'¡Aunque nos muramos de hambre, independencia!'" *La Prensa*, Apr. 25, 1936, 1; "La indep. divide la opinión política en P.R.," *La Prensa*, Apr. 25, 1936, 1; "Los borinqueños quieren un plan genuino de soberanía," *La Prensa*, Apr. 28, 1936, 1; Trías Monge, *Puerto Rico*, 95; Ayala and Bernabe, *Puerto Rico*, 111–12.

**93.** See various letters in "De nuestros lectores," especially from Max Ríos Ríos (Apr. 8, 1936, 4, and May 5, 1936, 4), Victor Fiol Ramos (May 8, 1936, 4), and Pilar Pacheco (Aug. 18, 1936, 4), *La Prensa*. Luisa A. Quintero, "De nuestros lectores," *La Prensa*, Sept. 8, 1936, 4.

**94.** WPA Federal Writers' Project, "Puerto Rican Political Alignments in New York," Sept. 1936, Spanish Book, WPA files, reel 269, folder 9.

**95.** "Agrupación de Puertorriqueños Ciudadanos de EU de A," 1936, Vando papers, series III, box 1, folder 7.

**96.** Pacheco had written many other letters to *La Prensa* on subjects like women in the Spanish Civil War, the hardships of women working in the embroidery business, and the discriminatory nature of rhetoric about crime in Harlem. Pilar Pacheco, "De nuestros lectores," *La Prensa*, Aug. 18, 1936, 4.

97. María Más Pozo, "De nuestros lectores," *La Prensa*, Jan. 12, 1931, 6.

98. Bhana, *United States and the Development of the Puerto Rican Status Question*, 20. About his opponent's vision of the island's "apparent independence," Marcantonio remarked: "Instead of offering genuine independence to the people of Puerto Rico, his bill offers them an American-controlled plebiscite and a commonwealth which will be under the thumb of the American Government. The independence subsequently offered by the Tydings bill would be considerably curtailed by the menacing presence of an American naval reservation. . . . At the same time the Tydings bill, with its tariff provisions, threatens to ruin the only present source of Puerto Rican income, which is the sale of their cash crops in the American market. His bill does not provide for the development of substitutes for the dominating and American-dominated sugar industry." "Puerto Rican Independence," 74th Cong., 2nd sess., *Congressional Record* 80, no. 6 (May 6, 1936): 6726.

99. "Marcantonio presenter esta semana otro proyecto de independencia a P.R.," *La Prensa*, Apr. 30, 1936, 1; Dietz, *Economic History of Puerto Rico*, 170; Tugwell, *Stricken Land*, 70. On the silence of most congressmen on Puerto Rican issues, see, for example, the debate over the Puerto Rican Reconstruction Administration, 76th Cong., 3rd sess., *Congressional Record* 86, part 6 (May 22, 1940): 6651–56, especially 6655.

100. Bhana, *United States and the Development of the Puerto Rican Status Question*, 28.

101. "10,000 Parade Here for Puerto Ricans," *New York Times*, Aug. 30, 1936, 24.

102. See Gerald Meyer, *Vito Marcantonio: Radical Politician, 1902–1954* (Albany: State University of New York Press, 1989), 152–54. Nationalist demonstrations in Harlem were becoming more frequent by 1934–35, as leaders in the *colonia* rode the wave of popularity of Nationalists in Puerto Rico, who capitalized politically on the worsening economic situation there. See "Instantáneas de la colonia, con los nacionalistas . . . ," *La Prensa*, Jan. 3, 1934, 2; "Manifestación independentista borinqueña," *La Prensa*, Sept. 3, 1935, 4. On demonstrations following the arrest of the eight Nationalists in 1936, see Germán Berrios, "De nuestros lectores," *La Prensa*, Mar. 2, 1936, 4.

103. WPA Federal Writers' Project, "Puerto Rican Political Alignments in New York," Sept. 1936, Spanish Book, WPA files, reel 269, folder 9.

104. On other politicians' assaults on Marcantonio for his radicalism and alleged ties to the Communist Party (there was some truth to these allegations), see Meyer, *Vito Marcantonio*, 41–42 and passim; on the campaigns of various politicians against Marcantonio and his radical politics in Puerto Rican East Harlem, see ibid., 168–69 and passim.

105. A. Reina, Agrupación Socialista Española, to Jesús Colón, May 25, 1935, Colón papers, series II, box 2, folder 5; "Convocatoria," flyer by the Comité Pro Democracia Española, Jan. 24, 1937, Vando papers, series III, box 2, folder 18. See also list of "Sociedades Afiliadas" printed by el Comité Antifascista Español, n.d., and "Llamamiento a todos los Mexicanos residentes en los Estados Unidos," flyer by the

Mutualista Obrera Mexicana, Vando papers, series III, box 2, folder 18. "La guerra española, tema predominante de las protestas del 'Día del Trabajo,'" *La Prensa*, May 3, 1937, 2. See also, generally, Robin D. G. Kelley, "This Ain't Ethiopia, but It'll Do," in Kelley, *Race Rebels: Culture, Politics, and the Black Working Class* (New York: Simon and Schuster, 1996).

**106.** Tugwell, *Stricken Land*, 70.

**107.** WPA Federal Writers' Project, "Puerto Rican Political Alignments in New York," Sept. 1936, Spanish Book, WPA files, reel 269, folder 9.

**108.** Organizers of the Nationalist demonstration had been issued a permit by the town's mayor, but the island's police chief and governor revoked the permit at the last minute because they believed the parade would end in violence. Demonstrators proceeded with the event anyway, and the local chief of police stationed 150 officers, armed with rifles and submachine guns, along the parade route. The source of the first shot was never determined, but photographs of the event reveal that the marchers, at least, were unarmed. Police opened fire on the crowd. See Mathews, *Puerto Rican Politics and the New Deal* (Gainesville: University of Florida Press, 1960), 310–15; Vega, *Memoirs*, 192.

**109.** Interview with José Ramón Giboyeaux, conducted by Rina Benmayor and Blanca Vázquez, Mar. 12, 1984, Costureras Project.

**110.** A WPA field-worker's notes on the "Defensa Cívica Hispano Americana," organized in 1936, remarked on the mixed-class support of García Rivera: "White collar workers . . . who work in various exporting firms" collaborated with "the older men [who] are cigarmakers and restaurant workers" in support of García Rivera's campaign. "Organizations—Defensa Cívica Hispano Americana," Dec. 29, 1938, Spanish Book, WPA files, reel 269, folder 7. See also Sánchez-Korrol, *From Colonia to Community*, 190–91.

**111.** City of New York Board of Elections, *Annual Report*, 1932–37 (New York: Board of Elections of the City of New York). The voter registration figures for the Seventeenth Assembly District for 1932, 1933, and 1937, for example, are as follows:

1932: 17,439 Democrats; 2,864 Republicans
1933: 15,185 Democrats; 2,328 Republicans
1937: 12,464 Democrats; 2,834 Republicans
García Rivera won 8,798 votes in the 1937 election, compared to 6,218 for Alterman.

**112.** "Los comités hispanos cerraron anoche con discursos su campaña en New York," *La Prensa*, Nov. 2, 1937, 1; "Los boricuas debemos de controlar el Distrito 17," *La Prensa*, May 17, 1938, 1. WPA Federal Writers' Project, "Puerto Rican Organizations in New York—Puerto Rican Political and Social League," May 19, 1936, Spanish Book, WPA files, reel 269, folder 7.

**113.** "Debe celebrarse una asamblea para la unificación de hispanos en Brooklyn," *La Prensa*, May 30, 1938, 1; "Formaron ya su delegación para la gran conferencia," *La Prensa*, Aug. 11, 1938, 3; "La unión de las sociedades borinqueñas fue acordada," *La Prensa*, Aug. 27, 1938, 1.

**114.** "'Nos hace falta un líder político hispano en N.Y.,'" *La Prensa*, June 7, 1938, 1;

"¿Cómo puede organizarse políticamente la colonia hispana de New York?" (interview with Oscar García Rivera), *La Prensa*, June 10, 1938, 3; Juan J. Blasini, "Cómo puede organizarse políticamente la colonia hispana de New York?" *La Prensa*, June 11, 1938, 3; María Luisa Lecompte de Varona, "De nuestros lectores," *La Prensa*, Aug. 6, 1938, 4.

**115.** "El Congreso Borinqueño se inicia hoy en Nueva York," *La Prensa*, Nov. 11, 1938, 1; Vega, *Memoirs*, 194.

**116.** Antonio T. Rivera, "¿Cómo puede organizarse políticamente la colonia?" *La Prensa*, May 24, 1938, 3; Pedro Damián Moreno, "¿Cómo puede organizarse políticamente la colonia?" *La Prensa*, June 22, 1938, 5; Ángel Reyes, "¿Cómo puede organizarse políticamente la colonia?" *La Prensa*, June 24, 1938, 3; and letter from Juan Tejada, "De nuestros lectores," *La Prensa*, June 24, 1938, 4.

**117.** Luis Raúl Rosas, "¿Cómo puede organizarse políticamente la colonia?" *La Prensa*, Aug. 9, 1938, 5; José Ferrer, "De nuestros lectores," *La Prensa*, May 21, 1938, 4; Libertad Narváez, "De nuestros lectores," *La Prensa*, Aug. 25, 1938, 4; "'Estoy en contra de los grupos regionales aquí,'" *La Prensa*, May 27, 1938, 1.

**118.** Libertad Narváez, "De nuestros lectores," *La Prensa*, Aug. 25, 1938, 4; Juan Ortega, "¿Cómo puede organizarse políticamente la colonia?" *La Prensa*, May 23, 1938, 3; J. E. López, "¿Cómo puede organizarse políticamente la colonia?" *La Prensa*, June 14, 1938, 3; Isabel O'Neill, "¿Cómo puede organizarse políticamente la colonia?" *La Prensa*, June 23, 1938, 3.

**119.** "Labor de solidaridad: La colonia puertorriqueña en Nueva York," *La Prensa*, June 6, 1938, 4. Dr. R. Marty Pérez, also from Puerto Rico, wrote a letter expressing similar sentiments about the duty of Puerto Rican New Yorkers to "produce a good impression" as citizens and reap the political benefits of this respectability. Dr. R. Marty Pérez, "¿Cómo puede organizarse políticamente la colonia?" *La Prensa*, June 25, 1938, 3.

**120.** Max Ríos Ocaña and Dr. D. Randolfo Marty, "De nuestros lectores," *La Prensa*, Jan. 10, 1939, 4, Jan. 18, 1939, 5, Feb. 17, 1939, 4, and Apr. 19, 1939, 5; "La Confederación Boricua cooperará en demandas beneficiosas para Pto. Rico," *La Prensa*, Apr. 27, 1939, 2.

**121.** "Los boricuas que viven en N.Y. deben de unirse," *La Prensa*, May 31, 1938, 1; "La unión podría ayudar grandemente a Pto. Rico," *La Prensa*, June 8, 1938, 1.

**122.** Sánchez, *Becoming Mexican American*, 245–48.

**123.** See "Comité Pro Diario Popular Hispano," flyer draft, May 1937, Colón papers, series II, box 2, folder 6; "Proyecto de carta-manifiesto a la colonia hispana de Nueva York y sus alrededores," n.d., Colón papers, series II, box 2, folder 6; Comité Pro Periódico Hispano, "Manifiesto," 1939, Colón papers, series II, box 2, folder 7; Isabel López, Hispanic Section the International Workers Order, letter-flyer, July 24, 1939, Colón papers, series II, box 2, folder 7; "Algunos de los párrafos más importantes del informe del compañero presidente, Jesús Colón . . . ," Aug. 6, 1939, Colón papers, series V, box 20, folder 7; Jesús Colón, "Manifiesto—A los españoles, puertorriqueños, cubanos, mexicanos y demás hispanos en todos los Estados Unidos," n.d. [1939], Colón papers, series III, box 10, folder 1.

**124.** José Cruz, "Pluralism and Ethnicity in New York City Politics: The Case of

Puerto Ricans" (paper presented at the New York State Political Science Association meetings, John Jay College, CUNY, Apr. 25, 2009).

**125.** "Puerto Rico Reconstruction Administration," 76th Cong., 3rd sess., *Congressional Record* 86, part 6, May 22, 1940, 6654.

**126.** Tugwell, *Stricken Land*, 73.

**127.** Vega, *Memoirs*, 202. "Puerto Rican Reconstruction Administration," 76th Cong., 3rd Sess., *Congressional Record* 86, part 6 (May 22, 1940): 6655.

**128.** The amendment under debate proposed cutting the PRRA's budget from $8 million to $3.5 million. A counteramendment, proposed by Rep. James P. McGranery (D-PA), would have cut the budget less, to $4.5 million; this was rejected by a vote of twenty-six to sixty-eight. "Puerto Rico Reconstruction Administration," 6651–56.

### Chapter Four

**1.** By 1947, that number reached more than 120,000. See Ira Rosenwaike, *Population History of New York City* (Syracuse, NY: Syracuse University Press, 1972), 121; and Clarence Senior, *The Puerto Ricans: Strangers—Then Neighbors* (Chicago: Quadrangle Books, 1961), 38.

**2.** House Committee on Immigration and Naturalization, "Temporary Restriction of Immigration," 71st Cong., 3rd sess., Feb. 17, 1931, report no. 2801, 13.

**3.** Charles S. Brown Jr. to William Jay Schieffelin, Esq., Mar. 21, 1935, La Guardia papers, reel 76, frame 727.

**4.** Charles E. Hewitt Jr., "Welcome: Paupers and Crime," *Scribner's Commentator* (Mar. 1940): 11–17, Covello papers, series X, box 103, folder 23.

**5.** Ibid.

**6.** The Philippines gained independence in 1946.

**7.** Robert Korstad and Nelson Lichtenstein argue that it was the "narrowing of public discourse in the early cold war era [that] contributed largely to the defeat and diffusion" of the labor movement in the late 1940s. Korstad and Lichtenstein, "Opportunities Found and Lost: Labor, Radicals, and the Early Civil Rights Movement," *Journal of American History* 75 (Dec. 1988): 811.

**8.** "Muchas sociedades hispanas se unen a la protesta de los boricuas en N. York," *La Prensa*, Apr. 15, 1940, 1; "Comité Puertorriqueño de Protesta" letterhead, including list of fifty-plus affiliated organizations, Vando papers, series III, box 2, folder 19; "El Comité de Protesta informa," *Brújula*, May 5, 1940, n.p.; "La colonia puertorriqueña se reune en asamblea para planear centro comunal," *La Prensa*, May 10, 1940, 2; letter to Representative Vito Marcantonio from Ruperto Ruiz, chairman, Puerto Rican Employees Association, May 8, 1940, Marcantonio papers, box 4, "Puerto Ricans: Correspondence—General" folder; Hewitt, "Welcome: Paupers and Crime," 14.

**9.** "C. E. Hewitt explica su artículo sobre Pto. Rico," *La Prensa*, May 1, 1940, 1; "Chas. E. Hewitt elogia a las mujeres de P. Rico en explicación de su artículo," *La Prensa*, July 1, 1940, 2.

**10.** The movement for "intercultural democracy," or "intercultural education," arose during the mid-1930s as an offshoot of educator Rachel Davis DuBois's work with children on tolerance and pluralism. (DuBois, who was white, was not related to W.E.B. Du Bois.) The list of directors and special consultants of DuBois's organization, Workshop for Cultural Democracy, read like a "who's who" of progressive and interracial politics in New York City and included Leonard Covello, W.E.B. Du Bois, A. Philip Randolph, Louis Adamic, and E. Franklin Frazier, as well as Puerto Rican writer and librarian Pura Belpré and numerous other lesser-known civic leaders. Rachel Davis DuBois to Mrs. Clarence Cameron White, Mar. 21, 1949, series II, box 3, folder 8, Belpré papers. Covello had lobbied the city since 1931 to build a school in Harlem where the neighborhood's diverse population of children could attend school together and learn constructive ways solving social conflicts. Benjamin Franklin's first location was on 116th Street near the East River, on the far eastern edge of the "Italian side" of East Harlem. Leonard Covello, "Intercultural Ed.—Curriculum," Covello papers, series VI, box 30, folder 12; and Covello, "An Experiment in Building Concepts of Racial Democracy," 1941, Covello papers, series III, box 22, folder 10.

11. Flyer, "The East Harlem Committee for Racial Cooperation Conference on Puerto Rican Needs in East Harlem," May 3, 1940, Covello papers, series VI, box 51, folder 12. More than eighty Harlem community leaders received invitations to this meeting, most of them Italian or Puerto Rican. "List of Names Receiving Invitations to the Racial Meeting," Covello papers, series VI, box 51, folder 12.

12. Christina Duffy Burnett and Burke Marshall, eds., *Foreign in a Domestic Sense: Puerto Rico, American Expansion, and the Constitution* (Durham, NC: Duke University Press, 2001), 1–17 and passim.

13. "Puerto Rican Independence," 78th Cong., 1st sess., *Congressional Record—Senate* 89, part 3 (Apr. 9, 1943): 3171–72.

14. Wenzell Brown, *Dynamite on Our Doorstep* (New York: Greenberg Press, 1945), and Vincenzo Petrullo, *Puerto Rican Paradox* (Philadelphia: University of Pennsylvania Press, 1947).

15. Rexford Guy Tugwell, *The Stricken Land: The Story of Puerto Rico* (New York: Doubleday, 1947), 69.

16. See letter from H. Ickes to Senator Millard Tydings, May 13, 1943, on the latter's Apr. 1943 independence bill, reprinted in 78th Cong., 1st sess., *Congressional Record* 89 (June 18, 1943): 6048–50. Ickes argued in this letter that there were other policy options besides independence and the "present dependency status," including, for a start, the election of a native governor. See also Charles Goodsell, *Administration of a Revolution: Executive Reform in Puerto Rico under Governor Tugwell, 1941–1946* (Cambridge, MA: Harvard University Press, 1965), 55–58.

17. "Message from the President," 78th Cong., 1st sess., *Congressional Record* 89 (Sept. 28, 1943): 7842.

18. "'Pto. Rico gozará de más libertades,' dijo H. Ickes," *La Prensa*, July 6, 1942, 1. Andrés Torres also talks about the reluctance of Congress in this period. Torres, *Between Melting Pot and Mosaic: African Americans and Puerto Ricans in the New York Political Economy* (Philadelphia: Temple University Press, 1995), 27.

**19.** "Convocatoria," Executive Committee of the Congreso Pro-Independencia de Puerto Rico, May 23,1943, Colón papers, series VI, box 21, folder 2. See also speech by the Nationalist Félix Benítez Rexach, praising FDR and the Atlantic Charter as beacons of hope for Puerto Rican *independentistas*, 78th Cong., 1st sess., *Congressional Record* 89, part 5 (June 18, 1943): 6049.

**20.** Testimony of Vito Marcantonio, 78th Cong., 1st sess., *Congressional Record* 89, part 5 (June 17, 1943): 6028.

**21.** Goodsell, *Administration of a Revolution*, 29, 159. The quotes are from the Subcommittee of the Committee on Insular Affairs, "Report on the Investigation of Political, Economic, and Social Conditions in Puerto Rico," 79th Cong., 1st sess., *Congressional Record* 91 (May 1, 1945): 27.

**22.** Goodsell, *Administration of a Revolution*, 59.

**23.** Bernardo Vega, *Memoirs of Bernardo Vega: A Contribution to the History of the Puerto Rican Community in New York*, edited by César Andreu Iglesias (New York: Monthly Review Press, 1984), 225.

**24.** "Conference on Puerto Rico's Right to Freedom: Independent Citizens Committee on the Arts, Sciences, and Professions," Jan. 5, 1946, Colón papers, series VI, box 21, folder 9; Vega, *Memoirs*, 225–26.

**25.** The *New York World-Telegram* ran two series of articles on Puerto Rican migrants, one in May 1947 and one in Oct. 1947, both titled "New York's Puerto Rican Influx."

**26.** "Relief Funds Being Spent without Proper Controls," *New York Times*, May 25, 1947, 1; "Officials Worried by Influx of Migrant Puerto Ricans," *New York Times*, Aug. 2, 1947, 15; "Guidance Is Asked for Puerto Ricans," *New York Times*, Oct. 28, 1947, 17.

**27.** *New York World-Telegram* articles: "Puerto Rico to Harlem—At What Cost?" May 1, 1947; "Little Puerto Rico, a Gigantic Sardine Can," May 2, 1947; "Puerto Rican Influx Overcrowds Schools," May 3, 1947; "Migrants Find Even More Misery in City," Oct. 20, 1947; "Migrants Hike Relief," Oct. 22, 1947; "Crime Festers in Bulging Tenements," Oct. 23, 1947; "Church Tackles Migrant Problem," Oct. 28, 1947; "Proposals to Ease Problem," Oct. 29, 1947—all n.p., from Vertical File, "Puerto Ricans, 1950s–60s," City Hall Library (hereafter CHL). "Puerto Ricans Crowd into New York," *PM*, Feb. 6, 1947, 12, Colón papers, series X, box 35, folder 4.

**28.** Letters from Agustín Crespo, Feb. 26, 1947, 4, and Aurelio Román Hernández, Oct. 25, 1947, 3, "De nuestros lectores," *La Prensa*; "Proponen asamblea magna de todos los organismos puertorriqueños aquí," *La Prensa*, Nov. 6, 1947, 2; "Fernós comenta sobre la publicidad al caso de puertorriqueños en N. York," *La Prensa*, Nov. 28, 1947, 2. Juan Marchand Sicardo, "De nuestros lectores," *La Prensa*, Oct. 22, 1947, 4. *La Prensa* series titled "Por la comunidad," including articles "Fecunda labor conjunta de los veteranos borinqueños en Nueva York," Sept. 27, 1947, 2; "Un boricua llegó pobre de recursos y prosperó notablemente," Oct. 4, 1947, 2; "La mujer puertorriqueña en la labor cultural hispánica aquí," Oct. 11, 1947, 2; "Agencias del gobierno de Puerto Rico en Washington y Nueva York," Oct. 15, 1947, 3. The series ran through Jan. 1948.

**29.** "Puerto Ricans Here Indignant about Inquiry," *New York Herald-Tribune*, Nov. 13, 1947, in Vertical File, "Puerto Ricans, 1950s–60s," CHL.

**30.** Isaías Encarnación, "De nuestros lectores," *La Prensa*, Mar. 3, 1947, 4.

**31.** Leonard Covello, to the principals in Districts 10 and 11, regarding Good Neighbor Federation conference titled "The Social Backgrounds of the Puerto Rican People," Covello papers, series X, box 104, folder 6.

**32.** Program, Annual Education Conference at Benjamin Franklin High School, Puerto Rican Employees' Association, May 24, 1942, Colón papers, series VI, box 21, folder 2; Ruperto Ruiz, president, Puerto Rican Employees' Association, to Leonard Covello, regarding "educational conference," May 24, 1942, Covello papers, series VIII, box 74, folder 2. See also reprint of *Herald Tribune* article, "Schools in City to Fit Courses to Puerto Ricans," Nov. 16, 1947, n.p., Covello papers, series X, box 103, folder 6.

**33.** Leonard Covello, "We Hold These Truths," manuscript, n.d. [1938], Covello papers, series III, box 5, folder 13; Leonard Covello to Benjamin Franklin High School students, Oct. 26, 1938, regarding reaction to "clashes," Covello papers, series VI, box 51, folder 13.

**34.** "Niños puertorriqueños, según prueba mental, al nivel de sus condicípulos," *La Prensa*, Jan. 14, 1948, 3. See also, for instance, "A Puerto Rican Story," radio broadcast from WFUV-FM, Fordham University, transcript reprinted in *American Unity* 5 (Sept.–Oct. 1956): n.p., publication of the Council against Intolerance in America, Covello papers, series X, box 103, folder 16. This program featured Joseph Montserrat, then director of the Migration Division and a former student of Leonard Covello's at Benjamin Franklin High School.

**35.** Bureau of Applied Social Research, Columbia University, New York Area Chapter of the American Statistical Association, "Puerto Rican Population of New York City," address by Clarence Senior, chairman, Oct. 21, 1953. See also Senior, "Migration and Puerto Rico's Problem Population," *Annals of the American Academy of Political and Social Science* 285 (Jan. 1953): 130–36, and Senior, "Migration and Economic Development in Puerto Rico," *Journal of Educational Sociology* 28 (Dec. 1954): 151–56.

**36.** Department of Labor, Migration Division, "Attitudes toward Immigrants, Old and New: A Persistent Myth and a Recurrent Theme," pamphlet, n.d., Covello papers, series X, box 107, folder 26.

**37.** Spanish-American Youth Bureau, "Comments and Suggestions Offered by Mr. Ruperto Ruiz, President of the Bureau, Relative to the Objectives for Improvement of the Puerto Rican Problems, Proposed by Commissioner of Welfare of the City of New York for the Mayor's Committee on Puerto Rican Affairs," n.d. [1949?], Covello papers, series X, box 102, folder 13.

**38.** Colón, "Manifiesto—a los españoles, puertorriqueños, cubanos, mexicanos y demás hispanos ...," n.d. [1939?], Colón papers, series III, box 10, folder 1; Colón, "Notas sobre el negro en los EU," n.d. [1948?], Sociedad Fraternal Cervantes, International Workers' Order (IWO), Colón papers, series V, box 19, folder 16; and Colón, "The Growing Importance of the Puerto Rican Minority in N.Y.C.," n.d. [1955?], Colón papers, series III, box 10, folder 1.

**39.** "Joint Conf. Discusses Minority Group Problems," Dec. 20, 1952, 8; "Here Is Why Puerto Ricans Crowd Harlem!" June 3, 1950, 1; "Confab to Strengthen Puerto Rican Unity: Same Bias Snags Both Groups Say," Dec. 13, 1952, 36; "Judge Hits Bias against Puerto Ricans," Oct. 17, 1953, 5, *New York Amsterdam News*, Brooklyn Council for Social Planning (hereafter BCSP) papers, box 63, folder 8.1.114, "Puerto Ricans—Press Clippings."

**40.** See Michael Lapp, "The Rise and Fall of Puerto Rico as a Social Laboratory, 1945–1965," *Social Science History* 19 (Summer 1995): especially 177–88. See also Manuel Maldonado-Denis, *Puerto Rico: A Socio-Historic Interpretation* (New York: Random House, 1972), 309–12 and passim.

**41.** Vega, *Memoirs*, 229.

**42.** "Bosquejo preliminar de materias que serán incluidas en el Almanaque Puertorriqueño de Nueva York," 1947, Colón papers, series V, box 15, folder 2. Colón, "Factual Report," n.d., Colón papers, series VI, box 21, folder 9.

**43.** Meeting minutes, La Unidad Fraternal Hispana, IWO, Oct. 29, 1947, Colón papers, series V, box 17, folder 11; Pilar Pacheco, "De nuestros lectores," *La Prensa*, Aug. 25, 1947, 4. "Imponente manifestación de protesta pro–Puerto Rico," *La Prensa*, Nov. 1, 1947, 1. Press release, National Maritime Union of America, National Headquarters, Oct. [1947], Covello papers, series X, box 103, folder 23; Vega, *Memoirs*, 229–30.

**44.** Vega, *Memoirs*, 225.

**45.** "Joint Conf. Discusses Minority Group Problems: 100 Attend All Day Meet," *New York Amsterdam News*, Dec. 20, 1952, 8, BCSP papers, box 63, folder 8.1.114, "Puerto Ricans—Press Clippings." "Ethical Issues in the News: Our Puerto Rican Neighbors and Citizens," radio address by Algernon D. Black, president, Society for Ethical Culture, Station WMCA, Jan. 18, 1948, Covello papers, series X, box 103, folder 6; letter from Algernon Black to Leonard Covello, Jan. 18, 1948, Covello papers, series X, box 105, folder 20; New York City Mission Society, "Religion at Work in New York," Dec. 30, 1947, Vertical File, "Puerto Ricans, 1950s–60s," CHL.

**46.** Quoted in Gerald Meyer, "Marcantonio and El Barrio," *CENTRO Journal* 4 (Spring 1992): 66–87; the source is a flyer dated Sept. 15, 1941, in "District Organizations, 1942–44," Vito Marcantonio papers.

**47.** Vega, *Memoirs*, 206.

**48.** Hispanic Section of the IWO, "Hispanic American Section from 1940–1944," Colón papers, series V, box 18, folder 7.

**49.** Ibid. See also materials on the "Conferencia Pro Periódico Liberación," a project of the Club Obrero Español, as in an open letter from the club's secretary, Joaquín Palomino, regarding the *conferencia*, Mar. 1946, Colón papers, series II, box 3, folder 3.

**50.** George Sánchez, *Becoming Mexican American: Ethnicity, Culture, and Identity in Chicano Los Angeles, 1900–1945* (New York: Oxford University Press, 1995), 248–49.

**51.** Hispanic Section of the IWO, "Hispanic American Section." See other IWO documents that illustrate the IWO's extensive efforts in antifascist organizing, including "Antifascism at Home," which included the prohibition of literature that was "antisemitic, antiblack, or against any other race." Hispanic Section of the IWO, "Report of Conference," Nov. 14, 1943, Colón papers, series V, box 18, folder 5.

**52.** IWO, "Resolution on Puerto Rican Independence," n.d. [1944], Colón papers, series V, box 18, folder 7.

**53.** The IWO sought to collaborate, at least initially, with the island's wartime governor Rexford Tugwell and with Luis Muñoz Marín's increasingly popular Popular Democratic Party, which had not yet formally renounced the goal of independence: "We may not be in full agreement with [Tugwell's] ultimate views for the solution of the status for Puerto Rico. But that does not bar us from being with him a hundred present [sic] and with Muñoz Marín's Popular Democratic Party in their efforts to develop the industries in Puerto Rico and give the Puerto Ricans there a higher standard of living." Hispanic Section of the IWO, "Hispanic American Section from 1940–1944," Colón papers, series V, box 18, folder 7.

**54.** Federal Bureau of Investigation, "Statement of Jesus Colon," July 10, 1944, Colón papers, series II, box 2, folder 11; Jesús Colón, "There Is a Crisis among the Leadership of the Puerto Rican Democrats in Brooklyn," manuscript, n.d., Colón papers, series III, box 13, folder 4.

**55.** "Welfare, Reds, Puerto Ricans," *New York World-Telegram*, Oct. 22, 1947, n.p. "Our Worst Slum: Can We Save It from Going Red?" *American*, Sept. 1949, 30–31, 129–31, Covello papers, series X, box 103, folder 17.

**56.** "O'Dwyer dice que no hay 'problema puertorriqueño,'" *La Prensa*, Aug. 8, 1947, 1; "Entrevista entre Piñero y O'Dwyer," *La Prensa*, Aug. 11, 1947, 4.

**57.** See Michael Lapp, "Managing Migration: The Migration Division of Puerto Rico and Puerto Ricans in New York City, 1948–1968" (PhD diss., Johns Hopkins University, 1991), 49, 108.

**58.** "46 Named to Help City Puerto Ricans," *New York Times*, Sept. 17, 1949, 28.

**59.** "City Acts to Help Its Puerto Ricans," *New York Times*, Sept. 12, 1949, 23; "46 Named to Help City Puerto Ricans."

**60.** "Analysis of the Mayor's Committee on Puerto Rican Problems," n.d. [1949], Colón papers, series IV, box 14, folder 2; "Interim Report of the City of New York Mayor's Committee on Puerto Rican Affairs in New York City" (list of members), n.d. [1952?], Covello papers, series X, box 110, folder 15.

**61.** Vito Marcantonio, "Third Speech—Puerto Ricans," Sept. 21, 1949, 2, American Labor Party papers, box 11, "Labor for Marc Endorsements," Rutgers University Archives.

**62.** See "ALP Facts: Municipal Campaign 1949, Puerto-Ricans in New York City," Colón papers, series VIII, box 26, folder 2. "Tres candidatos puertorriqueños al concejo municipal de New York hoy," *La Prensa*, Nov. 8, 1949, 1.

**63.** On the interconnection of Puerto Rican and New York City politics during the 1949 mayoral race, see Lapp, "Managing Migration," 57, 109; and Gerald Meyer, *Vito Marcantonio: Radical Politician, 1902–1954* (Albany: State University of New York Press, 1989), 169. See also "Woman Mayor a Visitor," *New York Times*, Oct. 14, 1949, 29; "Bias Is Laid to O'Dwyer," *New York Times*, Oct. 23, 1949, 88; "Puerto Ricans to Back O'Dwyer, Woman Mayor of San Juan Says," *New York Times*, Oct. 27, 1949,

1; "Puerto Rico en la campaña electoral neoyorquina," *La Prensa*, Oct. 28, 1949, 4; "De la campaña electoral," *La Prensa*, Nov. 1, 1949, 2; "La alcaldesa de San Juan corresponde a la visita del alcalde de Nueva York," *La Prensa*, Nov. 4, 1949, 4. On Governor Luis Muñoz Marín's ideological position vis-à-vis the cold war, see Lapp, "Rise and Fall of Puerto Rico," 185.

**64.** On this era of media hype about welfare fraud, see Michael B. Katz and Lorrin R. Thomas, "The Invention of Welfare in America," *Journal of Policy History* 10 (1998): 406–9.

**65.** "Statement by the Honorable Raymond M. Hilliard, Welfare Commissioner of the City of New York[,] upon his Arrival in Puerto Rico," Aug. 21, 1950, Vertical File, "Puerto Ricans—Social Welfare," CHL; "City Acts to Help Its Puerto Ricans"; "Services Extended for Puerto Ricans," *New York Times*, Oct. 5, 1949, 43; "Logros del Comité Asesor del Alcalde sobre Asuntos Puertorriqueños," *La Prensa*, Nov. 1, 1949, 4.

**66.** "City Seeks U.S. Aid for Puerto Ricans," *New York Times*, Apr. 21, 1950, 25. "Heller pide para P.R. todos los beneficios de la ley de Seguro Social," *El Diario*, Nov. 5, 1950, 1.

**67.** "Puerto Ricans Win Praise as Citizens," *New York Times*, Feb. 17, 1952, 56; "Puerto Rican Will to Work Stressed," *New York Times*, Feb. 25, 1953, 18, from reprint, "Puerto Rico and the U.S., Three Articles from the *New York Times* by Peter Kihss," Vertical File, "Puerto Ricans, 1950s–60s," CHL.

**68.** "Excerpts from Report of Mayor's Committee on Puerto Rican Affairs in New York City," Feb. 26, 1953, Leonard Covello papers, series X, box 110, folder 15. "City Acts to Help Its Puerto Ricans."

**69.** "Puerto Rico," *Newsweek*, Feb. 20, 1950, Vertical File, "Puerto Ricans, 1950s–60s," CHL.

**70.** Public Law 600 replaced the Jones Act. Another crucial limitation on Puerto Ricans' freedom in writing their constitution was that the constitution stipulate neither statehood nor independence for the island. See James Dietz, *Economic History of Puerto Rico: Institutional Change and Capitalist Development* (Princeton, NJ: Princeton University Press, 1986), 235–38; and José Trías Monge, *Puerto Rico: The Trials of the Oldest Colony in the World* (New Haven, CT: Yale University Press, 1997), 107–18.

**71.** "Puerto Rican Progress," *Washington Post*, reprinted in "Puerto Rican Progress, extension of remarks of Hon. Antonio M. Fernandez [Democrat] of New Mexico," 81st Cong., 2nd sess., *Congressional Record* 96, appendix (July 11, 1950): A5038–39.

**72.** Quoted in Dietz, *Economic History of Puerto Rico*, 238, from Juan Angel Silén, *Historia de la nación puertorriqueña* (Río Piedras, PR: Edil, 1973), 327. On the rise and fall of "Operation Bootstrap," see Dietz, *Economic History of Puerto Rico*, 182–310.

**73.** Peter J. Fleiss, "Puerto Rico's Political Status under Its New Constitution," *Western Political Quarterly* 5 (Dec. 1952): 635, 639. Fleiss quotes *Senate Report* no. 1779, 81st Cong., 2nd sess., June 6, 1950.

**74.** "Mueren 40 personas en la sangrienta revolución . . . ," *El Diario*, Oct. 31, 1950, 1–2, 4. "Denuncia la participación de los comunistas," *El Diario*, Oct. 31, 1950, 1–2, 8.

**75.** One *New York Times* editorial referred to the would-be assassins as "the crackpot, the revolutionary, or the disgruntled"; another grouped them with "the fanatic, the zealot, and the insane." "The President Spared," *New York Times*, Nov. 2, 1950, 30; Arthur Krock, "The Tragedy in Pennsylvania Avenue," *New York Times*, Nov. 2, 1950, 30. "Dos nacionalistas fallen en un desesperado intento de asesinar a Truman," *El Diario*, Nov. 2, 1950, 1, 2.

**76.** "Acontecimientos de P.R. convueven a la líder boricua liberal de N. York," *El Diario*, Nov. 2, 1950, 2; "Comité del alcalde expresa el sentir de puertorriqueños," *El Diario*, Nov. 3, 1950, 1; "Puerto Rico de duelo," *El Diario*, Nov. 3, 1950, 4.

**77.** Feb. 10, 1951, address by Harris L. Present, delivered at the third annual convention of Puerto Rican and Spanish-speaking organizations of New York City, Covello papers, series X, box 102, folder 13.

**78.** "Se cree en Washington que el atentado contra el presidente puede repercutir en el continente; Temor es que influya en elecciones de Guatemala," *El Diario*, Nov. 3, 1950, 3; ". . . La policía y el FBI creen tener evidencia que conecta a líderes rojos con la revolución . . . ," *El Diario*, Nov. 4, 1950, 1. The *New York Times* did not report on the student demonstration, although it did cover the more general question of Cuban support for the Puerto Rican Nationalists. See "Cuba Denies Drop in Amity for U.S.," Nov. 4, 1950, 6, and "U.S. Acts in Revolt, Seizes 4 on Island," Nov. 4, 1950, 6.

**79.** "Conclusions of the Conference on Migration," San Juan, Mar. 1–7 , 1953, 2, 12, Covello papers, series X, box 110, folder 10. See also Jorge Duany, *Puerto Rican Nation on the Move: Identities on the Island and in the United States* (Chapel Hill: University of North Carolina Press, 2002), 168–78.

**80.** "What the City Does Right," *New York Post*, July 29, 1953, n.p.; "Many Local Units Aid Puerto Ricans," *New York Times*, May 21, 1954, 24. "Fiesta Planned by Casita Maria," *New York Times*, Nov. 16, 1954, 33; "Puerto Rican Will to Work Stressed," 18; "N.Y. Puerto Ricans: The Search for a Job, 'A Place of My Own,'" *New York Herald-Tribune* [1957?], n.p., Vertical File, "Puerto Ricans, 1950s–60s," CHL.

**81.** "School Life Hard for Puerto Ricans," *New York Herald-Tribune*, Mar. 4, 1954, n.p., BCSP papers, box 63, folder 8.1.114, "Puerto Ricans—Press Clippings"; "N.Y. Puerto Ricans: A Cold New World," *New York Herald-Tribune*, Oct. 16, 1954, n.p., Vertical File, "Puerto Ricans, 1950s–60s," CHL.

**82.** See, for instance, Gertrude Samuels, "Two Case Histories out of Puerto Rico," *New York Times Magazine*, Jan. 22, 1954, 26–27, 57–60; and Robert Williams, "The Puerto Ricans in New York," *New York Post*, July 30, 1953, 14. Sidney Mirkin, "Some Puerto Ricans Feel Political Oats," *Daily News*, Jan. 7, 1955, 34.

**83.** United Parents Association, "Understanding Our New Neighbors: A Report of Goodwill Workshops, 1953–54," BCSP papers, box 63, folder 8.1.115.

**84.** Herbert Sternau, "Puerto Rico and the Puerto Ricans," pamphlet, Feb. 1958, Vertical File, "N.Y.C. Puerto Ricans," CHL, emphasis in original. Babby Quintero, "En Nueva York . . . del ambiente hispano," *La Prensa*, Nov. 13, 1951, 3.

**85.** Henry Miller, "New York City's Puerto Rican Pupils: A Problem of Acculturation," *School and Society* 76 (Aug. 30, 1952): 129–32, reprint, Covello papers, series X, box 103, folder 6; New York City Board of Education, "What Schools Are Doing for Puerto Rican Children," *Curriculum and Materials* 8 (May–June 1954): 12–13, Covello papers, series X, box 103, folder 6.

**86.** Robert Williams, "The City Fathers Love the Puerto Ricans—at the Polls," *New York Post*, July 31, 1953, n.p., Vertical File, "Puerto Ricans—Social Welfare," CHL; Mirkin, "Some Puerto Ricans"; "New York's Puerto Ricans: Their Position Is Improving," *New York Herald-Tribune*, Oct. 21, 1957, n.p., Vertical File, "N.Y.C.— National and Racial Groups," CHL.

**87.** "Survey of Spanish Market for *El Diario* Potential Advertisers," n.d. [1955], Vertical File, "Puerto Ricans—Surveys," CHL. *El Diario de Nueva York* was the main competitor of *La Prensa* until 1963, when its owner bought *La Prensa* and merged the two newspapers. See Nicolás Kanellos with Helvetia Martell, *Hispanic Periodicals in the United States, Origins to 1960: A Brief History and Comprehensive Bibliography* (Houston: Arte Público Press, 2000), 58–60.

**88.** "Puerto Rican Workers Performing Efficiently . . . in Mainland U.S. Plants," *America Continental*, Spring 1956, 54–55, Vertical File, "Puerto Ricans, 1950s–60s," CHL.

**89.** See Carmen Teresa Whalen, "Contested Citizenship: Puerto Ricans and the Question of Rights in the Post–World War II Era" (paper presented at the Latin American Studies Association XXII International Congress, Miami, Mar. 16–18, 2000).

**90.** Anonymous to Leonard Covello, n.d. [1952], Covello papers, series X, box 103, folder 23.

**91.** E. Virginia Massimine, *Challenges of a Changing Population: A Study of the Integration of Puerto Ricans in a West Side Community in Manhattan* (New York: Center for Human Relations Studies, New York University, 1954), 22.

**92.** Department of Church Planning and Research of the Protestant Council of the City of New York, "Midcentury Pioneers and Protestants: A Survey Report of the Puerto Rican Migration to the U.S. Mainland and in Particular a Study of the Protestant Expression among Puerto Ricans of New York City," Mar. 1, 1954, BCSP papers, box 63, folder 8.1.115. See also "New York's Puerto Ricans: Official Sweet-Talk Ignores Official Inaction," *New York Post*, July 22, 1953, 56.

**93.** Lapp, "Managing Migration," 136. In 1950, Mayor O'Dwyer had been appointed ambassador to Mexico, and his deputy Vincent Impellitieri became mayor for the remainder of O'Dwyer's term.

**94.** "Problems of Minority Groups," letter to the editor by Harris L. Present, *New York Times*, Dec. 29, 1955, 22.

**95.** "Madness in Washington," *New York Times*, Mar. 2, 1954, 24.

**96.** This was how Puerto Rican governor Rexford Tugwell (1941–46), a Roosevelt appointee and a member of his "brain trust," described the island's relationship to the United States in a recollection about how he and President Roosevelt viewed the role of Puerto Rico during World War II. Rexford Guy Tugwell, *The Art of Politics* (New York: Doubleday, 1958), 148. On the fears of PPD officials about

Nationalists' ties to other revolutionary movements in Latin America, see, for instance, "Se cree in Washington."

**97.** "Luisa Quintero defiende a Babby del cargo de 'antipuertorriqueño,'" *El Diario*, Nov. 5, 1957, 7; "'Fraternidad Colón' dice es 'divisionista' desfile puertorriqueño," *El Diario*, Nov. 6, 1957, 12; Vicente Hernández, "Tenemos derecho," letter to the editor, *El Diario*, Nov. 10, 1957, 13.

**98.** Alberto Sándoval-Sanchez, *José, Can You See? Latinos On and Off Broadway* (Madison: University of Wisconsin Press, 1999), 66.

**99.** Roberto Márquez, "One Boricua's Baldwin: A Personal Remembrance," *American Quarterly* 42 (Sept. 1990): 465.

**100.** See Sandoval-Sánchez, "*West Side Story*: A Puerto Rican Reading of 'America,'" in *Latin Looks: Images of Latinas and Latinos in the U. S. Media*, edited by Clara Rodríguez (Boulder, CO: Westview Press, 1997), 174–75. See also Ramón Grosfoguel with Chloe Georas, "'Coloniality of Power' and Racial Dynamics," in *Colonial Subjects: Puerto Ricans in a Global Perspective*, edited by Ramón Grosfoguel (Berkeley: University of California Press, 2003), 164–65. Christopher Rand, *The Puerto Ricans* (New York: Oxford University Press, 1958), 29.

**101.** Sandoval-Sánchez, "*West Side Story*," 169–70.

**102.** See Grosfoguel with Georas, "'Coloniality of Power,'" 43–60; César Ayala and Rafael Bernabe, *Puerto Rico in the American Century: A History since 1898* (Chapel Hill: University of North Carolina Press, 2007), 95–116; and, generally, Dietz, *Economic History of Puerto Rico.*

**103.** Gervasio Luis García, "I Am the Other: Puerto Rico in the Eyes of North Americans, 1898," *Journal of American History* 87 (June 2000): 55.

**104.** Dan Wakefield, *Island in the City* (Boston: Houghton Mifflin Company, 1959), 213.

### Chapter Five

**1.** Christopher Rand, *The Puerto Ricans* (New York: Oxford University Press, 1958), 151.

**2.** This is Michael Lapp's phrase. See Lapp, "Managing Migration: The Migration Division of Puerto Rico and Puerto Ricans in New York City, 1948–1968" (PhD diss., Johns Hopkins University, 1991), 49, 108.

**3.** Joseph Montserrat, interview with the author, Sept. 13, 2000; Ralph Ellison, *Invisible Man* (New York: Vintage International, 1995), introduction to 1981 edition, xv.

**4.** Luis Muñoz Marín, "Development through Democracy," *Annals of the American Academy of Social and Political Science* 285 (Jan. 1953): 3.

**5.** Michael Lapp, "The Rise and Fall of Puerto Rico as a Social Laboratory, 1945–1965," *Social Science History* 19 (Summer 1995): 185. See also Pedro Malavet, *America's Colony: The Political and Cultural Conflict between the United States and Puerto Rico* (New York: New York University Press, 2004), 68–72; and Jorge Duany, *Puerto Rican Nation on the Move: Identities on the Island and in the United States* (Chapel Hill: University of North Carolina Press, 2002), 122–36.

**6.** Charles Goodsell, *Administration of a Revolution: Executive Reform in Puerto Rico under Governor Tugwell, 1941–1946* (Cambridge, MA: Harvard University Press, 1965), 154. In 1945, Congress called it "the most expensive planning board under the American flag" and "supergovernment in Puerto Rico." Subcommittee of the Committee on Insular Affairs, "Report on the Investigation of Political, Economic, and Social Conditions in Puerto Rico," 79th Cong., 1st sess., *Congressional Record* 91 (May 1, 1945): 27.

**7.** Rexford Guy Tugwell, *The Stricken Land: The Story of Puerto Rico* (New York: Doubleday, 1947), 37.

**8.** Lapp, "Rise and Fall," 178, citing Arcadio Díaz Quiñones, "Tomás Blanco: La reinvención de la tradición," *Boletín del Centro de Investigaciones Históricas* 4 (1988–89): 173–74.

**9.** This is Angel Quintero Rivera's term, from "La ideología populista y la institucionalización universitaria de las ciencias sociales" (presentation at Encuentro de Historiadores de Puerto Rico conference, University of Puerto Rico, Feb. 15–16, 1990), quoted in Lapp, "Rise and Fall," 177–85.

**10.** President Roosevelt noted in a message to Congress in 1943 that Puerto Rico's population had grown from 950,000 (in 1898, presumably) to about 2,000,000, "making this one of the most densely inhabited areas on earth." He argued that birth control ought to be tried. "Government for Puerto Rico—Amendment to Organic Act," 78th Cong., 1st sess., *Congressional Record* 89, part 6 (Sept. 28, 1943): 7842. Tugwell disagreed; see Tugwell, *Stricken Land*, 35. On the history of population control and sterilization in Puerto Rico, see Annette Ramírez de Arellano and Conrad Seipp, *Colonialism, Catholicism, and Contraception: A History of Birth Control in Puerto Rico* (Chapel Hill: University of North Carolina Press, 1983); César Ayala and Rafael Bernabe, *Puerto Rico in the American Century: A History since 1898* (Chapel Hill: University of North Carolina Press, 2007), 207–8; and, generally, Laura Briggs, *Reproducing Empire: Race, Sex, Science and U.S. Imperialism in Puerto Rico* (Berkeley: University of California Press, 2002).

**11.** Clarence Senior, "Migration and Puerto Rico's Population Problem," *Annals of the American Academy of Social and Political Science* 285 (Jan. 1953): 130.

**12.** James Gregory, *The Southern Diaspora: How the Great Migrations of Black and White Southerners Transformed America* (Chapel Hill: University of North Carolina Press, 2005). "Urban 'adjustment' was the main issue of interest behind this research," p. 66, writes Gregory.

**13.** See Lapp, "Managing Migration," 49, 108.

**14.** Senior, "Migration and Puerto Rico's Population Problem," 135. See Lapp, "Rise and Fall," 181; and, generally, Duany, *Puerto Rican Nation on the Move*, 168–78.

**15.** Leonard Covello, notes on Raymond Hilliard's 1949 report on "The Puerto Rican Problem . . . ," n.d., Covello papers, series X, box 110, folder 1.

**16.** Senior, "Migration and Puerto Rico's Population Problem," 135. For a later perspective on this debate, see Clifford Hauberg, *Puerto Rico and the Puerto Ricans* (New York: Twayne Publishers, 1970), 131.

**17.** "Analysis of the Mayor's Committee on Puerto Rican Problems," n.d. [1949],

Colón papers, series IV, box 14, folder 2; for a discussion of this issue, see chapter 4, p. 000.

**18.** Erasmo Vando, "Carta abierta a Don Luis Muñoz Marín, president of the Senate of Puerto Rico," n.d. [1948], Vando papers, series III, box 2, folder 4.

**19.** "Man of the People," *Time*, May 2, 1949, 33–36; "The Bard of Bootstrap," *Time*, June 23, 1958, 30–38; see also Goodsell, *Administration of a Revolution*, 177–79, and, more generally, James Dietz, *Economic History of Puerto Rico: Institutional Change and Capitalist Development* (Princeton, NJ: Princeton University Press, 1986), chapter 5, "Growth and Misdevelopment," 240–310.

**20.** See Peter Novick, *That Noble Dream: The "Objectivity Question" and the American Historical Profession* (New York: Cambridge University Press, 1988), 281–319, 377–411.

**21.** "Columbia Accepts Puerto Rico Study," *New York Times*, Aug. 10, 1947, 54.

**22.** Ruperto Ruiz, "Reply to Governor of Puerto Rico, Jesús T. Piñero's Denial of Certain Existing Facts about the Needs of Puerto Ricans in New York City," Aug. 21, 1947, Covello papers, series VIII, box 73, folder 8.

**23.** Lawrence Chenault, *The Puerto Rican Migrant in New York City* (New York: Columbia University Press, 1938), 153.

**24.** C. Wright Mills, Clarence Senior, and Rose Kohn Goldsen, *The Puerto Rican Journey: New York's Newest Migrants* (New York: Harper and Brothers Publishers, 1950), 7, 15.

**25.** Ibid., vii.

**26.** Advertisement for *The Puerto Rican Journey*, by C. Wright Mills, Clarence Senior, and Rose Kohn Goldsen, *New York Times*, Nov. 3, 1950, 25.

**27.** Mills, Senior, and Goldsen, *Puerto Rican Journey*, 61, 94, 145. "La Univ. Columbia presenta su informe puertorriqueño," *La Prensa*, June 16, 1948, 1; "Texto del informe de la U. de Columbia sobre los puertorriqueños en New York," *La Prensa*, June 17–23, 1948; "Universidad de Columbia anula prejuicio," *El Boricua*, June 23, 1948, 1.

**28.** John Murra, review of *The Puerto Rican Journey*, *Hispanic American Historical Review* 31 (Nov. 1951): 680–81.

**29.** For a description of the terms used to describe race, see *Sixteenth Census of the United States, 1940, Puerto Rico, Population* (Washington, DC: U.S. Government Printing Office, 1943), 2.

**30.** Mills, Senior, and Goldsen, *Puerto Rican Journey*, 217; "La Univ. Columbia presenta."

**31.** Ira D. Reid, review of *The Puerto Rican Journey*, in *American Sociological Review* 15 (Dec. 1950): 820–21. See also, for example, Carey McWilliams, *Brothers under the Skin* (New York: Little, Brown, 1943), 216.

**32.** Irving L. Horowitz, "In Memoriam: The Sociological Imagination of C. Wright Mills," *American Journal of Sociology* 68, no. 1 (July 1962): 105–7. C. Wright Mills, *Listen, Yankee! The Revolution in Cuba* (New York: Ballantine Books, 1960); C. Wright Mills, *The Marxists* (New York: Dell, 1962).

**33.** Millard Hansen, "Training and Research in Puerto Rico," *Annals of the American Academy of Social and Political Science* 285 (Jan. 1953): 110.

**34.** "Conclusions of the Conference on Migration Held in San Juan, Puerto Rico, Mar. 1–7, 1953," Covello papers, series X, box 110, folder 10.

**35.** "Felisa, alcaldesa extraordinaria," *El Diario*, Dec. 4, 1955, D4.

**36.** Peter Kihss, "Puerto Rico Avoids New York Politics," *New York Times*, Mar. 9, 1953, 31; and Blaine Littell, "Puerto Ricans Want No Part of City Politics," *New York Herald Tribune*, Mar. 9, 1953, and Raymond Hilliard, chairman, Mayor's Committee on Puerto Rican Affairs, to Blaine Littell, *Herald Tribune*, Mar. 9, 1953, clippings, Brooklyn Council for Social Planning (hereafter BCSP) papers, box 63, folder 8.1.115.

**37.** For this analysis of the relationships linking liberals, social scientists, and Migration Division officials, I am greatly indebted to the work of historian Michael Lapp, "The Rise and Fall of Puerto Rico as a Social Laboratory, 1945–1965," *Social Science History* 19 (Summer 1995): 169–99. John H. Lewis, director of staff and community relations, "We Went to Puerto Rico," *The Welfarer*, Oct. 1953, 12, Covello papers, series X, box 105, folder 9.

**38.** Joseph Montserrat, interview with the author, Sept. 13, 2000. See also Andrés Torres, *Between Melting Pot and Mosaic* (Philadelphia: Temple University Press, 1995), 73, who cites James Jennings, *Puerto Rican Politics in New York City* (Lanham, MD: University Press of America, 1977), 76.

**39.** Board of Education of New York City, "The Puerto Rican Study, 1953–57" (New York: 1958), 2; Emilio Guerra, "The Orientation of Puerto Rican Students in New York City," *Modern Language Journal* 32 (Oct. 1948): 415–20.

**40.** Committee of the Association of Assistant Superintendents, "A Program of Education for Puerto Ricans in New York City," 1947, reprinted in *Bilingual Education in New York City: A Compendium of Reports*, edited by Francesco Cordasco (New York: Arno Press, 1978), 24.

**41.** Raymond Hilliard, commissioner of welfare, "The 'Puerto Rican Problem' of the City of New York Department of Welfare," report submitted to Mayor O'Dwyer, Sept. 6, 1949, Covello papers, series X, box 111, folder 1.

**42.** See Chenault, *Puerto Rican Migrant*, 85. WPA Federal Writers' Project, "Interview with Dr. Samuel Joseph of CCNY on Puerto Rican Survey," May 1936, and "Files of the Porto Rican Community Committee," June 19, 1936, Spanish Book, WPA files, reel 269, folder 9. The WPA field-workers who interviewed Joseph noted that, "according to Professor Joseph, the Puerto Ricans in the U.S. and especially New York are the least known of all the foreign groups in the country and yet from a sociological point of view [are] the most interesting."

**43.** Welfare Council of New York City, "Report of the Committee on Puerto Ricans in New York City," 1948; "Estudian ayuda a puertorriqueños en Nueva York," *La Prensa*, Jan. 13, 1947, 2.

**44.** "Interesante y nuevo informe sobre migración de Pto. Rico," *La Prensa*, Feb. 13, 1948, 2; "Migrant Aid Asked for Puerto Ricans," *New York Times*, Feb. 13, 1948, 23.

**45.** Jesse Dossick, "Fifth Workshop—Field Study in Puerto Rican Education and Culture," *Journal of Educational Sociology* 26 (Dec.1952): 177–86, Covello papers, series X, box 113, folder 2.

**46.** Ibid., 181–83.

**47.** "Children from Puerto Rico," special issue of *Curriculum and Materials* 8 (May–June 1954), Covello papers, series X, box 103, folder 6.

**48.** Irving Lorge and Frank Mayans, "Vestibule vs. Regular Classes for Puerto Rican Migrant Pupils," *Teachers College Record* 55 (Feb. 1954): 1; Mary Finocchario, "Puerto Rican Newcomers," *High Points*, June 1951, 1; Harold Fields, "Puerto Rico Trains a Willing People," *High Points*, Apr. 1958, 2. For an interesting discussion of the larger impact of the Board of Education's research on Puerto Rican students, see Madeleine López, "Investigating the Investigators: An Analysis of the Puerto Rican Study," *Centro Journal* 29 (2007): 60–85.

**49.** Boys' Athletic League, "One in Twenty: The Facts about the Puerto Ricans among Us—and What the Boys' Athletic League Is Doing about It," 1950, Vertical File, "Puerto Ricans, 1950s–60s," City Hall Library (hereafter CHL); Brooklyn Council for Social Planning, "Workshop Conference on Puerto Ricans," 1953, BCSP papers, box 66, folder 9.1.033; Department of Church Planning and Research of the Protestant Council of the City of New York, "Midcentury Pioneers and Protestants: A Survey Report of the Puerto Rican Migration to the U.S. Mainland . . . ," Mar. 1, 1954, BCSP papers, box 63, folder 8.1.115.

**50.** Casita María remains a vibrant Puerto Rican organization in New York.

**51.** Brooklyn Council for Social Planning, "Report on Survey of Brooklyn Agencies Rendering Services to Puerto Ricans," n.d. [1953], BCSP papers, box 66, folder 8.1.115; Jesús Colón, "Some Ideas about Concentration Work among the Puerto Ricans in Brooklyn," n.d. [1960?], Colón papers, series III, box 10, folder 1.

**52.** Spanish-American Youth Bureau, "Summary Statement of Aims and Purposes," n.d., BCSP papers, box 63, folder 8.1.109; Spanish-American Youth Bureau, "Program—Sixth Annual Convention," Feb. 6, 1954, BCSP papers, box 63, folder 8.1.109. Ruperto Ruiz, "Reply to Governor of Puerto Rico, Jesús T. Piñero's Denial of Certain Existing Facts about the Needs of Puerto Ricans in New York City," Aug. 21, 1947, Covello papers, series VIII, box 73, folder 8.

**53.** Graduate School of Public Administration and Social Service, New York University, *The Impact of Puerto Rican Migration on Governmental Services in New York City* (New York: New York University Press, 1957), 63 and passim.

**54.** "City Fathers Love Puerto Ricans at the Polls," *New York Post*, July 31, 1953, n.p.

**55.** Dan Wakefield, *Island in the City* (Boston: Houghton Mifflin, 1959), 265; Rev. Rubén Dario Colón et al., "Press Release," July 27, 1953, Colón papers, series VI, box 21, folder 9.

**56.** "Results of Balloting for Governor, Other State Offices," *New York Times*, Nov. 3, 1954, 18. Luis Hernández, candidate for New York State Assembly, Fourteenth Assembly District, Brooklyn, to "Dear Puerto Rican," Sept. 29, 1952, Colón papers, series IV, box 14, folder 1. This tone in the campaigns of Puerto Rican candidates was very common throughout the fifties. See, for example, "Promete luchar por el derecho de los boricuas," *El Diario*, Dec. 5, 1955, 3.

**57.** ALP, "Meet Two of Your Neighbors [Jesús Colón and José Giboyeaux for City Council on the American Labor Party ticket]," pamphlet, 1953, Colón papers, series IV, box 14, folder 1; Jesús Colón, "Some Independent Forms of Activity and

Mounting Pressure on the Democratic Party for Political Representation," section in "The Growing Importance of the Puerto Rican Minority in New York City," unpublished manuscript, n.d. [1956], Colón papers, series III, box 10, folder 1.

**58.** Council of Spanish-American Organizations, Fourth Annual Meeting, Apr. 14, 1956, Covello papers, series X, box 105, folder 3; Colón, "Growing Puerto Rican Minority."

**59.** Wakefield, *Island in the City*, 274.

**60.** A 1957 *Herald Tribune* article said that Puerto Ricans' registration campaigns that year had yielded eighty-five thousand voters. "New York Puerto Ricans: Their Position Is Improving," *Herald Tribune*, Oct. 21, 1957, Vertical File, "Puerto Ricans, 1950s–60s," CHL; Joseph P. Fitzpatrick, *Puerto Rican Americans: The Meaning of Migration to the Mainland* (Englewood Cliffs, NJ: Prentice-Hall, 1971), 57.

**61.** Colón, "Growing Importance of the Puerto Rican Minority." See various other statements by Puerto Rican candidates: "Nuestros candidatos," *Vida Hispana*, Nov. 2, 1952, 2; "Meet Two of Your Neighbors."

**62.** Colón, "Growing Importance of the Puerto Rican Minority"; "Acusa a 'políticos sordos' el desamparo boricuas NY" and "Felisa Rincón aconseja unidad a los boricuas," *El Diario*, Sept. 27, 1957, 4; "Unificación boricua," *El Diario*, Oct. 4, 1957, 15.

**63.** Dossick, "Fifth Workshop," 181–83; "Conference on the Problems of Negroes and Puerto Ricans in New York State," sponsored by the Urban League; Puerto Rican Department of Labor, Migration Division; NAACP; and Council of Spanish-American Organizations, Dec. 13, 1952, Covello papers, series X, box 105, folder 3; "Urban League Sets Visit to Puerto Rico," *New York Amsterdam News*, Sept. 18, 1954, 32.

**64.** Harlem Affairs Committee, "Can Negroes and Puerto-Ricans Unite for Mutual Progress?" n.d. [1954], Colón papers, series VI, box 21, folder 3; transcript, Jesús Colón speech, WABD-TV, Oct. 20, 1954, Colón papers, series IV, box 21, folder 1; speech by New York State assemblyman Felipe Torres (Bronx, Fourth Assembly District), Jan. 24, 1954, Colón papers, series VI, box 21, folder 6; Robert W. Justice, Harlem Affairs Committee, to "Dear Friend," Jan. 14, 1954, Colón papers series VI, box 21, folder 7; Jesús Colón, "As I See It from Here: Little Rock," *Daily Worker*, Oct. 8, 1957, Colón papers, series III, box 9, folder 10; Dolores Rodríguez, "The Special Election in the 14th A.D.: The Struggle for Puerto Rican Representation and for Negro–Puerto Rican Unity," [Communist] *Party Voice*, Colón papers, series VIII, box 26, folder 5; Jesús Colón, "A Letter to Paul Robeson," Apr. 12, 1955, p. 4, Colón papers, series II, box 4, folder 4.

**65.** "On Negro–Puerto Rican Political Unity," n.d. [1957?], Colón papers, series III, box 9, folder 14.

**66.** Herbert Hill, "Guardians of the Sweatshops," in *Puerto Rico and the Puerto Ricans: Studies in History and Society*, edited by Adalberto López and James Petras (New York: John Wiley and Sons, 1974), originally published in *New Politics*, 394–400.

**67.** There was some disagreement about when the committee for Puerto Ricans was established within the AFL-CIO; reported dates range from 1952 to 1955. Clarence Senior, *The Puerto Ricans: Strangers—Then Neighbors* (Chicago: Quadrangle

Books, 1961), 67–68; Colón, "Some Independent Forms of Activity"; Dan Wakefield, "The Vulnerable Stranger," *The Nation*, Apr. 13, 1957, 315–22; and Wakefield, *Island in the City*, 205–6. The *New York Times* and *La Prensa* reported in 1950 that the Migration Division had begun pressuring the AFL-CIO to examine the exploitation of the tens of thousands of Puerto Rican workers in New York; see "Unions Plan Help to Puerto Ricans," *New York Times*, Mar. 24, 1950, 27, and "Cooperan en la solución de los casos boricuas," *La Prensa*, Mar. 25, 1950, 2.

**68.** Colón, "Growing Importance of the Puerto Rican Minority"; Rand, *Puerto Ricans*, 143.

**69.** Hill, "Guardians," 388.

**70.** "Uniones obreras apoyan candidatura de Lumen Román," *El Diario*, Nov. 2, 1957, 4.

**71.** "Montserrat dice José M. Pérez usaba 'fraudulentamente' papel con el membrete de la oficina de Puerto Rico," *El Diario*, Oct. 9, 1957, 2. "Trabajadores boricuas en N.Y. aún están en garras de 'uniones fantasmas,'" *El Diario*, Nov. 7, 1957, 14.

**72.** "Obreros unen sus fuerzas contra unión 'fantasma,'" *El Diario*, Oct. 7, 1957, 4; "Líder obrero renuncia al no poder acabar con explotación de boricuas," *El Diario*, Oct. 9, 1957, 5.

**73.** Senior, *Puerto Ricans*, 101; Wakefield, *Island in the City*, 203; Hill, "Guardians," 392.

**74.** Senior, *Puerto Ricans*, 68–69.

**75.** Hill, "Guardians," 394. Hill makes an important point that there is an even more bleak reality hidden by the "average" wage noted in the study he cites, since that figure was calculated based on a range of hourly wages that included the relatively highly paid cutters ($4.00 per hour compared to the average wage of $2.40 per hour), who were nearly all white.

**76.** Presentation by Joseph Montserrat at Institute of the Welfare Council, Chicago, on changes in patriarchal family structure, Oct. 17, 1957, Covello papers, series X, box 109, folder 20.

**77.** Torres, *Between Melting Pot and Mosaic*, 69–70.

**78.** "1,400 City Police Shifted to Fight on Youth Crimes," *New York Times*, Sept. 1, 1959, 1. The Capeman murder was the second gang-related homicide incident of the week and one of fifty-one incidents of murder and non-negligent homicide in the first seven months of the year.

**79.** See, for instance, "Investigan relaciones de 'Drácula' con dos vendedores de narcótico" and "Combaten demoliciones en oeste de Manhattan," *El Diario*, Sept. 6, 1959, 4.

**80.** Harlem Legislative Conference report, Sept. 25, 1939, Marcantonio papers, series III, "Subjects: Harlem Legislative Conference" folder.

**81.** Wakefield, *Island in the City*, 232.

**82.** Quoted in Wakefield, *Island in the City*, 232, 236.

**83.** New York City Board of Education, "Strengthening Democracy," Mar. 1956, "A Program of Housing Education and Citizenship," vol. 8, no. 4.

**84.** Rand, *Puerto Ricans*, 104; "Piden se asigne porcentaje a cada grupo racial en viviendas públicas," *El Diario*, Oct. 7, 1957, 4.

**85.** "Altos alquileres hacen que gente se vaya de N.Y.," *El Diario*, Oct. 3, 1957, 14.

**86.** "Combaten demoliciones en oeste de Manhattan," *El Diario*, Sept. 6, 1959, 4.

**87.** Richard Perlman, *Delinquency Prevention: The Size of the Problem* (Washington, DC: U.S. Government Printing Office, 1960), 3. Children's Bureau of the U.S. Department of Health, Education, and Welfare, *The Children's Bureau and Juvenile Delinquency: A Chronology of What the Bureau Is Doing and Has Done in This Field* (Washington, DC: U.S. Government Printing Office, 1960), 32.

**88.** Erwin Schepses, "Puerto Rican Delinquent Boys in New York City," *Social Science Review* 23 (Mar. 1949): 51–61.

**89.** One difficulty in determining the real scope of delinquency among Puerto Ricans arose from the lack of an accurate census count of migrants; on this point, see Sophia Robinson, *Can Delinquency Be Measured?* (New York: Columbia University Press, 1936), cited in Lawrence Chenault, *Puerto Rican Migrant*, 131.

**90.** J. Cayce Morrison, *The Puerto Rican Study, 1953–57* (New York: Board of Education, 1958), 120–21. Clarence Senior, "The Newcomer Speaks Out: What Puerto Ricans Want and Need from Voluntary Agencies and the Public," National Conference on Social Welfare, June 1960, Covello papers, series X, box 103, folder 2. "Puerto Rican Unit Reports Lag Here," *New York Times*, Feb. 7, 1954, 60; Spanish-American Youth Bureau Conference Program, "Topic: Youth of Hispanic Origin and Delinquency," Feb. 26, 1955, and Spanish-American Youth Bureau Conference Program, "Topic: Community Efforts in Combating the Development of Juvenile Delinquency among Puerto Rican and Hispanic Youth," Feb. 25, 1956, Covello papers, series X, box 102, folder 13. Presentation by Joseph Montserrat at Institute of the Welfare Council, Chicago, on changes in patriarchal family structure, Oct. 17, 1957, Covello papers, series X, box 109, folder 20; "Muñoz niega juventud boricua sea culpable de crímenes y violencia," *El Diario*, Oct. 8, 1957, 2.

**91.** "Víctimas de pandillas juveniles simbolizan fracaso de comunidad," *El Diario*, Aug. 30, 1959, 3; "Juventud sigue bañando en lágrimas los rostros y corazones de madres," and "Pandilleros juveniles viven en un mundo aparte y hasta tienen su propio lenguaje," *El Diario*, Sept. 1, 1959, 9; "'Ganga' dice: Queremos ser buenos, pero nadie nos ayuda y todos nos persiguen," *El Diario*, Sept. 2, 1959, 5.

**92.** "Puerto Rican Community Takes Initiative to Combat Juvenile Delinquency in New York," press release by the Public Relations Committee of the Council of Puerto Rican and Spanish-American Organizations of Greater New York, Sept. 8, 1959, Covello papers, series X, box 106, folder 4.

**93.** "Civic Contribution by Puerto Ricans," *New York Herald-Tribune*, Sept. 8, 1959; "Responsible Action," *New York World-Telegram and Sun*, Sept. 11, 1959; and "Ethnology and Crime," *Washington Post and Times Herald*, Sept. 11, 1959, all reprinted by the Migration Division under the heading "Three Editorials on Delinquency," Covello papers, series X, box 106, folder 4. Senior, "The Newcomer Speaks Out," National Conference on Social Welfare, June 1960, p. 14, Covello papers, series X, box 103, folder 2.

**94.** Elisamuel Arroyo (S. Third Street, Brooklyn), "Manifestaciones le han sorprendido," "La opinión del lector," *El Diario*, Oct. 2, 1957, 13. Another example of the pairing of welfare dependency and juvenile crime is "From San Juan to Hell's Kitchen," *The Sign*, National Catholic Magazine, Nov. 1959, reprint, Covello papers, series X, box 103, folder 7.

**95.** "Officials Dispute Coddling Charge," *New York Times*, Sept. 5, 1959, 36; Eric Schneider, *Vampires, Dragons, and Egyptian Kings: Youth Gangs in Postwar New York* (Princeton, NJ: Princeton University Press, 1999), 188–97 and passim.

**96.** "Liebowitz Sued on Jury's Inquiry: Illegal Directive on Puerto Rican Migration Laid to Judge—Writ Is Sought," *New York Times*, Nov. 6, 1959, 19.

**97.** Rev. Joseph Fitzpatrick, "Delinquency and the Puerto Ricans," lecture, Oct. 8, 1959 (and delivered again in 1966), Covello papers, series X, box 106, folder 4.

**98.** Joseph Montserrat, "Statement for the Record of the U.S. Senate Subcommittee to Investigate Juvenile Delinquency," Sept. 25, 1959, Covello papers, series X, box 106, folder 4.

**99.** An earlier version of Senior's *"Strangers—Then Neighbors"* book was published as a pamphlet by Freedom Pamphlets in New York City [1952].

**100.** Dietz, *Economic History of Puerto Rico*, 238.

**101.** Michel Foucault, *Discipline and Punish: The Birth of the Prison* (New York: Vintage Books, 1979), 200; see also Hubert Dreyfus, "'Being and Power' Revisited," in *Foucault and Heidegger: Critical Encounters*, edited by Alan Milchman and Alan Rosenberg (Minneapolis: University of Minnesota Press, 2003), 42.

**102.** See Beatrice Bishop Berle, *80 Puerto Rican Families in New York City: Health and Disease Studied in Context* (New York: Columbia University Press, 1958); Elena Padilla, *Up from Puerto Rico* (New York: Columbia University Press, 1958); and Oscar Handlin, *The Newcomers: Negroes and Puerto Ricans in a Changing Metropolis* (Cambridge, MA: Harvard University Press, 1965).

**103.** Handlin, *Newcomers*, 111.

### Chapter Six

**1.** "Pandillas italianas atropellan y roban a estudiantes hispanos," *El Diario*, Nov. 2, 1951, 1; "Pandilla de italianos atropella hispanos en la Benjamin Franklin," *El Diario*, Jan. 17, 1952, 2.

**2.** "New York's Sorest Spot," *New York Tribune*, Nov. 21, 1938, n.p., Covello papers, series VI, box 51, folder 13.

**3.** On BFHS as a desegregated school, see Eric Schneider, *Vampires, Dragons, and Egyptian Kings: Youth Gangs in Postwar New York* (Princeton, NJ: Princeton University Press, 1999), 67. Anonymous letter to Leonard Covello, n.d., Covello papers, series VI, box 56, folder 9; Leonard Covello, "We Hold These Truths," manuscript, n.d. [1938], Covello papers, series I, box 5, folder 13; Covello to BFHS students, regarding reaction to "clashes," Oct. 26, 1938, Covello papers, series VI, box 51, folder 13; Covello, "An Experiment in Building Concepts of Racial Democracy," 1941, Covello papers, series VI, box 56, folder 10.

NOTES TO PAGES 201–204 | 317

**4.** See Mauricio Mazón, *The Zoot Suit Riots: The Psychology of Symbolic Annihilation* (Austin: University of Texas Press, 1984). For a discussion of the rise in concern about gang activity after 1943, see Schneider, *Vampires, Dragons*, 55–77.

**5.** Migration Division pamphlet, "Juan Q. Citizen," 1956, Vertical File, "Puerto Ricans," City Hall Library (hereafter CHL).

**6.** José Morales, interview with the author, Dec. 13, 2007; Antonia Pantoja, *Memoir of a Visionary: Antonia Pantoja* (Houston: Arte Público Press, 2002), 77–78.

**7.** It was exactly the kind of discourse of recognition that, as political theorist Nancy Fraser puts it, "promotes the goal that assimilation to majority or dominant cultural forms is no longer the price of equal respect." Nancy Fraser and Axel Honneth, *Redistribution or Recognition? A Political-Philosophical Exchange* (New York: Verso, 2003), 7.

**8.** The writings of Franz Boaz, Margaret Mead, and Ruth Benedict, among others, introduced the American public to the "culture concept," a theory of human societies that embraced relativism and rejected scientific racism. See David A. Hollinger, "Ethnic Diversity, Cosmopolitanism and the Emergence of the American Liberal Intelligentsia," *American Quarterly* 27 (May 1975): 1313–51; and Richard Weiss, "Ethnicity and Reform: Minorities and the Ambiance of the Depression Years," *Journal of American History* 66 (Dec. 1979): 566–85. In the early 1930s, Rachel Davis DuBois, a white progressive educator from the Midwest, devised an educational philosophy based on the ideas of essayist Horace Kallen, who had first advanced the idea of "cultural pluralism" in a 1915 *Nation* article titled "Democracy versus the Melting Pot: A Study of American Nationality" (*Nation* 100 [Feb. 18, 1925]: 190–94, 217–20). See Hollinger, "Ethnic Diversity," 142.

**9.** Leonard Covello, "Interview with *Sunday Morning*, Jan. 5, 1941," Jan. 6, 1941, Covello papers, series X, box 112, folder 10.

**10.** Leonard Covello, "Intercultural Ed—Curriculum Notes," n.d., Covello papers, series IV, box 30, folder 12; Covello, "An Experiment in Building Concepts of Racial Democracy—Examination on Racial Unit," 1941, Covello papers, series III, box 22, folder 10.

**11.** Leonard Covello, "The Community School and Race Relations," 7, Covello papers, series VI, box 54, folder 12; "Student 'Strikes' Flare into Riots in Harlem Schools," *New York Times*, Sept. 29, 1945, 1; "400 Police Watch Harlem Students," *New York Times*, Oct. 2, 1945, 25. See Schneider, *Vampires, Dragons*, 68–70, for an account of the event that is skeptical of its characterization as a "riot."

**12.** This focus on schools as the site of citizenship training was hardly an innovation of postwar liberals and cold warriors. American politicians and intellectuals had carried on debates about how to educate citizens sporadically since the Civil War. See, for example, David Snedden, *Education for Political Citizenship: A Critical Analysis of Certain Unsolved Problems of School Educations towards Superior Memberships in Democratic and Political Societies* (New York: Columbia University Teachers College, 1932).

**13.** Lorrin Thomas, "'What Have We Done—Except Talk?' Pluralism, Race, and Intercultural Democracy, 1925–1945" (paper, University of Pennsylvania, 1997).

14. Rita Mellone to Leonard Covello, Oct. 1, 1945, Covello papers, series VI, box 54, folder 12.

15. Ralph De Donato to Leonard Covello, Oct. 1, 1945, Covello papers, series VI, box 54, folder 12.

16. L. F. Coles to Leonard Covello, Oct. 10, 1945, Covello papers, series VI, box 54, folder 12.

17. I know this because of several cross-references to L. F. Coles in Mark Naison's book *Communists in Harlem during the Great Depression* (Urbana: University of Illinois Press, 1983), 54, 82, 93, 94, 111. L. F. Coles was a Harlem resident and a writer who conducted a regular correspondence with Walter White of the NAACP during the early to mid-1930s.

18. See Schneider, *Vampires, Dragons*, 54–62.

19. Leonard Covello, "East Harlem History," in "The Community Centered School," n.d., 60, Covello papers, series III, box 18, folder 10. See also Nicholas Montalto, "Multicultural Education in New York City Public Schools, 1919–1941," in *Educating an Urban People*, edited by Diane Ravitch and Ronald Goodenow (New York: Teachers College Press, 1981), 76; Montalto, *A History of the Intercultural Education Movement* (New York: Garland Publishing, 1982), 17, 24–25, and passim; and Peter Novick, *That Noble Dream: The "Objectivity Question" and the American Historical Profession* (New York: Cambridge University Press, 1988), 315.

20. Henry W. Thurston, *The Education of Youth as Citizens: Progressive Changes in Our Aims and Methods* (New York: Richard R. Smith, 1946), 1.

21. National Education Association, "Report of the Fifth National Conference on Citizenship" (Washington, DC, May 20–24, 1950), 11.

22. National Education Association, "Report of the Fourth National Conference on Citizenship" (New York, May 14–18, 1949), 83.

23. Committee of the Association of Assistant Superintendents, *A Program of Education for Puerto Ricans in New York City* (New York: Board of Education, City of New York, 1947), cited in Francesco Cordasco, ed., *Bilingual Education in New York City: A Compendium of Reports* (New York: Arno Press, 1978), 24, 28, 31.

24. Miscellaneous flyers for festivals sponsored by the Club Borinquén, 1948–1953, "pro ayuda del estudiante pobre puertorriqueño," "Festivals," Covello papers, series X, box 106, folder 10; Borinquén Club meeting minutes, Feb.–May 1955, Covello papers, series X, box 104, folder 6.

25. Note signed by J. Montserrat, with list of films in the Migration Division library, n.d., Covello papers, series X, box 106, folder 17.

26. "Puerto Rican Survey," n.d. [1948?], Covello papers, series X, box 113, folder 12.

27. Ibid.

28. MACPRA, "The Puerto Rican Pupils in the Public Schools of New York City," 18; Committee of the Association of Assistant Superintendents, "A Program of Education for Puerto Ricans in New York City," 1947, 103, both reprinted in Cordasco, *Bilingual Education*. As head of the Migration Division's Educational Section in 1956, Covello compiled a set of journal articles showing the extent to which psy-

chologists and educational experts had discredited the use of standard IQ tests on children whose first language was not English.

**29.** MACPRA, "Puerto Rican Pupils," 12.

**30.** Leonard Covello, under the auspices of the Good Neighbor Federation, to the principals in districts 10 and 11, regarding Good Neighbor Federation conference titled "The Social Backgrounds of the Puerto Rican People," n.d., Covello papers, series X, box 105, folder 6.

**31.** Letter from Mark McCloskey, director, Division of Community Education, Board of Education of New York City, to Leonard Covello, Oct. 8, 1947, and various letters in file "Correspondence, Misc., 1946–63," Covello papers, series X, box 106, folder 1.

**32.** "Schools in City to Fit Courses to Puerto Ricans—Franklin Principal Visited Island Background; 300 Boys in His Classes," *Herald Tribune*, Nov. 16, 1947 (reprint), and "There's a Far Brighter Story about NY's Puerto Ricans," *Pittsburgh Courier*, Jan. 10, 1948, n.p., Covello papers, series X, box 102, folder 17.

**33.** New York Puerto Rican Scholarship Fund of the Mayor's Committee on Puerto Rican Affairs, press release, July 23, 1953, Covello papers, series X, box 102, folder 9.

**34.** "State and City Colleges," *New York Times*, Feb. 22, 1950, 28; and "State University Tuition," *New York Times*, Apr. 5, 1955, 28.

**35.** New York Puerto Rican Scholarship Fund, press release.

**36.** Riverside Neighborhood Assembly, flyer, "Notes on New Neighbors," including clips from the *New York Times*, the *New York Herald Tribune*, *El Mundo* (San Juan), the *West Side News*, and *La Prensa*, Feb. 1953, announcing plans for the program. Participants were from twenty-one to twenty-five years of age. Colón papers, series X, box 35, folder 6.

**37.** Cecelia Nuñez, speech at the Hispanic Association Pro–Higher Education (HAPHE), "Puerto Rican Youth Conference," 1960, Covello papers, series X, box 102, folder 10; J. Cayce Morrison, *The Puerto Rican Study, 1953–1957* (New York: Oriole Editions, 1972), 85, 88, Colón papers, series X, box 35, folder 7. Higher Horizons was originally called the Demonstration Guidance project. It served children at several disadvantaged schools, about 85 percent of whom were reported to be African American or Puerto Rican.

**38.** George Sánchez, *Becoming Mexican American: Ethnicity, Culture, and Identity in Chicano Los Angeles, 1900–1945* (New York: Oxford University Press, 1993), 255.

**39.** Pantoja, *Memoir of a Visionary*, 68.

**40.** Ibid., 77–78, 98, and passim; José Morales interview.

**41.** Pantoja, *Memoir of a Visionary*, 74, 98.

**42.** Ibid., 76–77.

**43.** Ibid. See also Virginia Sánchez-Korrol, "Building the New York Puerto Rican Community, 1945–65: A Historical Interpretation," in *Boricuas in Gotham: Puerto Ricans in the Making of Modern New York City*, edited by Gabriel Haslip-Viera, Félix V. Matos Rodríguez, and Ángelo Falcón (Princeton, NJ: Markus Wiener Publishers, 2005), 11–12.

**44.** History Task Force, *Labor Migration under Capitalism: The Puerto Rican Experience* (New York: Monthly Review Press, 1980), 152; José Morales interview.

**45.** "The Puerto Rican needs more publicity. . . . The bad publicity of the summer of 1959 still affects him," proclaimed the program for the 1960 conference. Second Puerto Rican Youth Conference, "We the New Yorkers Contribute," 1960, Covello papers, series X, box 102, folder 10.

**46.** Pantoja, *Memoir of a Visionary*, 99; History Task Force, *Labor Migration under Capitalism*, 52.

**47.** Pantoja recalled that, during her tenure as excutive director of Aspira (1961–66), some of the strongest opposition to Aspira came from New York's Board of Education, which objected to the program's employment of unlicensed counselors to advise youth on educational issues and placed numerous restrictions on school-based Aspira clubs that it did not apply to other ethnic groups' clubs. Eventually, as the Aspira Club Federation gained in numbers, strength, and legitimacy, the school board stepped back from its opposition. Pantoja, *Memoir of a Visionary*, 103.

**48.** Pantoja, *Memoir of a Visionary*, 78; José Morales interview. José Cruz provides a thorough discussion of the political and generational tensions between the Migration Division on the one hand and the younger activists in organizations like the forum and Aspira on the other in "Puerto Rican Politics in New York City during the 1960s: Structural Ideation, Contingency, and Power," forthcoming in *The Politics of Inclusion and Exclusion: Identity Politics in Twenty-first Century America*, edited by David Ericson (New York: Routledge, 2011). See also Sherrie Baver, "Puerto Rican Politics in New York City: The Post–World War II Period," in *Puerto Rican Politics in Urban America*, edited by James Jennings and Monte Rivera (Westport, CT: Greenwood Press, 1985), 46; History Task Force, *Labor Migration under Capitalism*, 151–52.

**49.** David Pérez, "The chains that have been taken off slaves' bodies are put back on their minds," in Michael Abramson and the Young Lords Party, *P'alante: Young Lords Party* (New York: McGraw Hill, 1971), 65–68. On bilingual education activism, see James Jennings interview with Luis Fuentes, "Puerto Ricans and the Community Control Movement," in *The Puerto Rican Movement: Voices from the Diaspora*, edited by Andrés Torres and José E. Velázquez (Philadelphia: Temple University Press, 1998), 285; and "First Time for Spanish Report Cards," *New York Amsterdam News*, Nov. 11, 1967, 29. On *Aspira v. Board of Education*, filed on behalf of the 182,000 children in New York City public schools, see Puerto Rican Legal Defense Fund, pamphlet, 1974, 8, Vertical File, "Puerto Ricans," CHL. The PRLDF cited dropout rates for Puerto Ricans ranging from 60 to 90 percent in American cities, and a 20 percent rate of high school graduation on the mainland. Only 5 percent of Puerto Rican high school graduates attended college in the United States, compared to 50 percent nationally.

**50.** "The Growing Importance of the Puerto Rican Minority in N.Y.C.," n.d. [1955?], Colón papers, series III, box 2, folder 1.

**51.** Clara Rodríguez, "Economic Factors Affecting Puerto Ricans in New York," in *Labor Migration under Capitalism*, History Task Force of the Centro de Estudios Puertorriqueños (New York: Monthly Review Press, 1979), 205; and Herbert Hill,

"Guardians of the Sweatshops," in *Puerto Rico and the Puerto Ricans: Studies in History and Society*, edited by Adalberto López and James Petras (New York: John Wiley and Sons, 1974), 394.

**52.** U.S. Commission on Civil Rights, *Puerto Ricans in the Continental United States: An Uncertain Future* (report of the U.S. Commission on Civil Rights [no publisher/printer listed], Oct. 1976), 47.

**53.** Pete Hamell, "Coming of Age in Nueva York," *New York* (Nov. 1969): 33–47, reprinted in *The Puerto Rican Experience: A Sociological Sourcebook*, edited by Francesco Cordasco and Eugene Buccioni (New York: Rowman and Littlefield, 1973), 204.

**54.** Senior and Donald Watkins, "Toward a Balance Sheet of Puerto Rican Migration," in *The Status of Puerto Rico—Selected Background Studies for the U.S.-P.R. Commission on the Status of Puerto Rico* (Washington, DC: U.S. Government Printing Office, 1966), 160.

**55.** Hispanic American Labor Council, press release, May 16, 1954, Colón papers, series VI, box 21, folder 7.

**56.** Hill, "Guardians of the Sweatshops," 405, reprinted from *New Politics* (Winter 1963); "AFL-CIO Civil Rights Chairman Is Charged with Racial Bias," *New York Amsterdam News*, Sept. 10, 1960, 1; "ILGWU Answers Hill's Charges Item by Item," *New York Amsterdam News*, Jan. 12, 1963, 5.

**57.** From Gilberto Gerena Valentín, "Recommendations Regarding Civil Rights, Discrimination, Voter Registration and Police-Community Relations," in *Community Conference Proceedings, Puerto Ricans Confront the Problems of the Complex Urban Society: A Design for Change*, convened by Mayor John Lindsay, Apr. 15–16, 1967, Vertical File, "Puerto Ricans," CHL.

**58.** Figures on government employment from *U.S. Census of Population 1970, General Social and Economic Characteristics* (Washington, DC: U.S. Government Printing Office, 1973), tables 88, 92, 98, 25.

**59.** "Change of Brownsville School Site Pleases Still Worried Parents," *New York Amsterdam News*, Feb. 27, 1960, 19; "SCHOOL STRIKE! N.Y. City Parents September Sit-ins," *New York Amsterdam News*, July 23, 1960, 19; "Negroes and Puerto Ricans Boycott PS 81," *New York Amsterdam News*, Sept. 16, 1961, 24. For general discussion on Puerto Ricans and housing in the sixties, see Patricia Sexton, *Spanish Harlem* (New York: Harper and Row, 1965), 35–46; and Francesco Cordasco, "Spanish Harlem: The Anatomy of Poverty," *Phylon* 26 (Summer 1965): 195–96.

**60.** "Dr. Theobald Writes Letter to Parents," *New York Amsterdam News*, Sept. 10, 1960, 1.

**61.** On the school boycott issue, see, for instance, "Dr. Theobald Writes Letter to Parents," *New York Amsterdam News*, Sept. 10, 1960, 1. J. Fitzpatrick, "Puerto Ricans in Perspective: The Meaning of Migration to the Mainland," *International Migration Review* 2 (Spring 1968): 11.

**62.** "Breakdown of City's Schools by Race," *New York Amsterdam News*, Sept. 10, 1960, 6 ; "Negroes, Puerto Ricans Over One-Third Public School Register," *New York Amsterdam News*, May 13, 1961, 26. "Puerto Ricans Seek School Board Say," *New York Amsterdam News*, Aug. 26, 1961, 16. Program, "N.Y.C. honors its first public school to be named for a Puerto Rican. Carlos Tapia lived as a resident of Brooklyn where he gave exemplary service to his community and to all people, regardless of their race, color or creed," groundbreaking ceremony, May 25, 1964, Colón papers, series VI, box 21, folder 5.

63. "An Analysis of Factors Causing the School Strike at Gary, Indiana," *Monthly Summary of Events and Trends in Race Relations* 3 (Dec. 1945): 148; Diane Ravitch, *The Great School Wars* (New York: Basic Books, 1974), 198–226. Also see, generally, Randolph Bourne, *The Gary Schools* (1916; repr., Cambridge, MA: MIT Press, 1970).

64. "Puerto Rican Parents Organization Formed," *New York Amsterdam News*, Feb. 6, 1965, 33.

65. "Neighborhoods Urged to Fight Poverty," *The Worker*, Jan. 19, 1965, 2, Colón papers, series X, box 36, folder 4.

66. HARYOU-ACT was Harlem Youth Opportunities Unlimited—Associated Community Teams. See Pantoja, *Memoir of a Visionary*, 112–19; "New Agency to Help Puerto Ricans Is Opened," *New York Times*, June 7, 1966, 22; Cruz, "Puerto Rican Politics in New York City."

67. Puerto Rican Forum, "A Study of Poverty Conditions in the New York Puerto Rican Community" (1964), and Office of Mayor John Lindsay, "Puerto Ricans Confront Problems of the Complex Urban Society: A Design for Change," Apr. 15–16, 1967, Vertical File, "Puerto Ricans," CHL. On Gerena Valentín, see Baver, "Puerto Rican Politics," 47. Mayor Lindsey appointed him head of the City Human Rights Commission's Business and Employment Division. Gerena Valentín, "Recommendations Regarding Civil Rights, Discrimination, Voter Registration, and Police-Community Relations," 349–50, Vertical File, "Puerto Ricans," CHL.

68. News release, Office of the Mayor, John V. Lindsay, Apr. 21, 1967, John Lindsay papers, Subject Files 1966–73, cited by Cruz, "Puerto Rican Politics in New York City."

69. "'War on Poverty' Is the Theme for This Year's Puerto Rican Day Parade," *New York Amsterdam News*, June 3, 1967, 13.

70. Peter Kihss, "Puerto Rican Story: A Sensitive People Erupt," *New York Times*, July 26, 1967, 18. See also Hamell, "Coming of Age in Nueva York," 210.

71. Piri Thomas, testimony before the National Advisory Commission on Civil Disorders, Sept. 21, 1967, 9, in Joseph Boskin, "The Revolt of the Urban Ghettos, 1964–67," *Annals of the American Academy of Political and Social Science* 382, "Protest in the Sixties" (Mar. 1969): 1–14; *Down These Mean Streets* was reviewed on the cover of the *New York Times* Book Review the week it came out: Daniel Stern, "One Who Got Away," *New York Times*, May 21, 1967, BR1; Christopher Lehmann-Haupt, "A Talk with Piri Thomas," *New York Times*, May 21, 1967, BR44.

72. Experts were engaged in heated arguments at this moment over whether Operation Bootstrap was a resounding success or an abysmal failure; the island's average annual income had indeed risen dramatically since the 1940s. See Michael Meyerson, "Puerto Rico: Our Backyard Colony," *Ramparts*, June 1970, 115; he quotes himself from the *Wall Street Journal* (no date given): "Two million potential customers live on Puerto Rico, but the hopeful industrial planners see it as the shopping center for the entire Caribbean population of 13 million."

**73.** "New Book Scored by Puerto Ricans," *New York Times*, Nov. 16, 1966, 43. César Andreu Iglesias, "La clave del acertijo," the fourth of four parts of the review of *La Vida, El Imparcial*, Feb. 1967, Colón papers, series X, box 36, folder 8. See also Michael Harrington, "Everyday Hell," *New York Times*, Nov. 20, 1966, BR1; Frank Cordasco, "Another Face of Poverty," *Phylon* 29 (first quarter 1968): 88–92.

**74.** For a similar framing of the issue, see "The Puerto Ricans," *Newsweek*, June 15, 1970, 94, quoted in Clifford Hauberg, *Puerto Rico and the Puerto Ricans* (New York: Twayne Publishers, 1970), 143.

**75.** Jean Paul Sartre, preface to Frantz Fanon, *The Wretched of the Earth* (1961; repr., New York: Grove Press, 1967), 13–14.

**76.** Fredric Jameson, "Periodizing the Sixties," in *The Sixties without Apology*, edited by Sohnya Sayres, Anders Stephanson, Stanley Aronowitz, and Fredric Jameson (Minneapolis: University of Minnesota Press, 1984), 181.

**77.** Meyerson, "Puerto Rico," 119; "FBI Guards Powell after P.R. Threats," *New York Amsterdam News*, Aug. 11, 1962, 1. Powell had married a Puerto Rican woman, his second wife, in 1960.

**78.** Presentation by Juan Mari Bras (Estonian Hall, New York City, Mar. 14, 1963), Colón papers, series VI, box 21, folder 5.

**79.** La Misión Vito Marcantonio del MPI; MPI flyer for Jenaro Rivera performance, "Sobre 'La Otra Poesía'" [Sept. 9, 1967], Colón papers, series VI, box 21, folder 6. See also José Velázquez, "Coming Full Circle: The Puerto Rican Socialist Party, U.S. Branch," in *Puerto Rican Movement*, 49–50.

**80.** Puerto Rican Revolutionary Workers Organization (Young Lords Party), "Resolutions and Speeches, First Congress," Nov. 1972, 8, A la izquierda collection, Young Lords Party Publications and Pamphlets, reel 3.

**81.** "Puerto Rican Assn. Sets Next Seminar," *New York Amsterdam News*, Apr. 20, 1963, 5. See also "Fernos Sees Need to Clarify the Commonwealth Compact," *San Juan Star*, Aug. 12, 1965, n.p., series X, box 36, folder 6.

**82.** "A 'Plebiscite' That Is Not a Plebiscite; We Accuse the United States Government of Trying to Impose a Colonial Plebiscite on Puerto Rico," advertisement, *New York Times*, Apr. 2, 1967, 180; "Puerto Rico's Future," *New York Times*, Mar. 22, 1967, 31; "Puerto Rican Writers and Artists Support Plebiscite BOYCOTT," *Granma*, June 18, 1967, n.p., Colón papers, series X, box 36, folder 9.

**83.** "Leyes no permiten boricuas de N.Y. voten en el plebiscito: H. Badillo," *El Diario–La Prensa*, Mar. 7, 1967, 1; "Editorial: El plebiscito," *El Diario–La Prensa*, Feb. 3, 1967, 19.

**84.** José Lumen Román, "El plebiscito de Puerto Rico," *El Imparcial*, Jan. 30, 1967, n.p.; "Se opone voten boricuas viven EU—Ellos desconocen los problemas aquí," *El Diario–La Prensa*, Dec. 7, 1966, n.p.; "Mari Bras acusa a Muñoz de provocar la guerra civil," *El Diario–La Prensa*, Dec. 13, 1966, n.p.; "Considerarán hoy peregrinación de boricuas a San Juan desde N.Y.," *El Diario–La Prensa*, Apr. 24, 1967, n.p., Colón papers, series X, box 36, folder 9. Flyer, El Comité Boricuas Ausentes Pro–Voto Plebiscitario, "Preocupa a todos los puertorriqueños intención ELA de negar a ausentes oportunidad votar en plebiscito," Colón papers, series VI, box 21, folder 7.

"91% quiere votar en plebiscito de P. Rico," *El Diario–La Prensa*, Dec. 16, 1966, 22. The question of mainland Puerto Ricans participating in island plebiscites is still debated in the twenty-first century.

85. Letter to Senator James Eastland, chair of the Senate Judiciary Committee, from J. A. González-González, permanent delegate of the mission to the United Nations of the MPI, May 9, 1969, Colón papers, series VI, box 21, folder 7.

86. "Gran acto por ciudadanía, a pesar de independentistas," *El Diario–La Prensa*, Mar. 5, 1967, n.p.; "LBJ felicita a boricuas en cincuentenario ciudadanía," *El Diario–La Prensa*, Mar. 3, 1967, n.p.; Luisa Quintero, "Rocky proclama día ciudadanía de EU a boricuas," *El Diario–La Prensa*, Mar. 3, 1967, n.p., all in Colón papers, series X, box 36, folder 8. Press sheet with miscellaneous news articles on this event: "Día ciudadanía acaba a golpes," *El Mundo*, n.d., n.p.; "10 Held as Puerto Ricans and Police Scuffle Here," *New York Times*, Mar. 3, 1967, 20; "Independentistas dicen policías los golpearon," *El Diario–La Prensa*, n.d., n.p.; "Independence Backers Rally at NY Hotel," *San Juan Star*, n.d., n.p., Colón papers, series VI, box 21, folder 6.

87. American Youth for a Free World, "Fact Sheet on Puerto Rican Youth," n.d., Colón papers, series VI, box 21, folder 7. Flyer, "Liberation for Puerto Rico," Dec. 8, 1969, Colón papers, series VI, box 1, folder 7. "Gen. Van Fleet to Get Award from the Order of Lafayette," *New York Times*, Dec. 3, 1969, 48. See also Puerto Rican Revolutionary Workers Organization, "Resolutions and Speeches," 9.

88. MPI, Misión Vito Marcantonio, "A la comunidad puertorriqueño en NY," July 25, 1966; flyer, "Spring Mobilization Committee," "¡Ningún P.R. a Viet Nam!" Colón papers, series VI, box 21, folder 7. "Gran marcha contra la guerra sat. april 15," *Challenge*, Nov. 1, 1966, n.p.; "P.R. Anti-draft Pickets at U.N.," *Challenge*, Nov. 1, 1966, n.p., Colón papers, series X, box 36, folder 7. Full-page ad by organization called "Vietnam Protest," "A Warrant for the Arrest of: LBJ, McNamara, Dean Rusk, Gen'l Westmoreland . . . ," *San Juan Star*, Dec. 18, 1967, n.p.; "Demostración en P.R. en sepelio de joven soldado que murió en Viet Nam," *Granma*, July 5, 1966, n.p., Colón papers, series X, box 36, folder 7.

89. Peniel Joseph, *Waiting 'til the Midnight Hour: A Narrative History of Black Power in America* (New York: Macmillan, 2007), 124–25; "'Poder Negro' y MPI firman pacto para acciones conjuntas," *El Tiempo Nueva York*, Aug. 3, 1967, 16–17.

90. "'Poder Negro' y MPI firman pacto," 16–17.

91. "Conferencia de estudiantes condena intervención de E.U. en Puerto Rico," *El Imparcial*, Jan. 9, 1967, n.p., Colón papers, series X, box 36, folder 8. Teach-in on Puerto Rico, flyer, July 13, 1967, Colón papers, series VI, box 21, folder 7.

92. See Bobby Seale, *Seize the Time: The Story of the Black Panther Party and Huey P. Newton* (Baltimore: Black Classic Press, 1970); Harvard Sitkoff, *The Struggle for Black Equality, 1954–1980* (New York: Hill and Wang, 1981); Peniel Joseph, "Dashikis and Democracy: Black Studies, Student Activism, and the Black Power Movement," *Journal of African American History* 88 (Spring 2003): 182–203; Carlos Muñoz Jr., *Youth, Identity, Power: The Chicano Movement* (London: Verso, 1990); Benita Roth, *Separate Roads to Feminism: Black, Chicana, and White Feminist Movements in America's Second Wave* (New York: Cambridge University Press, 2004); Helen Zia, *Asian American Dreams: The Emergence of an American People* (New York: Farrar, Straus and Giroux,

2000); William Wei, *The Asian American Movement* (Philadelphia: Temple University Press, 1994).

**93.** Flyer, Comité Pro Defensa Ciudadana, Jan. 11, 1962, Colón papers, series VI, box 21, folder 7. On the "internal colonialism" theory, Ramón Gutiérrez argues that the idea of internal colonialism originated among Latin American development economists and dependency theorists. He identifies Mexican sociologist Pablo González Casanova's "Sociedad plural, colonialismo interno y desarollo" (*América Latina* 6 [1963]: 15–32) as the first published use of the term. Gutiérrez, "Internal Colonialism: An American Theory of Race," *DuBois Review* 1 (2004): 282. See also Mitchell Seligson, "The 'Dual Society' Thesis in Latin America: A Reexamination of the Costa Rican Case," *Social Forces* 51 (Sept. 1972): 91–98, who cites J. Colter, "The Mechanics of Internal Domination and Social Change in Peru," *Studies in Comparative International Development* 3 (Dec. 1967): 229–46; and George Dalton, "Theoretical Issues in Economic Anthropology," *Current Anthropology* 10 (Feb. 1969): 63–102. Robert Blauner, in "Internal Colonialism and Ghetto Revolt," *Social Problems* 16 (Spring 1969): 393–408, credits Kenneth Clark with some of the earliest published writings in the United States on the idea of internal colonialism, in *Dark Ghetto* (New York: Harper and Row, 1965) and *Youth in the Ghetto* (New York: HARYOU, 1964). There was a lot of cross-fertilization of this framework by the early sixties, and intellectuals in Africa were making similar arguments. See Katema Yifru, J. Rudolph Grimes, Ibrahim Abboud, Mongi Slim, Kwame Nkrumah, Louis Lansana Beavoqui, Leopold Sedar Senghor, and Alhaji Sir Abubaker Tafawa Balewa, "Africa Speaks to the United Nations: A Symposium of Aspirations and Concerns Voiced by Representative Leaders at the UN," *International Organization* 16 (Spring 1962): 303–30. Eldridge Cleaver probably published the first Black Power presentation of the internal colonialism argument in "The Land Question and Black Liberation," written in prison in the early to mid-sixties and later published in *Post-prison Writings and Speeches* (New York: Random House, 1967).

**94.** Meyerson, "Puerto Rico," 114.

**95.** Puerto Rican Revolutionary Workers Organization, "Resolutions and Speeches," 7–9 and passim.

**96.** Harrington, "Everyday Hell."

**97.** "Sixth Puerto Rican Youth Conference, Points to Ponder," Feb. 15, 1964, Covello papers, series X, box 102, folder 2; flyer, in English and Spanish, Independent Committee in Support of Mobilization for Youth and Social Progress (Lower East Side), Sept. 22, 1964, Colón papers, series VI, box 21, folder 7.

**98.** Hill, "Guardians of the Sweatshops," 413.

**99.** Flyer, Independent Committee in Support of Mobilization for Youth and Social Progress. See also Luis Aponte Parés, "The East Harlem Real Great Society: A Puerto Rican Chapter in the Fight for Self Determination," *Planners Network*, Mar.–Apr. 1999, www.virtualboricua.org/docs/nps01.htm.

**100.** Pablo "Yoruba" Guzmán, "Before People Called Me a Spic, They Called Me a Nigger," in *Palante*, 77. See also History Task Force, *Labor Migration under Capitalism*, 154; Iris Morales, personal communication with the author, June 10, 2008. See also Monte Rivera, "Organizational Politics of the East Harlem Barrio in the

1970s," in *Puerto Rican Politics in Urban America,* edited by James Jennings and Monte Rivera (Westport, CT: Greenwood Press, 1985), 63; Thomas Jackson, "The State, the Movement, the Poor," in *The Underclass Debate: Views from History,* edited by Michael B. Katz (Princeton, NJ: Princeton University Press, 1993), 413; Jeffrey Ogbar, "Puerto Rico en mi corazón: The Young Lords, Black Power, and Puerto Rican Nationalism in the U.S., 1966–1972," *Centro Journal* 18 (Spring 2006): 148–69.

**101.** "La March de los Pobres," *El Imparcial,* May 30, 1968, n.p.; "Puerto Rican Poor Organize March," *Daily World,* May 28, 1968, n.p., Colón papers, series X, box 37, folder 2. "Plan Puerto Ricans in D.C. March," *New York Amsterdam News,* Apr. 20, 1968, 4.

**102.** Hamell, "Coming of Age in Nueva York," 204, 205.

**103.** Migration Division, "Migration: Calendar Years 1955–1967," Colón papers, series VI, box 21, folder 6. United States Commission on Civil Rights, *Puerto Ricans in the Continental United States: An Uncertain Future* ([no pub. info.], Oct. 1976), 27. "Rising Hispanic Migration Heightens City Tensions," *New York Times,* Apr. 4, 1966, 1. See also History Task Force, *Labor Migration under Capitalism,* 151.

**104.** Biliana C. S. Ambrecht and Harry P. Pachon, "Ethnic Political Mobilization in a Mexican American Community: An Exploratory Study of East Los Angeles, 1965–1972," *Western Political Quarterly* 27 (Sept. 1974): 500–519. Noting that "titles of articles of this period are indicative of the Mexican American image in this society" (ibid., 512), the authors cite, as examples, Helen Rowan, "The Minority Nobody Knows," *Atlantic,* June 1967, 47–52, and "Invisible Minority," *Newsweek,* Aug. 29, 1966, 48.

**105.** H. Carl McCall, "The Fight on Poverty: An Alliance for Progress," *New York Amsterdam News,* July 1, 1967, 17.

**106.** "Program for Poor at City U. Expands," *New York Times,* Aug. 12, 1966, 33; the article was subtitled "first of 2000 who could not normally meet high standards enter in fall." After its introduction in 1965 as the "Pre-baccalaureate Program," CUNY renamed the program SEEK (Search for Education, Elevation, and Knowledge) a year later. The SEEK program generated periodic controversy, with critics charging that it forced the university to lower its standards for admission. On the issue of open admissions at CUNY, see "Education: Open Admissions Policy at CUNY Increases Percentages of Blacks and Puerto Ricans," *New York Times,* Sept. 20, 1970, 193, and "Slow Road to Parity," *New York Times,* May 24, 1976, 27.

**107.** Miguel "Mickey" Melendez, *We Took the Streets: Fighting for Latino Rights with the Young Lords* (New Brunswick, NJ: Rutgers University Press, 2005), 70. Iris Morales, personal communication with the author, Aug. 31, 2008.

**108.** Iris Morales attended SNCC, NAACP, and Human Relations Club meetings in high school, at Julia Richman High School; Columbia Oral History interview with Ron Grele, Nov. 19, 1984, 19–20. "Young Lords Win Church Battle," *New York Amsterdam News,* Jan. 3, 1970, 1. Aspira, "Sixth Puerto Rican Youth Conference, 2/15/64, Points to Ponder," Covello papers, series X, box 102, folder 2.

**109.** American Youth for a Free World, Information Committee, "El Mov. del 19 Nov." [1967], Colón papers, series VI, box 21, folder 6. "Rebels at Queens College Blockading Main Building," *New York Times,* Apr. 30, 1969, 1.

**110.** Puerto Rican Revolutionary Workers Organization, "Resolutions and Speeches," 4–5; Iris Morales, Columbia Oral History transcript, and Iris Morales, interview with the author, May 7, 2008; Melendez, We Took the Streets, 87–88.

**111.** Uncollected garbage in poor New York neighborhoods, and the health and safety risks it caused, was something residents had complained about consistently for more than a decade. See "Garbage Tide Rises in Brooklyn," *Daily World*, July 16, 1968, 3, Colón papers, series X, box 37, folder 2. Hauberg, *Puerto Rico and the Puerto Ricans*, 139–43. "Los Young Lords son una quinta columna . . . ," *El Tiempo Nueva York*, Feb. 18, 1970, n.p., Colón papers, series X, box 37, folder 7; "Marginalia," by Luisa Quintero, "No somos comunistas," *El Diario–La Prensa*, Feb. 17, 1970, 16. See also "The Puerto Rican Revolutionary Workers Organization: A Staff Study," Subcommittee to Investigate the Administration of the Internal Security Act and Other Internal Security Laws of the Committee on the Judiciary, United States Senate, 94th Cong., 2nd sess. (Washington, DC: U.S. Government Printing Office, Mar. 1976), 24.

**112.** Meléndez, We Took the Streets, 201.

**113.** Wakefield, *Island in the City*, 215, and especially chapter 6 on the "Civic Orientation Office," set up by volunteers from Public School 108. Rand, in *Puerto Ricans*, 168–69, describes it as a "'rent clinic,' but so much more."

**114.** "Young Lords Win Church Battle," *New York Amsterdam News*, Jan. 3, 1970, 1. Meléndez, We Took the Streets, 129; "Badillo Confers with Young Lords," *New York Times*, Feb. 1, 1970, 59; "Contempt Charges Are Dropped as Lords Reach Accord," *New York Times*, Feb. 25, 1970, 36; "House of Lords," *Time*, Jan. 12, 1970, 33. On the church leadership's response, see "Primera Iglesia Metodista unida: A la opinión pública," *El Tiempo Nueva York*, Mar. 1, 1970, n.p., Colón papers, series X, box 37, folder 7. "Will Felipe Leave the Young Lords?" *New York Amsterdam News*, Sept. 12, 1970, 24. Pablo Guzmán, "La Vida Pura: A Lord of the Barrio," in *Puerto Rican Movement*, 160. Kids were given buttons saying "Puerto Rican power" at the First People's Church in Dec. 1969, *Palante*, 143.

**115.** Pablo Guzmán, "La Vida Pura: A Lord of the Barrio," in *Puerto Rican Movement*, 157.

**116.** Pablo Guzmán, "The Young Lords Legacy: A Personal Account," *Proceedings from the Institute for Puerto Rican Policy Community Forum*, Apr. 8, 1995, 6, A la izquierda collection, reel 3.

**117.** Iris Morales, comments following showing of her film ¡Palante, siempre palante! at Rutgers University, New Brunswick, Apr. 3, 2008.

**118.** Guzmán, "Vida Pura," 166.

**119.** Iris Morales, "¡PALANTE, SIEMPRE PALANTE!" in *Puerto Rican Movement*, 216; Puerto Rican Revolutionary Workers Organization, "Resolutions and Speeches," 9; A. Philip Randolph, Joseph Montserrat, and James Baldwin, letter to the editor, *New York Times*, July 3, 1962, 13; "Puerto Rican Revolutionary Workers Organization: A Staff Study," 25–26.

**120.** "The Puerto Ricans," *Newsweek*, June 15, 1970, 94, quoted in Hauberg, *Puerto Rico and the Puerto Ricans*, 143. See also "Identity Crisis," *Newsweek*, Jan. 19, 1970, 62; "Puerto Rican Revolutionary Workers Organization: A Staff Study," 26.

**121.** Manuel Maldonado-Denis, "Puerto Ricans: Protest or Submission," *Annals of the American Academy of Political and Social Science* 382 (Mar. 1969): 26–31.

**122.** J. Fitzpatrick, "Puerto Ricans in Perspective: The Meaning of Migration to the Mainland," *International Migration Review* 2 (Spring 1968): 7–20. "Call Puerto Rican, Black Strife a Hoax," *New York Amsterdam News*, Dec. 6, 1969, 33. On black cultural nationalists' ties to Puerto Ricans, see, for instance, "Panther 21 Benefits," *New York Amsterdam News*, Feb. 14, 1970, 16; "Young Lords Calmed by LeRoi Jones," *New York Amsterdam News*, July 15, 1970, 1.

**123.** "Pickets to Protest Prisoner Hangings," *New York World Telegram*, Mar. 31, 1965, n.p.; "Boricuas piquetearán los sábados cuarteles policía," *El Tiempo*, Apr. 9, 1965, n.p., Colón papers, series X, box 37, folder 7.

**124.** Guzmán, "Young Lords Legacy," 14–15.

**125.** Torres and Velázquez, *Puerto Rican Movement*, 13–15, 89, 221.

**126.** Iris Morales, Columbia Oral History transcript, 92, 94. Pablo Guzmán, "Puerto Rican Barrio Politics in the United States," in *The Puerto Rican Struggle: Essays on Survival in the United States*, edited by Clara Rodríguez, Virginia Sánchez-Korrol, and José Oscar Alers (Maplewood, NJ: Waterfront Press, 1980), 124. Meléndez, *We Took the Streets*, 193. Puerto Rican Revolutionary Workers Organization, "Resolutions and Speeches," 12–13.

**127.** Baver, "Puerto Rican Politics," 50.

**128.** Johanna Fernández presentation (Schomburg Symposium, Taller Puertorriqueño, Philadelphia, Feb. 24, 2007).

**129.** Guzmán, "Young Lords Legacy," 14.

**130.** Abramson and the Young Lords Party, *Palante!*, 150.

**131.** Mark Kitchell, *Berkeley in the Sixties* (documentary film, 1990). To get an idea of the worldwide appeal of Maoism among young radicals throughout the sixties, see the review of a Finnish book on Mao, whose translated title is *Mao, Where Have You Got To?* in the *American Historical Review*; the review author refers to the book's discussion of "the parallel upsurges of revolutionary enthusiasm among the student generation all over the Western world generated by the Peace Movement, the anti–Vietnam War movements, and enthusiasm for Third World anti-imperialism and the search for a socialists 'third way' that would be neither communist nor social democratic." A. F. Upton, review of *Mao missa sä oot?* by Pirkko-Liisa Kastari, *American Historical Review* 106 (Dec. 2001): 1888–89.

**132.** *Quotations from Chairman Mao Tsetung* (1966; repr., Peking: Foreign Language Press, 1976), 39, 61, 72, and passim.

**133.** Iris Morales, Columbia Oral History transcript, 49.

**134.** Guzmán, "Puerto Rican Barrio Politics," 125.

**135.** Flyer, Agrupación de Puertorriqueños Ciudadanos de los Estados Unidos de América, 1936, Erasmo Vando papers, series II, box 1, folder 7.

**136.** Andrés Torres, "Introduction: Political Radicalism in the Diaspora—The Puerto Rican Experience," in *Puerto Rican Movement*, 4.

**137.** Hamell, "Coming of Age in Nueva York," 211.

**138.** "Pickets Ask Rocky to Abolish S.C.H.R.," *El Diario–La Prensa*, July 25, 1970, 26; "People's Action Party," *El Diario–La Prensa*, Feb. 1970, n.d., n.p.; "Discriminatoria la Comisión de Derechos Humanos," *Tiempo Martes*, Mar. 24, 1970, n.p., Colón papers, series X, box 37, folder 7.

**139.** Baver, "Puerto Rican Politics," 50.

**140.** Guzmán, "Puerto Rican Barrio Politics," 123, 125. See also Alfredo López, *The Puerto Rican Papers* (New York: Bobbs-Merrill Company, 1973), especially 262, 268–76.

**141.** Carmen Vivian Rivera, "Our Movement, One Woman's Story," in *Puerto Rican Movement*, 203.

**142.** "Hemos trabajado bien," a report on the First National Conference of Puerto Ricans, Mexican Americans and Educators on the Special Needs of Puerto Rican Youth (New York: Aspira, 1968), 64–66, reprinted in *Puerto Rican Experience*, 301; Antonia Pantoja, "Puerto Ricans in New York: A Historical and Community Development Perspective," *CENTRO Bulletin* 2 (Spring 1989): 21–31; José Morales interview.

**143.** History Task Force, *Labor Migration under Capitalism*, 152.

**144.** Catarino Garza, *Puerto Ricans in the U.S.: The Struggle for Freedom* (New York: Pathfinder Press, 1977), 14; Iris Morales, personal communication with the author, June 10, 2008.

**145.** Alfredo López, *The Puerto Rican Papers* (New York: Bobbs-Merrill Company, 1973), 292, 295, 291.

**146.** Carmen Whalen, "Bridging Barrio and Community Politics," in *Puerto Rican Movement*, 110.

**147.** Young Lords central committee member Juan "Fi" Ortiz, for example, went to Franklin; "Puerto Rican Revolutionary Workers Organization: A Staff Study," 9.

## Epilogue

**1.** Pablo Guzmán, "Puerto Rican Barrio Politics in the U.S.," in *The Puerto Rican Struggle: Essays on Survival in the U.S.*, edited by Clara Rodríguez, Virginia Sánchez-Korrol, and José Oscar Alers (Maplewood, NJ: Waterfront Press, 1980), 126.

**2.** History Task Force, Centro de Estudios Puertorriqueños, *Labor Migration under Capitalism* (New York: Monthly Review Press, 1980), 156.

**3.** Mike Davis, *Magical Urbanism: Latinos Reinvent the U.S. City* (New York: Verso, 2000), 123–30.

**4.** Juan M. García-Passalacqua, "The Grand Dilemma: Viability and Sovereignty for Puerto Rico," *Annals of the American Academy of Political and Social Science* 533, "Trends in U.S.-Caribbean Relations" (May 1994): 151–64; History Task Force, *Labor Migration under Capitalism*, 142; Rubén Berríos, "Independence for Puerto Rico: The Only Solution," *Foreign Affairs* 55 (Apr. 1977): 561–83.

**5.** U.S. Commission on Civil Rights, *Puerto Ricans in the Continental United States: An Uncertain Future*, report of the U.S. Commission on Civil Rights ([no publisher/printer listed] Oct. 1976), ii.

**6.** Catarino Garza, *Puerto Ricans in the U.S.: The Struggle for Freedom* (New York: Pathfinder Press, 1977), 17. Guzmán, "Puerto Rican Barrio Politics in the U.S.,"

126–27. Sherrie Baver, "Puerto Rican Politics in New York City: The Post–World War II Period," in *Puerto Rican Politics in Urban America*, edited by James Jennings and Monte Rivera (Westport, CT: Greenwood Press, 1985), 53. See two-part article "The Baron of the Bronx," by David González with Martin Gottlieb: "Power Built on Poverty: One Man's Odyssey," *New York Times*, May 14, 1993, A1; and "In an Antipoverty Empire, a Clinic is an Opportunity," *New York Times*, May 15, 1993, A1. The articles are about Vélez and his financial success built on a foundation of anti-poverty programs in the sixties, but the first also mentions Herman Badillo.

**7.** "30 in Puerto Rican Group Held in Liberty I. Protest," *New York Times*, Oct. 26, 1977, 30. See also "Four Who Got Clemency," *New York Times*, Sept. 7, 1979, B18.

**8.** Garza, *Puerto Ricans in the U.S.*, 38–39.

**9.** "Puerto Rico Aid Unit Cites Its Successes," *New York Times*, Oct. 4, 1977, 78.

**10.** Eugene Mohr, *The Nuyorican Experience* (Westport, CT: Greenwood Press, 1982), 116. Manuel Maldonado-Denis writes about the origins of *New Yorican* in 1976, *The Emigration Dialectic: Puerto Rico and the U.S.A.* (New York: International Publishers, 1980), 127–28; also see Garza, *Puerto Ricans in the U.S.*, 17. On cultural meanings and conflicts over the parallel term *Dominican-yorks*, see Jesse Hoffnung-Garskof, *Tale of Two Cities: Santo Domingo and New York after 1950* (Princeton, NJ: Princeton University Press, 2008), 7, 229–30.

**11.** Miguel Algarín and Miguel Piñero, eds., *Nuyorican Poetry: An Anthology of Puerto Rican Words and Feelings* (New York: William Morrow and Company, 1975), 24, 110, 111.

**12.** Ibid., 24.

**13.** Mohr, *Nuyorican Experience*, 97.

**14.** In this sense, Nuyorican activists would turn out to resemble the late-twentieth-century cultural nationalists who attempted, as Ramón Grosfoguel and Frances Negrón Muntaner argue, to navigate Puerto Rican politics outside of the restrictive colonial/national dichotomy—that is, to craft a political identity beyond the limitations of the traditional nation-state. Ramón Grosfoguel and Frances Negrón Muntaner, *Puerto Rican Jam: Rethinking Colonialism and Nationalism* (Minneapolis: University of Minnesota Press, 1997), 2.

**15.** On the activities of centrist Puerto Rican politicians in the seventies, see José Cruz, "Pluralism and Ethnicity in New York City Politics: The Case of Puerto Ricans" (paper presented at the New York State Political Science Association meetings, John Jay College, CUNY, Apr. 25, 2009).

**16.** Juan Flores, "Reclaiming Left Baggage: Some Early Sources for Minority Studies," *Cultural Critique* 59 (Winter 2005): 199.

**17.** These debates tended to focus on conflicts over claims for special group recognition in multicultural societies, such as the Québequois in eastern Canada. See, for instance, Will Kymlicka, *Multicultural Citizenship: A Liberal Theory of Minority Rights* (New York: Oxford University Press, 1995). Renato Rosaldo, "Whose Cultural Studies?" *American Anthropologist* 96 (Sept. 1994): 524–29.

**18.** Saskia Sassen published her groundbreaking study *The Mobility of Labor and Capital: A Study in International Investment and Labor Flow* (New York: Cambridge

University Press, 1988) in 1988, inaugurating globalization as a new field of academic study. Likewise, it was Nina Glick Schiller, Linda Basch, and Cristina Blanc-Szanton's 1992 book *Towards a Transnational Perspective on Migration: Race, Class, Ethnicity, and Nationalism Reconsidered* (New York: New York Academy of Sciences, 1992) that marked the real beginning of the new academic field of transnationalism studies in the United States.

**19.** See introduction, n. 56.

**20.** Mariana Mora, "Zapatista Anticapitalist Politics and the 'Other Campaign': Learning from the Struggle for Indigenous Rights and Autonomy," *Latin American Perspectives* 153 (Mar. 2007): 64; Richard Werbner, *Reasonable Radicals and Citizenship in Botswana* (Bloomington: Indiana University Press, 2004), especially 48–56; Deborah J. Yashar, "Contesting Citizenship: Indigenous Movements and Democracy in Latin America," *Comparative Politics* 31, no. 1 (Oct. 1998): 23–42. Benedict Kingsbury and Kirsty Gover, guest eds., "Indigenous Groups and the Politics of Recognition in Asia," *International Journal of Minority and Group Rights* 11, issue 1–2 (2004).

**21.** Andrés Torres, "Political Radicalism in the Diaspora: The Puerto Rican Experience," in *The Puerto Rican Movement: Voices from the Diaspora*, edited by Andrés Torres and José E. Velázquez (Philadelphia: Temple University Press, 1998). See also Carmen T. Whalen, "Bridging Homeland and Barrio Politics: The Young Lords in Philadelphia," in the same volume.

**22.** Oscar Handlin, *The Newcomers: Negroes and Puerto Ricans in a Changing Metropolis* (1959; repr., Cambridge, MA: Harvard University Press, 1965), 60.

**23.** Garza, *Puerto Ricans in the U.S.*, 9.

**24.** Pamphlet, Puerto Rican Legal Defense Fund, 1974, Vertical File, "Puerto Ricans," City Hall Library.

**25.** Manning Marable, *Race, Reform, and Rebellion: The Second Reconstruction and Beyond in Black America* (Jackson: University Press of Mississippi, 1991), 87.

**26.** Wendy Brown, *Politics Out of History* (Princeton, NJ: Princeton University Press, 2001), 14.

# Index

54; island politics and, 127–28; migrant understanding of, 43–44; in 1930s, 95, 97–106; in 1950s, 183–91; patronage and, 94; Puerto Rican candidates and, 112; reform efforts, 103–4

Ellison, Ralph, 167, 182–83, 197

Emigration Advisory Council, 152

employers, pro–Puerto Rican testimonies by, 159–60

employment: in Brooklyn versus Manhattan, 271n96. *See also* job discrimination; unemployment

employment offices, exclusion by, 279n40

English-language programs, 143–44; in Committee on Puerto Ricans report, 179–80

English-only literacy testing, 217; outlawing of, 185

ethnic conflicts: in East Harlem, 49–55; between Puerto Ricans and African Americans, 53–54, 111, 187–88, 234; between Puerto Ricans and Italians, 200; between Puerto Ricans and Jews, 7–8, 40–50, 53–54, 105

ethnic politics, during La Guardia years, 98

European immigrants: preferential treatment of, 56; Puerto Rican migrants versus, 138, 145, 197

Fanon, Frantz, 12, 222

Federación Libre de Trabajadores, 30, 37; Gompers and, 269n64

Federación Portorriqueña, *independentista* ideology of, 47

Feliciano, Joseph, 72

Fernández, Joanna, 237

Ferré, Luis, 226

Fiol Ramos, Victor, 52

First Spanish Methodist Church, Young Lords' takeovers of, 232–33, 235

Fitzpatrick, Joseph, 35, 196, 217, 234

Flores, Diego, 103–4

Flores, Jesús, 82

Flores, Juan, 248–49

Flores, William, 261n53

Foraker, Joseph B., 6–7

Foraker Act of 1900, 271n92; citizenship status and, 256n4; provisions of, 36

Ford, James W., 110–11

Foucault, Michel, 197

Fraser, Nancy, 15, 317n7

Frazier, E. Franklin, 300n10

Frias de Hempel, Luisa, 180

Fusion Party, 95; in 1933–34 elections, 97–98; Puerto Rican candidate of, 100–101; Puerto Rican voters and, 99

gang stereotypes, in *West Side Story*, 202

gang violence, 314n78. *See also* ethnic conflicts

garbage offensive, 232, 327n111

García, Chino, 247

García, Gervasio Luis, 165

García Rivera, Oscar, 102, 142, 162; defeat of, 130; election of, 124–30, 126f; Hewitt and, 137; housing crisis and, 191–92; labor support for, 129; mixed-class support of, 297n110

garment industry: exploitation of minorities by, 188–89; struggles in, 191–92

Garza, Catarino, 243, 245, 252

Garzón, Julio, 85

gender: complexion labels and, 74; norms for, 33–34

Gerena Valentín, Gilberto, 170, 215, 235; background, 274n1; on Puerto Rican exclusion from key institutions, 218–19

gerrymandering, 185

Gerstle, Gary, 20, 129

Giboyeaux, José, 116; in 1953 elections, 184
Giboyeaux, Ramón, 125
Gleason, Phillip, 11
Goldson, Rose Kohn, 172
Gómez, Manuel, named municipal magistrate, 183
Gompers, Samuel, Socialists and, 269n64
González, Juan, 234
Good Neighbor Policy, 129
Goodwill workshops, 158–59
Gordon, Maxine, 69
Great Depression: confronting race during, 56–91; impacts of, 8; migration during, 92–93; repatriation debate during, 288n7
Grele, Ron, 238–39
Gruening, Ernest, 117–18, 119–20
Guerra, Emilio, 180
Gutmann, Amy, 19
Guzmán, Pablo "Yoruba," 229, 230, 232, 233, 236, 239; on shift away from radical politics, 245–46

Habermas, Jürgen, 5, 16
Hamell, Pete, 215
Handlin, Oscar, 90, 198, 252
Hansen, Millard, 176
Harding, Warren G., 38, 269n67
Harlem: antipoverty groups in, 218; Communist Party in, 94; crime wave in, 87–88; Mayor's Commission on, 81; political alliances in, 187; racial/ethnic composition in 1935, 264n8; and riots of 1935, 73–83, 133. See also *barrios latinos*; East Harlem
Harlem Affairs Committee, 187
Harlem Puerto Rican community: versus Brooklyn community, 24–25; schism with Brooklyn community, 36
Harlem Riot of 1935, 75–83, 133; Left response to, 80; and Puerto Rican

invisibility, 76–77; and Puerto Rican nonalignment with African Americans, 75–76
Harriman, Averell, 225f
Harrington, Michael, 217–18, 228
HARYOU-ACT, 218, 322n66
Hayden, Tom, 227
Hegel, Georg, 12, 13
Hernández, Antonio, 192f
Hernández, Emilia, 45
Herndon, Angelo, 65
Heron, Gil Scott, 245
Hewitt, Charles, 134–35, 136; apologies by, 137–38; *colonia's* response to, 137–38
Higher Horizons program, 209–10, 214
Hill, Herbert, 190, 215
Hilliard, Raymond, 153, 154
Hispanic Association Pro-Higher Education, 212
Hispanic Parade, 162, 162f
Hispanic Young Adult Association: factions in, 211; goal of, 211
*hispanidad, latinidad* versus, 53
Hodson, William, 108
Homar, Lorenzo, 27–28
Home Relief Bureau: corruption in, 106; programs of, 106; protest at, 109–10. See also relief programs; welfare dependency
Honneth, Axel, 17, 19
hooks, bell, 17
Hoover, Herbert, Puerto Rican visit of, 62–63
Horne, Frank, 211
Hostos, Eugenia María de, 219
housing, 216; Committee on Puerto Ricans and, 179–80; crisis in, 192–93; Mayor's Commission and, 81; Mayor's 1967 conference and, 218–19; Migration Division and, 169–70; NYU study and, 183; PRRA promises for, 109; Spanish Voters Association and, 184;

New York City: African American migration to, 56–57; migration decline in 1960s, 214–15; postwar Puerto Rican population boom in, 135–36; Puerto Rican population in 1920s, 3, 24; Puerto Rican population in 1930s, 256n5; Puerto Rican population in 1940s, 133

Ngai, Mae, 57

numbers racket: in Manhattan versus Brooklyn, 44; Tapia and, 42, 43

Nuyorican, transition to, 245–53

Nuyorican poets, 14, 247–48

O'Brien, John, 97, 99–100

O'Dwyer, William, 152–54, 171, 179; reelection of, 155

Office of Employment and Identification, 169; Iglesias and, 67

"one-drop" rule, 74–75, 276n7

O'Neill, Isabel, 45, 82, 100, 111, 127

open enrollment policy, CUNY, 216–17

Operation Bootstrap, 12; controversy over, 322n72; failures of, 245; false claims about, 221; influence of, 242; liberal-PPD alliance and, 157; MACPRA and, 171; New York liberals and, 136; social science research and, 172

Operation Rapport, 190

oppression, Young Lords' theory of, 237, 238

Ortiz, Pedro, 105

Other America, The (Harrington), 217–18

overpopulation, Roosevelt's position on, 168–69

Pacheco, Pilar, 121–22, 147, 221, 295n96

Padilla, Elena, 198

Padrón, Lucila, 70

Pagán, José Victor, 72, 73f

Pantoja, Antonia, 213f, 242, 320n47;

Aspira and, 212–14; background, 210–11; on War on Poverty, 218. See also Aspira

Park, Robert, 12

Partido Nacionalista (Puerto Rico), 269n67; establishment of, 38

Partido Popular Democrático (PPD). See Popular Democratic Party (PPD)

patronage, ethnic voting blocs and, 94

People's Action Party, 240–41

People's Church, 232; Young Lords and, 232–33, 235, 238

Pérez, David, 213–14, 235

Pérez, José, 189

Piñero, Jesús, 152, 248; appointment as governor, 10, 141; Bureau of Employment and Migration and, 169

Piñero, Jesus, migrant studies and, 172

poets, Nuyorican, 14

police harassment/brutality, 54, 58; Lords' protest against, 234–35

political activism, in homeland versus metropole, 39–40

political activists: academia's nonrecognition of, 198–99; generational tensions of, 213–14; heterogenous, 241; internal disputes of, 241–42; nonradical, 241; radicalization of, 229–30. See also radical activists; specific groups

political assassinations, in Puerto Rico, 118

political identity, 3; defining, 4; evolving, 250–51; globally based movements and, 18; liberal versus communitarian theories of, 15–16; struggle for, 8. See also racial identity

political marginalization. See marginalization of Puerto Ricans

political organizations, women's roles in, 44–45

political parties (Puerto Rico), 36–37; alliances of, 37

status of, 6; U.S. military takeover of, 1; U.S.–Puerto Rican plebiscite in, 223–24; worker exploitation in, 170
"Puerto Rico" (Wells and Hansen), 175–76

Quintero, Babby, 120, 158
Quintero, Luisa, 120, 162

race: binary concept of, 74; in Brooklyn versus Manhattan communities, 26; changing concepts after World War II, 88–89; confronting during Depression, 56–91; increasing emphasis during 1930s, 58; intelligence testing and, 84; legal construction of, 57; rubric for determining, 174–75
racial categories, in U.S. census, 276n7
racial identity: changing attitudes toward, 186; discussion of, 64; hardening during 1930s, 8, 74, 94–95; job discrimination and, 66–69; in Latin America, 280n45; as Negro, 8, 59, 88; during 1930s, 59–66; pride in, 59; in Puerto Rico, 286n109; in Puerto Rico versus U.S., 69–70, 72; shift in, 230; as *trigueños*, 24, 264n7; of U.S. immigrant groups, 275n5
"racial incapacity" argument, 136
racial mixing, U.S. denial of, 74
racial violence, in South, 277n17
racism: anthropological influences on, 317n8; in anti–Puerto Rican rhetoric, 145–46; arrests and, 194; debate over, 59; immigration and, 57; Jones Act and, 5–6; organizations combating, 289n20; of Puerto Ricans, 61, 64, 87; World War II lessons on, 203–4
radical activists: and articulation of connection between colonialism/

racism and local politics, 238; international network of, 231; 1960s agenda of, 230–31; redistributive justice and, 252; shift away from, 245–46. *See also* political activists; Young Lords
Rainbow Coalition, 231
Ramírez Santibánez, José, 128
Ramos, Juan, 28, 243, 279n41
Ramos, Luis, 103
Ramos López, José, 149
Rand, Christopher, 164, 166, 189
Randolph, A. Philip, 110, 233, 300n10
Real Great Society, 229, 237
recognition: aspirations for, 4–5; challenge of, 11–14; and challenge to liberal assumptions, 202; beyond citizenship, 250; Colón and, 214; as core of political struggle, 49; debates over, 330n17; versus equality, 202; failures of, 221; French-Canadian example of, 261n51; group, 16, 240, 243; historical versus present significance of, 19; and language of human rights, 14; in Latin American contexts, 262n56; Latinos' struggle for, 17; beyond liberalism, 20; liberal versus communitarian theories of, 15–16; limited notions of, 251; meanings of, 12; in 1960s context, 13; old and new claims for, 237–44; political, 250; political goals in context of, 20; politics of, 13, 19; Puerto Rican movement and, 243; search for, 183–84; status model of, 261n50; struggle for, 14–21; and struggles in global south, 18; theoretical debates about, 249; theory of, 249–50; as unifying thread, 253
Recovery Party, 97–98, 105
redbaiting, 151–52; in selection of Mayor's Commission members, 282n67; as threat to political action, 166–67

HISTORICAL STUDIES OF URBAN AMERICA

*Edited by Timothy J. Gilfoyle, James R. Grossman, and Becky M. Nicolaides*

SERIES TITLES, CONTINUED FROM FRONTMATTER

*The Transatlantic Collapse of Urban Renewal: Postwar Urbanism from New York to Berlin*
by Christopher Klemek

*I've Got to Make My Livin': Black Women's Sex Work in Turn-of-the-Century Chicago*
by Cynthia M. Blair

*Puerto Rican Citizen: History and Political Identity in Twentieth-Century New York City*
by Lorrin Thomas

*Staying Italian: Urban Change and Ethnic Life in Postwar Toronto and Philadelphia*
by Jordan Stanger-Ross

*New York Undercover: Private Surveillance in the Progressive Era*
by Jennifer Fronc

*African American Urban History since World War II*
edited by Kenneth L. Kusmer and Joe W. Trotter

*Blueprint for Disaster: The Unraveling of Chicago Public Housing*
by D. Bradford Hunt

*Alien Neighbors, Foreign Friends: Asian Americans, Housing, and the Transformation of Urban California*
by Charlotte Brooks

*The Problem of Jobs: Liberalism, Race, and Deindustrialization in Philadelphia*
by Guian A. McKee

*Chicago Made: Factory Networks in the Industrial Metropolis*
by Robert Lewis

*The Flash Press: Sporting Male Weeklies in 1840s New York*
by Patricia Cline Cohen, Timothy J. Gilfoyle, and Helen Lefkowitz Horowitz
in association with the American Antiquarian Society

*Slumming: Sexual and Racial Encounters in American Nightlife, 1885–1940*
by Chad Heap

*Colored Property: State Policy and White Racial Politics in Suburban America*
by David M. P. Freund

*Selling the Race: Culture, Community, and Black Chicago, 1940–1955*
by Adam Green

*The New Suburban History*
edited by Kevin M. Kruse and Thomas J. Sugrue

*Millennium Park: Creating a Chicago Landmark*
by Timothy J. Gilfoyle

*City of American Dreams: A History of Home Ownership and Housing Reform in Chicago, 1871–1919*
by Margaret Garb

*Chicagoland: City and Suburbs in the Railroad Age*
by Ann Durkin Keating

*The Elusive Ideal: Equal Educational Opportunity and the Federal Role in Boston's Public Schools, 1950–1985*
by Adam R. Nelson

Block by Block: Neighborhoods and Public Policy on Chicago's West Side
by Amanda I. Seligman

Downtown America: A History of the Place and the People Who Made It
by Alison Isenberg

Places of Their Own: African American Suburbanization in the Twentieth Century
by Andrew Wiese

Building the South Side: Urban Space and Civic Culture in Chicago, 1890–1919
by Robin F. Bachin

In the Shadow of Slavery: African Americans in New York City, 1626–1863
by Leslie M. Harris

My Blue Heaven: Life and Politics in the Working-Class Suburbs of Los Angeles, 1920–1965
by Becky M. Nicolaides

Brownsville, Brooklyn: Blacks, Jews, and the Changing Face of the Ghetto
by Wendell Pritchett

The Creative Destruction of Manhattan, 1900–1940
by Max Page

Streets, Railroads, and the Great Strike of 1877
by David O. Stowell

Faces along the Bar: Lore and Order in the Workingman's Saloon, 1870–1920
by Madelon Powers

Making the Second Ghetto: Race and Housing in Chicago, 1940–1960
by Arnold R. Hirsch

Smoldering City: Chicagoans and the Great Fire, 1871–1874
by Karen Sawislak

Modern Housing for America: Policy Struggles in the New Deal Era
by Gail Radford

Parish Boundaries: The Catholic Encounter with Race in the Twentieth-Century Urban North
by John T. McGreevy

Made in the USA
Middletown, DE
21 February 2023

25287136R00217